THE LONGMAN COMPANION
TO THE FRENCH REVOLUTION

THE LONGMAN COMPANION
TO THE FRENCH REVOLUTION

THE LONGMAN COMPANION TO THE FRENCH REVOLUTION

COLIN JONES

LONGMAN

LONDON AND NEW YORK

Longman Group UK Limited,
Longman House, Burnt Mill, Harlow,
Essex CM20 2JE, England
and Associated Companies throughout the world.

Published in the United States of America
by Longman Inc., New York

First published 1988
First paperback edition 1990

British Library Cataloguing in Publication Data
Jones, Colin, 1947–
The Longman companion to the French revolution.
1. France – Politics and government – Revolution, 1789–1799
I. Title
944.04   DC155

ISBN 0-582-49417-6

Library of Congress Cataloging-in-Publication Data
Jones, Colin, 1947–
The Longman Companion to the French Revolution/Colin Jones.
p. cm.
Bibliography: p.
Includes index.
ISBN 0-582-49417 6 ppr
1. France – History – Revolution, 1789–1799.   2. France – History –
Revolution, 1788–1799 – Chronology.   I. Title.
DC148.J57 1988
944.04 – dc 19

87-24485
CIP

Set in Linotron 202 10½/12 pt Garamond

Produced by Longman Singapore Publishers (Pte) Ltd.
Printed in Singapore

CONTENTS

VIII. RELIGION AND IDEAS

IX. SOCIETY AND THE ECONOMY

LIST OF MAPS AND FIGURES

ABBREVIATIONS

adc	aide-de-camp
Ant	Antoine
Apr	April
AR	Ancien Régime
Ass./ass.	Assembly, assembly
assass	assassinated
Aug	August
B	Baptiste
battle	killed in battle
brum	brumaire
C500	Conseil des Cinq-Cents
C Anciens	Conseil des Anciens
CinC	Commander-in-Chief
CGD	Committee of General Defence
CGS	Committee of General Security
Ch	Charles
Civ Constn	Civil Constitution of the Clergy
Constit Ass.	Constituent Assembly
Convtn	Convention
CPS	Committee of Public Safety
dep	died while in deportation
dept	department, departmental
Dec	December
E	east, eastern
EG	Estates General
emgtn	died while in emigration
esp	especially
Et	Etienne
exctd	executed
Feb	February
flor	floréal
frim	frimaire
fruct	fructidor
Fs	François

germ	germinal
guill	guillotined
inc	including
J	Jean
Jan	January
jc	jour complémentaire
Jos	Joseph
JP	Justice of the Peace, *juge de paix*
Jq	Jacques
L	Louis
liv	livre(s)
Leg Ass.	Legislative Assembly
Mar	March
mess	messidor
N	north, northern
NE	north-east, north-eastern
nat	national
Nat Ass.	National Assembly
neol	neologism
Nic	Nicolas
niv	nivôse
Nov	November
Oct	October
P	Pierre
parl	parlement, parlementary
PEC	Provisional Executive Council
PGS	Procureur-Général Syndic
Ph	Philippe
pluv	pluviôse
prair	prairial
prov	provincial
rep	représentant, representative
rev	revolution, revolutionary
Rev Govt	Revolutionary Government
rpbc	republic
rpbcn	republican
S	south, southern
sc.	namely
SE	south-east, south-eastern
Sept	September
suic	committed suicide
SW	south-west, south-western
Th	Thomas

therm	thermidor
vendém	vendémiaire
vent	ventôse
W	west, western

PREFACE

This book would not have been written if there was not a widespread interest – among students, sixth-formers and members of the general public – in the French Revolution. It could not have been written without the vast mass of scholarship which for two centuries has built up on the subject. Yet it would not have needed to be written had there existed a basic source to which readers could turn for help and guidance with elementary points of information about the Revolution. The Revolution, even for those who have studied it a lifetime, is not easy to understand. Events move fast in the 1790s and in often bewildering and unanticipated directions. Hundreds of 'bit-part' players stud the course of events. Untranslatable French terms clog the prose of the most basic textbook. And it can prove bafflingly difficult to discover even the most apparently rudimentary factual information. What was the franchise from 1789 onwards, for example? When and how was feudalism finally abolished? Who were the ministers in the 1790s? Who were the commanders of the Revolutionary armies? And so on.

The present volume aims to come to the aid of those interested in the Revolution but who find it difficult. It includes:
- a detailed basic chronology
- subject chronologies and a great deal of useful information on major topics (finances, counter-revolution, political parties, etc.)
- detailed explanations of constitutional changes
- a thorough exposition of the machinery and impact of the Reign of Terror
- a guide to French Revolutionary expansion in Europe
- a biographical dictionary with brief details on over 500 of the dramatis personae of the Revolution. The aim here has been to highlight the minor figures – Chaumette, D'Eprémesnil, Catherine Théot, Vadier – as well as the more familiar figures like Mirabeau, Danton and Robespierre on whom basic information is not lacking
- a glossary of over 400 French Revolutionary terms in French, for readers who may feel confident with the meanings of *aristocrate* and *cahier de doléances*, but who may have more of a problem with an *Allobroge* or a *cul blanc*, and who might confuse a *sans-culotte* with a *sans-culottide*, an *appel au peuple* with an *appel nominal*, a *terrier* with a *terroriste*, a *fédéré* with a *fédéraliste*
- an explanation of the Revolutionary Calendar and a concordance.

Throughout the composition of this book, my rule of thumb has been to include material which I would have myself found useful when studying the Revolution as a general reader, and as an undergraduate and postgraduate. I have trawled widely amidst the oceans of scholarly writings on the Revolution, but am bound to have missed much. I found the most useful secondary sources to be the works of the Revolutionary *érudits* of the late nineteenth and early twentieth centuries: Jaurès, for example, Aulard (esp 1889–1923, 1889–97, 1910), Albert Mathiez (notably 1919, 1927), Marcel Marion (1914–31, 1923), Pierre Caron (1947), Georges Lefebvre (e.g. 1924, 1962, 1964) and of recent writers, one whose first publications were in the 1920s, and whose *Les Institutions de la France sous la Révolution et l'Empire* (1968) remains the best work of reference on the Revolutionary period, Jacques Godechot. Other helpful reference works by earlier scholars included those by Boursin and Challamel (1893), by Cahen and Guyot (1913), by Décembre-Alonnier (1866–8), by Duguit and Monnier (1898), by Helié (1880), by Robert *et al.* (1891), by Robinet *et al.* (1899) and by Walter (1941, 1951; and with A. Martin, 1936–43). Without the commitment and historical good sense of such scholars, on whose shoulders we all stand, a work such as this could not have been produced. Of more recent reference works, those by Cabourdin and Viard (1978), Connelly *et al.* (1985), Massin (1963, 1965) and Scott and Rothaus (1985) deserve mention.

I would like to record my thanks to colleagues and friends who have helped in the writing of the present book, though they are in no way responsible for remaining errors which are entirely original. My thanks go especially to my colleague at Exeter, Michael Duffy, who has shown a keen interest in the project from the start, has always been willing to read bits and pieces of the typescript and come up with challenging ideas for its improvement: the finished work owes much to his wisdom and his insight. Michael Sonenscher, Bill Wilson, Malcolm Cook, Mark Cleary, Hugh Gough, Peter Jones, and Lesley Sharpe have helped in different ways. Successive sets of French Revolution special subject students have had a lot tried out on them. Heather Eva, of the Inter-Library Loans section of the Exeter University Library, has shown great perseverance and patience. Mike Rouillard drew the maps. The index was compiled by Sarah Jones. My wife, Nicole Jones, has been encouraging throughout. The work is dedicated to two of our children. I would like to thank them – and Kelsey and Blanche: without them all, the book would doubtless have been written more quickly, but the period spent doing it would have been a lot less fun.

for Joe and Luke

I. POLITICAL CHRONOLOGY

1. EIGHTEENTH-CENTURY BACKGROUND

REIGN OF LOUIS XIV (1643–1715)

1701–13   War of Spanish Succession
1713   Treaty of Utrecht

REIGN OF LOUIS XV (1715–74)

1715–23   Regency government of Philippe, duc d'Orléans
1718–20   War of the Quadruple Alliance
1726–43   Administration of Cardinal Fleury
1733–8   War of Polish Succession
1737   Controller-General Orry introduces the royal *corvée* (forced labour service on road maintenance)
1740–8   War of Austrian Succession
1749   Controller-General Machault d'Arnouville introduces the *vingtième* tax
1756–63   Seven Years War: 'Diplomatic Revolution' bringing France into alliance with Austria for the first time
1761   'Family Compact' unites in alliance the Bourbons of France and Spain
1762   Suppression of the Jesuit order in France
1766   Lorraine passes to the king of France
1768   Corsica passes under French control
1771 (Apr)   Chancellor Maupeou abolishes the Paris parl, following several years of disputes

REIGN OF LOUIS XVI (1774–92)

1774 (Aug)   Turgot appointed Controller-General
   (Oct)   Recall of the Paris parl: Maupeou disgraced
1775 (Apr–May)   'Flour War' (*Guerre des farines*): popular disturbances, esp in the Paris region
1775–7   War Minister Saint-Germain introduces important military reforms

1776 (12 May)   Dismissal of Turgot, who is replaced as Controller-General by Clugny

1776 (18 Oct)   Death of Clugny. Taboureau des Réaux takes over as Controller-General, with Necker as Associate Director of the Treasury

1777 (29 June)   Taboureau retires, and Necker is appointed Director-General of the Finances

1778 (Feb)   Alliance with the American colonies against England, upon whom France declares war (10 July)

1779 (Aug)   Suppression of mortmain on royal domain land

1780 (Jan)   Abolition of some forms of judicial torture (*la question préparatoire*)

1781 (Jan)   Publication of Necker's *Compte-Rendu*

1781 (19 May)   Dismissal of Necker. Joly de Fleury appointed Controller-General (25 May)

1781 (28 May)   'Ségur ordinance' (administrative decree of the War Minister): four quarters of nobility required for direct access to the highest military ranks

1782 (July) Decree levying a third *vingtième* for the period 1783–6

1783 (30 Mar)   Le Fèvre d'Ormesson Controller-General

1783 (3 Sept)   Peace of Versailles between France, the American colonies, Spain and England

1783 (2 Nov)   Calonne appointed Controller-General

1785 (14 Apr)   New Compagnie des Indes created

1785 (Aug)   The 'Diamond Necklace Affair': widespread discrediting of Marie-Antoinette

1785 (10 Nov)   Treaty of alliance with Holland.

2. THE PRE-REVOLUTION (AUGUST 1786–APRIL 1789)

1786

20 Aug   Prompted by impending state bankruptcy, as the time-limit (31 Dec) on the third *vingtième* established in 1782 draws near, Controller-General Calonne proposes to Louis XVI a package of reform measures, notably:
- introduction of a unitary tax on land to replace the existing *vingtième*
- other tax reforms (stamp duty, extension of the state tobacco monopoly, reduction of *taille* and *gabelle*, etc)
- establishment of prov assemblies in all *pays d'élection*
- liberal economic reforms (freeing of the grain trade, commutation of the *corvée* into a money tax, suppression of internal customs barriers).

26 Sept   Anglo-French Trade Treaty (or 'Eden Treaty'): reduction in duty on the import of English manufactured goods, in return for reductions in duty on French wines and spirits entering England.

1787

22 Feb   OPENING OF THE ASSEMBLY OF NOTABLES, convoked to ratify the reforms proposed by Calonne (who dared not confront the Paris parl with them for fear of rejection): review of proposals to be done in committees, each of which is to be headed by a Prince of the Blood.

8 Apr   Following the hostile reception of the Ass. of Notables to the most important tax reforms, and thanks to subversive actions by his ministerial colleagues (esp Miromesnil and Breteuil), Calonne is dismissed and replaced as Controller-General by a nonentity, Bouvard de Fourqueux.

1 May   APPOINTMENT OF BRIENNE. Following his attempt (23 Apr) to rally support in the Notables for a modified reform programme, Louis XVI makes the conciliatory gesture of appointing one of Calonne's main adversaries in the Notables, Loménie de Brienne, archbishop of Toulouse and favourite of the queen, as head of the Royal Council of Finances, with Laurent de Villedeuil replacing Bouvard as Controller-General.

May   Brienne proposes a modified version of Calonne's reforms: a unitary land-tax; free trade in grain; the commutation of the *corvée* into a money tax;

4

a stamp duty on newspapers, petitions, etc; major economies in state expenditure; the establishment in the *pays d'élection* of prov assemblies (in which the 'doubling of the Third' will ensure the Third Estate deputies parity with those of the first two orders combined, and where voting will be by head, not order).

25 May   Following their refusal to ratify Brienne's reform programme, the Ass. of Notables is dispersed.

June/Oct   The Brienne ministry declines, mainly for financial reasons, to become militarily embroiled in the domestic crisis of the United Provinces, where combined Anglo-Prussian pressure is ousting French influence.

MAJOR REFORMS OF THE BRIENNE MINISTRY, June–Oct 1787

22 June–Sept: regulations introducing prov assemblies in all généralités
17 June: free trade in grain
27 June: commutation of the *corvée*
2 July: stamp duty introduced
9 Aug: major economies in the Royal Household introduced by Malesherbes
9 Oct: establishment of a War Council, on which Guibert is esp influential; in following months, a variety of military reforms is introduced (reduction in troops attached to the Royal Household, reform of officer training, reorganisation of the supply system, wage increases for troops of the line, introduction of a Prussian-style code of discipline)
13 Oct: further cuts in state pensions and Household sinecures
27 Oct: streamlining of financial administration
19 Nov: Edict of Toleration for Protestants (eventually passed by the Paris parl, 29 Jan 1788).

26 July   The Paris parl, which opposes Brienne's reforms, esp the unitary land-tax and the proposal to extend stamp duty, presents its remonstrances to the king, urging that the Estates General be called to approve new taxes.

 6 Aug   Following the resubmission to the parl of the land-tax decree (30 July) and the parl's rejection of the measure, a royal *lit de justice* is introduced to enact registration of this and the stamp duty decree.

 7 Aug   The parl refuses to recognise the validity of the *lit de justice* of 6 Aug.

14 Aug   The king orders the promulgation of the decree of 6 Aug and exiles the parl to Troyes.

Mid Aug   Demonstrations in Paris by the populace and the *basoche* in support of the parl; also, expressions of support from subaltern courts.

26 Aug   Brienne appointed Principal Minister, with Lambert replacing Ville-deuil (30 Aug) as Controller-General.

20 Sept   Following some weeks of negotiation, Brienne and the parl reach a compromise:
  • Brienne withdraws the land-tax and stamp-duty proposals
  • parl agrees to the imposition of two *vingtièmes*

- Brienne looks to the restructuring of financial administration and to further loans to tide the state over.

28 Sept   Parl returns to Paris from Troyes to the accompaniment of popular demonstrations in its favour.

Nov   Prov assemblies start to meet.

19 Nov   KING AGREES TO THE CONVOCATION OF THE EG. A *Séance royale* is held, to secure parl ratification of further loans: in the course of it the crown agrees that the EG should meet before 1792. The proceedings are transformed by the king into a *lit de justice,* entailing the forcible registration of the royal decrees, and when the duc d'Orléans protests (an act for which he is exiled, 20 Nov 1787–Apr 1788) he is quashed by Louis. The parl formally protests against the proceedings.

20 Nov   *Lettres de cachet* issued for the exile of Orléans and the arrest of two Orleanist councillors in the parl.

21 Nov   Louis formally expunges from the records of the parl all mention of their protests on 19 Nov.

26 Nov, 7 Dec 1787, 4 and 9 Jan 1789   Remonstrances of the parl in favour of its two councillors exiled on 20 Nov, and growing condemnation of the abuse of *lettres de cachet.*

1788

Apr   Fearing an imminent royal coup, the parl reiterates and generalises its opposition to 'despotism' in general.

3 May   Parl issues a 'Declaration of the Fundamental Laws of the Kingdom': attack on *lettres de cachet,* statement that the convocation of the EG is essential for all new taxes, etc.

4 May   *Lettres de cachet* issued against prominent parlementarians Goislard de Montsabert and Duval d'Eprémesnil, both of whom (5 May) take refuge in the parl, which refuses to hand them over to troops sent to arrest them.

6 May   Surrender of the two parlementarians, who are imprisoned.

8 May   THE 'MAY EDICTS'. Following the annulment of the preceding decrees of the parl, the Brienne ministry issues the famous 'May Edicts':
- reorganisation of the higher courts, with parls losing much judicial authority to new appeal (*grand bailliage*) courts
- creation of a Plenary Court (*Cour plénière*), comprising the Grand Chambre of the parl and the major ministers and dignitaries of the realm, to register all national legislation and financial measures relating to new taxes
- abolition of many minor courts
- abolition of torture (*question préalable*).

THE 'NOBLE REVOLT', Summer 1788

Wide-ranging opposition from the nobility to the May Edicts:

- most provincial parls join with the parl of Paris in remonstrating against the May Edicts
- pro-parl riots and disturbances in many urban centres
- *June:* The Ass. of the Clergy makes common cause with the parls, protests against the Plenary Court and accedes to a figure of only 1.8 million liv over two years as its *don gratuit* (as against the 8 millions requested by the government)
- *May–July:* riots in Rennes in support of the local parl, eventually forcing the Intendant of Brittany, Bertrand de Moleville, to flee
- *7 June:* 'Day of the Tiles' in Grenoble, with popular riots and demonstrations in support of the local parl against royal troops
- dissension in the officer corps of the army, with some officers showing sympathy for the parl cause
- protests from *ad hoc* assemblies of nobles in several provinces (Brittany, Béarn, Dauphiné, Languedoc, Provence)
- *14 June:* meeting of Grenoble notables from all three estates, headed by Barnave and Mounier, to support the parls: they urge the re-establishment of the prov estates of the Dauphiné and call for the convocation of the EG
- *21 July:* following on from the meeting of 14 June, representatives of the three estates of the Dauphiné meet in the chateau of Vizille, near Grenoble, and call for the reinstatement of the parls and for prov and nat representative bodies.

5 July   BRIENNE CAPITULATES TO THE NOBLE REVOLT. Brienne, who has endeavoured to counter the noble revolt by summoning popular support (e.g. allowing the return of prov estates in the Dauphiné and the Franche-Comté with a strong Third Estate element) is forced to make concessions by a sudden crisis in short-term credit, and agrees to call the EG. Informed opinion is solicited on the proposed EG's mode of business. (The latter decree creates greater latitude for freedom of the press.)

8 Aug   Further, more serious concessions from Brienne:
- suspension of the Plenary Court and the *grands bailliages*
- EG to meet 1 May 1789.

16 Aug   *DE FACTO* STATE BANKRUPTCY: the state is forced to suspend payment of the interest payments on some of its debts. As a camouflaged way of constraining state creditors into a forced loan, Brienne creates special treasury bills bearing 5 per cent interest.

25 Aug   Following court intrigues master-minded by Artois, Brienne loses the queen's favour and is forced to resign in favour of Necker. Popular rejoicings in Paris when the news filters through. Shortly afterwards, Garde des Sceaux Lamoignon resigns and is replaced by Barentin.

26 Aug NECKER DIRECTOR-GENERAL OF FINANCE: believing civil war imminent, he rejects Lamoignon's judicial reforms, restores the parls to their former powers and agrees that the EG may meet in Jan 1789 (later postponed to May 1789). He is able to borrow to tide the state over its feared bankruptcy, at least provisionally.

25 Sept Decree of the newly reinstated Paris parl: the EG should meet according to its 1614 form (with voting by order, and with the number of deputies in each estate approximately the same). The parl loses much of its popularity with this decree and also by its attempted censorship (Sept–Dec 1788) of pro-Third Estate pamphleteering.

5 Oct Convocation, on Necker's advice, of a second Ass. of Notables, to deliberate on the forms in which the EG is to meet in 1789.

6 Nov OPENING OF THE SECOND ASS. OF NOTABLES: it fails to reach any helpful conclusions.

28 Nov In one of a series of measures designed to end free trade in grain, the government decrees that no grain transactions are to take place outside the market-place.

5 Dec In an unsuccessful endeavour to recapture popular support the Paris parl supports double representation for the Third Estate in the EG (on 22 Dec it will renounce fiscal privilege).

12 Dec As the Ass. of Notables disperses, the Princes of the Blood (though not including Provence or Orléans) issue a memorandum, a kind of ultra-reactionary manifesto urging the king to stand by his loyal nobility, and resist demands for voting by head and the doubling of the Third Estate in the EG.

27 Dec *RESULTAT DU CONSEIL:* the basic decisions of the king's council on procedure in elections to the EG:
- assent to the 'doubling of the Third'
- freedom of the press to be observed
- elections within *bailliage* constituencies, with the number of deputies roughly proportionate to the size of the *bailliages*.

1789

24 Jan Regulations concerning electoral procedure finalised and sent out to the *bailliages*.

ELECTIONEERING AND THE EMERGENCE OF THE THIRD ESTATE AS AN AUTONOMOUS POLITICAL FORCE, AUTUMN 1788–SPRING 1789:
- establishment of clubs in Paris and the major prov towns
- campaign to petition the crown to grant the 'doubling of the Third' in the EG and voting by head (in order that the clerical and noble orders should not hold the whip hand)

- widespread political pampleteering: publication of e.g. Siéyès' *Qu'est-ce que le Tiers Etat?*, Target's *Lettre aux Etats-Généraux*, Desmoulins's *La France libre,* etc
- model cahiers drawn up and distributed, e.g. by members of the Société des Trente
- meeting of primary assemblies (Mar–Apr) and *bailliage* assemblies (late Apr: though in Paris, elections only close in May)
- drawing up of *cahiers des doléances*
- *30 Apr:* first meeting of the Breton Club at Versailles

STIRRINGS OF POPULAR REVOLT, AUTUMN 1788–SUMMER 1789:

- wine-growing areas still not recovered from crisis of over-production, 1778–87
- many textile areas in crisis, worsened in some cases by the Anglo-French Trade Treaty of 1786
- bad harvests, 1787, 1788
- *Jan–Mar 1789:* urban bread riots
- *Spring 1789:* peasant insurrections in Flanders, Franche-Comté and the Mâconnais
- unrest in Brittany, the northern frontier, the Paris region, Provence, etc
- *27–28 Apr 1789:* Réveillon riots in Paris among workers from the Faubourg Saint-Antoine, precipitated by alleged remarks of wall-paper manufacturer Réveillon urging reductions in wages.

3. THE ESTATES GENERAL AND THE CONSTITUENT ASSEMBLY (MAY 1789–SEPTEMBER 1791)

1789

2 May   Deputies to the EG presented to the king.

5 May   OPENING SESSION OF THE EG:
- vague and woolly opening statements by Louis XVI and Garde des Sceaux Barentin
- Necker announces that voting procedures are to be by order, not by head.

6 May   Deputies of the Third Estate, calling themselves *Députés des Communes,* refuse to meet as a separate chamber, though nobles (after voting 188/46) and clergy (134/114) agree to voting by order.

12–20 May   Final stages of Parisian elections to the EG.

23 and 25 May, 4–6 June   Attempts at conciliation between the three estates.

4 June   Death of the dauphin.

10 June   Following a month of deadlock, the 'Commons' make a final offer to the other orders to join them, and announce that they will proceed with the verification of powers on 12 June.

13 June   The first defectors from the clergy (3 *curés* from the Poitou, followed by 6 other clerical deputies on 14 June, and 10 on 16 June) present themselves in the 'Commons' to verify credentials.

17 June   ADOPTION OF THE TITLE 'NATIONAL ASSEMBLY'. Following a debate on 15 June, the 'Commons' vote (490/90) to adopt title of 'National Assembly' and to proceed, voting by head, with the work of nat reconstruction. Existing taxes are to be continued provisionally.

19 June   Clerical order agrees (149/137) to join the Nat Ass. for the verification of its deputies' credentials.

20 June   TENNIS COURT OATH (*serment du jeu de paume*): following the decision of the Royal Council to hold a *séance royale* in the presence of all deputies, the meeting-place of the Nat Ass. is closed; whereupon the deputies repair to a nearby tennis-court (*jeu de paume*) and there swear not to disperse until a constitution has been passed and is firmly established.

22 June   Two noble as well as many clerical deputies join the Nat Ass.

23 June   *SEANCE ROYALE* in the presence of the three orders: Louis overrules the

decrees of the 'Third Estate'; orders the three estates to meet separately; and introduces a reform programme, including fiscal equality (but not abolition of tithes or seigneurial dues and rents). When the king leaves the deputies remain in their places; confirm their previous decrees; and declare themselves constitutionally inviolable (493/34).

24 June   Most of the clergy join the Nat Ass., followed the next day (25 June) by 47 nobles led by Orléans.

25 June   407 Parisian electors who have participated in the second stage of the Parisian elections to the EG form an unofficial municipal council.

27 June   The king orders the rumps of the clerical and noble orders to take their places in the Nat Ass.; but simultaneously accedes to the demands of the hard-line faction at court and starts to call up the army round Paris and Versailles.

6 July   Appointment by the Nat Ass. of a Constitution Committee.

8 July   Against the background of popular disturbances in Paris, the Nat Ass. requests the king to withdraw troops from the Parisian area.

9 July   Nat Ass. adopts the title of 'National Constituent Assembly'.

11 July   KING DISMISSES NECKER, appointing the reactionary Breteuil as his principal minister with Broglie as War Minister.

12 July   News of Necker's dismissal reaches Paris, where it inspires popular revolt and middle-class defensive organisation:
  • demonstrations at the Palais-Royal
  • clashes with troops at the Tuileries
  • closure of the stock exchange (*Bourse*) in protest
  • gunsmiths looted, and arming begins
  • attacks on Paris customs-posts
  • looting and attacks on persons and property
  • *Gardes-françaises* refuse to fire on demonstrators and begin to fraternise.
Evening: meeting of the Parisian electors, who form a permanent committee and establish a bourgeois militia to keep order.

13 July   Further popular unrest in Paris: attack on the Saint-Lazare monastery; looting, erection of barricades.
At Versailles, the Nat Ass. declares itself in permanent session and reiterates its call for the removal of troops.

14 July   JOURNEE: THE STORMING OF THE BASTILLE. Attack on the Invalides, then the Bastille by the Paris crowd, aided by *Gardes-françaises*.

15 July   Louis, informed that the regular troops cannot be relied on in action in Paris, goes to the Nat Ass. to announce that he is ordering troops away from Paris and Versailles.
In Paris, the electors form themselves into the Commune, and elect Bailly as mayor, with Lafayette as commander of the Nat Guard.

16 July   RECALL OF NECKER.

17 July   King visits Paris: he is welcomed at the Hôtel-de-Ville by Bailly and dons the rev cockade.

Beginning of the emigration as the comte d'Artois leaves Paris, followed by Condé, Broglie, etc.

22 July Parisian crowds assassinate Bertier de Sauvigny, Intendant of Paris, and Foulon.

24 July Parisian local government passes into the hands of representatives of the 60 electoral districts.

THE 'GREAT FEAR' AND PEASANT REVOLUTION, 20 JULY–4 AUG

Following endemic unrest throughout the Spring and Summer, the 'Great Fear', a nationwide panic fear of economic crisis, brigands and aristocratic plots, sweeps France.

The peasants go on to attack châteaux and seigneurial personnel, often making bonfires of feudal documents.

Insurrection esp violent in the Franche-Comté, Normandy, Alsace, the Hainaut and the Mâconnais.

'MUNICIPAL REVOLUTION', JULY–SEPT

A variety of factors (food shortages, Necker's dismissal, the fall of the Bastille, etc) precipitate in most cities a transformation of local government, with a system emerging that is more democratic and less identified with the army and the king.

1 Aug Nat Ass. discusses the constitution and agrees to draw up a Declaration of Rights.

4 Aug THE 'NIGHT OF THE 4 AUG'. In a session introduced by Aiguillon and Noailles, the Ass. renounces feudal privilege. Abolition of: seigneurial rights on persons (those on property are to be redeemable); tithes; hunting rights; *corvées;* seigneurial justice; venality of office; prov and municipal privileges; etc.

Ministerial reshuffle, with the Fayettists seeming to benefit from the change in government policy.

5–11 Aug Decrees embodying the decisions taken on 4 Aug.

9 Aug Loan of 30 million liv decreed at $4\frac{1}{2}$ per cent interest (to be followed on 27 Aug by a further loan of 80 millions at 5 per cent which will be similarly undersubscribed).

26 Aug DECLARATION OF THE RIGHTS OF MAN AND THE CITIZEN.

29 Aug Re-establishment of free trade in grain.

10 Sept Despite the arguments of the *Monarchiens* (Mounier, Lally-Tollendal, etc), the Constit Ass. rejects a bicameral legislature (849/89).

11 Sept Ass. rejects an absolute veto for the king but allows a suspensive one (673/325).

15 Sept Louis criticises the decrees of 5, 11 and 26 Aug and refuses to endorse them.

CONTINUATION OF POLITICAL AGITATION, AUG–OCT

Economic crisis continues (irregular food supplies, worsened unemployment as a result of the emigration, closure of Paris charity workshops on 31 Aug, etc).

Political clubs begin to appear.

Political agitation, notably through newspapers and broadsheets. Further political deadlock over Louis's refusal to sanction key measures.

1 Oct   Constitutional Act: establishment of a constitutional monarchy, with the separation of powers. Markers laid down for the new constitution.

Banquet at Versailles for the Royal Bodyguard and the Royal Flanders Regiment in the course of which the nat cockade is trampled underfoot.

3–4 Oct   News of the Versailles banquet reaches Paris: demonstrations, crowd disturbances.

5–6 Oct   *JOURNEES* OF 5–6 OCT: Lafayette and the Paris Nat Guard accompany a crowd of demonstrators to Versailles to protest over economic hardship and the Flanders Regiment incident. During the night, a personal attack on the queen is narrowly avoided. The king agrees to sanction the Declaration of the Rights of Man and the abolition of feudalism, and then is forced to accompany the returning crowd to Paris, where the royal family is installed in the Tuileries palace.

6 Oct   Decree instituting the *contribution patriotique*: a once-and-for-all voluntary tax of a quarter of personal income.

9 Oct   Constit Ass. agrees to move its seat to Paris.

19 Oct   First session of the Constit Ass. in Paris.

21 Oct   Following grain riots in Paris in which a baker, François, is assassinated, a new martial law decree is passed.

22, 29 Oct   Debates on the distinction between 'active' and 'passive' citizens and on the creation of the *marc d'argent* qualification for deputies in the new constitution.

2 Nov   NATIONALISATION OF CHURCH PROPERTY (568/346): in return, the state will fund public worship and poor relief.

3 Nov   Suspension (*mise en vacances*) of the parls (which are formally abolished 6 Sept 1790).

7 Nov   Deputies excluded from ministerial office.

9 Nov   Constit Ass. establishes itself in the Salle du Manège in the Tuileries palace.

29 Nov   *Fédération* of national guards at Etoile, near Valence.

30 Nov   Corsica declared an integral part of France.

14–22 Dec   Decrees reorganising local government (depts, municipalities).

19 Dec   Sales of church lands begin, and assignats are issued for the first time.

22 Dec   Decree on primary elections to the forthcoming legislature.

1790

Jan–Feb   Elections to the new municipalities.

4 Feb   Louis attends Ass., and is greeted rapturously.

13 Feb   Prohibition of monastic vows and suppression of religious orders (except in teaching and assistance).

19 Feb   Execution of the marquis de Favras, counter-rev conspirator.

26 Feb   ORGANISATION OF FRANCE INTO 83 DEPTS.

8 Mar   Barnave, speaking for the Colonies Committee, gets the Ass. to approve powers of self-government for the colonies: the franchise within them is to be based on property-holding; mulattos are to have no political rights; and slavery is upheld.

W INDIAN COLONIES, SPRING–AUTUMN 1790.
28 May: an illegal assembly of planters in Saint-Domingue proclaims independence from France
3 June: mulatto rising in Martinique
29 Oct: mulatto rising in Saint-Domingue led by Ogé: it is soon crushed by the planters
25 Nov: beginning of disturbances among slaves in Saint-Domingue.

15 Mar   Ass. accepts the report of its Feudal Committee (chaired by Merlin de Douai) on the abolition of seigneurial rights and the redemption of feudal dues and rights.

16 Mar   Abolition of *lettres de cachet*.

21 Mar   Suppression of the *gabelle*.

Apr–June   Counter-rev uprisings at Nîmes, Montauban, Vannes, Toulouse, etc.

13 Apr   Right-wing and clerical backlash in the Ass., following a vote *not* to accept Dom Gerle's motion that catholicism should be the state religion.

17 Apr   Assignats recognised as currency.

29 Apr   Decree on free trade in grain.

9 May   Nationalisation of royal domain land.

21 May   Paris local government reorganised into 48 sections.

22 May   Ass. renounces wars of conquest.

10–12 June   Disturbances in Avignon over proposed annexation to France: the Francophile 'patriots' will prevail, though the Ass. delays a decision so as not to offend the Pope, ruler of Avignon and the Comtat Venaissin.

19 June   Abolition of titles of hereditary nobility, followed on 20 June by the suppression of orders of chivalry, etc.

12 July   CIVIL CONSTITUTION OF THE CLERGY: complete reorganisation of the Catholic Church in France.

14 July   FIRST *FETE DE LA FEDERATION* on the Champ de Mars in Paris to celebrate the first anniversary of the fall of the Bastille.

27 July   Treaty of Reichenbach: Prussia, Britain and Holland agree to allow Austria to reconquer the Austrian Netherlands (Belgium) which have been in revolt since late 1789.

9–31 Aug   Agitation within the Châteauvieux Regiment, which has been in open dispute with its officers at Nancy, is fiercely repressed as a 'mutiny' by Bouillé, on the orders of Lafayette, and with the approval (3 Sept) of the Ass.

14

16–24 Aug Decree reorganising the judiciary.

18 Aug Camp de Jalès (counter-rev assembly) in the Vivarais.

26 Aug Formal renunciation of the 'Family Compact' (*Pacte de famille*) with Spain.

 4 Sept RESIGNATION OF NECKER: formation over the next weeks of a Fayettist ministry (Duportail, Duport-Dutertre, de Lessart, . . .).

28 Oct Ass. debates France's dispute with the *princes possessionnés* (German princes with jurisdiction in enclaves within French frontiers who have been adversely affected by the Rev reforms).

31 Oct–5 Nov Abolition of internal customs barriers: France becomes an internally unified customs area.

23 Nov New land-tax (*contribution foncière*) introduced.

26 Nov Louis secretly accords Breteuil plenipotentiary powers to treat with European states.

27 Nov Decree ordering priests holding ecclesiastical office to take the oath to the constitution (sanctioned by Louis, 26 Dec).

12 Dec Austrian troops complete the reconquest of Belgium.

1791

 4 Jan Date by which ecclesiastical deputies in the Ass. must have sworn the oath of allegiance associated with the Civ Constn: in fact, most refuse to swear.

13 Jan Tax on movable wealth (*contribution mobilière*) introduced.

 5 Feb Election of first constitutional bishops.

19 Feb Abolition of municipal tolls (*octrois*).

28 Feb 'Chevaliers du poignard' conspiracy: the Tuileries is temporarily invaded by armed young nobles.

Mar Spain establishes a cordon sanitaire along the Pyrenees to restrain French ideological influence.

 2 Mar *Loi d'Allarde:* suppression of corporations and guild-masterships and state privileges for industry.
New tax on trades and professions (the *patente*).

10 Mar, 13 Apr Pope condemns the Civ Constn. Diplomatic relations with the papacy are broken (15 March).

 2 Apr Death of Mirabeau: his body is taken (4 Apr) to the newly created Panthéon.

18 Apr The royal family is prevented from leaving Paris for Saint-Cloud.

May French occupation of Avignon and the Comtat Venaissin.

 7 May Refractory priests permitted to conduct religious services.

COLONIAL ISSUES: THE W INDIES, SPRING–AUTUMN 1791

15 May: against a background of growing dissension in the W Indies (e.g. insurrection at Port-au-Prince, 4 March), the Ass. cedes coloured men of free parents (a tiny proportion of the coloured population) equality with whites. Slavery is maintained.

22 Aug: slave revolt in Saint-Domingue involving 100,000 black slaves. Over the next months, 2,000 whites and 10,000 blacks will die in savage fighting. Emergence of the slave-leader Toussaint l'Ouverture.

24 Sept: following stormy debates in the Constit Ass. pitting Barnave against Robespierre, the Ass. follows Barnave's suggestion and leaves matters relating to slaves and mulattos to the (planter-dominated) colonial assemblies.

27 Sept: abolition of slavery in France (sc. *not* in the colonies).

16 May   SELF-DENYING DECREE: on Robespierre's suggestion, deputies exclude themselves for standing for election to the Leg Ass.

18 May   Collective petitioning forbidden.

14 June   *LOI LE CHAPELIER:* workers' associations and strikes prohibited.

20 June   FLIGHT TO VARENNES. The king and the royal family are arrested before they meet up with royalist forces. The comte de Provence succeeds, however, in his simultaneous flight to Belgium.

21 June   Constit Ass. suspends Louis and sits in permanent session. The Paris Jacobins also sit *en permanence*. The frontiers are declared closed.

24 June   Extraordinary commissioners sent out to settle the frontier provinces. 'Petition of the 30,000' organised by the Cordeliers, declaring liberty and royalty incompatible.

25 June   Royal family re-enters Paris. The king is provisionally suspended from the exercise of power.

26 June   From exile, Bouillé accepts responsibility for 'abducting' the king.

9 July   *Emigrés* to pay threefold their tax load for 1791.

14 July   Second *Fête de la Fédération*.

16 July   Following heated debates (13–16 July), the Constit Ass. decrees:
   • the person of the monarch is inviolable
   • acceptance of the theory of the 'abduction' of the king
   • Louis only to be reinstated when he ratifies the new Constitution.
   Feuillant schism from the Jacobin Club. Only a handful of deputies (inc Robespierre, Pétion, Grégoire) remain with the Jacobins.

17 July   'MASSACRE OF THE CHAMP DE MARS': martial law proclaimed and Nat Guard opens fire on demonstrators in a mass meeting on the Champ de Mars supporting a Cordelier petition in favour of republicanism.

POST-CHAMP DE MARS REACTION, JULY–SEPT

As the Constit Ass. winds down, attacks on the popular movement and strengthening of the principle of authority:
   • harassment of popular clubs and militants, suppression of radical newspapers
   • *18 July:* decree on riot and sedition aimed at the Champ de Mars demonstrators

- *19–22 July:* law on municipal police
- *26 July:* law on seditious meetings
- *28 July, 19 Sept:* reorganisation of Nat Guard, limiting it to active citizens
- *27 Aug:* revision of the electoral law, and raising of the property franchise (though the *marc d'argent* qualification is dropped)
- *30 Sept:* law on political associations, restricting the publicity of their sessions.

5 Aug   As secret negotiations between the crowned heads of Europe redouble, the Ass. renounces wars of conquest.

15 Aug   Prohibition of the wearing of religious dress in public.

17 Aug   Decree calling on *émigrés* to return within a month.

27 Aug   PILLNITZ DECLARATION: Leopold II of Austria and Frederick-William II of Prussia threaten combined intervention.

The *émigrés* see this as a sell-out, but the Ass. feels menaced.

29 Aug–5 Sept   Elections to the Leg Ass.

3 Sept   Completion of the Constitutional Act.

12 Sept   FORMAL ANNEXATION OF AVIGNON AND THE COMTAT VENAISSIN.

13 Sept   KING ACCEPTS THE NEW CONSTITUTION: the following day he swears the oath of allegiance in the Ass.

30 Sept   FINAL MEETING OF THE CONSTIT ASS.

Law passed forbidding collective petitions and delegations (never enforced).

Amnesty for individuals sentenced for riot and revolt since 1788.

4. THE LEGISLATIVE ASSEMBLY (OCTOBER 1791–SEPTEMBER 1792)

1791

1 Oct FIRST MEETING OF LEG ASS.

9 Oct Report on counter-rev peasant disturbances in the W (Vendée, Deux-Sèvres, etc).

14 Oct Louis XVI's proclamation urging his brothers to return from voluntary exile.

20 Oct Brissot in the Convtn calls for military action to disperse the *émigrés*.

31 Oct Decree stripping the comte de Provence of his rights of succession unless he returns to France within two months (vetoed by Louis XVI on 11 Nov).

9 Nov Law against the *émigrés:* if they do not return they will be accounted conspirators against France and their lands sequestrated (vetoed by Louis on 11 Nov).

16 Nov Pétion elected mayor of Paris (beating Lafayette, whom the court opposed).

25 Nov Creation of a Comité de surveillance ('Search Committee') with powers to investigate crimes of *lèse-nation*.

29 Nov New oath demanded of refractory priests: they will be accounted suspects unless they take the civic oath within a week (vetoed by the king on 19 Dec).

Leg Ass. asks Louis to request the Electors of Trier and Mainz to disperse the *émigré* formations within their territories.

Late Nov–Dec Ministerial reshuffle, benefiting the Feuillants (and including the appointment on 7 Dec of Narbonne as War Minister).

14 Dec Louis publicly informs the Elector of Trier that he will regard him as an enemy of France if he has not dispersed the *émigrés* by 15 Jan 1792 (though he secretly intimates to the Holy Roman Emperor his wish for the opposite).

31 Dec Amnesty passed for the troops of the Châteauvieux Regiment involved in the Nancy mutiny of Aug 1790.

1792

1 Jan   Ass. decrees that the 'Era of Liberty' has started on 1 Jan 1789.

6 Jan   Elector of Trier disperses the *émigrés* (in fact, not wholly carried out).

18 Jan   Comte de Provence deprived of his rights to regency.

23–24 Jan, 14 and 24 Feb   Sugar and coffee shortages lead to demonstrations in Paris and crowd seizures of groceries.

25 Jan   Leg Ass. asks Louis to request that the Holy Roman Emperor renounce treaties which threaten French sovereignty (notably the Pillnitz Declaration).

Feb–Mar   Grain riots and *taxation populaire* in many regions, including (3 Mar) the lynching of the mayor of Etampes, Simonneau, for refusing to fix food prices.

1 Feb   Law on passports: all travellers to carry one.

9 Feb   Decree announcing the sequestration by the nation of *émigré* property.

1 Mar   Death of Holy Roman Emperor Leopold II. His son and successor, Francis II, is more belligerently counter-rev.

10–23 Mar   FORMATION OF A 'GIRONDIN MINISTRY' (Roland, Clavière, etc), following the Girondins' attempted impeachment of Foreign Minister de Lessart for failing to inform the Ass. of the Holy Roman Emperor's war preparations.

25 Mar   Further ultimatum to the Holy Roman Emperor.

4 Apr   Colonies: decree according equality of political rights to mulattos and free blacks in the colonies: an expeditionary force of 6,000 men is dispatched to the W Indies to enforce the decree.

6 Apr   The wearing of religious dress forbidden.

15 Apr   Festival in Paris in honour of the Suisses of Châteauvieux responsible for the Nancy mutiny who had been sent to the galleys.

20 Apr   DECLARATION OF WAR: Louis in the Leg Ass. where he announces that as Francis II has failed to meet his ultimatum, France is at war with 'the king of Bohemia and Hungary' (i.e. with the monarch and not his subjects; and with Francis II as Austrian ruler rather than as Holy Roman Emperor). The other German states will in fact make common cause with Austria against Rev France. Only seven deputies in the Ass. oppose the declaration of war.

War, Apr–June 1792

29 Apr: General Dillon murdered by his troops after an unsuccessful skirmish with the Austrians near Valenciennes

Late Apr: Custine occupies the territory of Porrentruy, near Basle.

18 May: the three army commanders (Lafayette, Rochambeau, Luckner), afraid to commit in battle raw and undisciplined troops, urge peace negotiations.

Mid June: French armies resume the offensive, but are soon driven back, and by early Aug are well inside French frontiers.

20 May Decree on the police of Paris: tightening up of controls on travellers and strangers.

23 May Brissot and Vergniaud in the Ass. attack the *Comité autrichien* ('Austrian committee').

27 May Non-juring priests to be deported on denunciation of 20 citizens (vetoed by king on 19 June).

29 May Dissolution of the king's bodyguard on the grounds that it is riddled with aristocrats.

3 June *Fête de la Loi:* elaborate state funeral ceremony organised by Girondin and Feuillant deputies for Simonneau, the mayor of Etampes who had been assassinated on 3 Mar for refusing to accede to popular demands for the fixing of food prices.

8 June Proposed establishment near to Paris of a camp of 20,000 *fédérés* (vetoed by the king on 19 June).

13 June Following disagreement with Roland over withholding the royal sanction from the laws of 27 May and 8 June, Louis dismisses Roland and his colleagues and appoints a Feuillant-based ministry which fails, however, to win the confidence of the Ass.

17 June Feuillant/Jacobin 'Commission des Douze' (a kind of embryonic CPS) established to aid ministers in the conduct of the war.

18 June At the head of his army, Lafayette calls for the Ass. to suppress the Jacobin clubs.

Abolition of seigneurial *droits casuels* on land, save where these are justified by a legal contract.

20 June JOURNÉE OF 20 JUNE: crowds demonstrate urging Louis to withdraw his veto on the laws of 27 May and 8 June. They invade the Tuileries and oblige him to don the *bonnet rouge* and drink the health of the nation (but he still maintains his veto).

28 June Lafayette in Leg Ass. calls for the suppression of the Jacobin clubs and the punishment of the 20 June demonstrators.

1 July Moderate 'Petition of 20,000' against the *journée* of 20 June.

2 July Despite the king's veto, the *camp des fédérés* is decreed.

4–5 July Law on *la patrie en danger:* when the Ass. makes this declaration, legislative and administrative bodies assume emergency powers.

6 July The dept authorities of Paris remove Pétion as mayor of Paris on account of his behaviour on 20 June.

7 July Attempt at reconciliation between warring factions in the Ass.: the *baiser Lamourette.*

10 July Ceding to attacks, the Feuillant ministers resign.

11 July With Prussian forces assembling on the French frontiers, the Leg Ass. declares *la patrie en danger:* administrative bodies to sit in permanent

session; Nat Guard dispatched to colours. (The king's veto may now be evaded legally under emergency powers.)

12 July   Call for 50,000 volunteers for the army.

13 July   Leg Ass. re-establishes Pétion as mayor of Paris.

14 July   Third *Fête de le Fédération*.

17 July   *Emigré* property, sequestrated since 9 Feb, may be placed on sale like ecclesiastical 'nat lands'.

20, 29 July   Unsuccessful secret negotiations with the king by Girondin deputies (Vergniaud, Guadet).

23 July   Petition originating from a committee of *fédérés* meeting at the Jacobin Club demanding the overthrow of the monarchy.

25 July   Breton *fédérés* arrive in Paris.

Convtn permits the Paris sections to sit *en permanence*.

War, July–Sept 1792

25 July: BRUNSWICK MANIFESTO (see below).

19 Aug: Allied troops enter France and head for Paris.

23 Aug: Capitulation of Longwy.

1 Sept: SURRENDER OF VERDUN, the last fortress between the Allied armies and Paris.

20 Sept: BATTLE OF VALMY: after an exchange of artillery fire, the Prussians retreat.

(In the W Indies, French troops dispatched to impose political equality for free blacks and mulattos arrive (Sept). Planters begin secret negotiations with the British. In Sept, Martinique and Guadeloupe declare for the Bourbons, though they are soon brought back into line.)

27 July   Establishment at the Paris Hôtel-de-Ville of a coordinating committee to plan the king's overthrow.

28 July–1 Aug   News filters through to Paris of the BRUNSWICK MANIFESTO, in which the Allied CinC threatens death for Nat Guardsmen and citizens opposing the advance of the Allies, and exemplary violence against Paris if the royal family is harmed.

30 July   Passive citizens permitted to join the Nat Guard.

Some Paris sections (which had already integrated passive citizens in the Nat Guard) begin to admit passive citizens to their assemblies.

1 Aug   Arrival in Paris of the *fédérés* from Marseille.

Municipalities are instructed to manufacture pikes for nat defence.

3 Aug   Petition from 47 of Paris's 48 sections demanding the overthrow of the king. The Ass. adjourns discussion of the issue until 9 Aug.

9 Aug   Ass. makes no decision on the fate of the king. A Commune insurrectionnelle established in Paris to plan his overthrow.

10 Aug   *JOURNEE* OF 10 AUG: OVERTHROW OF THE MONARCHY. Popular demonstrations and attacks on the Tuileries lead the Leg Ass.:

- to suspend the king from the exercise of his functions
- to vote for the establishment of a Nat Convtn, to be elected by universal manhood suffrage, and with the task of drawing up a new constitution
- to re-enact all decrees vetoed by the king
- to establish and define the powers of a Provisional Executive Council (PEC), or *Conseil exécutif provisoire* of six ministers
- to send out 12 *commissaires* with far-ranging powers into the provinces to rally support for the Convtn.

POWER INTERREGNUM, 10 AUG–20 SEPT 1792

Power shared three ways in rather inchoate fashion:

- Leg Ass.
- PEC (headed unofficially by Danton)
- Commune insurrectionnelle.

All three bodies send out commissioners into the provinces to suspend disloyal military and civilian officials, arrest suspects, set up patriotic committees, etc.

Disturbances in the provinces occasioned by the overthrow of the king, and sometimes stoked by the *émigrés*.

11 Aug   Leg Ass. grants municipalities powers to enforce general security, notably the right to arrest suspects.

Paris Commune prohibits the publication of royalist journals.

12 Aug   Louis and the royal family placed in the Temple prison.

14 Aug   All state functionaries inc priests to take an oath of allegiance to the new government.

Common lands to be subdivided (a hasty measure never properly implemented).

16 Aug   Paris Commune prohibits religious processions and ceremonies in public.

17 Aug   'Extraordinary Tribunal' established to try individuals who have committed counter-rev offences in the *journée* of 10 Aug. (It will achieve little, and will be dissolved on 29 Nov.)

18 Aug   Suppression of teaching and charitable congregations, and religious confraternities. All forms of AR religious association have now been suppressed.

19 Aug   Lafayette flees to the enemy (who imprison him).

20, 25 Aug   Abolition without indemnity of all feudal dues except where seigneurs can show title-deeds.

26 Aug   Members of the clergy who have not taken the oath of 14 Aug are to leave France within two weeks on pain of deportation to Guiana.

News of the fall of Longwy reaches Paris.

27 Aug   Primary elections to the Convtn begin.

28 Aug   Leg Ass. permits house-to-house searches (*visites domiciliaires*) for arms and suspects: large numbers of arrests and imprisonments in Paris.

2 Sept Second phase of elections to Convtn begin.

2–6 Sept 'SEPT MASSACRES' break out in Paris on news of siege and impending fall of Verdun. Over 1,000 inmates of Paris's prisons murdered, with the connivance of the Commune's Comité de surveillance. Danton rallies Paris to self-defence against the threat of enemy invasion.

4 Sept Leg Ass. urges Convtn to abolish monarchy when it meets.

9–16 Sept Decrees to permit requisitioning for grain.

10 Sept Gold and silver church ornaments are requisitioned by the Ass. for the war effort.

20 Sept Legalisation of divorce.

Registration of births, marriages and deaths becomes a state responsibility.

LAST SESSION OF THE LEG ASS.

BATTLE OF VALMY.

5. THE CONVENTION DOWN TO THE PURGE OF THE GIRONDINS (SEPTEMBER 1792–JUNE 1793)

1792

20 Sept   FIRST MEETING OF THE NAT CONVTN.

21 Sept   Convtn replaces the Leg Ass. in the Salle du Manège.

Decision that the new constitution should be ratified by the people in primary assemblies.

Unanimous vote to abolish the monarchy.

22 Sept   YEAR I OF THE RPBC PROCLAIMED.

Decree instituting new elections for administrative, municipal and judicial offices.

23–27 Sept   Girondin deputies in the Convtn attack Marat (over the Sept Massacres), Robespierre (for his alleged dictatorial tendencies) and the power of the Paris Commune. They urge the call-up of *fédérés* from the depts to protect the Ass. against Paris (though the *fédérés* who come to be based in Paris rally to the sections rather than the Girondins).

25 Sept   PROCLAMATION OF THE RPBC 'ONE AND INDIVISIBLE'.

War, Sept–Dec 1792

NORTH: Following Valmy, the Allied forces retreat beyond French frontiers, allowing the French under Dumouriez to liberate Verdun (8 Oct) and Longwy (22 Oct), before entering Belgium (27 Oct). The major French victory at JEMAPPES (6 Nov) throws open Belgium, which Dumouriez proceeds to occupy before entering the Netherlands in late Nov.

EAST: French offensive in the Rhineland, with Custine taking Speier (25 Sept), Worms (5 Oct), Mainz (21 Oct) and Frankfurt (23 Oct), and occupying the Palatinate (9 Nov). Prussia retakes Frankfurt on 2 Dec, and Custine falls back on Mainz for the winter.

SWITZERLAND: the French occupy Basle (30 Oct).

SOUTH-EAST: Anselme enters Nice (29 Sept); Savoy is liberated (Sept–Oct).

2 Oct   CREATION OF THE COMMITTEE OF GENERAL SECURITY (CGS), or *comité de sûreté générale*, with as yet vaguely defined police powers.

10 Oct   Brissot expelled from the Jacobin Club.

Ministerial reshuffle as Danton resigns from the Executive Council in order to take up his place in the Convtn.

16 Oct   The fate of the king is referred to the Legislation Committee.

18 Oct   Girondins attack Danton over irregularities in his accounts as Minister of Justice.

25 Oct–7 Nov   Further Girondin attacks on Robespierre, Danton, Marat.

7 Nov   Mailhe reports on behalf of the Legislation Committee: the Convtn has the power to pass sentence on the king.

13 Nov   THE DEBATE ON THE FATE OF THE KING BEGINS, with Saint-Just making a powerful maiden speech attacking Louis.

16 Nov   Executive Council declares freedom of navigation on the Scheldt, which contravenes the Treaty of Munster (1648) and upsets the Dutch and the British.

19 Nov   DECREE OF FRATERNITY (*secours et fraternité*) offering aid to oppressed peoples wishing to recover their liberty.

20 Nov   Discovery of compromising secret correspondence of the king in the *armoire de fer*.

26 Nov   Law on *émigrés* who had returned to France: they were to leave Paris within 24 hours, France within a week.

27 Nov   ANNEXATION OF SAVOY.

Nov–Dec   Serious peasant disturbances and price-fixing demonstrations in the Beauce region.

3 Dec   Convtn decrees that it will proceed with the trial of the king.

4 Dec   Death penalty for advocates of the re-establishment of monarchy.

6 Dec   Creation of a committee to draw up a list of charges against the king.

8 Dec   Roland introduces a law restoring free trade in grain.

10–11 Dec   KING'S TRIAL BEGINS. Louis is interrogated in the Convtn.

15 Dec   LAW ESTABLISHING REVOLUTIONARY ADMINISTRATION IN ALL CONQUERED TERRITORIES: sequestration of clerical lands and property of enemies of the regime; abolition of tithes, feudal dues; tax on the wealthy; all functionaries to swear an oath of allegiance.

16 Dec   Death penalty for threatening the unity and integrity of the Rpbc.

26 Dec   Speeches for the defence in the king's trial.

27 Dec   Girondins propose a referendum (the so-called *appel au peuple*) over the fate of the king.

1793

1 Jan   FOUNDATION OF THE COMMITTEE OF GENERAL DEFENCE (CGD), or *Comité de Défense générale*, to stimulate and help direct the war effort.

14 Jan   CONVTN VOTES ON THE KING: he is guilty (693/0 votes); and there will be no *appel au peuple* (424/283).

16–17 Jan CONVTN DECREES THE DEATH OF THE KING. The voting figures: 387/334.

19–20 Jan Deputies vote on question of reprieve for the king: no reprieve (380/310).

20 Jan Sentence of the king decreed.
Assassination of Lepeletier de Saint-Fargeau.

21 Jan EXECUTION OF LOUIS XVI.

22 Jan Resignation of Roland as Minister of the Interior.

24 Jan Funeral of Lepeletier de Saint-Fargeau.

28 Jan From exile, the comte de Provence declares himself regent of France during the minority of the imprisoned Louis XVII, and makes a statement urging the re-establishment of the AR.

31 Jan ANNEXATION OF NICE.

Jan–Mar War declared against various Italian states.

1 Feb FRANCE DECLARES WAR ON BRITAIN AND HOLLAND.

War, Feb–Apr 1793

NORTH: Dumouriez leads an ambitious offensive into Holland in Feb, and seizes Breda (25 Feb). On 1 Mar, the Austrians under Coburg counter-attack and take Aix-la-Chapelle and Liège, before inflicting a crushing defeat on the French at NEERWINDEN (18 Mar) which forces the French out of Belgium. After various acts of treachery, Dumouriez flees to the enemy (5 Apr).

EAST: Custine loses the Rhineland to Brunswick, who besieges the French outpost in Mainz (Apr).

5 Feb All state functionaries must produce a valid *certificat de civisme*.

13 Feb Deputation of the Paris sections (among which the propaganda of *enragé* militants such as Jacques Roux is having increasing influence) petitions the Convtn for legislation to lower bread prices.

15 Feb ANNEXATION OF THE PRINCIPALITY OF MONACO.

21 Feb LAW OF THE *AMALGAME,* which Dubois-Crancé had proposed for the Military Committee on 7 Feb (only properly implemented from Autumn 1793).

24 Feb *LEVÉE* OF 300,000 MEN for the armies.

24–27 Feb Consumer disturbances in Paris, notably over bread and soap prices, as economic disruption (caused by war, the depreciation of the assignat, the loss of colonial markets, unemployment in luxury trades, etc) grows apace.

Feb–Mar Various regions of Belgium vote for incorporation into France.

4 Mar Decree annulling commercial and alliance treaties of the AR.

7 Mar WAR DECLARED AGAINST SPAIN.

9 Mar CREATION OF REPS *EN MISSION:* deputies are to be sent out as delegates of the Convtn to each of the departments to levy men for the army and to rally the nation behind the war effort.

War in the Vendée, Mar–June 1793

Operations to enforce the military levy of 24 Feb trigger off peasant revolt in W France.

In Mar the rebels are successful in establishing control of many towns (Cholet, Machecoul, Parthenay), though they fail to take Les Sables-d'Olonne (23 and 25 Mar), from where liaison with the British fleet would have been possible.

In May, regular troops are sent against the rebels for the first time, but this does not halt the Vendéans's success: on 5 May, the rebels, now grouped in the 'Royal Catholic Army' (*armée catholique royale*) seize Thouars, and go on to seize Parthenay (9 May) and Fontenay (25 May).

9–10 Mar Attacks on the printing presses of Girondin newspapers in Paris. Attempt at organising a rev *journée* by the *enragés,* with Cordelier help.

10 Mar ESTABLISHMENT OF A REV TRIBUNAL for counter-rev offences. Precipitated by indifferent French fortunes at the front and by news coming in about the Vendée revolt.

17 Mar An assembly in Mainz approves incorporation into France.

18 Mar Death penalty for proponents of the *loi agraire.*

19 Mar DEATH PENALTY WITHOUT APPEAL FOR REBELS CAPTURED UNDER ARMS decreed, following news of the French defeat at Neerwinden (18 March).

21 Mar ESTABLISHMENT OF *COMITES DE SURVEILLANCE* to vet the movements of strangers in communes and sections and issue *certificats de civisme.*

23 Mar BISHOPRIC OF BASLE/REGION OF PORRENTRUY ANNEXED, and becomes the department of Mont-Terrible.

25 Mar Reorganisation of CGD, and renewal of its personnel.

26 Mar CGD assumes title 'Committee of Public Safety' (*Comité de Salut public*).
Decree ordering the disarming of suspects (ex-nobles, ecclesiastics, etc).

27 Mar Dumouriez at the front declares against the Convtn.

28 Mar Laws against *émigrés* codified and made more severe: *émigrés* are regarded as legally deceased.

29 Mar Restriction of press freedom: death penalty for inciting murder, violation of property, dissolution of the Ass., re-establishment of the monarchy.

1 Apr Dumouriez hands over to the Austrians War Minister Beurnonville and the four deputies sent to arrest him.

5 Apr After failing to turn his men against the Convtn in Paris, Dumouriez flees to the enemy, taking with him the duc de Chartres (the future King Louis-Philippe).
Marat, as president of the Jacobin Club, circulates all affiliated societies urging them to recall and dismiss deputies who voted the *appel au peuple* during the king's trial.

5–6 Apr ESTABLISHMENT OF A COMMITTEE OF PUBLIC SAFETY (*Comité de Salut public*) to be drawm from members of the Convtn. It is empowered to supervise the actions of the Executive Council and the administration and to pass decrees as it sees fit.

6 Apr Arrest and imprisonment of the duc d'Orléans.

9 Apr ESTABLISHMENT OF REPS *AUX ARMEES:* deputies are sent out *en mission* to each of the armies to supervise the high command and contribute to the war effort.

11 Apr Law stipulating that the assignat is to be regarded in transactions as equivalent to its face value.

13 Apr Death penalty for individuals advocating peace negotiations on a basis which would compromise French independence.

14 Apr On Guadet's instigation, Marat is impeached (voting figures 226/93, with 47 abstentions) over the circular letter of 5 Apr, and sent before the Rev Tribunal.

15 Apr 35 of Paris's 48 sections petition the Convtn over Marat's impeachment, and call for the expulsion of 22 notorious Girondins.

21 Apr Deportation of non-juring priests and of constitutional priests denounced by six citizens within a canton.

24 Apr Marat is acquitted by the Rev Tribunal.

30 Apr Codification of regulations relating to reps attached to the armies.

4 May ESTABLISHMENT OF A MAXIMUM ON GRAINS (the 'First Maximum').

10 May Convtn moves from the Salle du Manège to the Tuileries.

18 May 'Commission of Twelve' (*Commission des Douze*) established to investigate possible subversion by the Paris Commune and sections: its membership is packed with Girondins and their supporters.

20 May Forced loan on the rich decreed (followed by further measures, 22 June, 3 Sept).

24 May Commission of Twelve orders the arrest of Hébert for subversion in his newspaper, the *Père Duchesne;* and later of Dobsen and Varlet.

25 May Isnard viciously rejects the demand of the Commune that Hébert be released.

26 May Jacobin Club declares itself to be in a state of insurrection.
In the temporary absence of protesting Girondins, the Montagnard-dominated Convtn abolishes the Commission of Twelve.

27 May Release of Hébert, Dobsen and Varlet.

28 May Convtn re-establishes the Commission of Twelve.

28–9 May Establishment in Paris of an insurrectionary committee, prominent on which are Dobsen, Dufourny and Varlet.

29 May *Lyon:* moderates overthrow the radical municipal government.

31 May *JOURNEE* OF 31 MAY: sectional demonstration, influenced by the *enragés*, with demands:
  • exclusion of Girondins from the Convtn
  • revocation of the 'Commission of Twelve'
  • arrest of suspects
  • purges of all administrations

- establishment of an *armée révolutionnaire*
- voting rights for *sans-culottes* alone
- bread price to be fixed at 3 sous a liv
- aid to poor, needy and to families of soldiers.

Only the demand to revoke the Commission of Twelve is heeded.

2 June   JOURNEE OF 2 JUNE: PURGE OF THE GIRONDINS. Further popular demonstrations with the aid of Hanriot and the Paris Nat Guard lead to Convtn agreeing to the arrest of 29 Girondin deputies, plus the Girondin ministers Clavière and Lebrun.

6. THE CONVENTION FROM THE PURGE OF THE GIRONDINS TO THE OVERTHROW OF ROBESPIERRE (JUNE 1793–JULY 1794/THERMIDOR II)

1793

Federalism and counter-revolution, late Spring–Summer 1793

To counter-rev in W France is added the Federalist revolt, as at one time a majority of depts protest against the centralisation of power and the *journées* of 31 May and 2 June.

FEDERALISM: the main centres are Brittany and Normandy (where Buzot, Barbaroux and Pétion form an army against the Convtn); the SW (based in Bordeaux); Lyon; and the Midi (esp Nîmes, Avignon, Marseille and Toulon). In some localities (notably Lyon, Marseille, Toulon) federalism shades into outright counter-rev.

13 July: Brune defeats and diperses a Girondin army at the 'battle' of Pacy-sur-Eure; Buzot, Barbaroux and Pétion flee to Bordeaux.

17 July: Federalists in Lyon execute Jacobin ex-mayor Chalier who becomes a 'martyr of liberty'.

27 July: Avignon retaken by Carteaux.

9 Aug: SIEGE OF LYON by Kellermann begins.

25 Aug: MARSEILLE RETAKEN by Carteaux.

29 Aug: TOULON HANDS OVER THE PORT TO THE BRITISH: the French thus lose their Mediterranean fleet.

18 Sept: Bordeaux retaken by Tallien and Ysabeau.

9 Oct: LYON FALLS (at which time, only Toulon still holds out).

VENDÉAN REVOLT: Aided by the Rpbc's discomfiture with the Federalist Revolt, and despite the dispatch of regular troops to the area from May, the Vendéan rebels (from 12 June with Cathelineau as their CinC) continue to pose a serious threat in W France, and defeat French forces on several occasions.

8 June: Saumur falls to the Vendéans.

29 June: Vendéans fail to take Nantes. Cathelineau is killed, to be succeeded on 19 July by d'Elbée.

5 July: Vendéan victory at Châtillon.

18 July: Vendéan victory at Vihiers.

27 July: Vendéans capture Ponts-de-Cé and threaten Angers.

1 Aug: decision to transfer surrendered Mainz garrison to the Vendée, and to employ a scorched earth policy against the rebels.

13 Aug: battle of Luçon: Vendéans heavily defeated.

War, Spring–Summer 1793

Little goes right for the Rpbc, as Allied forces pour over French frontiers at numerous points.

NORTH: the British under York and the Dutch head for the Channel and besiege Dunkirk (21 Aug), while the Austrians defeat the French near Condé (8 May) and Valenciennes (21–23 May). They besiege fortresses on the Belgian frontier and take Condé (10 July) and Valenciennes (28 July) and then invest Le Quesnoy and Maubeuge.

RHINE: the Prussians under Brunswick besiege Mainz, which falls (23 July), and the French fall back into Alsace as the Prussians seize the Wissembourg lines and besiege Landau (13 Oct).

ALPS: Savoy is invaded by the Piedmontese with the French army, weakened by troop transfers to Lyon and Toulon, unable to react.

SOUTH-WEST: Spain advances over the frontier on both sides of the Pyrenees, and defeats the French near Perpignan in minor engagements.

W. INDIES: The British fail to bolster royalist revolt in Martinique (June). Sonthonax, commanding the French troops who are trying to maintain French rule over rebellious planters, is increasingly drawn into alliance with the slaves. He unofficially proclaims slave emancipation (29 Aug). A further British expeditionary force sets sail to aid the Saint-Domingue planters (Nov–Dec). Destruction and political chaos on this island will last into the late 1790s, lead to the political control from 1801 by the slave-leader Toussaint l'Ouverture, and write off the economic value of the colony to France.

June–July   Disturbances in Paris not over bread (fixed by the Commune at 3 sous) but over other commodities. Continuing *enragé* agitation.

3 June   *Emigré* lands to be sold in small plots.

4 June   Abolition of bounties to slave-traders (though no slave-trading has taken place since war began).

6–19 June   Protest against the expulsion of the Girondin deputies from the Convtn by the '75' (in fact, 76 deputies).

8 June   Robespierre persuades Convtn not to abolish the *comités de surveillance.*

10 June   Decree relating to the sharing out of common lands (a much more moderate law than the one hastily passed on 14 Aug 1792).

16 June   Cordeliers demand the formation of an *armée révolutionnaire.*

24 June   VOTING OF THE 1793 CONSTITUTION, following debates from 11 June. The constitution will be submitted for ratification to the nation's primary assemblies.

25 June   Jacques Roux presents a petition to the Convtn calling for radical economic legislation.

To combat federalism based round Avignon, the Convtn creates the dept of the Vaucluse.

26–8 June   Soap riots in Paris.

27 June   Closure of the Paris *Bourse* (stock exchange).

10 July   Renewal of the CPS: removal of Danton.

13 July   Assassination of Marat by Charlotte Corday. Robespierre introduces in the Convtn the (never-to-be-implemented) educational plans of Lepeletier de Saint-Fargeau.

16 July   Funeral of Marat.

17 July   FINAL SUPPRESSION OF ALL FEUDAL DUES (WITHOUT INDEMNITY). All seigneurial title-deeds are to be publicly burnt.

Measures taken by reps *en mission* to be regarded as provisional decrees of the Convtn.

23 July   Only one church bell is to remain in each parish. The remainder may be melted down for cannon.

26 July   DEATH PENALTY FOR HOARDERS: communes and sections are to appoint commissioners (*commissaires aux accaparements*) with powers of search and confiscation.

27 July   ROBESPIERRE VOTED ON TO THE CPS.

1 Aug   Convtn agrees to the implementation of a scorched earth policy in the civil war in the Vendée.

Convtn agrees to a decimal system of measurement.

3 Aug   All church bells are placed at the disposal of the Minister of War for possible melting down for the manufacture of cannon.

All British subjects in France are to be arrested.

6 Aug   In the Jacobin Club, Robespierre denounces Jacques Roux, whose *enragé* agitation is growing apace once more.

9 Aug   A public granary (*grenier d'abondance*) is to be established in each district (never really implemented).

10 Aug   Festival of the Unity and Indivisibility of the Rpbc in Paris commemorating the fall of the king. Results announced of the plebiscite ratifying the 1793 Constitution.

11 Aug   Robespierre baulks proposal in Convtn to hold primary elections under the 1793 Constitution.

12 Aug   The dept of the Rhône-et-Loire is to be split into two (Rhône, Loire), so as to separate rebellious Lyon from its provisioning area in the Forez.

14 Aug   Paris Commune forbids religious processions outside churches.

15 Aug   All state functionaries to take the civic oath to the new constitution.

16 Aug   Convtn accepts the idea of a conscript army advocated by the Commune and Paris sections.

Reps *en mission* are authorised to purge the regular authorities and introduce proven patriots in their place.

23 Aug *LEVEE EN MASSE* DECREED

24 Aug Suppression of joint-stock companies and societies (including the Caisse d'escompte and the Compagnie des Indes). Foundation of a consolidated national debt, the *Grand Livre de la Dette Publique.*

26 Aug Deportation from France of all priests who have not taken the civic oath.

2 Sept News reaches Paris of Toulon's surrender to the British fleet (29 Aug).

4 Sept Popular demonstration outside the Hôtel-de-Ville for more radical legislation.

5 Sept *JOURNEE* OF 5 SEPT: sections march on Convtn, which makes concessions:

- Terror the 'order of the day'
- introduction of a General Maximum
- arrests of suspects
- purge of rev committees
- establishment of an *armée révolutionnaire*
- gratuity of 40 sous for those attending sectional meetings; 3 liv for attendance of members of *comités de surveillance*
- expansion of the Paris Rev Tribunal
- only two sectional meetings per *décade.*

Arrest and imprisonment of Jacques Roux.

6 Sept Following on from the *journées* of 5–6 Sept, Collot-d'Herbois and Billaud-Varenne are elected to the CPS.

9 Sept Decree organising the Paris *armée révolutionnaire* (it will finally be put on a proper footing in Oct).

Sectional assemblies prohibited from sitting *en permanence.* This law will be circumvented by the most militant *sans-culottes* by the creation of sectional societies.

11 Sept GRAIN MAXIMUM DECREED: maximum price levels are introduced for grain and fodder.

Commissioners sent into the provinces by the ministers are henceforth to report direct to the CPS.

13–14 Sept Renewal of personnel on the Committee of General Security (CGS) under the guidance of the CPS.

15 Sept Decree renouncing France's former 'philanthropic' attitude in the conduct of war and authorising reprisals on the enemy.

17 Sept LAW OF SUSPECTS: definition of 'suspect' made wider; surveillance improved and placed under the authority of CGS.

18 Sept Arrest of leading *enragé* Varlet.

21 Sept The *enragé* Leclerc, threatened with arrest, suspends publication of his radical journal, the *Ami du peuple.*

Wearing of rev cockade by women made obligatory.

Navigation Act: overseas trade must be conducted in French vessels (in practice, this law is inoperable).

24–25 Sept   Robespierre fights off criticism of the CPS in the Convtn from left and right.

29 Sept   GENERAL MAXIMUM on all foodstuffs and commodities.

War and counter-rev Sept–Dec 1793

Within France, in the so-called 'anarchic' stage of the Terror, reps *en mission* with wide-ranging powers and often acting in variance from orders from Paris, are effective in rallying France in the 'war of national defence'. The Law of 14 Frim II is aimed to bring these often centrifugal forces more closely under central control. French fortunes improve on all fronts: the Allied forces are driven out of France; the Federalist revolt is ended, with the fall of Lyon (9 Oct) and Toulon (19 Dec); and the Vendéan revolt is brought more effectively under control.

NORTH: the British and Dutch are defeated in the important battle of HONDSCHOOTE, just outside Dunkirk (6–8 Sept), though the French subsequently suffer defeat at Menin (13 Sept). The Austrians are defeated too at WATTIGNIES (15–16 Oct) and driven back on Mons, which allows Maubeuge to be freed.

EAST: Hoche's offensive aimed at Kaiserslautern fails (28–30 Nov), but the French regroup in Dec and retake the Wissembourg lines, lift the siege of Landau (26 Dec) and drive the Austrians out of Alsace.

SOUTH: the Spanish are pushed out of France. Bordeaux (18 Sept) and Lyon (9 Oct) fall to the Rpbc, while on 19 Dec the British are forced to evacuate Toulon.

WEST: the defeat of Charette at Montaigu (16 Sept) is offset by the Vendéans's victory over Kléber at Tougoin (19 Sept). The Rpbc's victory at CHOLET (17–18 Oct) is important and crucial, however, and forces the rebels (who on 20 Oct replace d'Elbée with La Rochejacquelein as CinC) to make an unconvincing sortie to Granville, putatively to meet up with British forces (13–14 Nov). The rebels fall back towards the Loire, fail to take Angers (3–4 Dec), are heavily defeated in a street battle in Le Mans (13–14 Dec) and then decisively crushed at SAVENAY (23 Dec). The early months of 1794 will be marked by mass executions of rebels (Noirmoutier, Angers, Saumur, Laval, etc), esp through Turreau's 'infernal columns'.

3 Oct   Report of Amar of the CGS on the Girondins: large numbers of referrals to the Rev Tribunal ensue.

5 Oct   ADOPTION OF A REV CALENDAR. Convtn accepts reform of the calendar, with the Rpbcn era having begun 22 Sept 1792.

8 Oct   Liquidation of the Compagnie des Indes: sleight of hand over the decree by Delaunay and Fabre d'Eglantine with the aim of self-enrichment.

9 Oct   British manufactured goods prohibited entry into France.

10 Oct   On the recommendation of the CPS, the Convtn decrees that THE GOVERNMENT OF FRANCE WILL BE 'REVOLUTIONARY UNTIL THE PEACE'. The 1793 Constitution is put on ice – indefinitely, as it will prove.

12 Oct(?) Fabre d'Eglantine denounces to the CGS a 'foreign plot' against the Rpbc involving Proli, Desfieux, Pereira, Dubuisson.

12 Oct As news comes in of the surrender of Lyon, the Convtn decrees that 'Lyon will be destroyed'; it is to be renamed 'Ville-Affranchie', or 'Commune-Affranchie'.

16 Oct Execution of Marie-Antoinette.

24 Oct Fabre d'Eglantine reports on the introduction of the Rev Calendar.

[YEAR II (22 SEPT 1793–21 SEPT 1794)]

27 Oct/6 brum Establishment of a National Food Commission, the *Commission des subsistances*, to rationalise and enforce the Maximum.

29 Oct/8 brum Speeding up of the trial procedure in the Rev Tribunal.

30 Oct/9 brum Dissolution of women's political societies.

31 Oct/10 brum Execution of 20 of the leading Girondins, to be followed by Orléans (6 Nov), Madame Roland (9 Nov), Bailly (12 Nov), Barnave (29 Nov), Rabaut Saint-Etienne (5 Dec), etc.

1 Nov/11 brum CPS starts using *tutoiement* in its public and private correspondence; the practice becomes widespread.

5 Nov/15 brum List of civic festivals in the Rev Calendar approved by Convtn.

6 Nov/16 brum Convtn decrees that communes have the right to renounce the Catholic faith.

7 Nov/17 brum Clootz *et al.* persuade Gobel to renounce his priesthood and to resign as archbishop of Paris. Most ecclesiastical deputies follow his example and 'abdicate'. This triggers off a wave of dechristianising activity in Paris.

10 Nov/20 brum 'Festival of Liberty' in Paris: dechristianising activities; Notre-Dame cathedral designated the 'Temple of Reason'.

14 Nov/24 brum Chabot denounces the Compagnie des Indes fraud to the CGS.

18 Nov/28 brum Billaud-Varennes introduces the debate on the rev government (which will result in the Law of 14 Frim).

20 Nov/30 brum Danton returns to Paris from Arcis-sur-Aube and becomes the focus for the Indulgents.

21 Nov/1 frim Robespierre has 'foreign plotters' Proli, Pereira, Desfieux and Dubuisson excluded from the Jacobin Club, and denounces them in the Convtn (21 Nov, 28 Nov). He also attacks dechristianisation as 'aristocratic' and immoral.

22 Nov/2 frim Stipulations of the law of 3 June 1793 relating to the sale of *émigré* property extended to all forms of nat land.

23 Nov/3 frim Closure of Paris churches by the Commune.

24 Nov/4 frim Law establishing the nomenclature of the Rev Calendar.

26 Nov/6 frim Danton attacks dechristianisation and ultra-revs.

35

4 Dec/14 frim 'LAW OF REVOLUTIONARY GOVERNMENT' (= 'LAW OF 14 FRIMAIRE'): centralisation of power on the CPS; bureaucratisation of the Terror; etc.

5 Dec/15 frim Desmoulins launches *Le Vieux Cordelier*.

6 Dec/16 frim On the prompting of Robespierre, Cambon and Danton, the Convtn reaffirms the principle of freedom of worship.

7 Dec/17 frim Property of parents whose children are *émigrés* may be confiscated by the state.

17 Dec/27 frim Fabre d'Eglantine denounces to CPS Vincent and Ronsin, who are arrested.

19 Dec/29 frim Fabre d'Eglantine exposed as party to the Compagnie des Indes fraud.
Convtn institutes (in theory) compulsory primary education.

21 Dec/1 niv Collot-d'Herbois justifies the savage repression of Lyon, and wins the Convtn's approval.

24 Dec/4 niv Toulon, recaptured by Dugommier and Bonaparte on 19 Dec/29 frim, to be renamed 'Port-la-Montagne'.

25 Dec/5 niv Robespierre's report to the Convtn, 'On the principles of rev government'.

29 Dec/9 niv Dispatch of 58 reps *en mission* into the provinces to purge regular authorities and enforce the Law of 14 Frimaire.

[1794 (12 NIV II–11 NIV III)]

7 Jan/18 niv Robespierre denounces Desmoulins and his *Vieux Cordelier* in the Jacobin Club.

11 Jan/22 niv Grégoire reports on cultural issues: French to replace Latin on public monuments; denunciation of 'vandalism'; importance of preserving the nation's cultural patrimony.

12–13 Jan/23–24 niv Arrest of Fabre d'Eglantine over the Compagnie des Indes affair.

16 Jan/27 niv Marseille renamed 'Ville-sans-Nom' because of its federalist past.

1 Feb/13 pluv 10,000 million liv to be distributed among the depts in poor relief.
Establishment of a nat commission of arms (tantamount to a ministry of armaments).

2 Feb/14 pluv Following a Cordelier campaign in their support, Vincent and Ronsin are released.

4 Feb/16 pluv ABOLITION OF SLAVERY IN THE COLONIES.

5 Feb/17 pluv Robespierre's report to the Convtn, 'On the principles of political morality'.

21 Feb/3 vent Barère proposes a new General Maximum.

26 Feb, 3 March/8 and 13 vent   Saint-Just introduces the 'DECREES OF VENTOSE', intended to distribute the property of suspects among the poor.

War, Spring–Summer 1794
The victory of the Rpbc.
NORTH: though he loses Landrecies to Coburg (30 Apr), Pichegru goes on to defeat him at TOURCOING (18 May). The outcome of the battle of Tournai (22 May) is even, but following defeat at Hooglede (17 June) the Allies retreat. Charleroi is captured (25 June), and Coburg is defeated by Jourdan at the important battle of FLEURUS (26 June) which allows the French to push into Belgium and occupy it. On 9 therm (27 July), Pichegru is entering Antwerp; Jourdan, Liège.
SOUTH: the French offensive against Spain is successful: Catalonia is invaded and San Sebastian occupied (25 July). Invasion of Italy and Savoy begins.
W. INDIES: The British occupy Martinique and Guadeloupe. Based in Guadeloupe, however, Victor Hugues is from June leading resistance to the British in collaboration with the emancipated slaves.
SEA: technically, the French fleet loses to the British in sea battles off Brittany (28 and 29 May and the 'Glorious' First of June), but the action allows a crucial convoy of American grain to enter France safely. In the Mediterranean, the British occupy Corsica (10 Aug).

13–14 Mar/23–24 vent   Arrest of Cordelier leaders (inc Hébert, Ronsin, Vincent, Momoro) and 'foreign plotters' (Proli, Pereira, Dubuisson, Desfieux, Kock, etc) and their commitment to the Rev Tribunal.

13 Mar/23 vent   Against rumblings of insurrection in the Cordeliers Club over the trial of the Hébertists, Convtn decrees new measures against conspirators: tighter controls on public officials; looser definition of suspects; ex-nobles forbidden to reside in Paris, frontier towns, naval ports.

24 Mar/4 germ   EXECUTION OF THE HEBERTISTS, following a trial which is 'a parody of justice' (AULARD).

27 Mar/7 germ   Abolition of the Paris *armée révolutionnaire*.

29–30 Mar/9–10 germ   Arrest of Indulgents (Danton, Desmoulins, Delacroix, Philippeaux) plus assorted others (Westermann, Guzman, Espagnac, Háerault de Séchelles) and their referral before the Rev Tribunal.

1 Apr/12 germ   Abolition of *commissaires aux accaparements*.
Abolition of ministries and their replacement by 12 executive commissions.

5 Apr/16 germ   EXECUTION OF THE DANTONISTS, following a show trial (2–5 Apr/13–16 germ).

13 Apr/24 germ   Execution of assorted batch of alleged dissidents including the widows of Hébert and Desmoulins, plus Chaumette, Gobel, Dillon.

16 Apr/27 germ   At Saint-Just's instigation, a police law is passed: CPS assumes policing powers by the establishment of a *bureau de police générale* which

the CGS soon will resent; ex-nobles debarred from public office and forbidden to reside in Paris, fortresses or naval ports.

19 Apr/30 germ   Recall of 30 reps *en mission*.

Apr–May/flor-prair   The power of the Parisian *sans-culotte* movement is neutralised: the Commune is brought to heel by the arrest of Pache and his replacement as mayor of Paris by the CPS nominee Fleuriot-Lescot; Parisian sectional societies, which had sprung up following the limitations placed on sectional assemblies from 5 Sept 1793, are closed down under Jacobin and government pressure.

7 May/18 flor   DECREE INSTITUTING THE CULT OF THE SUPREME BEING, following a major speech in the Convtn by Robespierre, 'On the principles of political morality'.

8 May/19 flor   Dissolution of rev tribunals and commissions in the provinces (though the Rev Tribunal at Arras will be retained until 22 mess; and the commission at Orange is only established 10 May/21 flor).

11 May/22 flor   Barère introduces the *Grand Livre de Bienfaisance Nationale*, an ambitious pensions scheme for the rural poor.

20 May/1 prair   Attempt on the life of Collot-d'Herbois by Ladmiral.

23 May/4 prair   Arrest of Cécile Renault, would-be assassin of Robespierre.

4 June/16 prair   Robespierre unanimously elected President of the Convtn.

8 June/20 prair   FESTIVAL OF THE SUPREME BEING in Paris, with Robespierre as unofficial master of ceremonies.

10 June/22 prair   'LAW OF 22 PRAIRIAL': reform of the Rev Tribunal to make it produce more convictions. The 'Great Terror' begins.

15 June/27 prair   Vadier reports for the CGS to the Convtn on the case of the visionary and ultra-Robespierrist Catherine Théot: he turns the affair against Robespierre.

28 June/10 mess   Saint-Just brings to Paris news of the victory at Fleurus (26 June): he finds members of the CPS at daggers drawn.

22–3 July/4–5 therm   Failed attempt at reconciliation between CPS and CGS.

23 July/5 therm   Commune publishes list of maximum wage-rates, whose implementation would involve wage-cuts for urban workers.

26 July/8 therm   Robespierre attacks his opponents in the Convtn, and has Collot-d'Herbois and Billaud-Varenne expelled from the Jacobin Club. His enemies, orchestrated by Fouché and Tallien, regroup and establish a working relationship with key members of the Plain.

27 July/9 therm   *JOURNEE* OF 9 THERMIDOR: THE OVERTHROW OF ROBESPIERRE. A muddled day, in which things might have gone either way. The opponents of Robespierre have him (along with Couthon, Saint-Just, etc) arrested, prior to execution the following day.

7. THE THERMIDORIAN CONVENTION (JULY 1794/THERMIDOR II–OCTOBER 1795/ BRUMAIRE IV

1794/Year II

28 July/10 therm   Barère in Convtn supports the Thermidor coup, but defends the record and the role of the CPS.

29 July/11 therm   On Tallien's suggestion, a quarter of the personnel of the committees to be renewed each month, with re-eligibility after a month's absence. Prieur de la Côte-d'Or and Jean Bon Saint-André are replaced on the CPS by Tallien and Thuriot.

Mass purge of Robespierrists from membership of the Jacobin Club. Over 100 Robespierre supporters from the Commune will be executed in following days.

1 Aug/14 therm   Repeal of the Law of 22 Prairial. Major personnel changes in the CGS.

2 Aug/15 therm   Former nobles and priests are excluded from public office.

3 Aug/16 therm   The law of the previous day excluding priests and ex-nobles from public office is repealed.

5–10 Aug/18–23 therm   Mass release of suspects from Paris prisons.

6 Aug/19 therm   Paris Nat Guard not to have a single commander, but a commanding committee of five members.

10 Aug/23 therm   Reorganisation of the Rev Tribunal: its proceedings are to be less summary in future.

13 Aug/26 therm   Reps en mission are in future to serve for only limited periods: reps en mission in the provinces, three months: reps aux armées, six months.

21 Aug/4 fruct   Sectional assemblies only to meet once every 10 days.

24 Aug/7 fruct   LAW ON REV GOVT. Restructuring and decentralisation of government: creation of 16 committees, 12 of which to be assisted by the commissions exécutives; powers of CPS restricted to war and diplomacy; power centred on the three 'committees of government' (CPS, CGS, Legislation Committee).

Restrictions placed on the work of comités révolutionnaires: they are only to exist in communes with a population over 8,000 and in district chefs-lieux, while in Paris they are to number 12 in future, not 48.

29 Aug/12 fruct   In Convtn, Lecointre attacks Billaud-Varenne and Collot-d'Herbois, who resign from the CPS.

31 Aug/14 fruct   Decree reorganising (and limiting the powers of) the Paris Commune.

3 Sept/17 fruct   Fréron, Lecointre and Tallien expelled from the Jacobin Club.

5 Sept/19 fruct   Jacobin Club adopts a radical programme (enforcement of Law of Suspects, strengthened Rev Tribunal, exclusion of priests and nobles from public office, etc).

7 Sept/21 fruct   General Maximum to be observed for the whole of year III (though in fact, increasing non-observance is soon apparent).

15 Sept/29 fruct   Appointment as CinC in W France of Hoche, who decides on a policy of firmness allied with conciliation (amnesty, release of prisoners, etc).

18 Sept/2 jc   On Cambon's prompting and for largely financial reasons, the state suspends payment of the religious budget.

[YEAR III (22 SEPT 1794–22 SEPT 1795)]

War, Autumn 1794–Winter 1795
French fortunes prosper after Fleurus, not least because the Allies fall out with each other, notably over the Third Polish Partition.
The French cross the Roer (2 Oct 1794) and drive the Austrians back across the Rhine. In late Dec, Pichegru crosses the Meuse and his cavalry captures the ice-bound Dutch fleet on the Helder (23 Jan). He occupies Holland. The war with Spain prospers too.

28 Sept/7 vendém   The Legislation Committee is permitted to designate appointees to all regular authorities.

8 Oct/17 vendém   Prohibition on the meeting of Parisian sectional assemblies.

16 Oct/25 vendém   Prohibition of collective petitioning and reciprocal affiliation of clubs (a measure aimed at the Jacobins).

9 Nov/19 brum   Fréron's *jeunesse dorée* attacks the Jacobin Club.

11 Nov/21 brum   In the Convtn, Romme sums up the prosecution case against Carrier over his conduct in Nantes.

12 Nov/22 brum   CLOSURE OF THE JACOBIN CLUB, following a further brawl involving the *jeunesse dorée*.

15 Nov/25 brum   Maintenance of penalties against the *émigrés*.

Nov 1793–Jan 1794   Purge of militant *sans-culottes* in the Paris sections.

24 Nov/4 frim   Decision to send Carrier before the Rev Tribunal.

8 Dec/18 frim   Decision to allow the recall to the Convtn of the '75' (the deputies who had protested against the purge of the Girondins in June 1793). This decision moves the Convtn markedly towards the right.

9 Dec/19 frim   Report to the Convtn recommending the abolition of the Maximum.

16 Dec/26 frim   Execution of Carrier.

24 Dec/4 niv   SUPPRESSION OF THE MAXIMUM and all trade controls.

27 Dec/7 niv   Commission established to examine the past conduct of the 'Four' (Billaud-Varenne, Collot-d'Herbois, Vadier and Barère).

28 Dec/8 niv   Reorganisation of the Rev Tribunal, weakening its powers.

Containment of the Vendée, Dec 1794–Nov 1795

2 Dec: Convtn offers an amnesty to rebels who lay down arms within a month; and Hoche, as generalissimo in the W, combines the velvet glove approach (offers of amnesty) with the iron fist (repressive mobile columns).

Jan 1795: Negotiations.

17 Feb: PEACE OF LA JAUNAYE with Charette: amnesty; no imposition of military service; freedom of worship.

20 Apr: PEACE OF LA PREVALAYE with Chouans: same conditions as for Charette.

May–June: Disturbances in W recommence, encouraged by the death in prison of 'Louis XVII' and the more hard-line approach of Louis XVIII (formerly comte de Provence).

27 June: QUIBERON BAY EXPEDITION: landing of *émigrés* from British warships in S Brittany. The forces fail to break out of the peninsula, however (July), and after several defeats at the hands of Hoche, surrender (20–21 July). Execution of 748 rebels.

15 Nov: Failure of British force with the prince de Condé to establish a bridgehead on the Ile de Yeu off Poitou.

White Terror in the provinces, Dec 1794–Summer 1795

Attacks on former militants and the purchasers of nat lands stimulated by the retreat from policies of Terror, anti-terrorist legislation and by some Thermidorian reps *en mission* (Isnard, Boisset, etc). Esp vicious in the Lyonnais, the Rhône valley and the SE, where the actions of murder gangs with royalist links like the Compagnies de Soleil, de Jésus and de Jéhu are prevalent. Massacres of political prisoners at Lyon (2 Feb, 24 Apr and 4 May), Nîmes (23 Feb), Aix (11 May, 14 Aug), Tarascon (25 May and 28 June), Marseille (5 June) etc. Rising of Jacobin society in Toulon easily crushed (23 May).

[1795 (12 NIV III–11 NIV IV)]

3 Feb/15 pluv   Assembly in Amsterdam proclaims the 'Batavian Rpbc'.

9 Feb/21 pluv   Busts of Marat and Lepeletier removed from the hall of the Convtn, under pressure from the *jeunesse dorée* (who also have Marat's remains removed from the Panthéon, 8 Feb).

19 Feb/1 vent   Suppression of *comités révolutionnaires* in communes with a population under 50,000.

21 Feb/3 vent   FORMAL SEPARATION OF CHURCH AND STATE. Public worship is authorised in private dwellings.

23 Feb/5 vent   All officials discharged since 10 therm II to return to their home communes and to remain there under the surveillance of the municipalities.

2 Mar/12 vent   Arrest decree issued against the 'Four'.

8 Mar/18 vent   Recall to the Convtn of deputies outlawed under the Terror for Girondin affiliation or federalist offences (Isnard, Lanjuinais, Louvet, etc).

11 Mar/21 vent   The CGS is empowered to appoint *commissaires de police* throughout France.

14 Mar/24 vent   Convtn allows its Legislation Committee to appoint administrators, municipal officials, etc at local level.

17 Mar/27 vent   Popular demonstration from the Paris faubourgs protesting against economic hardship.

21 Mar/1 germ   Police law: death penalty for individuals marching on the Convtn issuing seditious threats.

22 Mar/2 germ   Debate in the Convtn on the 'Four' which leads (29 March/9 germ) to a decision to indict.

1 Apr/12 germ   JOURNEE OF 12 GERMINAL: popular demonstration in the Convtn hall calling for the implementation of the 1793 Constitution and the introduction of measures against economic hardship. Convtn declares a state of siege and restores order. A committee is to be established to review and amend the 1793 Constitution.

1–2 Apr/12–3 germ   JOURNEE OF 13 GERMINAL. In riposte against the *journée* of 12 germ, the 'Four' are deported to Guiana; eight Montagnards inc Amar, Thuriot and Léonard Bourdon are arrested, to be followed over the next few days by further arrests, inc that of Cambon.

War, Spring–Autumn 1795

With natural frontiers now secured, the French agree peace terms with Prussia (Apr), Holland (May) and Spain (July), leaving Austria and Britain as the main opponents. On 28 Sept 1795, however, Russia allies itself with Britain and Austria. In June–July, French forces occupy Bilbao and Vittoria in N Spain, while in Italy Schérer enjoys some success, notably in the battle of Loano (23–5 Nov 1795). The main theatre is still in Germany, however. Here the 1795 campaign starts late. Luxembourg falls to the French (26 June) and Jourdan crosses the Rhine and attempts to invade Germany (6 Sept). Austrian forces drive him back, however, and he is defeated at Höchst, while Pichegru is defeated outside Mannheim (19 Oct). The Austrian forces invade the Palatinate.

4–5 Apr/15–16 germ   TREATY OF BASLE WITH PRUSSIA. France evacuates the right bank of the Rhine. In secret clauses, Prussia cedes to France Holland and the left bank of the Rhine.

10 Apr/21 germ   Disarming of the 'terrorists' of year II.

11 Apr/22 germ   Repeal of the laws of 21 March 1793 and 23 vent II in regard to definitions of suspects and alleged enemies of the Rpbc.

17 Apr/28 germ   SUSPENSION OF THE LAW OF REV GOVT OF 14 FRIM II.

18 Apr/29 germ   'Commission des Onze' (moderate rpbcns and constitutional monarchists mostly) to draft a new constitution.

26 Apr/7 flor   Abolition of the institution of reps *en mission*.

29 Apr/10 flor   Sectional disturbances in Paris following reductions in bread doles.

 6 May/17 flor   Fouquier-Tinville and 14 jurymen from the Rev Tribunal sentenced to death.

16 May/17 flor   TREATY OF THE HAGUE WITH HOLLAND (now the Batavian Rpbc). Offensive and defensive alliance, with Holland pledging naval and military support to the French war effort; France retains Dutch Flanders until a general peace; and, in secret clauses, Holland agrees to maintain a French occupation force of 25,000 men.

20 May/1 prair   JOURNEE OF 1 PRAIRIAL: somewhat aimless popular insurrection, demanding bread and the 1793 Constitution. The Convtn is overrun and a number of ex-Montagnards compromise themselves in supporting the rebels. The hall of the Convtn is retaken by the government committees.

21 May/2 prair   JOURNEE OF 4 PRAIRIAL. Convtn outfaces another attempt at insurrection.

23 May/4 prair   Rebellious faubourgs overrun by troops, and repression by military commission set in motion: sectional militants and a number of Montagnard deputies are arrested. Six of the latter (Duquesnoy, Romme, Duroy, Goujon, Bourbotte, Soubrany) will be sentenced to death, but will attempt suicide before arriving at the scaffold, thus becoming the 'martyrs of Prairial' (16–17 June/28–9 prair). Rühl had avoided trial by committing suicide, Albitte and Prieur de la Marne by fleeing. Also, decree prohibiting women from attending any political assembly.

24 May–1 June/5–13 prair   Government purge of the sections.

29 May/10 prair   Disarming of all individuals suspected of terrorism in the past. 'Less well-off' citizens are exempted service in the Nat Guard.

30 May/11 prair   Churches made available for use (by rota) of constitutional and refractory clergy.

31 May/12 prair   SUPPRESSION OF THE REV TRIBUNAL.

 1 June/13 prair   Arrest of former ultra-rev reps *en mission* Javogues, Mallarmé, Dartigoëyte, Baudot, etc.

 8 June/20 prair   DEATH OF 'LOUIS XVII' in the Temple prison.

12 June/24 prair   Authorities forbidden to use the adjective *'révolutionnaire'*.

16–17 June/28–29 prair   Death of the 'martyrs of Prairial'.

21 June/3 mess   Sliding scale of depreciation for the assignat established.

24 June/6 mess   VERONA DECLARATION by the new Louis XVIII: a hard-line policy in the event of his return, including the execution of the regicides and the restoration of AR privilege.

27 June/9 mess   Quiberon Bay expedition (see above).
Establishment of a unified police force for the capital, the Paris Police Legion.

20 July/2 therm   Half the land-tax to be paid in grain.

21 July/3 therm   Hoche's victory over the Quiberon Bay forces complete.

22 July/4 therm   TREATY OF BASLE WITH SPAIN (to be followed by the alliance Treaty of San Ildefonso, 19 Aug 1796). Mutual restoration of conquests; Spain cedes France Spanish Santo Domingo.

5 Aug/18 therm   Formality of *certificats de civisme* abolished.

8–9 Aug/21–22 therm   Convtn decrees arrest of six ex-Montagnard deputies, inc Fouché.

22 Aug/5 fruct   CONSTITUTION OF YEAR III AGREED, accompanied (22 and 30 Aug/5 and 13 fruct) by the 'LAW OF TWO-THIRDS': two-thirds of the next legislature to be drawn from the ranks of the Convtn.

23 Aug/6 fruct   Closure of clubs and popular societies.

6 Sept/20 fruct   Primary assemblies meet for constitutional referendum.

[YEAR IV (23 SEPT 1795–21 SEPT 1796)]

23 Sept/1 vendém   Electoral ratification of the new constitution announced: the Constitution of Year III is proclaimed as a fundamental law of the state.

28–29 Sept/6–7 vendém   Law codifying and regulating freedom of worship: priests have only to promise to submit to the Rpbc (a dilution of earlier policy which soons brings back large numbers of refractory priests).

1 Oct/9 vendém   FORMAL ANNEXATION OF BELGIUM.

5 Oct/13 vendém   Royalist *JOURNEE* OF 13 VENDEMIAIRE: royalist rising prompted by the 'Law of Two-thirds'; dispersed by troops under Barras, with Bonaparte's assistance. Three royalist deputies arrested.

7 Oct/15 vendém   Law of Suspects repealed.

8 Oct/17 vendém   Suppression of Parisian sectional assemblies.

12 Oct/20 vendém   Elections.

25 Oct/3 brum   LAW OF 3 BRUM IV: public office denied to *émigrés* and their relatives and to individuals who have expressed seditious opposition to the laws in primary or electoral assemblies; wives of *émigrés* obliged to return to place of domicile in 1792 and to remain there under municipal surveillance; anti-priest legislation of 1792 and 1793 reimplemented in entirety.
List of national festivals announced.

Education law: Institut established, primary and secondary education reorganised.

26 Oct/4 brum   LAST MEETING OF THE CONVTN. Amnesty proclaimed for political prisoners (with the exception of *émigrés*, the deported deputies Billaud-Varenne and Collot-d'Herbois, the Vendémiaire rebels and counterfeiters of assignats).

8. THE DIRECTORY DOWN TO THE FRUCTIDOR COUP (OCTOBER 1795/BRUMAIRE IV–SEPTEMBER 1797/FRUCTIDOR V)

1795/Year IV

26–28 Oct/4–6 brum   A committee of the Convtn forms the 'Electoral Assembly of France' to designate two-thirds of the new councils by co-optation from among existing deputies in the Convtn, under the provisions of the 'Law of Two-thirds'.

3 Nov/12 brum   The Directory (elected by the councils on 31 Oct/9 brum) assumes office.

6 Nov/15 brum   Babeuf's *Tribun du peuple* starts a new series of publication.

16 Nov/25 brum   Opening of the Panthéon Club.

22 Nov/12 frim   Temporary suspension of the sale of nat lands.

5 Dec/14 frim   Arrest warrant issued for Babeuf, who goes into hiding.

10 Dec/19 frim   Forced loan introduced (poorly implemented).

26 Dec/5 niv   Exchange at Basle of Louis XVI's daughter, 'Madame Royale', for seven rpbcn captives (Bancal, Beurnonville, Drouet, etc).

1796 (11 NIV IV–11 NIV V)

2 Jan/12 niv   Creation of a Police Minister (*Ministre de Police générale*).

19 Feb/30 pluv   ISSUE OF ASSIGNATS CEASES, and assignat printing-presses are ritually broken.

26 Feb/7 vent   Directory orders the closure of the Panthéon Club and neo-Jacobin societies.

9 Mar/19 vent   Oath of hatred of royalty imposed on all functionaries.

18 Mar/28 vent   ISSUE OF *MANDATS TERRITORIAUX*, a new paper currency which collapses almost instantaneously.

War, Spring 1796–Winter 1797
As W France is pacified, war passes from nat defence to external expansion.

WEST: the capture and execution of rebel leaders Stofflet (25 Feb 1796) and Charette (29 Mar) help pacify the W, and in June 1796, the army of the West is disbanded. Some of the troops form an army of Ireland under Hoche. The French fleet does in fact set sail for Ireland (Dec), but a storm makes the expedition a fiasco.

SEA: despite the French—Dutch—Spanish alliance, British naval superiority is confirmed in the battle of Cape Saint Vincent (14 Feb 1797).

GERMANY: intended to be the main theatre of war, events here are indecisive, and the initiative passes to Italy. The Rhine-and-Moselle army under Moreau and the Sambre-and-Meuse army under Jourdan advance separately into S Germany (31 May 1796). The Austrians retreat across the Black Forest before Moreau who beats them off at Neresheim (11 Aug) before reaching and occupying Munich. Jourdan defeats the Austrians at Altenkirchen (4 June), is then defeated at Wetzlar (15 June), but goes on to occupy Frankfurt (16 July). Several minor German states sign armistices in the face of the French invasion threat. The two French armies fail to effect a junction, however, and when Jourdan is defeated at Amberg (24 Aug) and Würzburg (3 Sept), they both retreat and recross the Rhine (Sept—Oct).

ITALY: Bonaparte is appointed to succeed Schérer with the army of Italy (2 Mar), and in a whirlwind campaign transforms the war effort. Battles at MONTENOTTE (11–12 Apr), MILLESIMO (13 Apr), DEGO (13–14 Apr) and MONDOVI (21 Apr) split the Austrians from the Piedmontese, who fall back towards Turin. The king of Piedmont signs the Armistice of Cherasco (26 Apr), to be followed by the Treaty of Paris (15 May). Bonaparte now turns on the Austrians, defeats them at LODI (10 May), enters Milan (15 May) and, after defeating the Austrians at BORGHETTO (30 May), moves E to besiege the key fortress of Mantua.

The dukes of Parma and Modena sign an armistice with the French (9, 17 May), Bologna and Ferrara surrender (19–20 June), Naples signs an armistice (6 June) and the Pope comes to terms (23 June). Livorno is occupied by the French (27 June). Against the Directory's wishes, Bonaparte organises on 16 Oct the 'Cispadane Rpbc' (Modena, Bologna, Ferrara, Reggio, etc). On four occasions the Austrians try to relieve Mantua, but despite some temporary set-backs, Bonaparte defeats them at LONATO (3 Aug), CASTIGLIONE (5 Aug), BASSANO (8 Sept), ARCOLA (14–17 Nov) and RIVOLI (14–15 Jan 1797) before the French finally take the city (2 Feb 1797).

30 Mar/10 germ   Babeuf sets up the Insurrectionary Committee for his 'Conspiracy of Equals'.

16 Apr/27 germ   Councils decree the death penalty for those advocating the 1793 Constitution, the restoration of the monarchy or the *loi agraire*.

17 Apr/28 germ   Tightening up of regulations regarding the political press.

30 Apr–2 May/11–13 flor   Disbandment of the Paris Police Legion, which the babouvists have infiltrated.

10 May/21 flor Arrest of Babeuf and Buonarroti, followed by vigorous pursuit, orchestrated by Carnot, of their alleged followers. Expulsion from Paris of former Conventionnels, suspects, amnestied terrorists, etc.

15 May/26 flor PEACE OF PARIS with Piedmont: cession of Nice and Savoy to France; French troops allowed to occupy key locations.

17 July/29 mess Abolition of the compulsory quotation for the *mandat territorial*.

31 July/13 therm *Mandats territoriaux* only accepted at their market value in sales of nat lands.

19 Aug/2 fruct TREATY OF SAN ILDEFONSO with Spain: mutual territorial guarantee, and defensive and offensive alliance. Spain will declare war on England, 5 Oct/4 vendém V.

26–27 Aug/9–10 fruct Babouvist prisoners dispatched from Paris to Vendôme where they are to be tried by the High Court.

4 Sept/18 fruct As the *mandat territorial* crumbles, Belgian church lands are put on sale.

9–10 Sept/23–24 fruct Failure of babouvist Grenelle Camp rising. Military commission established to try those involved.

[YEAR V (22 SEPT 1796–21 SEPT 1797)]

Oct–Dec Anglo-French peace preliminaries at Lille: no agreement.

10 Oct/19 vendém The military commission established after the Grenelle Camp rising pronounces 32 death sentences (inc the Conventionnel Javogues).

16 Oct/25 vendém PROCLAMATION OF THE CISPADANE RPBC by Bonaparte.

31 Oct/10 brum Law forbidding import of English manufactured goods, even in foreign vessels.

6 Nov/16 brum Auction sales for nat lands re-established.

4 Dec/14 frim The Law of 3 Brum IV reaffirmed as regards *émigrés* and their families; the law is extended to those amnestied on 4 brum IV for political offences and to left-wing Conventionnels. The clauses relative to refractory priests are, however, waived.

6 Dec/16 frim Directory recalls *commissaires aux armées* and suppresses the post: generals have a freer hand over conquered territory.

[1797 (12 NIV V–11 NIV VI)]

15 Jan/26 niv First meeting of the Theophilanthropy sect.

30 Jan/11 pluv Arrest of the royalist conspirator Brotier and his counter-rev cell.

War, Spring–Summer 1797

The centre of interest is again in Italy, where Bonaparte's success brings the Austrians to terms.

ITALY: Following the capture of Mantua (2 Feb 1797), Bonaparte secures his rear by signing with the Pope the PEACE OF TOLENTINO (19 Feb) and moves NE against the Austrians, who suffer defeat at MALBORGHETTO (23 Mar), and are driven back to Leoben. On 18 Apr, Bonaparte signs the PEACE PRELIMINARIES OF LEOBEN which will lead on to the TREATY OF CAMPO-FORMIO (18 Oct). After disturbances in a number of cities, the French occupy Venetia, to which the Venetian authorities capitulate (16 May). France also engineers a *coup d'état* in Genoa (22 May), whereupon Bonaparte intervenes and establishes the 'Ligurian Rpbc' (6 June). On 9 July, he proclaims the 'Cisalpine Rpbc' (the Cispadane Rpbc plus parts of Lombardy and W Venetia).

GERMANY: In early 1797, the French under Hoche cross the Rhine and defeat the Austrians on the Lahn at NEUWIED (18 Apr) before news of Leoben filters through.

4 Feb/16 pluv   WITHDRAWAL OF REV PAPER CURRENCY: withdrawal of the *mandat territorial*, and return to metallic currency.

19 Feb/1 vent   TREATY OF TOLENTINO with the Pope: formal cession of Avignon and the Comtat Venaissin to France; Pope renounces claims to Bologna, Ferrara, Romagna; he pays 15 million liv and makes other concessions regarding the war.

20 Feb/2 vent   Babeuf trial starts at Vendôme.

4–5 Mar/14–15 vent   Drawing of lots to designate outgoing Conventionnels from the councils in the forthcoming elections.

20 Mar/30 vent   Law obliging all electors in electoral assemblies (which meet from the following day) to swear oath of hatred of monarchy and anarchy.

18 Apr/29 germ   LEOBEN PEACE PRELIMINARIES with Austria: peace between France and Austria, though a congress of German states will be held to establish a general peace *vis-à-vis* the Holy Roman Empire as a whole; Belgium and Lombardy are to be ceded to France; Lombardy, part of W Venetia and the Cispadane Rpbc will form the 'Cisalpine Rpbc'; part of French-occupied Venetia to be given to Austria in compensation. Sentencing of the accused in the Brotier trial: no capital sentences.

Germ-flor   ELECTIONS OF YEAR V: crushing defeat for Directorials (only 13 out of 216 ex-Conventionnels elected); victory for the right.

20 May/1 prair   The first session of the councils following the elections. Barthélemy, the candidate of the right, will replace Letourneur as Director.

27 May/8 prair   DEATH OF BABEUF. Sentenced to death by the Vendôme high court the previous day, Babeuf and Darthé attempt suicide. They are guillotined.

6 June/18 prair   New land-tax.

PROCLAMATION OF THE LIGURIAN RPBC at Genoa.

9 June/21 prair   Freedom of the grain trade decreed (though in practice this has been the situation for several months).

20 June/2 mess   Foundation of *cercles constitutionnels* in Paris; soon provincial branches are appearing.

27 June/9 mess   Laws of 3 brum IV and 14 frim V relating to *émigrés*, etc, repealed.

July–Sept   Resumed Anglo-French peace preliminaries: no agreement will be reached.

1 July/13 mess   With evidence of Pichegru's royalism and treachery accumulating, the Directors get Hoche to dispatch troops from the E frontier to W France via Paris.

9 July/21 mess   PROCLAMATION OF THE CISALPINE RPBC by Bonaparte.

14 July/26 mess   Ministerial reshuffle, including Talleyrand as Foreign Minister, with Hoche offered (he will not accept) the Ministry of War. This frightens the moderate majority in the Councils at the prospect of an army-led coup, especially as it is soon apparent that Hoche's men are within the 'constitutional zone' around Paris from which the constitution debars troops.

23 July/5 therm   Directory agrees to Councils' suppression of political clubs (a measure aimed against the *cercles constitutionnels*).

2 Aug/15 therm   New tax on movable wealth.

8 Aug/21 therm   Augereau, Bonaparte's nominee, is made commander of an army based in Paris. This force harries right-wing youths in the city.

12 Aug/25 therm   As a precaution against Hoche, whose army is threatening Paris, the increasingly right-wing Councils allow the arming of certain (esp the wealthy) Paris sections.

15 Aug/28 therm   First nat synod in Paris of the constitutional Church.

24 Aug/7 fruct   Laws of 1792 and 1793 against the non-juring clergy are repealed (though the law of 7 vendém IV remains intact).

4 Sept/18 fruct   *JOURNEE* OF 18 FRUCTIDOR: '*COUP D'ETAT* OF FRUCTIDOR'. Emergency legislation forced through the Councils by 'Triumvirs' (Directors Barras, La Révellière-Lépeaux and Reubell) supported by the army; military occupation of Paris; elections annulled in 49 departments; 177 deputies removed; 65 persons deported (inc Carnot, Barthélemy, Pichegru). Repressive legislation follows.

9. THE DIRECTORY FROM FRUCTIDOR TO BRUMAIRE (SEPT 1797/FRUCTIDOR V–NOVEMBER 1799/BRUMAIRE VIII)

1797/Year V

4–5 Sept/18–19 fruct THE 'DIRECTORIAL TERROR', unleashed by the 'Triumvirs' of Fructidor (Barras, Reubell, La Révellière-Lépeaux): a phase of purges and radical policies which will last down to early 1798, as the mood in political circles becomes leftish again. Major policy changes and initiatives include:

- press law (5–8 Sept/19–22 fruct): right-wing press decimated, notably by a further decree of 7 Dec/17 frim
- establishment of military commissions to try and execute *émigrés*, conspirators, etc (down to Mar 1799 they will pronounce approximately 160 death sentences)
- political clubs reopened (law of 7 therm V repealed)
- law of 3 Brum IV relating to non-eligibility for office of *émigrés* and opponents of the regime re-established (law of 7 fruct V repealed)
- priests troubling public order to be deported
- electors and jurymen are to swear an oath of hatred of royalty and anarchy
- Directory accords itself emergency powers to dismiss and replace judicial, municipal and administrative officials.

8 Sept/22 fruct Merlin de Douai and François de Neufchâteau replace Carnot and Barthélemy as Directors.

[YEAR VI (22 SEPT 1797–21 SEPT 1798)]

30 Sept/9 vendém 'BANKRUPTCY OF THE TWO-THIRDS': repudiation of two-thirds of the nat debt, to be followed by a similar measure regarding the state's other financial commitments on 14 Dec/24 frim.
Decree subjecting newspapers and journals to a stamp tax.

16 Oct–3 Nov/25 vendém–13 brum Further negotiations at Lille with the British.

18 Oct/27 vendém   TREATY OF CAMPO FORMIO with the Austrians: cession of Belgium to France; most of Venetia ceded to Austria; French acquisition of Ionian Isles (formerly Venetian); Austria recognises the 'Cisalpine Rpbc'; congress with the states of the Holy Roman Empire at Rastadt to negotiate a general peace; in secret clauses, Austria agrees that France should keep the left bank of the Rhine, and that part of W Germany should be incorporated into the 'Helvetian Rpbc', while France agrees to support Austrian compensation in Germany, notably its claim to Salzburg.

War and international relations, Autumn 1797-Spring 1798

Military operations are less significant, following Campo-Formio. From 16 Nov 1797 the French and the states of the Holy Roman Empire continue to discuss the terms of a general peace in the Congress of Rastadt, though continued French gains in Italy and Switzerland make this eventuality unlikely.

NORTHERN EUROPE: French influence in Holland is affirmed by coups of 22 Jan 1798 and 12 June 1798. In Switzerland, the Vaud is occupied (Jan 1798), the treasury at Berne seized (13–14 Feb) and the pro-French 'Fructidorian' coup of 16 June 1798 leads to the organisation of the Helvetian Rpbc. Meanwhile, the Army of England under Bonaparte created on 26 Oct 1797 waits patiently at the Channel. By Feb 1798, Bonaparte suggests to the Directory a campaign in Egypt, and in Apr the Army of the Orient is formed.

EGYPT: Bonaparte's fleet sets sail on 19 May for Egypt, manages to avoid the British fleet and captures Malta *en route* (11 June).

ITALY: A Roman Rpbc is organised (15 Feb 1798) following a riot in Rome in the course of which General Duphot is assassinated (28 Dec 1797). The French make an alliance and commercial treaty with the Cisalpine Rpbc (21 Feb 1798) and similar arrangements with the Roman Rpbc on 28 Mar, obliging them to help finance the armies

SEA: British naval superiority is confirmed in their victory over the Dutch at CAMPERDOWN (11 Oct 1797), though the joint Dutch–Spanish–French alliance keeps the British out of the Mediterranean.

 4 Nov/14 brum   The right bank of the Rhine is formed into four depts.

12 Nov/22 brum   Establishment of a direct tax agency in each department under the control of the Ministry of Finance.

17 Nov/27 brum   All candidates for state civil service to have attended state schools.

24 Nov/4 frim   Tax on doors and windows.

28 Nov/8 frim   Opening of the Congress of Rastadt.

29 Nov/9 frim   Ex-nobles accorded the status of aliens in regard to citizenship: not permitted to assume public office.

[1798 (12 NIV VI–11 NIV VII)]

18 Jan/29 niv   In an attempt to repress the brigandage prevalent in many areas, the Councils decree the death penalty, to be meted out by military commissions, for criminal outrages (highway robbery, breaking and entering, etc) committed by more than two persons.

28 Jan/9 pluv   ANNEXATION OF THE FREE CITY OF MULHOUSE.

31 Jan/12 pluv   In order to bar entry to undesirables, the Councils in future empowered to verify the credentials of all new deputies.

5 Feb/17 pluv   Private (sc. Catholic) schools to be kept under the surveillance of municipalities.

12 Feb/24 pluv   Outgoing Councils to elect the new Director, *prior to* the results of the Year VI elections.

15 Feb/27 pluv   PROCLAMATION OF THE ROMAN RPBC.

23 Feb/5 vent   Political rights and attendance in primary assemblies are denied to those who have enjoyed civil or military responsibilities with rebels.

5 Mar/15 vent   Directory approves Bonaparte's plan for an Egyptian campaign.

20 Mar/30 vent   Beginning of the elections of Year VI, which the Directors manipulate so as to exclude left-wing and right-wing critics of the regime. In particular, they encourage the formation of 'schismatic' electoral assemblies, so as to allow themselves a choice of candidates.

3 Apr/14 germ   Observance of the Rev Calendar made mandatory.

26 Apr/7 flor   ANNEXATION OF GENEVA.

11 May/22 flor   *JOURNEE:* THE COUP OF 22 FLOREAL. Following a poor Directorial showing in the elections, the 'coup' sees the annulment of numerous elections, where left-wing candidates have been returned, and the endorsement by the Directors of safe candidates voted by 'schismatic' electoral assemblies. Approximately one-quarter of legislative, one-third of non-legislative (judicial, administrative) candidates are excluded.

15 May/26 flor   Treilhard replaces François de Neufchâteau as Director.

18 May/29 flor   Directors to appoint all presidents, public prosecutors and court officials in criminal tribunals until the Year VII elections.

19 May/30 flor   Bonaparte embarks for Egypt

War and international relations, Summer 1798–Autumn 1799

Bonaparte's Egyptian campaign holds centre stage in mid 1798. Soon, however, the situation worsens: reverses in Italy lead to Naples joining Britain and Russia in an anti-French alliance (29 Dec 1798), the Egyptian campaign brings in Turkey (9 Sept 1798), while France declares war on Austria again and on Tuscany on 12 Mar 1799, an act closely followed by the outrage at Rastadt (28 Apr 1799) when French envoys engaged in negotiations with the Holy Roman Empire are attacked and several assassinated. By early summer, an invasion of France seems a distinct possibility, and war fever mounts.

ITALY: Neapolitan troops attack the Roman Rpbc (22 Nov 1798). The French under Championnet riposte, and on 23 Jan 1799 enter Naples, whereupon Championnet, disregarding the orders of the Directory, establishes a 'Parthenopean Rpbc' (26 Jan 1799). Further N, the French seize Tuscany (Mar). But the Army of Italy under Schérer is defeated by the Austrians and Russians at MAGNANO (5 Apr), and Moreau is defeated on 27 Apr at CASSANO, which allows the Russians into Milan (28 Apr) and later Turin (27 May). The Army of Naples, abandoning Naples to the British fleet and peasant counter-rev (May), comes N to help, but is defeated in its turn by the Russians at TREBBIA (17–19 June 1799). The Cisalpine Rpbc collapses. Bonaparte's achievements of 1796–7 are almost entirely annulled.

NORTHERN EUROPE: A French expedition to Ireland under Humbert fails to make an impression (Aug 1798). In Belgium, the French have to put down a peasant uprising (Oct–Dec) provoked by the Jourdan Law on conscription. The French cross the Rhine and attack the Austrians, but suffer defeat at STOKACH (25 Mar 1799) and retreat.

EGYPT: Bonaparte smashes the native Mameluke army in the BATTLE OF THE PYRAMIDS (21 July 1798) and enters Cairo (23 July). However, on 1 Aug Nelson destroys the bulk of the French fleet at anchor in Aboukir Bay. The French occupy Egypt, then push N into Syria (10 Feb 1799) where they are checked by Turkish forces. Despite some successes, they fail to take Acre from the British occupying forces (17 Mar–21 May 1799) and retreat into Egypt. Here, Bonaparte crushes the Turks in the battle of ABOUKIR (25 July 1799). Shortly afterwards, he decides to return to France.

6 July/18 mess   Domiciliary raids permitted for one month against royalists.

4 Aug/17 therm   *Décadi* to be observed: all reference to the old calendar prohibited.

30 Aug/13 fruct   Law on the celebration of decadal festivals.

5 Sept/19 fruct   JOURDAN LAW (*Loi Jourdan*): introduction of conscription, followed (24 Sept/3 vendém VIII) by the call-up of 200,000 men.

9 Sept/23 fruct   Ordinary citizens as well as public officials to utilise the Rev Calendar.

[YEAR VII (22 SEPT 1798–22 SEPT 1799)]

18 Oct/27 vendém   Establishment of an *octroi* (municipal toll) in Paris.

9 Nov/19 brum   Those sentenced in the Fructidor coup are to be assimilated to the *émigrés* unless they present themselves for punishment.

25 Nov/5 frim   Re-establishment of *commissaires aux armées* to supervise the activities of generals.

[1799 (12 NIV VII–10 NIV VIII)]

26 Jan–7 pluv   PROCLAMATION OF THE PARTHENOPEAN RPBC at Naples.

12 Mar/11 vent   FRANCE DECLARES WAR ON AUSTRIA AND TUSCANY.

10 Apr/22 germ   The captured Pope Pius VI is brought to France: he will be interned at Valence.

17 Apr/28 germ   Additional call-up under the provisions of the Jourdan Law. Replacement (conscripts arranging for a substitute to take their place) is permitted for the first time.

Apr/germ   Year VII elections: Directorial intervention restricts the effect of strong anti-Directorial feeling in the country. Partly in response to the war situation the new 'third' is to the left.

9 May/20 flor   Siéyès (whose hostility to the Constitution of Year III is notorious) replaces Reubell as Director.

20 May/1 prair   The new Councils meet.

War, Autumn 1799

NORTH: A British expeditionary force lands in Holland and links up with a Russian force. They take the Dutch fleet on the Texel (31 Aug), but the British are held and then driven back at BERGEN and ALKMAAR (19 Sept, 2 Oct). The Convention of Alkmaar (18 Oct) ends hostilities in the Netherlands as the British evacuate.

ITALY/SWITZERLAND: Exposed by defeats in Italy and Germany, the French retreat into Switzerland and hold off the Allies at the first battle of ZURICH (4 June). Italian cities (e.g. Siena, 28 June; Florence, 7 July) are occupied by counter-rev Italian forces, and the French garrison at Mantua falls (30 July). Besides the defeat at Zurich in June, the French suffer defeat at TREBBIA (17–19 June) and NOVI (15 Aug). They recover, however, to be victorious in the second battle of ZURICH (25–30 Sept), and reoccupy the left bank of the Rhine. On 23 Oct Czar Paul recalls Russian troops from W Europe.

INSIDE FRANCE: In order to add to the Rpbc's problems as the Austrians and Russians attack the frontiers, Louis XVIII uses his networks to rekindle revolt within France, which has been stimulated by the new conscription requirements: there is a royalist uprising in the Haute-Garonne region, which is crushed at Montréjeau (20 Aug); Frotté rallies Norman peasants under the royalist flag; there are surprise attacks in Anjou and Brittany on e.g. Vannes, Saint-Brieuc, Le Mans, Nantes, Vire, Cholet. The second battle of Zurich helps douse down internal sedition.

16 June/28 prair   At loggerheads with the Directory, and stimulated by indifferent French fortunes in the war, the Councils sit *en permanence*.

17 June/29 prair   The councils elect the pro-Jacobin Gohier as Director in place of Treilhard, whose election in Year VI it annuls on procedural grounds.

18 June/30 prair   *COUP D'ETAT* OF 30 PRAIRIAL: '*JOURNEE* OF THE COUNCILS'. The build-up of pressure in the Councils leads to a purge of the Directory (1–2 mess) with General Moulin and Roger Ducos replacing Merlin de Douai and La Révellière-Lépeaux.

22–3 June/4–5 mess   Beginnings of a ministerial reshuffle following the Prairial coup, to be accompanied by purges of administrative personnel.

28 June/10 mess   Forced loan urged in the Councils. Under the prescriptions of the Jourdan Law, all classes of conscripts are called up.

6 July/18 mess   First meeting of the neo-Jacobin Club du Manège.

12 July/24 mess   'Law of Hostages' (*loi des otages*): authorities permitted to take 'hostages' from among the families of *émigrés*.

20 July/2 therm   Fouché appointed Minister of Police.

30 July/12 therm   Oath of hatred of monarchy imposed.

1 Aug/14 therm   The press law of 19 fruct V is repealed: press freedom is re-established.

6 Aug/19 therm   The application of a forced loan is decreed.

13 Aug/26 therm   Closure of the Club du Manège organised by Police Minister Fouché.
News reaches Paris of the royalist insurrection in Haute-Garonne (5 Aug): councils permit domiciliary raids for a month.

20 Aug/3 fruct   Haute-Garonne rebels defeated at Montréjeau.

29 Aug/12 fruct   Death of Pope Pius VI at Valence.

2–3 Sept/16–17 fruct   Anti-press laws: both left- and right-wing newspapers are suppressed.

14 Sept/28 fruct   Siéyès contrives to have the Jacobin favourite, Bernadotte, replaced as War Minister by the more moderate Dubois-Crancé.
Resisting pressure from the left, the C500 refrains from declaring *la patrie en danger* (voting: 245/171).

[YEAR VIII (23 SEPT 1799–22 SEPT 1800)]

25–30 Sept/3–8 vendém   Masséna victorious over Austro-Russian forces in the second battle of Zurich.

9 Oct/17 vendém   As French successes (Alkmaar, Zurich) relieve the military situation, Bonaparte arrives from Egypt, landing at Fréjus.

14 Oct/22 vendém   Bonaparte arrives in Paris, and triggers off a flurry of conspiratorial politics.

Oct/vendém, brum   Unsuccessful counter-rev risings in W France.

15, 18 Oct/23, 26 vendém   Suppression of *commissaires civils* attached to the armies.

23 Oct/1 brum   Lucien Bonaparte elected president of the C500. Following defeats in Switzerland and Holland, Czar Paul recalls Russian troops from W Europe.

9–10 Nov/18–19 brum   *COUP D'ETAT* OF 18 BRUMAIRE. BONAPARTE OVER-
THROWS THE DIRECTORY AND ESTABLISHES THE CONSULATE. The new
constitution will be proclaimed 13 Dec/22 brum.

II. THE FRAMEWORK OF
GOVERNMENT

1. THE ANCIEN RÉGIME CONSTITUTION

The idea of a constitution as a single text defining the powers of the state and the relationships between citizens dates from the late eighteenth century, when it was popularised by the American, then the French Revs. Prior to 1789, like other W European states (cf. Britain), France was governed by a kind of 'customary constitution', a pot-pourri of written texts, established practices and sometimes disputed conventions which did not, however, lack a certain cogency and acceptance. Perhaps the most important element within the AR constitution were the so-called 'fundamental laws of the kingdom' which were allegedly hallowed by tradition and based on general consent. By the eighteenth century, they included:

- inalienability of the crown
- Salic law relating to the royal succession (i.e. daughters and their issue excluded from succession)
- primogeniture in the royal house
- catholicity of the ruler
- inalienability of royal domain.

The phrase 'fundamental laws of the kingdom' was sometimes also applied to the way in which the king ruled. It was accepted, for example, that the king could:

- pass laws
- create state officials and appoint ministers
- declare war and peace
- maintain supreme judicial power
- monopolise the issue of currency
- levy taxes.

Beyond this, however, definitions became murkier, though from mid-century the parls utilised arguments stressing the contractual nature of kingship and the responsibility of the monarchy towards the 'nation'. The Paris parl came to maintain, for example, notably in its decree of 3 May 1788, that the 'fundamental laws' included the following royal duties:

- the protection of property and the upholding of the 'freedoms' (privileges) of corporative and provincial bodies
- respect for the inviolability of magistrates

- acceptance that the parls registered all laws. (Although the parls could issue 'remonstrances' against any law, it was accepted that the king was within his powers to hold a *lit de justice*, in respect to normal legislation, to override these objections and enforce registration)
- agreement that new taxes could be established only with the assent of the nation as expressed by the EG.

On all these counts, the monarch was said to be trespassing on established convention in the pre-rev period, 1787–8.

2. PROCEDURE RELATING TO THE ESTATES GENERAL, 1789

From the decision in 1788 to convene the EG in May 1789 onwards, controversy raged over the procedures which were to be observed. Some general guidelines were set down in the *Résultat du conseil* of 27 Dec 1788, which conceded that the number of deputies representing the Third Estate should be equivalent to the combined strengths of the other two orders. It made no decision, however, on the thorny question of voting by head, which remained unresolved until the meeting of the EG. The Electoral Regulation of 24 Jan 1789, supplemented by a series of minor decrees, contained the basic framework for elections to the EG:

GENERAL PRINCIPLES

The principle was established that all Frenchmen (women were excluded, as they were to be from all electoral consultations throughout the 1790s and beyond) were invited to communicate their wishes and elect representatives to the EG. It was established that.

- letters of convocation were to be read out at parish mass
- the basic electoral constituency was to be the *bailliage* (*sénéchaussée* in the S)
- the number of representatives to be elected within each constituency was related to size and population
- not all *bailliages* and *sénéchaussées* were constituencies: the smaller ones were to be regarded as *bailliages secondaires* which did not elect direct to the EG, but to *bailliages principaux* or *grands bailliages*
- there was to be no mandating of deputies
- the nobility and clergy were to elect about 250 deputies each, the Third Estate about 500
- the clergy, nobility and Third Estate were to form separate electoral assemblies in *bailliages* throughout France
- at all stages of the electoral process, election of representatives was to be accompanied by the drawing up of lists of grievances (*cahiers de doléances*); the EG would only receive the general *cahiers* drawn up at *grand bailliage* level.

FRANCHISE

First Estate (clergy): The *bailliage* ass. was to be attended by all benefice-holders and (providing they could arrange for a locum in their parish during their absence) by all parish clergy outside the towns. Representation for other types of clergy was indirect:

- *chapters:* one representative for every 10 canons, and one for all the other 20 members of the clergy attached to the chapter
- *other religious communities:* one representative (this included female communities, who would need, however, to send a male proxy)
- *towns:* non-beneficed parish clergy to meet in parish assemblies and to elect 1 representative for 20 participants, 2 for 20–40, etc.

Second Estate (nobility): All fief-holders to be convoked (female fief-holders could send a proxy). Attendance at the *bailliage* ass. to be open to individuals with purchased or inherited nobility, male, over 25 years old, French or naturalised, and domiciled within the *bailliage*.

(Nobles and clerics possessing fiefs outside their place of residence were entitled to attend more than one ass. through proxies.)

Third Estate: A complex system of indirect, multi-stage elections. At all stages, those involved were to be male, 25 years old, French or naturalised, domiciled locally and on the tax rolls. (In practice, this was not far removed from manhood suffrage.) This estate could choose its representatives from any of the three orders (the nobles and clergy were confined to members of their own order).

LEVEL ONE
- *countryside:* parish-level primary assemblies sent deputies to the *bailliage* ass. at the rate of 2 representatives for a village with up to 200 households (*feux*), 3 for 200–300 households, etc
- *towns:* assemblies of all guilds and corporations elected representatives at the rate of 1 for up to 100 members, 2 for 200–300 and so on. (Wealthier guilds and members of the liberal arts were allowed to double the rate)
- the 'non-incorporated' inhabitants met in a municipal ass. (in larger cities, there might be parish assemblies) to elect representatives at the rate of 2 for up to 100 inhabitants, 3 for 200–300, etc

LEVEL TWO (towns only)
The town ass. brought together representatives of the corporate and non-corporate assemblies. (In towns without guilds, there was to be a single municipal ass.) These then drew up the town *cahier des doléances* and elected representatives to the general ass. of the *bailliage*. In most towns, the number of representatives was four, but in larger ones, a higher number was fixed by the regulation.

LEVEL THREE
In *bailliages principaux* which had *bailliages secondaires* within them, a preliminary

meeting and elections were held to reduce representation at the general *bailliage* ass. to one-quarter of existing strength.

LEVEL FOUR

General ass. of the *bailliage*. The general *cahier* of the *bailliage* was then drawn up, and representatives to the EG elected in numbers designated by the regulation. Voting in this ass. was by secret ballot; at all other levels of the electoral process it was open and by acclamation.

THE CASE OF PARIS

Special provision was made for elections to all three orders in Paris by separate electoral regulations issued on 28 March, 13 Apr and 2 May 1789. A division was made between Paris *extra-muros* (the surrounding countryside; formally, the *prévôté* and *vicomté* of Paris) and *intra-muros*. Special preliminary meetings of the nobility were held to elect to the general ass. In regard to the Third Estate, no guild assemblies were permitted, and a framework of 60 districts was established each of which drew up *cahiers* and elected representatives to a municipal ass. of electors which comprised about 400 individuals. These in turn elected 20 representatives to the EG. Those eligible to take part in the electoral process for the Third Estate had to be 25 years old, French or naturalised, resident in Paris for the previous year, and pay capitation tax of 6 liv (the final requirement was waived in the case of graduates of the University of Paris).

3. DECLARATION OF THE RIGHTS OF MAN AND THE CITIZEN (26 AUG 1789)

17 articles. 'The death certificate of the Ancien Régime' (GODECHOT) and 'the credo of the new age' (MICHELET), the Declaration set the political agenda for constitutional discussion within the Constit Ass. A composite document, planned by the Constitution Committee created on 6 July 1789, and re-formed on 14 July and 12 Aug, it showed the influence of Mirabeau, Mounier, Siéyès and Champion de Cicé. A liberal, but hardly democratic document.

Man's natural and imprescribable rights: liberty, property, security, freedom from oppression (*not* equality, though it was stated that 'men are born and remain free and equal in rights').

Rights of the individual: equality before the law; religious toleration; freedom of expression and the press; freedom from arbitrary arrest; equal opportunity; fiscal equality.

Property 'a sacred and inviolable right'.

Rights of the nation: sovereignty resides in the nation (not the monarch); monarch subordinate to the law; elected assemblies as the expression of national sovereignty; laws of elected assemblies the expression of the general will; right to tax; subordination of the army to the nation; responsibility of ministers and functionaries.

Separation of powers.

4. THE 1791 CONSTITUTION
(3 SEPT 1791)

Ratified by the monarch, 13 Sept. 210 articles. Prefaced by the 1789 Declaration of the Rights of Man. The work of the Constitution Committee, created on 6 July 1789 and supplemented from 23 Sept 1790 by a Revision Committee (which included Barnave, Alexandre de Lameth, Duport, Buzot and Pétion).

The most important provisions had been introduced gradually since late 1789, e.g. that the legislature should be unicameral (10 Sept 1789); that the king's veto should only be suspensive (11 Sept 1789); the provisional stipulations of the Constitutional Act (1 Oct 1789); provisions for primary elections (22 Dec 1789); etc.

From 10 Aug 1792, following the overthrow of the king, the constitution was modified by a number of provisional expedients and, increasingly by the forces of the Terror (See below, IV).

FUNDAMENTAL DISPOSITIONS GUARANTEED BY THE CONSTITUTION

Personal freedoms listed in the Declaration of the Rights of Man (equality before the law; religious toleration; freedom of opinion and of the press; freedom from arbitrary arrest; equality of opportunity; fiscal equality): PLUS freedom of assembly; freedom to petition; freedom to elect religious ministers.

Property inviolable except where public necessity requires its sacrifice.

State financially responsible for financing public worship.

State to provide public assistance (to succour abandoned children, relieve infirmity, provide work for the able-bodied); public education (free schooling); a code of civil law; and a programme of national festivals.

FORM OF GOVERNMENT

A constitutional monarchy, enshrining indirect, representative democracy and characterised by the separation of powers (judiciary, legislature, executive) and a property franchise.

Executive: 'King of the French': personally inviolable, holding a monopoly of the executive power and ruling under the authority of the law:

- appoints ministers (no prime minister, but ministers for the Interior, Finance, Justice, the Army, the Navy and Foreign Affairs). Ministers are neither to hold high judicial office nor to sit in the legislature, though they may be inter- pellated and even impeached by the latter
- forms, with the six ministers, the *Conseil du roi*
- has a civil list of 25 million liv per annum
- head of the armed forces
- conducts foreign policy
  BUT
- has no initiative in legislation
- has no powers to pass decrees
- has no effective block on legislation, only a suspensive veto, operative for two sessions of the Leg Ass. following the session in which the veto is imposed (thus usually between four and six years)
- has no powers of sanction over financial matters
- is obliged to swear an oath of loyalty to the constitution.

NOTE: the king was suspended from office on 10 Aug 1792, and the monarchy was abolished 21–22 Sept 1792

Legislature: the 'Legislative Assembly'

- unicameral
- two-year mandate
- composed of 745 members, elected by the depts in a ratio dependent on the latter's population, size and wealth
- has sole initiative in legislation
- fixes public expenditure and the size of the armed forces
- may impeach ministers before the National High Court.

FRANCHISE

The constitution distinguished between 'passive citizens' who enjoyed the civic rights enshrined in the Declaration of the Rights of Man but did not vote, and 'active citizens' who enjoyed both civic and political rights. All details below refer only to males.

Passive citizens (approx 2.7 millions):

- born in France of a French father
- born abroad of a French father, following return and taking of the civic oath
- born in France of a foreign father, and domiciled in France
- former French subjects exiled for religious beliefs, after returning to France and taking the civic oath

- foreigners domiciled in France for five years, and who have their own business, or property, or have married a French wife, after taking the civic oath
- naturalised foreigners.

Loss of citizenship:

- naturalisation by a foreign power
- affiliation to an international chivalric or monastic order
- condemnation either in person or by proxy for an offence involving loss of civic rights.

Active citizens (approx 4.3 millions):

- a French citizen who has taken the civic oath
- 25 years old
- domiciled one year in place of residence
- pays tax equivalent to the value of three days' work (from 15 Jan 1790 it was agreed that a day's work should be reckoned to be 1 liv [20 sous])
- on rolls of the Nat Guard
- not a servant, nor a slave
- not a bankrupt
- not awaiting trial
- not a Jew (this provision was waived, 27 Sept 1791).

(NOTE: the decree of 11 Aug 1792 formally abolished the distinction between passive and active citizens. To vote in elections for the Convtn, the following conditions sufficed: male; 21 years old; domiciled for 1 year; worked, or lived off private income; not a servant.)

'Electors' (1 per 100 participants in primary assemblies: approx 60,000):

- owners or tenants of property assessed at the value equivalent to between 100 and 400 days' work, depending on the size of the locality and the nature of possession

(NOTE: from 22 Dec 1789, it was planned that electors would have to pay taxes equivalent in value to 10 days' work. This requirement made more stringent in the above way on 27 Aug 1791; yet elections were too far advanced for the new stipulation to enter into force.)

Deputies:

- deputies were not to be executive or judicial agents. They could only serve for two successive legislatures, but could serve again after a gap of one legislature
- on 11 Aug 1792 it was decreed that deputies had to be at least 25 years old.

(NOTE: from 22 Dec 1789 it was planned that deputies should own land and pay taxes equivalent to the notorious *marc d'argent*, worth about 50 liv. Although this requirement was dropped in the 1791 Constitution (which permitted any active citizen to be elected), the elections were were so far advanced that the *marc d'argent* requirement was in fact operative in 1791.)

MODE OF ELECTION

A two-tier system:
- primary assemblies in each town or canton comprising all active citizens
- electoral assemblies in each dept comprising individuals chosen in the primary assemblies as electors
- number of deputies per dept dependent on its size, population and wealth.

(NOTE: all citizens were permitted to attend primary assemblies in the election for the Convtn under the provisions of a decree of 11 Aug 1792.)

5. THE CONSTITUTION OF 1793 OR YEAR I (24 JUNE 1793)

159 articles. The Convtn had chosen a Constitution Committee on 11 Oct 1792, and Condorcet presented its final report to the Convtn on 15 Feb 1793. The plan was too closely identified with the Girondins, however, and it was defeated. In late May, when the Montagnards had achieved ascendancy over the Girondins, the matter was referred to an *ad hoc* committee attached to the CPS, chaired by Hérault de Séchelles and including Couthon and Saint-Just. Their hurried report was debated from 11 June onwards.

The Constitution was never to be implemented: the decree of 10 Oct 1793 stated that the government of France was to be 'revolutionary until the peace'. Thus many of the expedients adopted since 10 Aug 1792 remained in force throughout the period of 'Rev Govt' (See below, IV).

DECLARATION OF RIGHTS OF MAN AND THE CITIZEN

- Aim of society is the 'common happiness'.
- Rights of Man: equality [*sic*], liberty, security, property.
- Personal rights: equality before the law; freedom of expression and of the press; equality of opportunity; freedom from arbitrary arrest; freedom of worship, assembly, petition; right to trial; right to resist oppression; freedom of trade and industry.
- No slavery; and domestic service not recognised as a legal status.
- No loss of property rights except in cases of public necessity.
- Sovereignty an attribute of the nation.
- Public assistance 'a sacred debt'; and education to be organised by the state.
- Right to insurrection when the government violates the people's rights 'the most sacred of rights and the most imprescribable of duties'.

FORM OF GOVERNMENT

A republic, with a high degree of concentration of power upon the legislature, and with a measure of direct democracy.

Legislature:
- unicameral
- one-year mandate, with elections each 1 May
- proposes laws: they are implemented unless, within 40 days, 10 per cent of the primary assemblies in over half of the depts object; and if this level of objection is achieved, the measure is submitted to a referendum of all voters.

Executive: executive council of 24 members, chosen by the legislature from a list prepared by the depts at the rate of one nomination per dept. Renewable by half each legislature. The council responsible to the legislature which may interpellate ministers to give explanations for policy decisions.

FRANCHISE

Universal male suffrage accorded with the following conditions:
- 21 years old, born and domiciled in France
- for foreigners of the same age who had been domiciled in France for one year; who were in work or lived on private income; who had acquired property; who had married a French woman, adopted a child or old person; or who were naturalised.

Loss of French citizenship:
- naturalisation by a foreign power
- condemned or awaiting trial for an offence involving loss of civic rights
- acceptance of functions or favours of an undemocratic (*non populaire*) government.

MODE OF ELECTION

Two-tier electoral system:
- primary assemblies composed of individuals domiciled in the canton for six months were to form groups of population between 200 and 600 individuals, who chose 'electors' at the rate of 1 for 200 citizens, 3 for between 300 and 600
- electoral assemblies comprising groups of primary assemblies with a joint population of between 39,000 and 41,000 individuals, who elected a deputy
- the assemblies need not respect departmental boundaries
- voting not by ballot, but by acclamation.

6. THE CONSTITUTION OF YEAR III OR 1795 (22 AUGUST 1795/5 FRUCTIDOR III)

408 articles. The work of a Constitution Committee established on 3 Apr 1795/14 germ III, and elected on 18 Apr/29 germ. The so-called 'Commission des Onze' comprised moderate republicans with a sprinkling of constitutional royalists (La Révellière-Lépeaux, Louvet, Thibaudeau, Daunou, Lesage, Lanjuinais, etc with, as *rapporteur*, Boissy d'Anglas).

DECLARATION OF THE RIGHTS AND DUTIES OF MAN AND THE CITIZEN

Rights of Man: liberty, equality, security, property.
Individual rights: equality before the law; freedom from arbitrary arrest; right to trial; fiscal equality.
No slavery.
Separation of powers.
Duties: to defend and serve society; to live under society's laws; to respect its agents; military service.
Violation of laws equivalent to a declaration of war on society.

(NOTE: formulations culled largely from former Declarations, but with no mention of men being born 'free and equal in rights'. Rights were counterbalanced by duties for the first time. No mention of freedom of opinion and the press [these were dealt with within the Constitution]; no mention of religious freedom [the state had just separated from the church]; and no mention of education or public assistance.)

FORM OF GOVERNMENT

A rpbc, but one which, in contrast with the 1793 Constitution, was to be liberal rather than democratic and characterised by the separation rather than the concentration of powers and by a property suffrage rather than universal male suffrage.

72

Legislature:
- bicameral
- mandate three years
- number of deputies fixed according to population
- one-third of the legislature renewable each year
- Conseil des Cinq-cents (500 members) had initiative in legislation
- Conseil des Anciens (250 members) approved or rejected measures, but had no powers of initiative or amendment
- no ministers, executive agents or executive committees to be drawn from within the legislature
- each council to have a bodyguard of 1,500 men
- each member of the councils to receive an annual allowance equivalent to the value of 30,000 myriagrammes (300 kg) of wheat.

Executive:
- a Directory of five members
- C500 presented a list of 10 candidates for each place on the Directory; the C Anciens voted on this by secret ballot
- mandate of Director five years, but for the first five years of its existence outgoing Directors were to be designated by lot
- signature of three Directors necessary to validate a Directorial decision
- potential Directors to be 40 years old and either current or former members of the councils or former ministers
- responsible for internal and external security; commanded army; appointed ministers (who did not form a council but were individually responsible to the Directors); appointed generals, major state functionaries
- may suggest legislation on an issue to the councils; and may decree edicts relating to the execution of the law
- had a bodyguard of 220 men
- salary of 50,000 myriagrammes (500 kg) of wheat.

FRANCHISE

The property franchise returned, though without the distinction between passive and active citizens.

Citizens/voters (*c.* 5 millions) males:
- born in France
- resident for one year
- 21 years old
- on civic lists of canton (entry on which from Year XII would require a knowledge of reading and writing and the exercise of a profession)
- paying direct taxes *or* having fought in the army

- foreigners resident seven years in France, paying taxes and owning property or having a French wife.

(NOTE: individuals who did not meet the tax requirements of the law could be enfranchised on the payment of a sum equivalent to three days' work in lieu of taxes.)

Loss of citizenship:
- naturalisation by a foreign power
- affiliation to an international chivalric or monastic order
- acceptance of functions or pensions from a foreign power
- condemnation for an offence entailing civic degradation
- bankruptcy
- entry into domestic service
- judicial interdiction as insane
- seven consecutive years' residence outside France.

(NOTE: from 3 brum IV/15 Oct 1795, voting rights were also removed from refractory priests, *émigrés* and their relatives and the law of 14 frim V/4 Dec 1796 did the same for Montagnard members of the Convtn who had been amnestied in Year IV; the law of 27 June 1797/9 mess V re-enfranchised these groups, but the law of 3 brum IV was reimposed on 19 fruct V/5 Sept 1797.)

Electors (*c*. 30,000):
Membership of electoral assemblies, for second round of voting:
- 25 years old
- owner or tenant of property evaluated at between 100 and 200 (depending on the locality) days' work

Deputies:
- for the C500: 25 years old (30 from Year VII), domiciled in France for 10 years
- for the C Anciens: 40 years old; married or a widower; domiciled in France for 15 years.

MODE OF ELECTION

Two-tiered voting:
- primary (cantonal, or part-cantonal) assemblies composed of between 450 and 900 individuals choosing electors at the rate of 1 for up to 300 voters, 2 for 300–500, 3 for 500–700, 4 for 700–900
- electoral assemblies at departmental level
- voting by secret ballot.

III. THE EXECUTIVE

1. THE ROYAL FAMILY: THE LAST BOURBONS

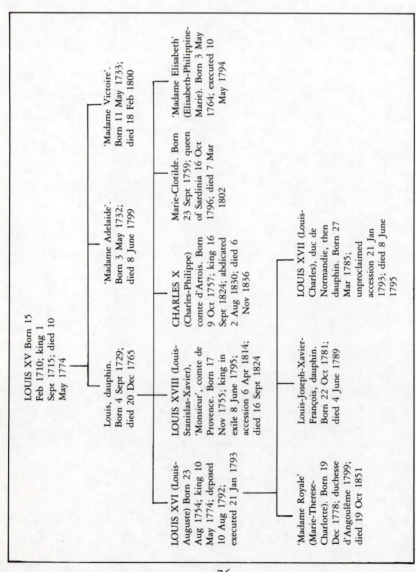

Figure 1 The Bourbon family tree.

2. MINISTERS, 1787–1799

THE PRE-REVOLUTION, 1787–12 JULY 1789

Principal Minister
Calonne (as Controller-General), 2 Nov 1783–8 Apr 1787
Loménie de Brienne (from 1 May as Head of the Council of Finances; from 26 Aug 1787 as Principal Minister), 1 May 1787–25 Aug 1788
Necker (as Director-General of Finances), 26 Aug 1788–12 July 1789

Finance (*Contrôleur-général des finances*) (see also Principal Minister)
Calonne, 2 Nov 1783–8 Apr 1787
Bouvard de Fourqueux, 14 Apr–1 May 1787
Laurent de Villedeuil, 3 May–28 Aug 1787
Lambert, 30 Aug 1787–30 Nov 1790

Justice (as Maupeou, the Chancellor since 1768, was in disgrace throughout Louis XVI's reign, the effective Justice Minister was his deputy, the Keeper of the Seals, or Garde des Sceaux)
Miromesnil, 24 Aug 1774–8 Apr 1787
Lamoignon, 29 Apr 1787–14 Sept 1788
Barentin, 19 Sept 1788–15 July 1789

Royal Household (*Maison du Roi*)
Baron de Breteuil, Oct 1783–July 1788
Laurent de Villedeuil, Aug 1788–15 July 1789

Foreign Affairs (*Affaires étrangères*)
Comte de Vergennes, 8 June 1774–13 Feb 1787
Comte de Montmorin, 14 Feb 1787–12 July 1789

War (*Guerre*)
Marquis de Ségur, 23 Dec 1780–29 Aug 1787
Comte de Brienne, 24 Sept 1787–28 Sept 1788
Comte de Puységur, 30 Nov 1788–12 July 1789

Navy (*Marine*)
Marquis de Castries, 7 June 1780–25 Aug 1787
Comte de Montmorin (as caretaker), 25 Aug 1787–24 Dec 1787
Comte de la Luzerne, 24 Dec 1787–12 July 1789

Without Portfolio
Duc de Nivernais, June 1787–(?)1788
Lamoignon de Malesherbes, June 1787–July 1789
Comte de Saint-Priest, 7 Dec 1788–12 July 1789

'THE MINISTRY OF THE 100 HOURS', 12–16 JULY 1789

President of the Royal Council: Baron de Breteuil
War: Duc de Broglie
Garde des Sceaux: Barentin
Foreign Minister: Duc de la Vauguyon
Household: Laurent de Villedeuil

FROM THE BASTILLE TO MAR 1792

Finance (from 27 Apr 1791, Minister of Public Revenue and Taxes [*Contributions et revenus publics*]
Necker, 16 (effectively 29) July 1789–4 Sept 1790 (as 'Prime Minister of Finance')
Lambert, 30 Aug 1787–30 Nov 1790, as Controller-General
Lessart, 4 Dec 1790–25 Jan 1791, then 25 Jan–18 May 1791 as both Finance and Interior Minister
Tarbé, 18 May 1791–15 Mar 1792

Justice (Garde des Sceaux until 27 Apr 1791, then Minister of Justice)
Barentin, 19 Sept 1788–3 Aug 1789
Champion de Cicé, 4 Aug 1789–21 Nov 1790
Duport-Dutertre, 21 Nov 1790–22 Mar 1792

Interior (Royal Household until 7 Aug 1790, then Interior Minister)
Comte de Saint-Priest, 19 July 1789–24 Dec 1790
Lessart, 25 Jan–20 Nov 1791
Cahier de Gerville, 27 Nov 1791–15 Mar 1792

Foreign Affairs
Comte de Montmorin, 16 July 1789–20 Nov 1791
Lessart, 20 Nov 1791–10 Mar 1792

War
Comte de Saint-Priest, 16 July–4 Aug 1789
La Tour du Pin, 4 Aug 1789–21 Oct 1790
Duportail, 16 Nov 1790–3 Dec 1791
Comte de Narbonne, 7 Dec 1791–10 Mar 1792

Navy
Comte de la Luzerne, 16 July 1789–23 Oct 1790
Comte Claret de Fleurieu, 24 Oct 1790–12 May 1791
Comte de Thévenard, 16 May–17 Sept 1791
Comte Bertrand de Moleville, 4 Oct 1791–15 Mar 1792

'THE GIRONDIN MINISTRY', MAR–JUNE 1792

Finance: Clavière, 23 Mar–13 June 1792
Justice: Duranthon, 13 Apr–3 July 1792
Interior: Roland de la Platière, 23 Mar–13 June 1792
Foreign Affairs: Dumouriez, 17 Mar–16 June 1792
War: Marquis de Grave, 10 Mar–8 May 1792
Servan, 9 May–12 June 1792
Dumouriez, 12–16 June 1792
Navy: Lacoste, 15 Mar–10 July 1792

FROM THE GIRONDIN MINISTRY TO 10 AUGUST
1792

Finance
Duranthon, 13–16 June 1792
Beaulieu, 18 June–29 July 1792
Delaville-Leroux, 30 July–10 Aug 1792

Justice
Dejoly, 3 July–10 Aug 1792

Interior
Mourgues, 13–18 June 1792
Marquis de Terrier de Monciel, 18 June–17 July 1792
Champion de Villeneuve, 20 July–10 Aug 1792

Foreign Affairs
Marquis de Chambonas, 17 June–23 July 1792
Bigot de Sainte-Croix, 1–10 Aug 1792

War
Lajard, 16 June–24 July 1792
Baron d'Abancourt, 24 July–10 Aug 1792

Navy
Vicomte du Bouchage, 21 July–10 Aug 1792

FROM THE OVERTHROW OF THE MONARCHY TO THE ABOLITION OF MINISTERS

Finance
Clavière, 10 Aug 1792–2 June 1793
Destournelles, 13 June 1793–1 Apr 1794/12 germ II

Justice
Danton, 10 Aug–8 Oct 1792
Garat, 9 Oct 1792–19 Mar 1793
Gohier, 20 March 1793–1 Apr 1794/12 germ II

Interior
Roland de la Platière, 10 Aug 1792–23 Jan 1793
Garat (as caretaker from 23 Jan), 19 Mar–19 Aug 1793
Paré, 20 Aug 1793–1 Apr 1794/12 germ II

Foreign Affairs
Lebrun-Tondu, 10 Aug 1792–21 June 1793
Deforgues, 21 June 1793–1 Apr 1794/12 germ II

War
Clavière (as caretaker), 12–21 Aug 1792
Servan, 21 Aug–3 Oct 1792
Pache, 18 Oct 1792–2 Feb 1793
Beurnonville, 4 Feb–11 Mar 1793
Bouchotte, 4 Apr 1793–1 Apr 1794/12 germ II

Navy
Monge, 12 Aug 1792–13 Apr 1793
Dalbarade, 13 Apr 1793–1 Apr 1794/12 germ II

FROM THE ABOLITION OF MINISTERS TO THE DIRECTORY

From 1 Apr 1794/12 germ II, ministries were abolished, and replaced by 12 administrative commissions. Ministers were restored from the first days of the Directorial regime, and the commissions were abolished on 25 Feb 1796/6 vent IV.

UNDER THE DIRECTORY

Finance
Faipoult, 8 Oct 1795/16 vendém III – 5 Jan 1796/15 niv IV

Ramel-Nogaret, 14 Feb 1796/25 pluv IV – 20 July 1799/2 therm VII
Robert Lindet, 23 July 1799/5 therm VII – 9 Nov 1799/18 brum VIII

Justice
Merlin de Douai, 3 Nov 1795/12 brum IV – 4 Jan 1796/14 niv IV
Génissieu, 5 Jan 1796/15 niv IV – 2 Apr 1796/13 germ IV
Merlin de Douai, 3 Apr 1796/14 germ IV – 18 Sept 1797/2 jc V
Lambrechts, 24 Sept 1797/3 vendém VI – 21 June 1799/3 mess VII
Cambacérès, 20 July 1799/2 therm VII – 24 Dec 1799/3 niv VIII

Interior
Bénézech, 3 Nov 1795/12 brum IV – 2 Sept 1797/16 fruct V
François de Neufchâteau, 16 July 1797/28 mess V – 14 Sept 1797/28 fruct V
Letourneux, 14 Sept 1797/28 fruct V – 17 June 1798/29 prair VI
François de Neufchâteau, 17 June 1798/29 prair VI – 23 June 1799/5 mess VII
Quinette, 25 June 1799/7 mess VII – 9 Nov 1799/18 brum VIII

Police (*Police générale*)
Merlin de Douai, 5 Jan 1796/15 niv IV – 3 Apr 1796/14 germ IV
Cochon de l'Apparent, 3 Apr 1796/14 germ IV – 13 July 1797/25 mess V
Lenoir Laroche, 16 July 1797/28 mess V – 26 July 1797/8 therm V
Sotin de la Coindière, 26 July 1797/8 therm V – 13 Feb 1798/25 pluv VI
Dondeau, 13 Feb 1798/25 pluv VI – 16 May 1798/25 pluv VI
Lecarlier d'Ardon, 16 May 1798/27 flor VII – 1 Nov 1798/11 brum VII
Jean-Pierre Duval, 1 Nov 1798/11 brum VII – 23 June 1799/5 mess VII
Bourguignon-Dumolard, 23 June 1799/5 mess VII – 20 July 1799/2 therm VII
Fouché, 20 July 1799/2 therm VII – 14 Sept 1802/27 fruct X

Foreign affairs (*Relations extérieures*)
Delacroix de Contaut, 7 Nov 1795/16 brum IV – 16 July 1797/28 mess V
Talleyrand, 16 July 1797/5 therm V – 20 July 1799/2 therm VII
Reinhard, 20 July 1799/2 therm VII – 29 Nov 1799/8 frim VIII

War
Aubert-Dubayet, 6 Nov 1795/15 brum IV – 8 Feb 1796/19 pluv IV
Pètiet, 8 Feb 1796/19 pluv IV – 4 July 1797/16 mess V
Schérer, 23 July 1797/5 therm V – 7 Feb 1799/19 pluv III
Milet-Mureau, 7 Feb 1799/19 pluv VII – 17 July 1799/29 mess VII
Bernadotte, 3 July 1799/14 mess VII – 14 Sept 1799/28 fruct VII
Dubois-Crancé, 14 Sept 1799/28 fruct VII – 10 Nov 1799/19 brum VIII

Navy
Truguet, 1 Nov 1795/10 brum IV – 18 July 1797/30 mess V
Pléville le Peley, 16 July 1797/28 mess V – 27 Apr 1798/8 flor VI
Bruix, 27 Apr 1798/8 flor VI – 30 July 1799/12 therm VII
Bourdon de Vatry, 30 July 1799/12 therm VII – 23 Nov 1799/2 frim VIII

3. THE DIRECTORS, 1795–1799

1 Nov 1795/16 brum V
LA REVELLIERE-LEPEAUX, LETOURNEUR, REUBELL, BARRAS, CARNOT
Siéyès was originally elected by the C Anciens, but refused to hold office. He was replaced by Carnot.

26 May 1797/7 prair V
LA REVELLIERE-LEPEAUX, BARTHELEMY, REUBELL, BARRAS, CARNOT
In replacement of Letourneur (designated by lot), the C Anciens elected Barthélemy (138 votes), who had headed the poll in the C500 with 309 votes.

8 Sept 1797/22 fruct V
LA REVELLIERE-LEPEAUX, MERLIN DE DOUAI, REUBELL, BARRAS, FRANCOIS DE NEUFCHATEAU
In replacement of Barthélemy and Carnot (proscribed in the *coup d'état* of 18 fruct V), the C Anciens elected Merlin de Douai (74 votes in the first poll) and François de Neufchâteau (111 votes in the second poll).

15 May 1798/26 flor VI
LA REVELLIERE-LEPEAUX, MERLIN DE DOUAI, REUBELL, BARRAS, TREILHARD
In replacement of François de Neufchâteau (designated by lot), the C Anciens elected Treilhard (166 votes) who had headed the poll in the C500 with 234 votes.

16 May 1799/22 flor VII
LA REVELLIERE-LEPEAUX, MERLIN DE DOUAI, SIEYES, BARRAS, TREILHARD
In replacement of Reubell (designated by lot), the C Anciens elected Siéyès (118 votes, as against 74 for Duval). Heading the poll in the C500 had been General Lefebvre (338 votes), Siéyès (236) and Duval (216).

16–18 June 1799/28–30 prair VII
LA REVELLIERE-LEPEAUX, MERLIN DE DOUAI, SIEYES, BARRAS, GOHIER
In replacement of Treilhard (whose election was now annulled on constitutional grounds), the C Anciens elected Gohier (164 votes). Voting in the C500: Lefebvre, 345 votes; Dupuis, 330; Gohier, 329.

18 June 1799/30 prair VII
LA REVELLIERE-LEPEAUX, ROGER DUCOS, SIEYES, BARRAS, GOHIER

In replacement of Merlin de Douai (who resigned under pressure in the *coup d'état* of 30 prair), the C Anciens elected Roger Ducos (153 votes). Voting in the C500: Lefebvre, 324; General Masséna, 316; Dupuis, 311; Roger Ducos, 309.

20 June 1799/2 mess VII
MOULIN, ROGER DUCOS, SIEYES, BARRAS, GOHIER

In replacement of La Révellière-Lépeaux (who resigned under pressure in the *coup d'état* of 30 prair), the C Anciens elected General Moulin (105 votes). Voting in the C500: Masséna, 304; Dupuis, 302; Martin, 300; Lefebvre, 300; Lacrosse, 292; Moulin, 260.

4. THE CONSULATE, 1799

9 Nov 1799/18 brum VIII
Provisional Consular Commission: BONAPARTE, SIEYES, ROGER DUCOS

13 Dec 1799/22 frim VIII
Consuls: BONAPARTE, CAMBACERES, LEBRUN

IV. THE STRUCTURE OF THE TERROR: THE INSTITUTIONS OF REVOLUTIONARY GOVERNMENT, 1792–1795

1. 'REVOLUTIONARY GOVERNMENT'

Contemporaries took the term 'revolutionary' to mean *not* 'pertaining to the Rev', *but rather* 'provisional', 'exceptional', the opposite of 'constitutional'. The phrase 'rev govt' may thus be applied to the whole period from 10 Aug 1792 to 26 Oct 1795/4 brum IV. For all this period, France was being governed outside the framework of a constitution, and for virtually all of it by a nat ass., the Convtn, specifically established to devise a rpbcn constitution. Military necessity required that the separation of powers, the keystone of any constitutional government, was provisionally in abeyance. The rpbcn constitution, finally approved on 24 June 1793, was never to be implemented: the law of 10 Oct 1793 declared that France's system of government was to be 'rev until the peace'; and the Thermidorian Convtn devised a less democratic constitution, the Constitution of Year III.

The period is often referred to as the 'Terror', the policy and institutions of intimidation and repression of political opponents. Very crudely, four periods of 'Rev Govt' may be discerned.

(i) The 'First Terror', 10 Aug–20 Sept 1792. The emergency government which lasted from the overthrow of the monarchy to the first session of the Convtn. Power shared between Leg Ass., the Provisional Executive Council of Ministers (PEC) and the Paris Commune. Most notable event, the 'Sept Massacres' (2–6 Sept).

(ii) Foundations of the Great Terror, 21 Sept 1792–2 June 1793. Rule of the Convtn down to the purge of the Girondins. Most of the organs of the Terror were established: Committee of General Security (CGS) (2 Oct 1792); Rev Tribunal (10 Mar 1793), reps *en mission* (9 Mar), death for rebels (19 March), comités de surveillance (21 Mar), Committee of Public Safety (CPS) (6 Apr), reps *aux armées* (9 Apr), 'First' Maximum (4 May).

(iii) The 'Great Terror', Spring/Summer 1793–9 Thermidor. The period of dominance of the CPS. The build-up of the legislative arsenal of the Terror was accelerated by the Federalist Revolt and the declaration (5 Sept 1793) that Terror was the 'order of the day': law on hoarding (27 July 1793), *levée en masse* (23 Aug), Law of Suspects (17 Sept), General Maximum (29 Sept), adoption of the Rev Calendar (5 Oct), suspension of the constitution 'until the peace' (10 Oct), Law on Rev Govt of 14 Frimaire II (6 Dec). Some historians distinguish an 'anarchic' phase of the Terror down to 14 Frimaire during which the CPS lacked the means of full control over the Terror in the provinces, and a 'bureaucratic' phase inaugurated by 14 Frimaire – though in practice it took several months for the law to be operational. The Terror accelerated with the execution of Hébertists (24 Mar 1794/4 germ II) and Dantonists (5 Apr/16 germ) and the streamlining of the Rev Tribunal by the Law of 22 Prairial (10 June).

(iv) the 'Thermidorian Reaction', 27 July 1794/9 therm II–26 Oct 1795/4 brum IV, and the White Terror. Aftermath of the overthrow of the 'Great CPS' at Thermidor. The Thermidorian Convtn kept the framework of emergency government but removed many of the features of the Terror. Reorganisation of the CPS and the committees of government (29 July 1794/11 therm II, 24 Aug/7 fruct), closure of the Jacobin Club (12 Nov/22 brum III), abolition of the Maximum (24 Dec/4 niv), suspension of the Law of 14 Frimaire II (17 Apr 1795/28 germ III), abolition of reps *en mission* (26 Apr/7 flor) and the Rev Tribunal (31 May/12 prair), voting of the Constitution of Year III (22 Aug/5 fruct), closure of clubs and popular societies (23 Aug/6 fruct), repeal of the Law of Suspects (7 Oct/15 vendém IV). White Terror in Paris and the provinces: authorities connived in harassment of and vigilante attacks against ex-terrorists.

On 12 June 1795/12 prair III, it was forbidden to use the term *révolutionnaire* in regard to any administrative organ.

2. THE COMMITTEE OF PUBLIC SAFETY (*COMITÉ DE SALUT PUBLIC*)

The basis of government from its inception on 6 Apr 1793 down to the end of the Convtn, the Committee had its most heroic hour at the height of the Terror from the Summer of 1793 down to Thermidor.

ORIGINS

Although there were precursors to a strong executive power located within the Nat Ass. (e.g. the 'Commission des Douze' established on 17 June 1792 to bolster the work of ministers in the face of the war), the CPS has its origins in the decision of the Convtn on 1 Jan 1793 to create a 'Committee of General Defence' (CGD), composed of representatives sitting in the Ass., which was to coordinate with the council of ministers to ensure a more effective prosecution of the war effort. It was composed of three representatives from seven key committees (war, finance, colonies, navy, diplomacy, constitution, commerce). Among the initial 21 members were Barère, Bréard, Cambon, Dubois-Crancé and Siéyès and the Girondins Brissot, Boyer-Fonfrède, Gensonné, Guadet, Kersaint and Lacaze.

On 25 Mar, the Convtn attempted to make it more effective by enlarging its membership; extending its powers to cover 'all measures necessary for the internal and external defence of the Rpbc'; and renaming it the 'Committee (or 'Commission') of Public Safety'. Wider discussion of the revised committee's powers, 3–5 Apr, led to the creation of the CPS proper on 6 Apr, and the election of its first members.

EARLY HISTORY

The nine members of the new committee, renewable monthly, were to:
- deliberate in secret (the CGD had always operated in open session)
- supervise the activities of ministers, and of agents of the executive
- pass decrees collectively relating to 'general defence, external and internal'
- report weekly to the Convtn.

Danton's primacy from 6 Apr to 10 July made the committee in some senses 'a Danton ministry' (AULARD). The *journées* of 31 May and 2 June 1793 led to changes in its personnel; an increased division of labour among members of the committee; and greater control over the activities of ministers. Military and diplomatic setbacks led to a major reshuffle from July onwards, and the replacement of Danton as dominant personality by Robespierre. By September, the personnel of the 'Great CPS' was in place, and with the exception of Hérault de Séchelles (arrested 18 Mar 1794, executed 5 Apr) they would remain in office down to Thermidor. Monthly renewals of membership became a formality.

PERSONNEL, 6 APR 1793–9 THERMIDOR

(See p. 90).

POWERS OF THE 'GREAT CPS'

The CPS was at once the heart of government and the nerve-centre of the war effort. The law of 6 Apr had stated that it was to ensure the 'surveillance and acceleration of action of administration entrusted to ministers', but by June it was acting as the executive force itself. On 28 July 1793 it was empowered to issue arrest warrants against suspects. On 2 Aug, it was granted 50 million liv for secret expenses. On 14 Sept, it nominated the membership of the other great 'committee of government', the CGS. Its supervisory activities over other authorities was confirmed in the decree of 10 Oct 1793 which proclaimed government 'rev until the peace': ministers, generals, other constituted authorities were placed under its orders; and for the first time it was to nominate generals for approval by the Convtn. On 25 Nov/5 frim, reps *en mission* were placed directly under the committee's orders. The Law of 14 Frimaire II on Rev Govt enshrined its primacy: it was further empowered to dismiss functionaries and to conduct foreign policy. The law of 13 Mar 1794/23 vent II permitted it to replace dismissed functionaries with its own nominees. On 1 Apr 1794/12 germ II the abolition of ministries confirmed the CPS's dominance of the executive, while the Law of 27 Germinal (16 Apr) establishing a *bureau de police générale* gave it police powers which made it a potential rival of the CGS.

Throughout the Terror, finance was out of the hands of either of the two committees of government and resided in the Finance Committee.

POLITICAL ORIENTATION OF THE 'GREAT CPS'

Left: Robespierre, Couthon, Saint-Just, Prieur de la Marne, Jean Bon Saint-André

Composition of the Committee of Public Safety, 1793

	6 Apr (votes)	7 Apr	30 May	June	10 July (votes)	27 July	14 Aug	6 Sept	30 Sept
CAMBON	278	*	*	*					
DANTON	233	*	*	*					
DELACROIX de l'Eure-et-Loir	151	*	*	*					
DELMAS	347	*	*	*					
GUYTON-MORVEAU	202	*	*	*					
BREARD	325	*	*	*	192				
BARERE	360	*	*	*	178	*	*	*	BARERE
TREILHARD	167	*	*	*					
DEBRY	227	*							
Robert LINDET		*	*	*	100	*	*	*	LINDET
RAMEL		*							
MATHIEU		*	*	*	176				
COUTHON			*	*	176	*	*	*	COUTHON
HERAULT DE SECHELLES			*	*	175	*	*	*	HERAULT DE SECHELLES
SAINT-JUST			*	*	126	*	*	*	SAINT-JUST
BERLIER					178				
GASPARIN			*	*	178	*			
JEAN BON SAINT-ANDRE			*	*	192	**	**	*	JEAN-BON SAINT-ANDRE
THURIOT			*	*	155				
PRIEUR DE LA MARNE					142	**	***	**	PRIEUR DE LA MARNE
ROBESPIERRE						*	*	*	ROBESPIERRE
CARNOT							*	*	CARNOT
PRIEUR DE LA COTE-D'OR							*	*	PRIEUR DE LA COTE-D'OR
BILLAUD-VARENNE								*	BILLAUD-VARENNE
COLLOT-D'HERBOIS								*	COLLOT-D'HERBOIS

Ultra-Left: Billaud-Varenne, Collot-d'Herbois

Right: Thuriot (down to 20 Sept 1793), Lindet, Carnot, Prieur de la Côte-d'Or.

DIVISION OF LABOUR WITHIN THE 'GREAT CPS'

Robespierre: main policy link with the Convtn, the Jacobins and the Commune; also religion; and (with Saint-Just and Couthon) major policy strategy and political police.

Saint-Just: war organisation

Barère: liaison with the Convtn and other authorities; education and welfare; diplomacy

Billaud-Varenne, Collot-d'Herbois: correspondence with reps *en mission* and with other departmental authorities

Lindet: food supply

Carnot: war strategy and personnel

Prieur de la Côte-d'Or: arms, gunpowder, war industries in general

Jean Bon Saint-André, Prieur de la Marne: usually away *en mission;* the former was effectively Minister of the Navy

Hérault de Séchelles: diplomacy.

The rough-and-ready division of labour can be seen in the authorship of CPS decrees during Prairial II (20 May–18 June 1794) (*Palmer 1941*):

	Lindet	Prieur de la Côte-d'Or	Carnot	Barère	Saint-Just	Robespierre	Couthon	Collot-d'Herbois	Billaud-Varenne
Supply & transport (195)	183	7	1	4	–	–	–	–	–
Munitions (120)	4	114	2	–	–	–	–	–	–
Army, Navy (143)	2	9	130	1	1	–	–	–	–
Personnel & police (21)	3	–	1	7	1	8	1	–	–
Public opinion, welfare, propaganda (24)		5	2	11	–	1	2	3	–
Admin, miscellaneous (105)	15	22	41	11	2	5	5	4	–
TOTAL (608)	207	157	177	34	4	14	8	7	0

DURING THE THERMIDORIAN REACTION

On 29 July 1794/11 therm II it was agreed that the personnel of the committee should be renewable by a quarter each month, and two days later six new members (including Thuriot, Tallien, Treilhard and Bréard) were elected in place of Robespierre, Couthon, Saint-Just and Hérault de Séchelles (all deceased), Jean Bon Saint-André and Prieur de la Marne. Sixty-eight deputies sat on the committee down to the end of the Convtn, the most dominant personalities being Cambacérès, Siéyès and Boissy d'Anglas.

The law of 24 Aug 1794/7 fruct II reorganised the committee system. The primacy of the CPS ended; it was entrusted with diplomacy, military operations, war supply, trade and imports, requisitions; but it lost its police bureau; and control over administration and justice passed to the Legislation Committee, which assumed a far more important role than hitherto. The centralising force of the 'committees of government' under the Terror was increasingly lost, and the committee system disappeared with the advent of the Directory.

3. THE COMMITTEE OF GENERAL SECURITY (*COMITÉ DE SÛRETÉ GÉNÉRALE*)

A virtual police ministry under the Great Terror, the CGS was with the CPS (to which it was subordinate) one of the 'committees of government' which effectively conducted the 'Great Terror' from the summer of 1793 down to Thermidor.

ORIGINS AND EARLY HISTORY

The idea of a committee to investigate acts of treason and serve as a political police dates back to the Constit Ass., which on 28 July 1789 established the so-called Search Committee (*Comité des recherches*) to investigate crimes of *lèse-nation*. The Leg Ass. created as its successor a *Comité de surveillance*, 25 Nov 1791, which was to bring those accused of *lèse-nation* before the High Court. From 10 Apr 1792, its authority was enlarged and it was empowered to arrest suspects. The Convtn kept the committee in being, and on 2 Oct 1792 renamed it the Committee of General Security (*Comité de sûreté générale*). It was entrusted with the tasks of:

- surveillance over state security
- correspondence with regular authorities
- prosecution of foreign agents, former servants of the crown, counterfeiters, etc
- reporting regularly to the Convtn.

From 17 Oct 1792, its membership of 30 (half of whom were to be renewed every two months) was largely Montagnard (Hérault de Séchelles, Basire, Chabot, Lavicomterie, Drouet, Tallien, Bernard de Saintes, Ingrand, etc). Following a concerted Girondin attack on the committee, new elections on 3 Jan 1793 gave the Girondins a clear majority on the committee for the first time. The Montagnards counter-attacked, blaming the CGS for the assassination of Lepeletier de Saint-Fargeau on 20 Jan 1793. Henceforth there were only to be 12 members; and of the 12 first elected (who included Basire, Chabot, Legendre, Tallien, Duhem), only one (Lasource) was a Girondin. Despite frequent personnel changes (Garnier de Saintes entered the committee in Mar, Carrier in Apr, etc), the CGS remained a Montagnard fief, and it was for this reason that the Girondins preferred to refer surveillance of the Paris Commune in May 1793 to the ill-fated 'Commission of Twelve' (*Commission des Douze*) rather than the CGS.

Following the purge of the Girondins, personnel changes continued, the most prominent members of the committee in the summer of 1793 being Basire, Chabot, Amar, Drouet, Guffroy, Laignelot, Lavicomterie, Legendre, Moïse Bayle and Dartigoëyte. On 9 Sept, it was agreed that membership should be restricted to 12. On 14 Sept, the CPS (whose authority over the CGS was to be reaffirmed in the laws of 10 Oct 1793 and 14 Frimaire II) presented a list of 12 nominees, which the Convtn endorsed. With some changes, these constituted the 'Great CGS' of the height of the Terror.

PERSONNEL OF THE 'GREAT CGS'

Name (with date of election to CGS if later than 14 Sept 1793)	Individuals who left CGS prior to 9 Thermidor	Member of CGS on 9 Thermidor
Amar		AMAR
Moise Bayle		MOISE BAYLE
Boucher Saint-Sauveur	Resigned 1 Oct 1793	
David		DAVID
Dubarran (13 Oct 1793)		DUBARRAN
Guffroy	Resigned 7 Mar 1794	
Jagot (13 Oct 1793)		JAGOT
Elie Lacoste (22 Nov 1793)		ELIE LACOSTE
Laloy (13 Oct 1793)	Resigned 3 Nov 1793	
Lavicomterie		LAVICOMTERIE
Lebas		LEBAS
Lebon	Withdrew from Oct 1793	
Louis du Bas-Rhin (13 Oct 1793)		LOUIS
Panis	Withdrew Jan–Mar 1794	
Rühl		RUHL
Vadier		VADIER
Voulland		VOULLAND

POWERS OF THE 'GREAT CGS'

Under the Terror, the tasks of the CGS were as follows:
- surveillance of state security
- control over all matters relating to persons and 'police' (the latter term was wider than mere policing functions and denoted administrative matters)
- maintenance of rev laws
- counter-espionage
- action against counterfeiting of assignats.

An extremely copious correspondence with the provinces and wide-ranging powers endorsed in the Law of 14 Frimaire II gave the CGS control over the conduct of the Terror in the provinces. It worked in harness with the CPS, with which it had a weekly meeting to discuss matters of common interest and with which it cooperated on major security matters (e.g. trial of the Dantonists).

By Spring 1794, relations with the CPS were marked by growing disharmony. The CGS resented the Police Law of 16 Apr/27 germ which created a rival *bureau de police générale* in the CPS; Robespierre's civic religion inaugurated on 7 May/18 flor; and the CPS's failure to consult it over the Law of 22 Prairial. A number of members of the CGS were to be among the Thermidor conspirators (though Lebas shared Robespierre's fate).

AFTER THERMIDOR

Personnel changes on 1 Aug 1794/14 therm II saw the political complexion of the committee change drastically. Henceforward, a quarter of the membership of the committee was changed each month. The law of 24 Aug/7 fruct further affected its powers: it lost the rivalry of the police bureau of the CPS which was dissolved; its membership was increased; and the size of its staff reduced. It was still a 'committee of government', though now alongside the Legislation Committee as well as the CPS. The committee played a crucial role in the Thermidorian Reaction: it supervised the release of those imprisoned under the Terror; it was entrusted with the appointment of *commissaires de police* throughout France (11 Mar 1795/21 vent III), and with the disarming of ex-terrorists (10 Apr 1795/21 germ III); and it enjoyed extensive rights of censorship over royalist and radical newspapers.

4. THE LAW OF REVOLUTIONARY GOVERNMENT OF 14 FRIMAIRE II (4 DEC 1793)

The charter of Rev Govt, this law ratified the primacy which since mid 1793 the CPS and, to a lesser extent, the CGS had developed in the exercise of power; and it helped the CPS enforce a tighter grip over the various organs of rev government. In the depts, increased power was given to the district authorities; and a new official, the *agent national,* was created at district and municipal level to facilitate the implementation of rev legislation. A bureaucratic tightening-up of administrative procedures, the law also constituted a political counterblast to the powers and ambitions of the Paris Commune and the more adventurous reps *en mission.* The system it erected was severely damaged in the aftermath of Thermidor, and the law was repealed on 17 Apr 1795/28 germ III.

THE CENTRE OF GOVERNMENT

The Convtn:
'the sole centre of impulsion of government'.

Committees of government, Executive Council:
- all regular authorities and functionaries under the 'inspection' of the CPS as regards rev legislation (as stated in the law of 10 Oct 1793), and of the CGS as regards police and personnel (as stated in the law of 17 Sept 1793)
- CPS and CGS make monthly reports to the Convtn
- Executive Council to ensure surveillance of military, judicial and administrative legislation, and to report to the CPS every 10 days
- although the Convtn appoints generals, ministers appoint subaltern officers after CPS approval
- CPS entrusted with the conduct of diplomacy.

MAIN REGULAR AUTHORITIES IN THE DEPTS

Districts ensure surveillance of the execution of rev legislation (and report direct to the government, without passing through the departmental level of authority); *departments* supervise taxes, industry, communications and national lands; *courts*

96

handle civil and criminal legislation; while at the front, surveillance of military measures is in the hands of *commanders* and other military agents

- dept authorities, military commanders and courts report every 10 days to the Executive Council; but districts report direct to the CPS and CGS
- application of rev legislation is the responsibility of the municipalities and *comités de surveillance* (or *comités révolutionnaires*) who report every 10 days to the district authorities (in Paris, the *comités* report direct to the CGS)
- all regular authorities are to provide monthly synopses of their activities to the body responsible for their supervision
- no authority is to issue decrees interpreting the law or adding to it, nor to release prisoners on anyone's authority except the CPS, CGS, reps *en mission* and the Convtn
- no regular authority is to be itinerary or peripatetic.

AGENTS NATIONAUX

The elected posts of departmental PGS and district *procureur-syndic* are abolished

- they are replaced by *agents nationaux* who are attached to each district as well as municipality and who are to ensure the execution of the law and to denounce any negligence on the part of officials
- the agents are to be drawn from the ranks of former *procureur-syndics,* municipal *procureurs* and their substitutes, and to be approved by the Convtn following purges of the regular authorities conducted by reps *en mission*
- unlike all other authorities, they are permitted to be peripatetic within their area of jurisdiction
- district agents are to report to the CPS and CGS every 10 days; municipal agents and *comités de surveillance* are to report to the district authorities.

REPRÉSENTANTS EN MISSION AND OTHER AGENTS

Roving commissioners may be reps *en mission,* agents of the Executive Council, of the CPS or of the *Commission des subsistances*

- reps *en mission* to keep strictly to ensuring the maintenance of rev legislation, requisitioning, etc
- they are also to purge all regular authorities, and to report to the CPS on the operation within a month
- they are to report to the CPS every 10 days
- none is to go beyond his mandate and all are to keep within the geographical area ascribed them
- executive and subsistence agents are to be approved by the CPS and to report to the reps *en mission.*

OTHER REVOLUTIONARY AGENCIES

Reps *en mission* may appoint their own agents, or *commissaires,* but the authority of the latter lapses when the reps are recalled

- these *commissaires* may not be sent into another area on the authority of themselves or the reps
- there are to be no congresses or mergers of popular societies or *comités de surveillance* (on the lines of *comité central de surveillance, commission central révolutionnaire*) on the grounds that these hinder the efficacy of government and smack of federalism
- all *armées révolutionnaires* formerly created by reps *en mission* are abolished
- no armed force of any description is to perform home raids, which are the responsibility of the regular authorities
- prohibition of the levying of armed forces, or of new taxes, forced or voluntary loans, except by' decree.

PROMULGATION OF LAWS

The laws of the Convtn are to be printed in a journal, the *Bulletin des Lois de la République,* which is under a special commission of four members of the Convtn responsible to the CPS

- the *Bulletin* to be sent out daily to all regular authorities and state functionaries
- laws are to be read to the public each *décadi* by the mayor or by some other municipal official
- translations are to be provided into the main *patois* and, for propaganda purposes, into foreign languages.

5. PRESIDENTS OF THE CONVENTION

The post of president of the Convtn was an elective one, held normally for a fortnight (one and a half *décades*, from Oct 1793). The choices of the Convtn reflect the political complexion and atmosphere of the Ass. Presidents played a role in several key rev *journées*.

1792

20 Sept	Rühl (as oldest member present)
21 Sept	Pétion
4 Oct	Delacroix
18 Oct	Guadet
1 Nov	Hérault de Séchelles
15 Nov	Grégoire
19 Nov	Barère
13 Dec	Defermon
27 Dec	Treilhard

1793

10 Jan	Vergniaud
24 Jan	Rabaut Saint-Etienne
7 Feb	Bréard
21 Feb	Dubois-Crancé
7 Mar	Gensonné
21 Mar	Debry
4 Apr	Delmas
18 Apr	Lasource
2 May	Boyer-Fonfrède
16 May	Isnard
30 May	Mallarmé
13 June	Collot-d'Herbois
27 June	Thuriot
11 July	Jean Bon Saint-André

25 July	Danton
8 Aug	Hérault de Séchelles
22 Aug	Robespierre
5 Sept	Billaud-Varenne
19 Sept	Cambon
3 Oct	Charlier

YEAR II

22 Oct/1 brum	Moïse Bayle
6 Nov/16 brum	Laloy
21 Nov/1 frim	Romme
6 Dec/16 frim	Voulland
21 Dec/1 niv	Couthon

(1794)

5 Jan/16 niv	David
20 Jan/1 pluv	Vadier
4 Feb/16 pluv	Dubarran
19 Feb/1 vent	Saint-Just
6 Mar/16 vent	Rühl
21 Mar/1 germ	Tallien
5 Apr/16 germ	Amar
20 Apr/1 flor	Robert Lindet
5 May/16 flor	Carnot
20 May/1 prair	Prieur de la Côte-d'Or
4 June/1 prair	Robespierre
19 June/1 mess	Elie Lacoste
5 July/16 mess	Louis du Bas-Rhin
19 July/1 therm	Collot-d'Herbois
3 Aug/16 therm	Merlin de Douai
18 Aug/1 fruct	Merlin de Thionville
1 Sept/15 fruct	Bernard de Saintes

YEAR III

22 Sept/1 vendém	André Dumont
7 Oct/16 vendém	Cambacérès
22 Oct/1 brum	Prieur de la Marne
6 Nov/16 brum	Louis Legendre

24 Nov/4 frim	Clauzel
6 Dec/16 frim	Reubell
21 Dec/1 niv	Bentabole

(1795)

6 Jan/17 niv	Letourneur
20 Jan/1 pluv	Rovère
4 Feb/16 pluv	Barras
19 Feb/1 vent	Bourdon de l'Oise
6 Mar/16 vent	Thibaudeau
24 Mar/4 germ	Pelet de la Lozère
5 Apr/16 germ	Boissy d'Anglas
20 Apr/1 flor	Siéyès
5 May/16 flor	Vernier
26 May/7 prair	Mathieu
4 June/16 prair	Lanjuinais
19 June/1 mess	Louvet
4 July/16 mess	Doulcet de Pontécoulant
19 July/1 therm	La Révellière-Lépeaux
3 Aug/16 therm	Daunou
19 Aug/2 fruct	Marie-Jos Chénier
2 Sept/16 fruct	Berlier

YEAR IV

23 Sept/1 vendém	Baudin des Ardennes
8 Oct/16 vendém	Génissieu

6. COMMITTEES

Committees of the Ass. continued to play a part in government under the Convtn. The dominance of the CPS and CGS clouds the less glamorous but nevertheless effective role which these played in preparing measures prior to discussion and voting in the Convtn and in dealing with most matters coming up from the depts. The most important of the other committees was the FINANCE COMMITTEE, chaired by Joseph Cambon. All financial matters were kept outside the purview of the 'committees of government', and all questions of financial strategy (e.g. over assignats; e.g. the law of 15 Dec 1792 relating to financial exactions within conquered territories) were in the hands of this key committee. The MILITARY COMMITTEE also played an important role in the organisation of the war effort from late 1792. Carnot and Prieur de la Côte-d'Or were among its members, as were Dubois-Crancé, Gasparin and Châteauneuf-Randon.

The full list of committees of the Convtn in existence under the Terror is as follows:

1. CPS
2. CGS
3. Legislation
4. Finance
5. Dispatches
6. 'Central Commission' (for the preparation of the agenda)
7. Military supply and contracts
8. Assignats and currency
9. Correspondence
10. Petitions
11. War
12. Decrees, minutes of sessions
13. Archives
14. Inspectors of the hall of session
15. Education
16. Public assistance
17. Division (administration of depts)
18. Liquidation and accounts
19. Alienation and domains
20. Agriculture, trade, navigation, communications
21. Navy, colonies.

The committee system was revised after Thermidor with the aim of producing a 'pairing' with the executive commissions which since 1 Apr 1794 had replaced ministries (See above, III, 2). The law of 24 Aug 1794/7 fruct II established 16 committees, all of whose membership was to be renewable by one-quarter each month:

1. CPS
2. CGS
3. Legislation
4. Finance
5. Education
6. Agriculture and arts
7. Trade and supply
8. Public works
9. Communications, postal services
10. Military
11. Navy, colonies
12. Public assistance
13. Division
14. Decrees, archives
15. Petitions, correspondence, dispatches
16. Inspectors of the meeting-hall.

The law of 7 fruct accorded the LEGISLATION COMMITTEE a new importance, and for the remainder of the Convtn's rule it figured, with the CPS and CGS, as one of the 'committees of government'. In particular, it took over from the pre-Thermidorian CPS correspondence with all dept, district, administrative and judicial bodies; and from 28 Sept 1794/7 vendém III it appointed to vacant places within these authorities (from 4 Mar 1795/14 vent III, without even having to consult the Convtn).

7. MINISTERS AND EXECUTIVE COMMISSIONS

(For ministerial personnel, see II. 2)

The overthrow of the king placed an added onus on the revitalised executive council of ministers created on 10 Aug 1792 (PEC). Ministers were now elected by the Ass., though not from among its members. The importance of ministers was, however, attenuated in late 1792 by the Girondins' distrust of the executive and, from Jan 1793, by the existence of the CGD, then the CPS. The CPS's position of dominance was ratified by the Law of 14 Frimaire II, by which time the executive existed only as a kind of 'homage to the dogma of the separation of powers' (AULARD).

On 1 Apr 1794/12 germ II, ministries were abolished outright, and replaced by 12 executive commissions, the chairmen of which acted as departmental heads under the authority of the CPS to which they were obliged to report direct each day. The Convtn approved membership of the commissions based on lists submitted by the CPS. The commissions were:

1. Civil administration, police, law courts
2. Education
3. Agriculture and the arts
4. Trade and food supply
5. Public works
6. Public assistance
7. Communications, postal services
8. National income
9. Organisation and movement of land armies
10. Navy, colonies
11. Arms, gunpowder
12. Foreign affairs.

After Thermidor, as part of the decentralisation of government, commissions reported not to the CPS but to the Convtn committee which covered their work.

8. NATIONAL FOOD COMMISSION, OR *COMMISSION DES SUBSISTANCES*

This body constituted the economic arm of the Rev Govt. Established on 27 Oct 1793, the commission was kept closely under the stewardship of Robert Lindet of the CPS and he liaised with other Convtn committees, notably those of finance, war, trade and agriculture. It contained over 500 staff at the height of the Terror (the CPS only had 400), and was empowered, like the CPS and Executive Council, to send out agents into the provinces for specific tasks and for intelligence-gathering. Its control over the economy far exceeded anything similar in France's past.

Its functions, chief among which was the enforcement of the Maximum, were extremely broad:

- supervision of agricultural and industrial production (notably by means of the price maximum)
- control of the labour force for the war effort (it could requisition labour for war industries, for example, and utilise garrisoned soldiers and prisoners of war for road repairs and to gather in the harvest)
- control of trade and communications, including imports and exports (partly through the Maximum, partly through specific legislation)
- enforcement of the Maximum
- diffusion of economic propaganda among producers
- compilation of economic statistics and collection of data.

After Thermidor, the commission was in theory maintained in its rights (law of 7 Sept 1794/21 fruct II prolonging the Maximum). But in fact the economic policy of the Terror was increasingly bypassed and the commission was run down. On 24 Dec 1794/4 niv III the Maximum and all government regulation of the economy was ended.

9. REPRÉSENTANTS EN MISSION

'Liaison agents' (GODECHOT), 'organisers and stimulants' (COLIN LUCAS), acting for the CPS in the provinces and alongside generals in the armies, the reps *en mission* in many ways constituted the key agents of the prov Terror. Themselves members of the Convtn, they had virtually plenipotentiary powers for much of 1793 and early 1794.

ORIGINS

The idea of 'commissioners' (*commissaires*) sent out from Paris with wide-ranging powers over the normal administrative bodies was not new, and indeed owed something to the office of Intendant, or *Commissaire départi*, under the AR (just as in some respects it prefigured Napoleon's prefects). Both the Constit Ass. and the Leg Ass. had occasionally utilised this expedient, but it was under the pressure of war and in the state of emergency following the overthrow of the monarchy in Aug 1792 that the post of *commissaire de la Convention* or rep *en mission* became a regular standby of government. During the power interregnum between 10 Aug and 20 Sept 1792, the Leg Ass., the PEC and the Paris Commune all sent out roving commissioners into the provinces to gather intelligence and to rally the nation behind the Rpbc.

REPRÉSENTANTS EN MISSION DOWN TO 14 FRIMAIRE

The Convtn continued the practice of sending out its members *en mission* from autumn 1792. The scale of the practice was amplified in March and Apr 1793 during the war emergency of those months. On 9 Mar, the Convtn divided the country into 41 sections of 2 departments each, and sent to each section 2 of its members with orders to call established authorities to account; to re-establish public order; to arrest suspects; to check on the proper functioning of the grain trade; and (particularly) to ensure that the levy of 300,000 men for the army established by the law of 24 Feb 1793 was being properly carried out. On 10

106

Mar, reps were empowered to arraign suspects before the newly created Rev Tribunal, and on 3 Apr to arrest and even deport suspects.

On 9 Apr, the Convtn sent out reps to be attached to the armies: there were to be three reps to each army, who were to have 'unlimited powers for the exercise of the functions delegated to them', these functions relating to everything relevant to the war effort (generalship, supply, recruitment, etc). On 30 Apr, the powers of reps *aux armées* were redefined and codified: they supervised and could suspend agents of the Executive Council and suppliers and could provisionally replace military commanders; appointed their own agents to act in their place as need arose; arrested individuals and sent them before the Rev Tribunal; supervised supply and recruitment and could requisition Nat Guardsmen; and acted as a source of propaganda and morale among the men. Renewable by half every month, they were to report weekly to the Convtn and daily to the CPS.

A second wave of reps *en mission* to the provinces occurred following the Federalist revolt of June–July 1793, though some of the Mar batch remained in the provinces. In particular, 18 were dispatched to the depts most affected by federalism on 16 Aug. By a law of 17 July, the Convtn stipulated that the decrees of the reps had the force of laws of the Convtn, while on 16 Aug reps were permitted to condemn to 10 years in irons any individual who obstructed their work. The reps in Mar had been sent to their native depts; this practice was forbidden on 5 July 1793.

The reps often found themselves working alongside agents of the CPS. The latter always encouraged its agents to work closely with reps *en mission*, though some, such as Marc-Antoine Jullien, acted effectively as CPS spies on the activities of the reps. Also working in the provinces were agents of the Executive Council. This proved a source of friction, and clashes of competence continued to occur, even though the CPS worked throughout 1793 to reduce the powers and activities of executive agents. Closer control of the latter was a feature of the great law of 14 Frimaire II (4 Dec 1793).

THE *REPRÉSENTANTS EN MISSION* FROM 14 FRIM II TO 9 THERMIDOR

The laws of 10 Oct 1793 and 14 Frimaire extended the control of the CPS over the reps *en mission*. The latter law was preceded by a decree of 5 frim/27 Nov which placed the reps directly under the orders of the CPS, thus clearing up any ambiguity as to their relations with the Executive Council. The Law of 14 Frimaire was esp important in that it submitted all other types of agents under the authority of the reps, and authorised the reps to institute purges of regular authorities and, in the absence of elections, to appoint replacements. The excessive powers which some reps had assumed were trimmed by clauses which forbade them to exceed the geographical or administrative limits to ˜their *missions* and repressing the use of agents and the levying of forced loans and *armées révolutionnaires*. The creation of the *agents nationaux* was also a straw in the wind which pointed towards the ultimate running down of the system of reps *en mission*.

A further wave of reps was dispatched *en mission* on 29 Dec 1793/9 niv. All reps in the provinces were recalled to Paris by the CPS decree of 13 Mar 1793/23 vent II, though this often took some time to operate, and further reps were sent into the provinces for specific purposes throughout 1794.

NATURE OF ACTIVITY

The fact that reps *en mission* were elected representatives of the people gave them great authority. About half of the members of the Convtn served as reps at some stage, and this included members of the 'Great' CPS (Saint-Just, Jean Bon Saint-André, Prieur de la Marne, etc).

The wide-ranging, virtually plenipotentiary powers enjoyed by the reps could be used in a variety of ways within the general framework of rallying the country for the war effort. Their surveillance ranged over all regular authorities, which they were empowered to purge, as well as the military. They also kept closely in touch with, and attempted to galvanise, local militants in *comités de surveillance*, popular societies, *armées révolutionnaires*, etc. Some of them, keen anti-clericals themselves, introduced dechristianising policies; others, radical social policies (forced loans, requisitions, etc). The Law of 14 Frimaire attempted to curb the rather free-wheeling activities of some reps.

STRENGTHS AND WEAKNESSES OF THE SYSTEM OF *REPRÉSENTANTS EN MISSION*

The scale and effectiveness of the activity of the reps *en mission* varied enormously. The CPS paid particular attention to the reps attached to the armies, who indeed often showed great ingenuity, enthusiasm and even physical courage in the exercise of their duties. The extent of CPS control over other reps *en mission* – and indeed the overall effectiveness of the system – depended on other factors such as distance from Paris, the temperament of individual reps, the political persuasion of depts, etc. The best-known reps are the most enthusiastic: great social levellers and organisers like Saint-Just in Alsace, cruel exponents of rev justice like Carrier at Nantes or Laignelot and Lequinio at Brest, or dechristianising radicals like Fouché in the Nièvre, Laplanche in the Loiret, Lebon in the Pas-de-Calais and Nord. There was a perceived danger of their over-enthusiastic activities proving counter-productive and alienating provincial opinion, and from late 1793 the CPS worked to establish closer control over them, notably in ensuring the implementation of the Law of 14 Frimaire. Recent studies have pointed out how decentralising the institution could be; yet it is also true to say that at no prior stage of French history had the central government a more effective means of enforcing its will than the reps *en mission*.

AFTER THERMIDOR

A clear indication of the efficacy of the institution was the fact that the Thermidorians preferred to utilise it rather than abolish it. The law of 13 Aug 1794/26 therm II limited the length of period of authority of reps *en mission* to three months, reps *aux armées* to six. Reps were now used for purposes of 'White' terror, purging local administrative bodies of Jacobins and ex-terrorists, e.g. Fréron in the Midi in late 1794. It was only when the Constitution of Year III was in the final stages of gestation that the institution was abolished (26 Apr 1795/7 flor III).

SELECT LIST OF *REPRÉSENTANTS EN MISSION* AND THE CENTRE OF THEIR ACTIVITIES

Paris Region and the North

Departments	Représentants	Period of activity
Armée du Nord	Cochon, Gasparin, Debry	Feb–Apr 1793
Armée des Ardennes	Camus, Quinette, Lamarque, Bancal, Carnot	Mar 1793
Aisne, Ardennes	Saint-Just, Deville	Mar–Apr 1793
Aube, Yonne	Turreau, Garnier de l'Aube	Mar–May 1793
Marne, Meuse	Thuriot, Pons de Verdun	Mar 1793
Nord, Pas-de-Calais	Carnot, Lesage-Senault	Mar 1793
Armée du Nord	Carnot, Gasparin, Duhem, Lequinio *et al.*	Apr–July 1793
Somme	André Dumont, Chabot (Lebon from Aug)	July–Sept 1793
Armée du Nord	Carnot, Levasseur, Hentz, Elie Lacoste	Aug 1793
Armée de la Moselle	Jean Bon Saint-André, Prieur de la Marne	Aug 1793
Nord, Pas-de-Calais	Billaud-Varenne, Niou	Aug 1793
Oise, Aisne	Collot-d'Herbois, Isoré, Lejeune, Lequinio	Aug–Sept 1793
Armée du Nord	Chasles	Aug 1793–Feb 1794
Marne, Haute-Marne	Rühl	Sept–Nov 1793
Oise	Levasseur, André Dumont	Oct 1793

Departments	Représentants	Period of activity
Armée de la Moselle	Saint-Just, Le Bas	Oct 1793–Jan 1794
Oise, Pas-de-Calais (+Somme from Sept)	André Dumont	Oct 1793–Apr 1794
Pas-de-Calais	Lebon	Oct–Dec 1793
Seine-et-Oise	Levasseur	Nov 1793
Aube, Marne	Bo	Dec 1793–Jan 1794
Paris, Seine-et-Oise	Crassous	Dec 1793–Feb(?) 1794
Eure-et-Loir, Orne	Bentabole	Dec 1793–Apr 1794
Paris, Oise, Aisne, Seine-et-Marne	Isoré	Jan–Apr 1794
Pas-de-Calais, Nord	Lebon	Dec 1793–July 1794

The East

Departments	Représentants	Period of activity
Ain, Isère	Amar, Merlino	Mar–May 1793
Jura, Côte-d'Or	Prost, Léonard Bourdon	Mar–May 1793
Armée du Rhin	Merlin de Thionville, Reubell *et al.*	Apr–Aug 1793
Ain, Doubs, Côte-d'Or, Jura	Bassal, Garnier de l'Aube	June–Aug 1793
Saône-et-Loire, Loire	Javogues	July 1793–Feb 1794
Jura + surrounding depts	Bassal, Bernard de Saintes	Aug–Dec 1793
Idem	Prost	Sept 1793–Apr 1794
Alsace	Saint-Just, Lebas	Sept 1793–Jan 1794
Armée du Rhin	Baudot, Lacoste	Nov 1793–Mar 1794
Côte-d'Or, Saône-et-Loire	Bernard de Saintes	Dec 1793–Apr 1794
Meuse, Moselle	Mallarmé	Dec 1793–?
Armée du Nord	Saint-Just, Lebas	Jan–Feb & Apr–July 1794
Armée du Rhin	Bourbotte	Apr–Nov 1794

The Lyonnais and the South-East

Departments	Représentants	Period of activity
Hautes-Alpes, Basses-Alpes	Barras, Fréron	Mar–Apr 1793
Bouches-du-Rhône, Drôme	Moïse Bayle, Boisset	Mar–June 1793
Armée des Alpes	Albitte, Dubois-Crancé *et al.*	Apr–Oct 1793
Armée d'Italie	Barras *et al.*	Apr–Aug 1793
Vaucluse	Rovère	June–Nov 1793
Armée d'Italie, Toulon	Ricord, Aug. Robespierre	July 1793–Jan 1794

Departments	Représentants	Period of activity
Armées du Var, des Alpes, Marseille, Toulon	Barras, Fréron	Sept 1793–Jan 1794
Rhône-et-Loire & surrounding depts	Couthon, Châteauneuf-Randon, Maignet	Aug–Oct 1793
Idem	Collot-d'Herbois (from Dec, Méaulle), Fouché	Nov 1793–Apr 1794
Hautes-Alpes, Alpes-Maritimes, Var	Ricord	Dec 1793–July 1794
Bouches-du-Rhône, Vaucluse	Maignet	Dec 1793–Aug 1794
Ain, Mont-Blanc	Albitte	Jan–May 1794
Ain, Rhône-et-Loire	Méaulle	Apr–July 1794

The South-West

Departments	Représentants	Period of activity
Aveyron, Tarn	Bo, Chabot	Mar–May 1793
Gers, Landes	Dartigoëyte	Mar–June 1793
Lot-et-Garonne, Gironde	Paganel, Garrau	Mar–May 1793
Gironde, Lot-et-Garonne	Mathieu, Treilhard	Apr–July 1793
Lot, Dordogne	Elie Lacoste, Jean Bon Saint-André	Mar–May 1793
Cantal, Lozère	Malhes, Châteauneuf-Randon	June–Aug 1793
Dordogne, Cantal, & surrounding depts	Taillefer	Aug–Nov 1793
Ardèche, Drôme	Boisset	Aug–Dec 1793
Gironde & surrounding depts	Baudot	Aug–Nov 1793
Idem	Tallien, Ysabeau	Aug 1793–Mar 1794
Lot-et-Garonne	Paganel	Aug–Nov 1793
Lot, Dordogne	Roux-Fazillac	Sept–Dec 1793
Hérault, Lozère	Châteauneuf-Randon	Oct 1793–Feb 1794
Lot	Paganel	Nov–Dec 1793
Corrèze, Puy-de-Dôme	Roux-Fazillac	Dec 1793–July 1794
Gers, Haute-Garonne	Dartigoëyte	Dec 1793–Oct 1794
Ardèche, Aude & surrounding depts	Boisset	Dec 1793–Feb 1794
Aveyron, Tarn	Paganel	Dec 1793–(?)
Lot, Cantal	Bo	Jan–Feb 1794
Aveyron, Lozère	Bo	Apr–May 1794
Gironde & surrounding depts	Garnier de Saintes	June–Aug 1794

The West

Departments	Représentants	Period of activity
Loir-et-Cher	Tallien, Goupilleau	Mar 1793
Loiret, Nièvre	Collot-d'Herbois, Laplanche	Mar–Apr 1793
Côtes-du-Nord, Ille-et-Vilaine	Billaud-Varenne, Sevestre	Mar–Apr 1793
Maine-et-Loire, Sarthe	Richard, Choudieu	Mar–Apr 1793
Seine-Inférieure, Somme	Pocholle, Saladin	Mar–Apr 1793
Loire-Inférieure, Mayenne	Fouché, Villers	Mar–May 1793
Loiret	Bourbotte	Mar–May 1793
Manche, Oise	Le Carpentier, Bourdon de l'Oise	Mar–June 1793
Armée de l'Ouest	Bourbotte	June 1793–?Jan 1794
'Departments of the Centre & West'	Philippeaux, Fouché, Méaulle, Esnuë-Lavallée	June-Autumn 1793 (Fouché in the Nièvre, Sept)
'Norman depts'	Carrier, Pocholle	July–Aug 1793
'Breton depts'	Carrier, Pocholle	Aug–Dec 1793
Manche, Orne (& surrounding depts from Sept)	Le Carpentier (with Garnier de Saintes from Sept)	Aug–Dec 1793
Charente, Charente-Inférieure, & then Rochefort	Lequinio	Sept 1793–May 1794
Brest	Prieur de la Marne, Jean Bon Saint-André	Sept 1793–Jan, and May–June 1794
Loiret, Cher	Laplanche	Aug–Oct 1793
Armée des Côtes de La Rochelle	Merlin de Thionville, Reubell	Aug–Dec 1793
Calvados & surrounding depts	Laplanche	Oct 1793–Jan 1794
Côtes-du-Nord, Finistère	Laplanche	Dec 1793
Loire-Inférieure, Morbihan	Carrier	Dec 1793–Feb 1794
Ille-et-Vilaine, Mayenne	Esnuë-Lavallée, Dubouchet	Dec 1793–Mar 1794
Loir-et-Cher, Sarthe	Garnier de Saintes	Dec 1793–May 1794
Finistère	Laignelot	Jan–Feb 1794
Ille-et-Vilaine, Mayenne	Laignelot	May–Aug 1794
Ille-et-Vilaine & surrounding depts	Le Carpentier	Dec 1793–Aug 1794

10. THE REVOLUTIONARY TRIBUNAL

This extraordinary law court, which was almost synonymous with the Terror, was in existence from 10 Mar 1793 to 31 May 1795/12 prair III.

The 1791 Constitution established a High Court for treasonable offences but it was little used. Neither was a special criminal court (*Tribunal criminel*) created on 17 Aug 1792 to try individuals accused of counter-rev offences committed during the *journée* of 10 Aug 1792 (it was suppressed on 29 Nov 1792).

The war crisis of spring 1793 resuscitated the idea, and on 10 Mar 1793 the Convtn established a *Tribunal criminel extraordinaire* whose remit covered counter-rev activities, including moves to re-establish the monarchy, attacks on liberty, equality, the unity and indivisibility of the Rpbc and the state's internal or external security. The court was to judge without appeal, and punishment was to be meted out within 24 hours of the sentence. There were to be five judges (three for a sentence), a public prosecutor and two assistants and a number of jurymen drawn from Paris and the surrounding depts, all of whom were elected by the Convtn. Six members of the Convtn (from 5 Apr 1793, the public prosecutor) drew up indictments.

On 27 March 1793, the Convtn invited depts to send to the Rev Tribunal all cases which seemed within its jurisdiction; and on 5 Sept 1793 the tribunal was expanded in size – henceforward four sections worked concurrently – to take account of the increasing workload.

To expedite the trial of the Girondins, a decree was passed on 29 Oct 1793/8 brum II which allowed juries to restrict proceedings to three days if they chose. The police law of 16 Apr 1794/27 germ II urged that suspects be sent to Paris 'from all points of the Rpbc', and centralisation was intensified by the law of 8 May 1794/19 flor II which gave the Paris Rev Tribunal exclusive jurisdiction over counter-rev offences. The Law of 22 Prairial (10 June 1794) completed this chilling rationalisation of rev justice: public cross-examination of defendants was abolished, as were defence counsels; 'moral' as well as material evidence of guilt was admitted; defence witnesses did not have to be heard; and the sole verdicts which the tribunal could pronounce were restricted to death or acquittal. The law initiated the 'Great Terror', a speeding-up of sentences from which there was widespread revulsion after Thermidor.

The Paris Rev Tribunal was not the only court to judge according to the precepts of rev justice (*révolutionnairement*), and indeed more sentences were passed outside Paris, especially in areas of civil war and unrest. Other instances of rev justice comprised:

Departmental criminal courts. Though often too legalistic and slow for most enthusiastic supporters of the Terror, the dept *tribunal criminel* accounted for a large number of death sentences.

Military commissions. Established on 9 Oct 1792 to try *émigrés*, these consisted of five judges, either civilians or soldiers, who followed in the wake of the armies. They could try cases expeditively and without appeal, and the sole sentence they could return was death. Under the provisions of the law of 19 Mar 1793, rebels found under arms or with royalist cockades could be referred to military commissions (though they might also be referred to the criminal courts). Other types of rebels and political offenders were subsequently referred to these commissions, especially under the influence of enthusiastic reps *en mission*. They were often known by the name of the leading judge, e.g. the Commission militaire Bignon in the Maine-et-Loire.

Other civilian emergency courts. Some were carbon copies of the Paris Rev Tribunal, e.g. the tribunals created at Rochefort, on 29 Oct 1793, and at Brest on 5 Feb 1794/17 pluv II by reps *en mission* Lequinio and Laignelot. Other civilian commissions were called *commissions populaires, extraordinaires* or *révolutionnaires* and were usually created by reps *en mission*. They tried rebels without a jury, without appeal and sometimes without a public prosecutor. The laws of 14 frim II (4 Dec 1793) and 8 May 1794/19 flor seemed officially to abolish provincial rev tribunals, but in fact they often continued under different names or with tacit CPS support. The infamous Commission at Orange, for example, was created on 10 May/21 flor, after the moves towards judicial centralisation.

Only the Paris Rev Tribunal survived the post-Thermidor reaction, and this was soon run down. The Law of 22 Prairial was repealed on 1 Aug 1794/14 therm II. The Rev Tribunal's proceedings were made less sanguinary, with better guarantees for a fair trial, by laws of 10 Aug/23 therm II and 28 Dec 1794/8 niv III, and it was finally suppressed altogether on 31 May 1795/12 prair III.

(*See page 115, opposite*) More recent suggestions that as many as half a million people died in the Vendée area may be disregarded, but it seems likely that between 150,000 and 200,000 individuals perished in that region in 1793–4 from the civil war and its consequences (hunger, epidemic disease, death at the hands of the Vendéan rebels, etc). (*Lebrun*, 1986)

11. THE IMPACT OF THE TERROR

The figures here provided are derived from *Greer* (*1935*), which is still regarded as authoritative. As Greer readily admits, however, the figure of 16,594 individuals sentenced to death under rev jurisdictions is only part of the total number of victims of the Terror. To it must he adds:

- deaths in prison among the approx 500,000 individuals incarcerated for rev offences: perhaps 10,000–12,000 deaths
- persons executed without trial under civil war conditions, esp in W France: perhaps 10,000–12,000 deaths

In all, he suggests a figure of 35,000–40,000. (* see footnote at the bottom of page 114)

GEOGRAPHY OF THE TERROR

Abbreviations:

First column:

F	Department where federalism was most deeply rooted
I	Departments invaded by or threatened by enemy forces
R	Departments outside the Vendéan area where popular royalism was most marked
V	Departments with courts involved in the suppression of the Vendéan revolt
C	Departments where chouannerie rife

Third column:

TC	Tribunal criminel
TR	Tribunal révolutionnaire
CMil	Commission militaire

Department	No. of death sentences	Court(s)
Ain (F)	6	TC Bourg
Aisne	5	TC Laon
Allier	4	TC Moulins
Basses-Alpes	NIL	
Hautes-Alpes	NIL	
Alpes-Mar. (I)	9	TC Nice
Ardèche (R)	20	TC Privas

Department	No. of death sentences	Court(s)
Ardennes (I)	12	TC Charleville
Ariège	4	TC Foix
Aube	NIL	
Aude	1	TC Carcassonne
Aveyron (R)	36	TC Rodez (33); CMil (3)
Bouches-du-Rhône (F, R)	409	TR Marseille (286); CMil Leroy (123)
Calvados (F, C)	7	TC Caen
Cantal	11	TC Aurillac
Charente	3	TC Angoulême
Charente-Inf. (V)	107	TC Saintes (3); TR Rochefort (40); CMil La Rochelle (60)
Cher	6	TC Bourges
Corrèze	9	TC Tulle
Corse (Golo, Liamone)	NIL	
Côte-d'Or	28	TC Dijon (12); CMil Auxonne (16)
Côtes-du-Nord (F, C)	32	TC Saint-Brieuc (25); CMil Lamballe (7)
Creuse	3	TC Guéret
Dordogne	21	TC Périgueux
Doubs (I)	75	TC Besançon (73); CMil Besançon (2)
Drôme	2	TC Valence
Eure (F)	4	TC Evreux
Eure-et-Loir	1	TC Chartres
Finistère (F, C)	80	TC Quimper (4); CMil, later TR Brest (76)
Gard (F)	136	TC Nîmes
Haute-Garonne	45	TC Toulouse (15); TR Toulouse (30)
Gers	12	TC Auch (2); CMil Auch (1); Commission extraordinaire de Bayonne, Auch (9)
Gironde (F, R)	299	CMil Lacombe
Hérault	36	TC Montpellier
Ille-et-Vilaine (V, C)	509	TC Rennes (87); CMil Brutus Magnier (265); CMil Frey (or Vaugeois), 86; CMil Saint-Malo (71)
Indre	4	TC Châteauroux
Indre-et-Loire	22	TC Tours (2); CMils (20)
Isère	3	TC Grenoble
Jura (F)	2	TC Lons-le-Saulnier

116

Department	No. of death sentences	Court(s)
Landes (I)	31	TC Mont-de-Marsan (6); Commission extraordinaire de Bayonne, Dax and Saint-Sever (25)
Loir-et-Cher	3	TC Blois
Loire (F, R)	87	TC Montbrison (3); TC Feurs (20); Commission de justice populaire, Feurs (15); CMil, later CRév, Feurs (49)
Haute-Loire (R)	52	TC Le Puy
Loire-Inf. (V)	3,548	TC Nantes (276); CMil Lenoir (244); CMil Bignon (2,905); CMil Paimbœuf (3); CMil Ancenis (23); CMil Machecoul (15); CMil Châteaubriant (16); CMil Guérande (2); CMil Légé (64)
Loiret	4	TC Orléans
Lot	13	TC Cahors
Lot-et-Garonne	5	TC Agen
Lozère (R)	87	TC Mende
Maine-et-Loire (V, C)	1,886	TC Angers (9); CMil Parein-Felix (1,160); 'Commission recenseur' (648); CMil Proust (36); other CMils (33)
Manche (F)	61	TC Coutances (22); CMil Granville (38); CMil Cherbourg (1)
Marne	7	TC Châlons-sur-Marne
Haute-Marne	2	TC Chaumont
Mayenne (F, C)	495	CMil Volcler (453); CMil Proust (28); CMil Parein-Felix (12); CMil Bignon (2)
Meurthe (I)	10	TC Nancy
Meuse (I)	14	TC Saint-Mihiel
Mont-Blanc (I)	5	TC Chambéry
Morbihan (V, C)	37	TC, later TR Vannes
Moselle (I)	45	TC Metz (40); CMil Metz (1); TC Army of the Moselle (3); T *armée rév*, Bitche (1)
Nièvre	2	TC Nevers
Nord (I)	157	TC Douai (8); TR Cambrai (149)
Oise	12	TC Beauvais
Orne (V)	187	TC Alençon
Pas-de-Calais (I)	392	TC Arras (49); TR Arras (343)
Puy-de-Dôme	17	TC Riom
Basses-Pyr. (I)	50	TC Pau (1); CMil Pau (8); Commission extraordinaire Pau (9); Commission extraordinaire Bayonne (26); Tribunal militaire, Army of the Eastern Pyrenees (2); unknown (4)

Department	No. of death sentences	Court(s)
Hautes-Pyr.	5	TC Tarbes
Pyr-Orient. (I)	48	TC Perpignan (14); various CMils (34)
Bas-Rhin (I)	54	TC Strasbourg (22); TR Strasbourg (29); CMil Haguenau (3); CMil Wasslenheim (1)
Haut-Rhin	12	TC Colmar (11); Commission extraordinaire (1)
Rhône (F, R)	1,880	Commission de justice populaire, Lyon (113); Commission de justice militaire, Lyon (99); Commission rév, Lyon (1,665); Tribunal militaire, armée républicaine (3)
Saône-et-Loire	6	TC Chalon-sur-Saône
Haute-Saône	NIL	
Sarthe (V, C)	225	TC Le Mans (146); CMil Le Mans (1); first CMil Sablé (23); second CMil Sablé (32); Commission Bignon (12); Commission Proust (11)
Seine	2,639	TR
Seine-et-Marne	NIL	
Seine-et-Oise	5	TC Versailles
Seine-Inf.	9	TC Rouen
Deux-Sèvres (V)	103	TC Niort (80); CMil Niort (23)
Somme	2	TC Amiens
Tarn	9	TC Albi (7); Tribunal, district of Gaillac (2)
Var (F, R)	309	TC Grasse (27); Commission rév, Toulon (282)
Vaucluse (F)	442	TC Avignon (47); TC Bédoin (63); Commission populaire, Orange (332)
Vendée (V)	1,616	TC Fontenay-le-Comte (47); CMil Fontenay-le-Comte (192); CMil Les Sables-d'Olonne (127); CMils Noirmoutier (1250)
Vienne	33	TC Poitiers
Haute-Vienne	13	TC Limoges
Vosges	10	TC Epinal (also at Mirecourt)
Yonne	2	TC Auxerre

SYNOPSIS OF THE GEOGRAPHY OF TERROR

Deaths per department

No. of death sentences per dept	No. of depts	No. of deaths	%
None	6	–	–
1–9	31	139	0.8
10–24	14	199	1.2
25–49	10	371	2.2
50–99	8	546	3.3
100–199	5	690	4.2
200–999	8	3,080	18.6
Over 1,000	5	11,569	69.7
TOTAL		16,594	

Main centres by region

	No. of deaths	%
Paris	2,639	15.9
Area of Vendée rebellion (Charente-Inf, Ille-et-Vilaine, Loire-Inf, Maine et-Loire, Mayenne, Morbihan, Orne, Sarthe, Deux-Sèvres, Vendée)	8,713	52.5
Area of armed federalism round Lyon (Rhône, Loire)	1,967	11.9
Area of armed federalism in the Midi (Bouches-du-Rhône, Gard, Var, Vaucluse)	1,296	7.8
Other areas	1,979	11.9
TOTAL	16,594	

Types of court

	No. of deaths	%
Paris Tribunal Révolutionnaire	2,639	15.9
Tribunal criminel or revolutionnaire (depts)	3,124	18.8
Military Commission (approx 50)	8,339	50.3
Civil Commission & other (less than 20)	2,492	15.0
TOTAL	16,594	

SOCIAL AND SEXUAL INCIDENCE OF THE TERROR

Global figures, inc Paris

	No	%	of whom women	% of each category
Old nobility	878	6.2	} 226	21.36
Robe nobility	278	2.0		
Upper middle class	1,964	14.0	137	6.98
Lower middle class	1,488	10.6	90	6.05
Clergy	920	6.5	126	13.70
Working classes	4,389	31.2	389	8.86
Peasantry	3,961	28.1	281	7.09
Unknown	200	1.4	65	32.50
TOTAL	14,080	–	1,314	9.33

Paris Revolutionary Tribunal
(*Paris figures from Godfrey 1951, which differ slightly from those of Greer 1935*)

Nobles	533	19.4
Clergy	240	8.7
Upper middle class	903	32.9
Lower middle class	540	19.7
Workers	478	17.4
Unknown	53	1.9
TOTAL	2,747	–

CAUSES OF INDICTMENTS FOR REVOLUTIONARY OFFENCES

	No.	%
Emigration	212	1.5
Intelligence with the enemy	457	3.1
Sedition	10,456	72.1
Federalism	427	2.9
Treason	96	0.7
Conspiracy	703	4.9
Offences involving trees of liberty	12	0.1
Counter-rev opinions	1,302	9.0
Refractory clergy	293	2.0
Concealment of refractory clergy	32	0.2
Economic offences (hoarding, traffic in assignats, counterfeiting)	119	0.8
Corruption	104	0.7
False witness	11	0.1
Other	273	1.9
TOTAL	14,497	–

CALENDAR OF THE TERROR, 1793–4

(Paris figures from Godfrey 1951, which differ slightly from those of Greer 1935)

	Month	Overall Total		Paris Rev Tribunal	
		No.	%	No.	%
1793	March	22	0.1	–	–
	Apr	210	1.5	7	0.3
	May	58	0.4	9	0.3
	June	99	0.7	15	0.6
	July	36	0.3	13	0.5
	Aug	22	0.2	5	0.2
	Sept	72	0.5	21	0.8
	Oct	179	1.3	48	1.8
	Nov	491	3.5	54	2.0
	Dec	3,365	23.9	76	2.8
1794					
	Jan	3,517	25.0	71	2.6
	Feb	792	5.6	62	2.2
	Mar	589	4.2	126	4.5
	Apr	1,099	7.8	244	9.1
	May	780	5.5	339	12.6
	June	1,157	8.2	659	24.5
	July	1,397	9.9	935	34.8
	Aug	86	0.6	6	0.3
	Unkown	110	0.8	–	–
	TOTAL	14,080	–	2,690	–

12. *COMITÉS DE SURVEILLANCE, OR COMITÉS RÉVOLUTIONNAIRES*

'Watch committees' at local level, 'the most active and perhaps the most violent agents of the Terror' (AULARD) which played a crucial part in the application of the Terror. It has been suggested that between 300,000 and 800,000 individuals passed under their surveillance during the Terror – between 1 and 4 per cent of the total population.

ORIGINS

Many committees dated back to the law of 11 Aug 1792 when the Leg Ass, in the crisis following the overthrow of the king, decreed that dept, district and municipal authorities were to assume responsibility for 'general security'. In the early days there were dept committees (in about 30 localities) as well district and municipal committees. The best known at this stage, however, was the Comité de surveillance of the Paris Commune which was largely responsible for the 'Sept Massacres' (2–6 Sept 1792).

As the war threat became more menacing in early 1793, the committees grew more numerous, though their form and inspiration varied. In some places, popular societies, elsewhere municipalities, elsewhere reps *en mission* stimulated their establishment and staffed them with nominees. Some were called *comités de salut public* in the early days. The phrase *'comité révolutionnaire'* became more widespread as time went on. The functions they assumed usually involved searching out political offenders, checking passports, cross-examining strangers and requisitioning for arms.

LAW OF 21 MARCH 1793

A clear response to the grim internal and external problems besetting France, the law decreed:
- each commune (each section in towns over 25,000) was to establish a committee
- the committee was to have 12 members, none of whom was an ecclesiastic or ex-noble or their agent

- they were to be elected, with 100 supporters for each nomination to the committee for every 1,000 head of population in the locality
- they were to receive declarations from foreigners resident within their commune; and were to issue *certificats de civisme* to those who could find six citizens to act as guarantors for them (foreigners without a job or property in the locality were to have their guarantors pledge half the value of their property for them)
- foreigners involved in riot or conspiracy were to be punished by death
- *certificats de civisme* were also to be accorded to all indigenous adult males who had a job, duly acquitted their civic reponsibilities and had four guarantors in the locality.

The committees' powers were less drastic than they might appear, however (the sectional committees in Paris saw their powers actually reduced by this law, and they had no powers of arrest). This, the fact that the electoral regulations were too stringent, and the fact that many surveillance committees were still in existence from before 21 Mar meant that the pace of introduction of the committees was slow down to Sept.

Introduction of *comités de surveillance* in a number of departments, Spring–Summer 1793:

Department	No. *established Spring–Summer 1793*	Total no. *known*
Alpes-Maritimes	0	7
Calvados	27	268
Creuse	1	6
Doubs	20	83
Loire	22	92
Loire-Inférieure	1	48
Manche	6	27
Nord	18	25
Puy-de-Dôme	0	10
Sarthe	1	6
Seine-Inférieure	9	290
Yonne	6	13
TOTAL	111 (= 12.7%)	875

From mid 1793, their membership was often purged by reps *en mission*, which helped make their social composition more democratic.

FROM THE LAW OF SUSPECTS TO 14 FRIMAIRE II

The powers and importance of the committees were widened by the Law of Suspects of 17 Sept 1793. They were henceforward empowered, with very little direct surveillance, to draw up lists of suspects who were to be arrested. By 'suspect', the law understood:

- 'enemies of liberty' and 'supporters of tyranny' and federalism
- those who could not show they had a job or performed their civic duties as enjoined by the law of 21 Mar
- those refused *certificats de civisme*
- suspended or dismissed public officials
- ex-nobles and their relatives who had not a proven record of support for the Rev
- those who had emigrated in the period from 1 July 1789 to 8 Apr 1792.

The lists of those arrested were to be sent regularly to the CGS. The committees could also have other types of offenders arrested (the actual arrest process being in the hands of local Nat Guardsmen or gendarmes), but had to produce more ample justification.

The Law of 14 Frimaire II (4 Dec 1793) ratified the importance of the committees, according them, with the municipalities, a key role in ensuring the application of rev legislation. They were to report every 10 days to the *agent national* of their district; membership was no longer elected, but nominated by reps *en mission;* and all supra-communal committees were suppressed.

ACTIVITY UNDER THE 'GREAT TERROR'

Rural committees tended to be far less active than urban ones, while there was a great deal of variation between towns (in Nantes, the committee was responsible for 4,000–5,000 arrests, in Nancy 72 and in Carcassonne 54). The degree of activity often depended on the assiduity of local reps *en mission*. Besides political policing (delivery of passports and *certificats de civisme,* arrest of suspects, assistance to the municipality in recruiting), the more active committees also engaged in economic police activity (application of the Maximum, assisting food supply, etc). Saint-Just's Laws of Ventôse (Feb–Mar 1794) entrusted the committees with drawing up lists of suspects whose property was to be sequestrated.

There was a tendency for them to be over-zealous and anti-rural. In this they were encouraged by the vaguely worded law of 13 Mar 1794/23 vent II which defined as 'traitors to the country':
- those who favoured the corruption of citizens
- those who subverted the public authorities or public morale
- those who excited anxiety about the food supply of Paris
- those who harboured *émigrés*
- those who advocated a change in the rpbcn form of government, etc.

Many committees intensely resented the CPS decree of 9 July/21 mess II that all imprisoned peasants except those guilty of flagrant revolt were to be freed. Reps *en mission,* who used them extensively, had to try to control the committees' propensity to over-enthusiasm and partiality as best they could.

AFTER THERMIDOR

By the law of 24 Aug 1794/7 fruct II, committees existing in communes with a population of less than 8,000 were suppressed, except where the locality was a district *chef-lieu* (in Paris, their number was reduced from 48 to 12); they were to have a quarter of their members renewed every three months; they were placed more securely under the authority of the CGS; members had to be over 25 years old and know how to read and write; and they were given an daily indemnity of 5 liv. The law of 20 Sept 1794/4 jc II, obliged committees to give motives for refusing to grant *certificats de civisme*.

Increasingly purged of terrorists, the committees now presided over the release of former suspects; and were mostly concerned with refractory priests and questions of food supply. The law of 19 Feb 1795/1 vent III suppressed them in all communes with a population of less than 50,000. On 11 Apr/22 germ, the vague definitions of suspects outlined in the laws of 17 Sept 1793 and 23 vent II were repealed. From 12 June/24 prair, they were forbidden to call themselves *'révolutionnaires'*. The Constitution of Year III had no place for them.

13. POPULAR SOCIETIES

A crucial adjunct to the work of the Rev Govt at local level. Originally expressions of grass-roots militancy, they were increasingly sucked into the bureaucratic system and lost much of their vitality in Year II even before Thermidor signalled their demise.

At first 'friends of the constitution' the societies normally followed the lead of the Paris Jacobins and renamed themselves the 'friends of equality and liberty' from 1792. 'Reservoirs of patriots' (COLIN LUCAS), they served as agencies of surveillance, propaganda, civic education, general welfare and police.

The societies in Paris tended to lose out to the sectional assemblies and also the Jacobin Club. In the provinces, the number of societies within a single locality declined, esp following the proscription of the Girondins and the crushing of the Federalist revolt. By the autumn of 1793 most communes had only one society, which was normally affiliated to the Jacobins. Membership was less upper middle class than before, with a heavier admixture of petty traders and small artisans.

An indication of the importance the government attached to the societies came on 13 June 1793 when the Convtn prohibited the regular authorities from forbidding meetings of the popular societies, while on 25 July individuals responsible for disrupting meetings were threatened with five years in irons. On 13 Sept, they were required to denounce errant functionaries and agents to the committees of government; and on 13 Nov/23 brum II they were asked to provide lists of the most patriotic citizens for public office.

The standby of reps *en mission,* who by the Law of 14 Frimaire II were instructed to consult with popular societies over purges of personnel from the regular authorities, they grew in self-confidence in early 1794, and frequently dominated municipal bodies and *comités de surveillance.* On 4 Feb 1794/16 pluv II, the CPS instructed them to conduct a purge on their own members, and on 16 Apr/27 germ they were instructed to exclude foreigners and ex-nobles.

Though most societies welcomed the overthrow of Robespierre, they were soon disillusioned with his successors. On 16 Oct 1794/25 vendém III, the affiliation, federation and collective petitioning of societies was forbidden. The purges of ex-terrorists often instigated by Thermidorian reps *en mission* and the closure of the Jacobin Club on 11 Nov/21 brum further reduced their vitality and conviction. All were closed down by the decree of 23 Aug 1795/6 fruct III.

14. ARMÉES RÉVOLUTIONNAIRES

These 'people's armies' were para-military bands of militants who acted as enthusiastic missionaries for the Terror, esp in rural areas.

There was talk about establishing such a body to help enforce rev legislation from early 1793 in *enragé* circles. On 2 June, under pressure from the sections, the Convtn actually decreed the establishment of an *armée révolutionnaire* in Paris of 6,000 men, but nothing was done to implement this decision until the *journées* of 4–5 Sept when, with terror on 'the order of the day', an *armée révolutionnaire* was instituted 'to curb counter-rev, execute rev laws and protect the transport of food'. A force of some 7,000 men, under the generalship of the Hébertist, Ronsin, was soon on a regular footing, and was being utilised in facilitating requisitioning and in repressing counter-rev movements in the Paris region.

The Convtn agreed to the creation of only a Parisian force, but *armées révolutionnaires* sprang up, in some cases before Sept 1793, in 56 depts. Esp strong in the Midi, the *armées* contained about 30,000 men in all. Usually, the forces were the creation of enthusiastic reps *en mission*, though often the latter acceded to spontaneous local demands for such a body. They were perhaps most effective in ensuring the provisioning of the cities and in their dechristianising activities (the detachment of 2,000 men from the Paris *armée* sent to the siege of Lyon was particularly notorious in this respect).

It was their penchant for dechristianisation as well as their links with Hébertist extremists which disenchanted the CPS with *armées révolutionnaires*. The Law of 14 Frimaire (4 Dec 1793) abolished all provincial *armées* (in theory: in practice the abolition was often circumvented for a number of months) and following the execution of the Hébertists, Barère in the name of the CPS proposed the dissolution of the Paris *armée,* to which the Convtn assented on 27 Mar 1794/7 germ II.

V. INTERNATIONAL RELATIONS
AND WAR

1. THE MAIN EUROPEAN STATES IN THE REVOLUTIONARY ERA

Austria (see also HOLY ROMAN EMPIRE)

Rulers (as archdukes of Austria, kings of Bohemia and Hungary): Joseph II, 29 Nov 1780–20 Feb 1790;   Leopold II, 30 Sept 1790–1 Mar 1792 (formerly Grand Duke Leopold I of Tuscany);   Francis II, 12 July 1792–1835.

Principal ministers: Prince Kaunitz, 1753–92 (Lord Chamberlain & Chancellor); Philip, Count Cobenzl, 1792–Mar 1793 (Vice-Chancellor, Lord Chamberlain & Chancellor);   Baron Thugut, 1793–1800 (Head of State Council).

Relations with France: hostile as soon as the lives of Louis XVI and Marie-Antoinette (sister of Joseph II and Leopold II) were threatened. Declaration of Pillnitz issued, Aug 1791. War declared by France, 20 Apr 1792. Prominent in the main campaigns, 1792–7. The continental backbone of the First Coalition. Leoben Peace Preliminaries, 18 Apr 1797, followed by the Treaty of Campo-Formio, 17 Oct 1797. Deteriorating relations, however, led France to declare war, 12 Mar 1799 (to last to 1801).

Austrian Netherlands (Belgium)

Austrian territory under the AR. Following widespread opposition to reforms introduced by Joseph II, 1787, full-scale revolt against Austrian rule broke out in 1789 and was only put down in Dec 1790.

Relations with France: at war following France's declaration of war against Austria, 20 Apr 1792. Occupied by French forces, 1792–3, 1794–5. Annexed 1 Oct 1795; confirmation of the annexation, Treaty of Campo-Formio, Oct 1797.

Baden

Margrave: Charles Frederick, 1738–1806.

Relations with France: joined Coalition 21 Sept 1793. Armistice 25 July 1796, followed by peace treaty, 22 Aug.

Bavaria

Electors: Charles Theodore, Elector Palatine, 1777–16 Feb 1799;   Maximilian IV, 16 Feb 1799–1825.

Relations with France: a rather unwilling Coalition partner to Austria originally. Peace treaty, 7 Sept 1796. Treaty with Russia, 20 Sept 1799.

Belgium, see AUSTRIAN NETHERLANDS

Brunswick
Duke: Charles William Ferdinand, 1780–1806.
Relations with France: providing troops for the Allies from March 1793. Treaty with England, 8 Nov 1794. The duke served as CinC of Prussian troops until late 1793 and led the Allied invasion force in 1792.

Denmark
King: Christian VII, 1766–1808.
Principal ministers: Andreas Peter, Count Bernsdorff (1784–21 June 1797), Foreign Minister; Christian Günther, Count Bernsdorff (June 1797–1819), State Secretary.
Relations with France: neutral.

England, see GREAT BRITAIN

Genoa (Republic)
Doge: Rafaele Ferrari, 1787–89; Alerame Maria Pallavicini, 1789–91; Michel-Angelo Cambiaso, 1791–93; Giuseppe Maria Doria, 1793–95; Giacomo Maria Brignole, 1795–97.
Relations with France: neutral 1792–6 (inc neutrality treaty, 22 Dec 1793). Treaty 9 Oct 1796, but under French pressure became the 'Ligurian Rpbc', 6 June 1797.

Great Britain
King: George III, 1760–1820.
Principal Ministers:
1. *First Lord of the Treasury and Chancellor of the Exchequer*
   William Pitt, 1783–1801
2. *Foreign Affairs*
   Marquis of Camarthen (from 1789 = duke of Leeds), 1783–Apr 1791
   William Wyndham Grenville, Apr 1791–1801
3. *Secretary of War*
   Henry Dundas, July 1794–1801
4. *Secretary at War*
   William Windham, July 1794–1801
5. *Home Affairs*
   William Wyndham Grenville, June 1789–Apr 1791
   Henry Dundas, Apr 1791–July 1794
   Duke of Portland, July 1794–1801
6. *First Lord of the Admiralty*
   Earl of Chatham, 1788–Dec 1794
   Earl Spencer, Dec 1794–1801
7. *Master-General of the Ordnance*
   Duke of Richmond, 1784–Feb 1795
   Marquis Cornwallis, Feb 1795–1801
Relations with France: France declared war 1 Feb 1793. Britain was the only power to remain at war with France throughout the 1790s. British troops served on the

continent from 1793 to 1795 and in 1799. Abortive French expedition to Ireland, 1796. Abortive peace talks in 1796, 1797.

Hesse-Cassel
Duke: William IX, 1785–1808.
Relations with France: at war following France's declaration of war with Austria, 20 Apr 1792, and joined the Coalition, 10 Apr 1793. Became a neutral following the Treaty of Basle between France and Prussia, 5 Apr 1795, as the latter guaranteed the neutrality of N German states. Signed a separate peace treaty with France, 28 Aug 1795.

Hesse-Darmstadt
Duke: Ludwig IX, 1768–1830.
Relations with France: joined the Coalition, 5 Oct 1793. Neutral following the Treaty of Basle between France and Prussia. Subsidy treaty with Britain [*sic*], 10 June 1796.

Holy Roman Empire (see also AUSTRIA)
Emperor: Joseph II, 1765–20 Feb 1790;   Leopold II, 30 Sept 1790–1 Mar 1792; Francis II, 12 July 1792–1806.
Relations with France: most major constituent parts of the Empire (apart from British Hanover) joined the Allies 1792. The imperial Diet consented to imperial engagement in a number of decisions from Nov 1792 to Apr 1793. Imperial negotiations for a general peace following the Treaty of Campo Formio between France and Austria, Nov 1797–Apr 1799, concluded unsuccessfully.

Milan, Mantua
Duchies ruled direct by Austria until their merger into the Cisalpine Rpbc in 1797.

Modena
Duke: Ercole III, 1780–1803 (1796 effectively).
Relations with France: drawn into conflict in N Italy, 1795–6 and occupied by French troops. Armistice, 12 May 1796. Civil disputes led to French military intervention and the merger of the state into the Cispadane Rpbc, 15 Oct 1796.

Naples
King: Ferdinand IV, 1759–1825 (also known as King of Sicily and King of Two-Sicilies).
Relations with France: king briefly recognised the French Rpbc 18 Nov 1792, but then allied with Britain against France, 12 July 1793. Armistice 5 June 1796, followed by a peace treaty, 10 Oct. Following alliance with Austria (9 May 1798), Russia and Britain (29 Dec 1798), and following an attempt by the king militarily to dislodge the French from the Roman Rpbc, France declared war, 9 Dec 1798. The victories of French armies led to the declaration of the 'Parthenopean Rpbc', 26 Jan 1799, but the French were forced to evacuate during the 1799 Italian campaigns, and the old regime was restored.

Netherlands, see UNITED PROVINCES

The Papacy

Popes: Pius VI, 1775–29 Aug 1799; Pius VII, 14 Mar 1800–23.

Relations with France: diplomatic relations were broken over the Civil Constitution of the Clergy and the French annexation of Avignon. The Papal States were invaded during Bonaparte's Italian campaign, June 1796. Armistice of Bologna agreed, 23 June. Bonaparte detached Bologna and Ferrara to the Cispadane Rpbc, and marched on Rome to force the Pope to accept the new land settlement in N Italy. The Peace of Tolentino, 19 Feb 1797, followed: the Pope agreed to French demands. French intervention continued and on 11 Jan 1798, the Roman Rpbc was proclaimed. French occupying forces were forced out briefly following attack by the king of Naples in Nov 1798, and then during the summer campaign of the Second Coalition in 1799.

Poland

Effectively wiped off the map of Europe by the Polish Partitions of 1793, 1795.

King: Stanislas Augustus II, 1764–22 Nov 1795.

Relations with France: the Rpbc admired the resistance to partition shown by the Poles under Kosciusko, 1794–5.

Piedmont

A monarchy (the kingdom of Sardinia) whose territory included the island of Sardinia as well as Savoy and Piedmont.

Kings: Victor Amadeus III, 1773–16 Oct 1796; Charles Emmanuel IV, 16 Oct 1796–1802.

Relations with France: war declared 27 July 1792. Savoy and Nice invaded by the French, late 1792. Joined the First Coalition, 25 Apr 1793. Following defeats by Bonaparte, and the Armistice of Cherasco (26 Apr 1796), a peace treaty was signed, 15 May 1796 (in which she accepted the loss to France of Nice and Savoy). Alliance treaty with France, 5 Apr 1797. Turin was occupied by French troops, June–July 1798, the rest of the main towns in Dec. A rpbcn constitution was agreed, the king left the mainland for the island of Sardinia, but the Directory decided to annex the territory rather than to create another 'sister rpbc'.

Parma

Duke: Ferdinand, 1765–1802.

Relations with France: occupied by the French in early 1796. Armistice 8 May 1796, followed by a peace treaty, 5 Nov.

Portugal

Rulers: Queen Maria I, 1777–1816.

Relations with France: entered the First Coalition, 26 Sept 1793. Peace Treaty following Campo-Formio, 20 Aug 1797. Joined Second Coalition, 16 Dec 1798.

Prussia

Kings: Frederick William II, 1786–97; Frederick William III, 16 Nov 1797–1840.

Principal ministers: Heinitz, 1777–1802, Secretary of State; Hertzberg, 1763–July 1791, Foreign Affairs; Alvensleben, 1 May 1791–1802, Foreign Affairs; Bischoffswerder, 1790–7, Foreign Affairs; Karmer, 1779–14 Feb 1795, Minister of Justice; Goldbeck, 14 Feb 1795–1808, Minister of Justice.

Relations with France: Co-signatory with Austria of the Declaration of Pillnitz, Aug 1791. Made common cause with Austria following the latter's involvement in war with France 20 Apr 1792. An important contributor in the fighting 1792–4, she agreed a separate peace treaty with France in the Treaty of Basle, 5 Apr 1795, and also agreed to guarantee the neutrality of N German states.

Russia

Czars: Catherine II ('the Great'), 1762–17 Nov 1796; Paul, 17 Nov 1796–1801.

Relations with France: a fierce counter-rev opponent of France, who allied with Austria on 12 July 1792, Catherine II was preoccupied with the Polish Partitions (1793, 1795) and failed to offer significant material support in W Europe. Under Paul I, however, following an alliance with Britain (18 Dec 1798), Russian troops were drafted W and fought in Italy and Switzerland under Suvarov and in Holland. The czar recalled his troops in Oct 1799.

Sardinia, see PIEDMONT

Sicily, see NAPLES

Spain

Kings: Charles III, 1759–13 Dec 1788; Charles IV, 13 Dec 1788–1808

Principal ministers: Count Floridablanca, 1777–28 Feb 1792; Count Aranda, 28 Feb 1792–15 Nov 1792; Godoy, 1792–1808.

Relations with France: France declared war, 7 Mar 1793. Joined First Coalition, 25 May 1793. Peace Treaty of Basle, 22 Sept 1795, followed by the alliance Treaty of San Ildefonso, 19 Aug 1796: cession of Santo Domingo to France. Spain subsequently declared war on Britain, 5 Oct 1796.

Sweden

Kings: Gustav III, 1771–29 Mar 1792; Gustav IV, 29 Mar 1792–1809.

Relations with France: though Charles III had been a vociferous opponent of Rev France, Sweden remained neutral throughout the 1790s.

Switzerland

Relations with France: neutral in the First Coalition Wars, the confederacy lost territory to the Cisalpine Rpbc (Oct 1797) and to France (1798), but became in 1798 a 'sister-rpbc', the Helvetian Rpbc.

Turkey

Sultans: Abdul Hamid I, 1774–7 Apr 1789; Selim III, 7 Apr 1789–1807.

Relations with France: involved in fighting against Russia and Austria in the early 1790s. Threatened by the French Egyptian expedition. War on France, 9 Sept 1798. Alliance with Russia (23 Dec 1798) and Britain (5 Jan 1799).

Tuscany
Grand Dukes: Leopold I, 1765–20 Feb 1790; Ferdinand III, 21 July 1790–1801.
Relations with France: neutral 1792–5 (though a fief of Austria). Treaty with France, 9 Feb 1795. British use of the port of Livorno (Leghorn) led the French to occupy it in June 1796. Peace treaty and declaration of neutrality, Mar 1797. France declared war, 12 Mar 1799, and occupied the duchy, only to evacuate it under Austro-Russian military pressure.

Two Sicilies, see NAPLES

United Provinces
Head of state: Prince William V, 1751–95
Relations with France: France declared war, 1 Feb 1793. Invaded by the French in Feb 1793 and again from late 1794–5. At the Treaty of the Hague, 16 May 1795, it was transformed into the Batavian Rpbc, a 'sister rpbc' under French control and occupation.

United States of America
Presidents: George Washington, 1 Jan 1789–4 Mar 1797; John Adams, 4 Mar 1797–1801.
Other key posts: Vice-President John Adams, 1789–97, Thomas Jefferson, 1797–1801; Secretary of State, 1789–95, Thomas Jefferson (who had also served as ambassador in Paris, 1783–9).
Relations with France: neutral, though in theory at first still allied (1778 treaty). French seizures of US ships trading with Britain led to a state of virtual warfare, 1798–1800.

Venice
Doges: Paolo Renier, 1779–13 Feb 1789; Luigi Manin, 9 Mar 1789–12 May 1797.
Relations with France: recognised the French Rpbc in late 1793, and remained studiously neutral. Treaty, 16 May 1797. This did not prevent her being partitioned between France, the Cisalpine Rpbc and Austria at Campo-Formio, Oct 1797.

Württemberg
Dukes: Charles Eugene, 1737–24 Oct 1793; Ludwig Eugene, 24 Oct 1793–20 May 1795; Frederick Eugene, 20 May 1795–23 Dec 1797; Frederick II, 23 Dec 1797–1816.
Relations with France: war in association with Austria from Apr 1792. Armistice 25 Sept 1795, followed by a peace treaty, 7 Aug 1796.

2. FRENCH ANNEXATIONS, 1791–1799

Austrian Netherlands (or BELGIUM) (1 Oct 1795)

Occupied from Nov 1792 to Mar–Apr 1793, then again from 1794 to 1795. Fifteen decrees, 1–30 Mar 1793, had concerned annexation of specific areas within Belgium. Departments were organised from 1 Oct 1795. The Austrians agreed to its cession at Campo-Formio, Oct 1797. Vendée-style counter-rev episodes, involving clergy and peasants, broke out on a number of occasions, 1798–9.

Avignon and Comtat Venaissin (14 Sept 1791)

Both territories were papal enclaves on the Rhône. Avignon had voted for incorporation on 10 June 1790, but the French government did not wish to offend the Pope over this issue. By Sept 1791, however, relations with the Papacy were at a low ebb following the Civ Constn, and the Ass. decided that the popular wish within the papal enclaves to join France was a sufficient moral and legal title to justify annexation. Split up at first between the depts of the Bouches-du-Rhône and the Drôme, the bulk of former papal territory was regrouped as the dept of the Vaucluse during the Federalist crisis, 25 June 1793. The Pope only accepted the cession at the Treaty of Tolentino, 19 Feb 1797.

Belgium, see AUSTRIAN NETHERLANDS

Dutch Flanders (16 May 1795)

Dutch Flanders, from Venloo to Maestricht, plus the S Gueldre and part of Dutch Limburg were ceded to France by the Treaty of the Hague which organised the Batavian Rpbc. Part of the region was organised into depts on 1 Oct 1795, the rest on 4 Nov 1797.

Geneva (15 Apr 1798)

Of strategic importance once France built up its empire in N Italy. The presence of French troops bullied this Swiss canton to accept annexation (Cf. Mulhouse). The region was organised into the dept of the Léman, 25 Aug 1798.

Ionian Islands (18 Oct 1797)

A windfall from the partition with Austria of the Venetian Rpbc in the Treaty of Campo-Formio. French administrators had arrived in the islands in June 1797. Reoccupied by Russia, 1798–9.

Left bank of the Rhine

The S Rhineland was occupied at first in late 1792–early 1793 and then again from 1794. French-manipulated local assemblies on 14, 20 and 30 Mar 1793 saw nearly 100 communities from the Palatinate, the Zweibrucken region and elsewhere vote for incorporation. The margrave of Baden ceded small enclaved territories to the French in a treaty, 7 Aug 1796. Even though part of the area was organised into depts (1 Oct 1795, 4 Nov 1797) and was recognised by the Austrians at Campo-Formio, it remained a pawn with which to negotiate right through the 1790s, and was not officially annexed until 1801.

Monaco (15 Feb 1793)

This tiny principality was occupied by French troops from late 1792 and became part of the dept of the Alpes-Maritimes in 1793.

Montbéliard (10 Oct 1793)

The duke of Württemberg agreed to the cession of this enclaved territory, 7 Aug 1796. It was incorporated into the dept of the Doubs.

Mulhouse (1 Mar 1798)

This Swiss free city, enclaved within French territory, was bullied into agreeing to annexation. It was incorporated into the dept of the Haut-Rhin.

Nice (31 Jan 1793)

Occupied by French forces Aug 1792, it voted in favour of annexation. The adjacent area of Tende (including Ventimiglia and Onaglia) was incorporated on 10 Oct 1793. Both areas formed part of the Alpes-Maritimes dept. The king of Piedmont agreed to their cession, 15 May 1796.

Piedmont (*de facto* 1798)

Partly and sporadically occupied by the French since 1792, this territory of the king of Sardinia fell wholly under French control once Bonaparte embarked on his Italian campaigns. Piedmont-Sardinia was forced out of the war by the Armistice of Cherasco (26 Apr 1796) and the Treaty of Paris (15 May). French troops occupied Turin in June–July 1798, and other major cities by the end of the year. The Directory made it clear that it envisaged annexation, and not the formation of another 'sister rpbc', but *de facto* control did not give way to *de jure* annexation until 1802.

Porrentruy (23 Mar 1793)

Part of the AR diocese of Basle, the region was occupied from late 1792. The inhabitants voted freely for annexation. At first the 'Rauracian Rpbc', the area was organised as the dept of Mont-Terrible.

Salm (2 Mar 1793)

This tiny principality enclaved within French territory was incorporated into the dept of the Vosges.

Savoy (27 Nov 1792)

Part of the kingdom of Sardinia, the region was occupied from June–July 1792. The inhabitants, galvanised by Doppet and the Club des Allobroges in Paris, seem to have been enthusiastic for annexation. The king of Piedmont agreed to the cession 15 May 1796.

3. THE ADOPTION OF FRENCH-STYLE CONSTITUTIONS IN EUROPE, 1791–1799

1. **Geneva,** 22 Mar 1791, 5 Feb 1794, 6 Oct 1796.
2. **Poland,** 3 May 1791.
3. **Bologna,** 4 Dec 1796 (before its incorporation into the Cispadane Rpbc).
4. **Cispadane Rpbc,** 27 Mar 1797.
5. **Cisalpine Rpbc (I),** 9 July 1797.
6. **Ligurian Rpbc,** 2 Dec 1797.
7. **Cisalpine Rpbc (II),** 9 Dec 1797.
8. **Valais (Switzerland),** 16 Mar 1798.
9. **Roman Rpbc,** 20 Mar 1798.
10. **Helvetian Rpbc,** 12 Apr 1798.
11. **Batavian Rpbc,** 23 Apr 1798.
12. **Cisalpine Rpbc (III),** 10 Sept 1798.
13. **Parthenopean Rpbc,** 23 Jan 1799.
14. **Lucca,** 15 Feb 1799.

NB. With the exception of the Polish and the first two Genevan constitutions, all the constitutions listed above were heavily influenced by the French Constitution of Year III. The adoption of such a constitution implied the acceptance of the most fundamental principles of the Rev:

- the rights of man
- broad suffrage (universal manhood suffrage in the Cispadane, Batavian, Helvetian and first Cisalpine constitutions)
- bicameral legislature (except in Naples)
- Directory-style executive, and separation of powers
- abolition of feudalism
- economic freedom and the abolition of guilds
- financial, judicial and military reforms
- religious reforms (in fact, the least widely adopted, esp in Italy, where Bonaparte went along with catholicism as the majority religion)
- rational division of territory, and organisation into depts.

4. THE 'SISTER REPUBLICS'

Batavian Republic (1795–1801)
Formerly the United Provinces, on which France declared war on 1 Feb 1793. French troops invaded some S parts in Feb – Mar 1793, then occupied the whole state in late 1794–5. Created by the Treaty of the Hague with Dutch provisional government, 16 May 1795, which also stipulated that the Dutch were to ally with France in the war, and make substantial payments towards the war effort; and that part of Dutch territory (notably Dutch Flanders) was to be incorporated into France.

Constitutional wrangles between unitarians and federalists, 1795–7, led to a French-backed Fructidor-style coup on 22 Jan 1798, and the imposition of a unitarian constitution, 23 Apr 1798. A coup on 12 June 1798, on the lines of the 22 Floréal coup in France, also had French backing. Departments were organised from 1798.

The Dutch army and navy fought alongside the French, albeit with little success, from 1795 onwards.

Cisalpine Republic (1797–9, and 1800–2)
Model 'sister rpbc' which was created following Bonaparte's overrunning of N Italy in the 1796 and 1797 Italian campaigns. Lombardy had been occupied militarily since Apr–May 1796, but the composition of the new rpbc in 1797 proceeded as follows:

- following secret clauses in the Peace Preliminaries of Leoben with Austria (Apr), the Rpbc was proclaimed in Lombardy (May)
- in July, the duchy of Modena, Massa-Carra and the Cispadane Rpbc were added
- in Oct, the Valtellina was added
- at Campo-Formio (18 Oct), it was agreed that Brescia and Bergamo, from the partitioned Venetian Rpbc, were to be added.

A constitution was drafted on 9 July 1797, but this was subject to amendment, and a constitution was only agreed 9 Dec 1797. A Fructidor-style *coup d'état* on 13 Apr 1798 led to the introduction of a new one on 10 Sept 1798. The reforms associated with the imposition of constitutional rule were extensive here, and the rpbc also had considerable financial and economic burdens imposed on it by the French, notably in a commercial alliance treaty of 21 Feb 1798.

Overrun during the 1799 Italian campaign, the rpbc was restored in 1800.

Cispadane Republic (1796–7)

The first 'sister rpbc' organised by Bonaparte following his brilliant successes in 1796–7.

Instituted Dec 1796 following demonstrations by pro-French Jacobin minorities in a number of cities, and formed by a merger of the duchy of Modena (inc Reggio) and the papal territories of Bologna and Ferrara. A Directory-style constitution was introduced, 27 Mar 1797, but shortly afterwards the rpbc was merged into the larger Cisalpine Rpbc.

Helvetian Republic (1798–1803)

Another product of Bonaparte's Italian campaigns, for the strategic importance of Italy required better French control of communications passing through the Swiss confederacy.

The Valtellina was lost to the Cisalpine Rpbc (Oct 1797), Mulhouse (Mar 1798) and Geneva (Apr) were incorporated into France. The rump of Switzerland was invaded and despite widespread resistance, a constitution was agreed on 12 Apr 1798 for the 'Helvetian Rpbc' which was instituted in Sept 1798. The Rpbc fell apart in the 1799 campaigns, but was reconstituted when French fortunes improved after Brumaire.

Ligurian Republic (1797–1805)

Formerly the Rpbc of Genoa which had studiously maintained neutrality from 1792 to 1796. In May 1797, however, Genoese Jacobins demonstrated and persuaded Bonaparte to send in the Army of Italy in their support. The new 'Ligurian Rpbc' was proclaimed on 6 June 1797, with a constitution agreed on 2 Dec 1797. A Fructidor-style coup on 31 Aug 1798 brought the regime more closely under French control.

Neapolitan, or Parthenopean Republic (1799)

The short-lived Neapolitan Rpbc (the word 'Parthenopean' was for Parisian consumption only) was created following an attack by the king of Naples on the Roman Rpbc in Aug 1798. The attack failed, Championnet led French troops S and Naples was overrun, with its ruler fleeing to Sicily. Though Championnet had no orders from the Directory to proceed in the way he did, and in spite of the policy of caution urged by civil commissary Faipoult, he introduced a constitution (23 Jan 1799) and proclaimed a rpbc (26 Jan).

In May–June 1799, the needs of beleaguered French forces in N Italy, and the peasant anti-French counter-rev insurrection organised by Cardinal Ruffo, forced the French to evacuate Naples, and the king returned.

Roman Republic (1798–9)

Northern parts of papal territory (Bologna, Ferrara) had been lost to the 'Cispadane Rpbc' in 1796. Pro-French demonstrations in Rome in Dec 1797 ended in the French General Duphot being assassinated in crowd disturbances, and this diplomatic incident was used by the French to send in their forces. Linking up with local Jacobins, Berthier and the Army of Italy established the 'Roman Rpbc' on 12 Feb 1798. A constitution was agreed on 20 Mar 1798, and on 28 Mar a commercial treaty with France brought the area under tight French control. The new regime resisted the attempt of the king of Naples to destabilise it in Aug 1798. The Italian campaigns of 1799 led to its collapse, however.

5. MILITARY ORGANISATION: CHRONOLOGY

1781–8 Major military reforms introduced by Brienne (administrative stream-lining, new disciplinary code, cuts in posts, etc) stimulate discontent among the officer corps, who show sympathy for their fellow nobles in the parls: the government is consequently unable to rely on the loyalty of troops in areas affected by the 'Noble Revolt' (e.g. Rennes, Grenoble).

Spring 1789 Army utilised for internal policing (grain trade, peasant disturbances, etc).

14 July 1789 Defection of large numbers of *Gardes-françaises* helps in the capture of the Bastille. Troop mutinies and indiscipline elsewhere in France during the summer crisis.

July–Aug 1789 Emergence of the 'Nat Guard' from emergency call-ups of bourgeois militias, etc, to combat aristocratic forces and protect property.

4 Aug 1789 'Night of 4 Aug': abolition of venality of office (inc in military posts).

5, 10 Aug 1789 Nat Ass. endorses existence of Nat Guard. (Organisation of the new force will take place 1790–1.)

Autumn 1789 Beginning of emigration of officers. Growing discord between aristocratic officer corps and the men.

30 Nov 1789 Naval mutiny at Toulon.

16 Dec 1789 Voluntary enlistment to be the basis of recruitment.

28 Feb 1790 Decree on the army: no foreign mercenaries without the approval of the legislature; no venality; soldiers enjoy rights as citizens; active citizenship a reward for 16 years' military service; Nat Ass. sets budget limits for the armed forces.

Apr 1790–Summer 1791 Disputes and mutinies over problems of discipline and politics in garrisons throughout France.

12 June 1790 AR militias incorporated into the Nat Guard; only active citizens to be members of the Nat Guard.

6 June 1790 Law on military discipline: loss of active citizenship for mutiny.

14 July 1790 *Fête de la Fédération* in Paris attended by Nat Guardsmen from throughout France.

9 Aug 1790 Mutiny of the Swiss Châteauvieux Regiment and other troops at Nancy.

143

16 Aug 1790   Ass. decrees the Nancy mutineers guilty of *lèse-nation*. Bouillé is called in to repress the insurrection: from late Aug, hundreds killed on both sides, over 20 executed, over 40 sent to the galleys, etc.

14 Sept 1790   Law on military discipline: no corporal punishments except forced drinking of water for drunkards; military councils and tribunals (inc officers and men) for disciplinary proceedings.

21 Sept 1790   Law on promotion: a mixture of election, seniority and appointment.

28 Jan 1791   New rule book for tactics and manœuvres: the basis of the conduct of war in the rev decade and under Napoleon.

4 Mar 1791   Regular army size fixed at 150,000 men.

28 Apr 1791   Law on the Nat Guard: it is reiterated that only active citizens may be members.

1 May 1791   Soldiers may attend clubs out of duty hours.

13 June 1791   Special oath of allegiance for officers. Recommendation that battalions of volunteers be levied to complement regular forces.

20 June 1791   Flight to Varennes highlights France's military vulnerability and triggers a massive wave of officer emigration: by early 1792, 60 per cent of the officer corps has emigrated.

21 June 1791   Battalions of 'Nat Volunteers' from the Nat Guard put at the disposal of commanders: men to be paid double the regular rate, and to enlist for one year.

24 June 1791   Generals can suspend suspect officers.

3 July, 4 Aug 1791   Number of 'Nat Volunteers' set at 26,000 (over 100,000 by Aug).

19 Sept 1791   As part of a general movement against popular militancy in the wake of the Massacre of the Champ de Mars, clubs are forbidden to correspond with army units.

29 Sept 1791   Law on organisation of the Nat Guard: active citizens between 18 and 60 serve without payment; officers elected for one year; military discipline to be observed.

31 Dec 1791   Amnesty for troops involved in the Nancy mutiny of Aug 1790. (They will be fêted in Paris on 15 Apr 1792.)

20 Apr 1792   Opening of the Rev Wars: France declares war on Austria.

8 June 1792   Proposed establishment near Paris of a military camp of *fédérés*, 20,000 strong. (The law will be vetoed by the king on 19 June; but the Leg Ass. overrules the veto on 2 July.)

4 July 1792   Law on *la patrie en danger*.

11 July 1792   Declaration of *la patrie en danger:* regular authorities are given emergency powers, and the Nat Guard is placed on full alert.

12 July 1792   *Levée* of 50,000 men for the army decreed.

30 July 1792   Former passive citizens may enlist in the Nat Guard.

21 Dec 1792   Convtn accepts the principle that volunteers and line troops should have the same pay.

1 Jan 1793 CGD established to coordinate the war effort.

7 Feb 1793 Dubois-Crancé, for the Military Committee, proposes the *amalgame:* assimilation of Nat Volunteers and troops of the line through the process of *embrigadement*, where infantry units are re-formed in *demibrigades* comprising one battalion of line soldiers, two battalions of volunteers. All men to receive the higher wages of the volunteers; election of officers, etc.

21 Feb 1793 Convtn accepts the *amalgame* (though its implementation will be slow).

24 Feb 1793 *Levée de 300,000 hommes:* the 300,000 recruits to be volunteers where possible, though local authorities are allowed to introduce an element of compulsion where necessary. Reps *en mission* are sent into the provinces to enforce this unpopular law, which sparks off the Vendée revolt.

6 Apr 1793 Creation of the CPS, taking over the prosecution of the war effort from the CGD.

9 Apr 1793 Establishment of reps *aux armées.*

23 July 1793 Only one church bell obligatory in a parish (by the complementary law of 3 Aug, all church bells are put at the disposal of the War Ministry and may be melted down for cannon).

12 Aug 1793 *Amalgame* decreed for all infantry regiments.

Late 1793–early 1794 Reps *en mission* requisition for military supplies, enforce the *amalgame,* implement the Terror, etc.

16 Aug 1793 The Paris sections petition the Convtn for the introduction of conscription.

23 Aug 1793 The *levée en masse:* introduction of universal obligation for military service; population divided into 'requisitions'; the 'first requisition', comprising the seven *classes d'âge* from 18 to 25 years old, is called up. The army swells dramatically in size: soon there are three-quarters of a million men under arms, and the same number under military authority in the war effort.

26 Aug 1793 CPS decree: iron grilles to be melted down for the war effort.

9 Sept 1793 A Parisian *armée révolutionnaire* is created, following a decision made on the rev *journée* of 5 Sept. Spread of similar 'people's armies' in the provinces during the autumn to enforce the Terror and stimulate the war effort.

4 Dec 1793/14 frim II Law of 14 Frimaire on Rev Govt: generals owe total obedience to the CPS; prov *armées révolutionnaires* to be disbanded.

27 March 1794/7 germ II Disbandment of the Paris *armée révolutionnaire.*

2 Apr 1794/13 germ II Company of balloonists formed: it will participate in the battle of Fleurus.

1 June 1794/13 prair II Creation of the *Ecole de Mars,* a rpbcn military academy (to be disbanded, 21 Oct 1794/30 vendém III).

19 July 1794/1 therm II Reduction of the practice of election of officers.

1794–7   Desertion on a massive scale: army less than 400,000 strong in 1797.

23 May 1795/4 prair III   Military commissions to judge cases of armed sedition (a measure aimed at the Paris faubourgs following the *journées* of Prairial).

29 May 1795/10 prair III   In the aftermath of the Prairial *journées*, 'less well-off' citizens are dispensed from the obligation of service in the Nat Guard.

18 Sept 1795/2 jc III   Suppression of military councils, and harshening of military discipline.

13 Nov 1795/23 brum IV   Creation of *commissaires aux armées:* not as independent or as powerful as reps *aux armées*.

6 Dec 1796/16 frim V   Abolition of *commissaires aux armées*.

Aug–Sept 1797   Use of military commissions following the *coup d'état* of Fructidor against royalists, ex-*émigrés*, etc.

18 Jan 1798/29 niv VI   Military commissions established to stamp out brigandage.

25 Nov 1798/5 frim VII   *Commissions civiles aux armées* appointed.

5 Sept 1798/19 fruct VI   Jourdan Law: universal obligation to conscription for males over 20 years old; to be operative for *classes d'âge* of 20 years from 24 Sept 1798, at which stage the 'first requisition' of those levied under the law of 24 Aug 1793 will have served 5 years. Call-up of 200,000 men decided soon after (24 Sept/3 vendém, etc).

28 June 1799/10 mess VII   All conscript classes called up under the provisions of the Jourdan Law.

15, 18 Oct 1799/23, 26 vendém VIII   Abolition of *commissions civiles aux armées*.

6. COMMANDERS OF FRENCH REVOLUTIONARY ARMIES
(CLERGET 1905)

* = army in existence at the fall of the Directory

Army before Lyon (*armée devant Lyon*), see ARMY OF THE ALPS

Army before Toulon (*armée devant Toulon*), see ARMY OF ITALY

Army of the Alps (*armée des Alpes*). Created from the Army of the Midi, 1 Oct 1792. On 1 Nov, subdivided into the Army of Savoy and the Army of Italy; the Army of Savoy was renamed Army of the Alps on 29 Nov 1793. From 8 Aug to 29 Oct 1793 part of the Army was detached, as the 'Camp before Lyon', to besiege the Federalist stronghold. Suppressed 21 Aug 1797. (See also ARMY OF ITALY.)

1 Oct–13 Nov 1792   Montesquiou
25 Dec 1792–5 May 1793, 2 June–18 Oct 1793   Kellermann (in Aug, at Lyon)
25 Sept–28 Oct 1793   Doppet (at Lyon until 18 Oct)
18 Nov–22 Dec 1793   Carteaux
21 Jan–6 July 1794   Alexandre Dumas
 1 Dec 1794–5 Apr 1795, 5 May–7 Oct 1795   Moulin (from 5 Apr, under Kellermann, CinC of the Armies of Italy and the Alps)
 8 Oct 1795–13 Sept 1797   Kellermann

Army of the Ardennes (*armée des Ardennes*). Formed from part of the the Army of the North, 1 Oct 1792. Dumouriez unofficially called the left the 'Army of Belgium', late 1792–3. Reorganised and reduced in size, Mar, Oct 1793. Merged into the Army of the Sambre-and-Meuse, 29 June 1794.

1 Oct–29 Dec 1792   Dumouriez (i/c the Army of the North)
30 Dec 1792–11 Jan 1793, 23 Feb–10 March 1793   Valence
12 Jan–22 Feb 1793   Lanoue and Leveneur (under Miranda of the Army of the North)
11 Mar–4 Apr 1793   Dumouriez (i/c the Army of the North)
 5–28 Apr 1793   Dampierre
29 Apr–28 July 1793   Lamarche (under Custine of the Army of the North, 28 May–16 July)
29 July–10 Aug 1793   Kilmaine (i/c the Army of the North)
11 Aug–12 Sept 1793   Houchard (ditto)
13–23 Sept 1793   Jourdan (ditto)
 4 Nov–3 Dec 1793   Ferrand (under Jourdan of the Army of the North)

4 Dec 1793–3 Feb 1794   Murat-Sistières (ditto)
4 Feb–2 June 1794   Charbonnier (ditto)
9 June–28 Sept 1794   Desjardin (ditto)
3 June–1 July 1794   Jourdan (under Pichegru of the Army of the North)

Army of Belgium (*armée de la Belgique*), see ARMY OF THE ARDENNES

Army of the Brest Coasts (*armée des côtes de Brest*). Subdivision of the Army of the Coasts created 30 Apr 1793. On 6–8 Sept, the Army of Mainz merged with it. The Mainz force, plus part of the Army of the Brest Coasts, composed the Army of the West, 2 Oct 1793. Merged with the Army of the Cherbourg Coasts and the Army of the West to form the Army of the Ocean Coasts, 26 Dec 1795.
  1 May–5 Oct 1793   Canclaux
  6 Oct 1793–6 May 1794   Rossignol (i/c the Army of the West, 14 Nov–2 Dec)
  7 May–10 Oct 1794   Moulin
24 Oct–9 Nov 1794   Alexandre Dumas
10 Nov 1794–30 Apr 1795   Hoche (i/c the Cherbourg coasts)
24 Dec 1795–8 Jan 1796   Hédouville

Army of the Centre (*armée du Centre*), see ARMY OF THE MOSELLE

Army of the Cherbourg Coasts (*armée des côtes de Cherbourg*). Created 30 Apr 1793 from the right of the Army of the Coasts. Merged with Armies of the West and the Brest Coasts to form the Army of the Ocean Coasts, 26 Dec 1795.
  1 May 1793–25 July 1793   Wimpfen
26 July–1 Dec 1793   Sepher
  2 Dec 1793–5 Jan 1794   Beaufort
  2 Jan–30 Aug 1794   Vialle
  1 Sept 1794–30 Apr 1795   Hoche (i/c the Army of the Brest Coasts)
  1 May–11 Nov 1795   Aubert-Dubayet

Army of the Coasts (*armée des Côtes*). Created 31 Jan 1793, and subdivided into the Armies of the Brest Coasts and the Cherbourg Coasts, 30 Apr 1793.
31 Jan–14 Apr 1793   La Bourdonnaye

Army of the Danube (*armée du Danube*). Created 2 Mar 1799 from the 'Army of Observation', formerly part of the Army of Mainz. Subdivided into the Army of the Danube and the Army of the Rhine, 7–13 June 1799. Reincorporated into the Army of the Rhine, 24 Nov 1799.
  7 Mar–8 Apr 1799   Jourdan
  9 Apr–29 Nov 1799   Masséna (periodically with the Armies of Helvetia and the Danube)

Army of the Eastern Pyrenees (*armée des Pyrénées Orientales*). Created from the left of the Army of the Pyrenees, 30 Apr 1793. Suppressed by decrees of Aug and Sept 1795 and dissolved following the conclusion of peace with Spain.

14 May–16 Aug 1793   Flers
18–28 Sept 1793   Dagobert
29 Sept–11 Oct 1793   Daoust
12 Oct–21 Nov 1793   Turreau (on paper only: local reps *en mission* prevented him assuming command, Daoust remaining in charge)
28 Nov–20 Dec 1793   Doppet
21 Dec 1793–15 Jan 1794   Daoust
16 Jan–17 Nov 1794   Dugommier
17 Nov 1794–29 May 1795   Pérignon
30 May–15 Sept 1795   Schérer
16 Sept–12 Oct 1795   Lamer

* **Army of England** (*armée d'Angleterre*). Created 26 Oct 1797.
26 Oct 1797–12 Apr 1798   Bonaparte
27 Mar–7 Oct 1798, 2 Nov 1798–2 Jan 1799   Kilmaine
 2 Jan–22 June 1799   Moulin
20 July–14 Nov 1799   Michaud
15 Nov 1799–16 Jan 1800   Hédouville

Army of Germany (*armée d'Allemagne*). Created from the merger of the Armies of the Rhine-and-Moselle and the Sambre-and-Meuse, 29 Sept 1797. Subdivided into the Armies of the Rhine and of Mainz, 9 Dec 1797.
 7 Oct–13 Dec 1797   Augereau

Army of Helvetia (*armée d'Helvétie*). Created 8 Mar 1798 from troops on the Swiss border from the Armies of Italy and the Rhine. Merged into the Army of the Danube 21 Apr 1799.
 8–27 March 1798 Brune
28 Mar–10 Dec 1798   Schawemburg
11 Dec 1798–4 Apr 1799   Masséna

Army of the Interior (*armée de l'Intérieur*)
  I. Created 4 Sept 1792 and almost at once merged into the Armies of the North and the Centre. Reconstituted 21 Oct 1792 as force comprising *fédérés* and Nat. Volunteers. Renamed Reserve Army (*armée de Réserve*) 1 Mar 1793. Became the Army of the La Rochelle Coasts 12 July 1793.
21 Oct–1792–28 Apr 1793   Berruyer
  II. Created 12 July 1795. Suppressed 22 Sept 1796.
12 July–4 Oct 1795   Menou
 5–26 Oct 1795   Barras (seconded by Bonaparte)
27 Oct 1795–9 March 1796   Bonaparte
10 Mar–21 Sept 1796   Hatry

Army of Ireland (*armée française en Irelande*). Organised 20 July 1796 at Brest. Dissolved, 9 Feb 1797.
 1 Nov–23 Dec 1796, 19 Jan–9 Feb 1797   Hoche

* **Army of Italy** (*armée d'Italie*). Created 1 Nov 1792 from the right of the Army of the Alps; from 4 Sept to 28 Dec 1793 most of it was renamed the 'Army before Toulon'. The latter was suppressed 25 Aug 1793, and its forces reallocated among armies in the S. On 3 Feb 1798, the army was subdivided into the Army of Italy and the Army of Rome; and on 8–21 July 1799, into the Army of Italy and the Army of the Alps, though the latter was reincorporated, 29 Aug–1 Sept.

7 Nov–25 Dec 1792   Anselme
26 Dec 1792–9 Feb 1793   Brunet
10 Feb–4 May 1793   Biron
 5 May–8 Aug 1793   Brunet (under Kellermann of the Army of the Alps from
   2 June)
 9 Aug 1793–20 Nov 1794   Dumerbion (until 18 Oct 1793 under Kellermann)
 5 Sept–6 Nov 1793   Carteaux (besieging Toulon)
16 Nov–28 Dec 1793   Dugommier (besieging Toulon)
21 Nov 1794–5 May 1795   Schérer
 6 May–28 Sept 1795   Kellermann (i/c the Army of the Alps)
29 Sept 1795–26 Mar 1796   Schérer
27 Mar 1796–16 Nov 1797   Bonaparte
22 Dec 1797–3 Apr 1798   Berthier
 4 Apr–27 July, 19 Aug–31 Oct 1798   Brune
 1 Nov 1798–31 Jan 1799   Joubert (i/c the Army of Rome)
12 Mar–26 Apr 1799   Schérer (i/c the Army of Naples)
27 Apr–4 Aug 1799   Moreau (ditto)
21 July–31 Aug 1799   Championnet (under Joubert of the Army of the Alps)
 5–15 Aug 1799   Joubert
15 Aug–20 Sept 1799   Moreau
21 Sept–30 Dec 1799   Championnet

Army of the La Rochelle Coasts (*armée des côtes de La Rochelle*). Created 30 Apr 1793 from the Reserve Army (formerly Army of the Interior). Merged into the Army of the West, 2 Oct 1793.
28 May–16 July 1793   Biron
31 July–24 Aug 1793, 1 Sept–5 Oct 1793   Rossignol
25–30 Aug 1793   Santerre

Army of Mainz (*armée de Mayence*).
   I. Garrison of Mainz redeployed 6–8 Sept 1793 in W France, following the fall of the city in July, into the Army of the Brest Coasts, and then merged into the Army of the West.
   II. (Or 'Army before Mainz' [*armée devant Mayence*].) Right of the Army of the Rhine besieging Mainz from Nov 1794 to mid 1795.
   III. Created 9 Dec 1797 following subdivision of the Army of Germany. The so-called 'Army of Observation' formed part of it, Jan–Mar 1799.
16 Dec 1797–9 July 1798   Hatry
30 July–7 Oct 1798   Joubert

1 Nov 1798–6 Mar 1799   Jourdan (with command of the Army of Helvetia from 5 Nov 1798)

Army of the Mediterranean (*armée de la Méditerranée*), see ARMY OF THE ORIENT

Army of the Midi (*armée du Midi*). Created 13 Apr 1792. Subdivided into the Army of the Alps and the Army of the Pyrenees 1 Oct 1792.
13 Apr–1 Oct 1792   Montesquiou (from 29 Sept, Anselme called his troops in the Nice area 'Army of the Var', though without authorisation)

Army of the Moselle (*armée de la Moselle*). From 14 Dec 1791, 'Army of the Centre'. Renamed Army of the Moselle from 1 Oct 1792. On 29 June 1794, most of the force was merged with the Army of the Ardennes and the right of the Army of the North into the Army of the Sambre-and-Meuse; and the remainder was merged with the rump of the Army of the Rhine into the Army of the Rhine-and-Moselle on 3 Mar 1795.
14 Dec 1791–11 July 1792 (Army of the Centre)   Lafayette
12 July–1 Sept 1792   Luckner (i/c the Army of the Rhine)
 2 Sept–7 Nov 1792   Kellermann (subordinate to Generalissimos Luckner, down to 18 Sept, then Dumouriez down to 5 Oct)
15 Nov 1792–23 Jan 1793   Beurnonville (under Custine of the Army of the Rhine)
24 Jan–28 Mar 1793   Ligniville (ditto)
29 Mar–28 Apr 1793   d'Aboville
29 Apr–2 Aug 1793   Houchard
 3 Aug–29 Sept 1793   Schauenbourg
30 Sept–30 Oct 1793   Delaunay
31 Oct 1793–18 March 1794   Hoche
19 Mar–1 July 1794   Jourdan (from 2 June, i/c the future components of the Army of the Sambre-and-Meuse)
2 July 1794–9 Feb 1795   Moreaux

Army of Naples (*armée de Naples*), see ARMY OF ROME

Army of the North (*armée du Nord*). Created 14 Dec 1791. From 1 Oct 1792, subdivided into the Army of the Ardennes and the Army of the North. The left of the Army of the Ardennes (the so-called 'Army of Belgium') was reincorporated 1 Mar 1793. On 29 June 1794, the right merged into the Army of the Sambre-and-Meuse. The rump was reduced in status to an occupying force in the Batavian Rpbc, 26 May 1795. Suppressed 25 Oct 1797.
14 Dec 1791–18 May 1792   Rochambeau
19 May–11 July 1792   Luckner
12 July–19 Aug 1792   Lafayette (assisted by Arthur Dillon)
18 Aug–28 Sept 1792   Dumouriez
28 Sept–25 Nov 1792   La Bourdonnaye (under Generalissimo Dumouriez from 20 Oct, who entered Belgium commanding the Armies of the Ardennes and the North)

26 Nov 1792–28 Feb 1793   Miranda (from 2 Feb under Dumouriez)
2 Feb–9 March 1793   Dumouriez (i/c the Army of the Ardennes)
6 Apr–8 May 1793   Dampierre (ditto)
28 May–16 July 1793   Custine (ditto)
17 July–10 Aug 1793   Kilmaine (ditto)
11 Aug–23 Sept 1793   Houchard (ditto)
25 Sept–9 Nov 1793, 15 Nov 1793–12 Jan 1794   Jourdan (ditto)
9 Feb–18 Oct 1794   Pichegru (ditto, to June 1794)
19 Oct–4 Dec 1794   Moreau
5 Dec 1794–20 Mar 1795   Pichegru
21 March 1795–29 Mar 1796   Moreau
4 Apr–15 Sept 1796   Beurnonville
16 Sept 1796–24 Sept 1797   Dejean
25 Sept–7 Nov 1797   Beurnonville

Army of Observation (*armée d'Observation*), see ARMY OF MAINZ

Army of the Ocean Coasts (*armée des côtes de l'Océan*). Created 26 Dec 1795 from the merger of the Armies of the West, the Brest Coasts and the Cherbourg Coasts. Dissolved in Aug–Sept 1796.
5 Jan–22 Sept 1796   Hoche

*Army of the Orient (*armée de l'Orient*). Created 5 Mar 1798, though it was known down to Aug as the 'Army of England', then the 'Army of the Mediterranean'.
8 May 1798–22 Aug 1799   Bonaparte
25 Aug 1799–14 June 1801   Kléber

Army of the Pyrenees (*armée des Pyrénées*). Created 1 Oct 1792 from the right of the Army of the Midi. Subdivided into the Army of the Eastern Pyrenees and Army of the Western Pyrenees on 30 Apr 1793.
3 Oct 1792–16 Feb 1793, 5–30 Apr 1793   Servan

* Army of the Rhine (*armée du Rhin*).
I. Created 14 Dec 1791. Subdivided into the Army of the Rhine and the Army of the Vosges, 1 Oct 1792. The latter was reincorporated, 1 Mar 1793. The right became the Army before Mainz (*armée devant Mayence*) 29 Nov 1794. Merged with the Army of the Moselle to become the Army of the Rhine-and-Moselle in Mar–Apr 1795.
14 Dec 1791–6 May 1792   Luckner
7 May–20 July 1792   Lamorlière (under Luckner of the Army of the Moselle)
21 July–25 Dec 1792   Biron (under Luckner until 19 Sept; under Custine of the Army of the Vosges from 30 Oct)
26 Dec 1792–14 March 1793   Deprez-Crassier (under Custine)
15 Mar–17 May 1793   Custine (i/c the Army of the Moselle from 9 Apr)
30 May–18 Aug 1793   Beauharnais (under Houchard of the Army of the Moselle until 2 Aug)

18 Aug–29 Sept 1793   Landremond
27 Oct 1793–13 Jan 1794   Pichegru (under Hoche of the Army of the Moselle
   from 26 Dec)
14 Jan 1794–10 Apr 1795   Michaud
 4 Dec 1793–13 Feb 1794   Kléber (Army besieging Mainz)
II. Subdivision of the Army of Germany, created 9 Dec 1797. Suppressed 29 Jan
   1798 and troops later incorporated into the Army of Helvetia.
14 Dec 1797–3 Feb 1798   Augereau
III. Reformed from subdivision of the Army of the Danube, 7–13 June 1799.
   The rump of the Army of the Danube was reincorporated, 24 Nov 1799.
28 Dec 1799–4 May 1801   Moreau

Army of the Rhine-and-Moselle (*armée du Rhin-et-Moselle*). Created 3 Mar 1795
from merger of the Armies of the Rhine and the Moselle. Merged into the Army
of Germany 29 Sept 1797.
20 Apr 1795–4 Mar 1796   Pichegru
21 Apr 1796–30 Jan 1797, 10–27 Mar 1797, 20 Apr–9 Sept 1797   Moreau

Army of Rome (*armée de Rome*). Created 3 Feb 1798 from the Army of Italy.
Suppressed 28 March it was, however, kept on a separate footing and reconstituted on 18 Oct. On 24 Jan 1799 Championnet proclaimed it the Army of
Naples. Reincorporated into the Army of Italy in July–Aug 1799.
20–25 Feb 1798   Masséna
26 Feb–27 March 1798   Dallemagne
28 March–25 July 1798   Saint-Cyr
26 July–19 Nov 1798   Macdonald
20 Nov 1798–23 Jan 1799 (as Army of Naples) 24 Jan–27 Feb   Championnet
28 Feb–3 Aug 1799 (as Army of Naples)   Macdonald

Army of the Sambre-and-Meuse (*armée du Sambre-et-Meuse*). Created 29 June
1794 from the merger of the Army of the Ardennes, the left of the Army of the
Moselle and the right of the Army of the Rhine. Merged into the Army of
Germany 29 Sept 1797.
 2 July–20 Dec 1794   Jourdan
21 Dec 1794–28 Feb 1795   Hatry
 1 Mar 1795–21 Jan 1796, 29 Feb–30 July 1796, 8 Aug–23 Sept
   1796   Jourdan
22 Jan–28 Feb 1796, 31 July–7 Aug 1796, and (with Beurnonville from 14
   Dec), 14 Dec 1796–23 Jan 1797   Kléber
23 Sept 1796–23 Jan 1797 (with Kléber from 14 Dec)   Beurnonville
26 Feb–30 July 1797, 14 Aug–18 Sept 1797   Hoche (i/c the Army of the
   Rhine-and-Moselle from 10 Sept)

Army of Savoy (*armée de Savoie*), see ARMY OF THE ALPS

Army of the Var (*armée du Var*), see ARMY OF THE MIDI

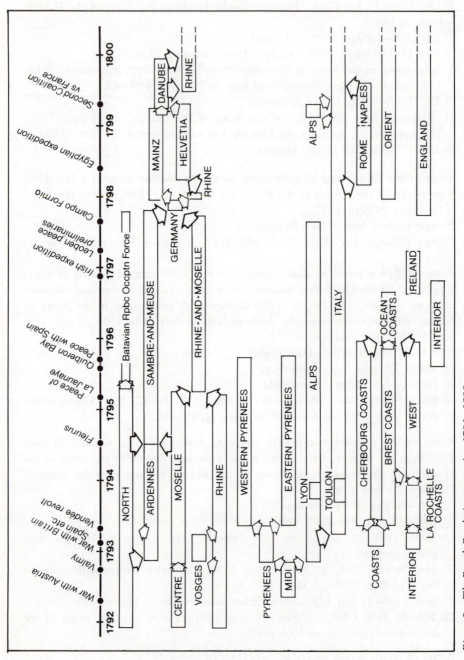

Figure 2 The French Revolutionary armies, 1791–1800.

Army of the Vosges (*armée des Vosges*). Created 1 Oct 1792 from the expeditionary force of the Army of the Rhine. Reincorporated into the Army of the Rhine, 1 Mar 1793.

1 Oct 1792–1 Mar 1793   Custine

Army of the West (*armée de l'Ouest*). Created from merger of the Mainz garrison and the Army of the Brest Coasts, 2 Oct 1793. Merged into the Army of the Ocean Coasts 26 Dec 1795.

6–27 Oct 1793   Léchelle
28 Oct–13 Nov 1793   Chalbos
14 Nov–4 Dec 1793   Rossignol
5–25 Dec 1793   Marceau
26 Dec 1793–17 May 1794   Turreau
18 May–6 Sept 1794   Vimeux
7 Sept–23 Oct 1794   Alexandre Dumas
24 Oct 1794–6 Sept 1795   Canclaux
11 Sept–17 Dec 1795   Hoche
18 Dec 1795–6 Jan 1796   Willot

Army of the Western Pyrenees (*armée des Pyrénées Occidentales*). Created 30 Apr 1793 from the left of the Army of the Pyrenees. Suppressed Aug–Sept 1795 and dissolved following the conclusion of peace with Spain.

1 May–4 July 1793   Servan
11 July–31 Aug 1793   Delbecq
5 Oct 1793–30 Aug 1794   Muller
1 Sept 1794–12 Oct 1795   Moncey

Reserve Army (*armée du Réserve*), see ARMY OF THE INTERIOR.

7. ARMY STRENGTHS

Line army, 1789 (Scott 1978)

102 infantry regiments (79 French, 11 Swiss, 8 German, 3 Irish, 1 Liégeois)	112,000
12 light infantry battalions	4,500
62 cavalry regiments (2 carabiniers, 24 heavy cavalry, 18 dragoons, 12 chasseurs, 6 hussars)	33,000
Artillery	6,600
TOTAL	156,100 men
(Plus *c.* 75,000 militia theoretically available)	

Line army at the time of the amalgame law (Feb 1793) (Scott 1978)

98 line regiments	125,000
14 light infantry battalions	8,500
64 cavalry regiments	35,000
Artillery	10,000
	178,000 men

Revolutionary armies under the Terror

	1793	*Early 1794*
North	120,000	245,822
Ardennes	40,132	37,630
Moselle	83,268	103,323
Rhine	114,557	98,390
Alps	40,489	43,042
Italy	29,274	60,551
Eastern Pyrenees	24,446	70,508
Western Pyrenees	30,000	50,782
La Rochelle Coasts	41,110	—
Cherbourg Coasts	15,481	27,388
Brest Coasts	32,539	34,379
Troops besieging Lyon	12,000	—
West	—	22,519
Other home forces	400,000	?
TOTAL	983,296	794,334

Ministerial estimates, 1794–9

Aug 1794	732,474
Aug 1795	484,363
Aug 1796	396,016
Aug 1797	381,909
Feb 1799	326,000
Oct 1799	264,983

8. BATTLES

French victory unless otherwise stated.

Aboukir, 25 July 1799. Egyptian campaign.
French (Bonaparte), 7,700; Turks (Ahmed Pasha), 18,000. Turks attempting to invade Egypt, which the French have occupied the previous year. About 13,000 Turkish casualties.

Aboukir Bay, see NILE.

Acre (siege of), 17 Mar–21 May 1799. French failure.
French, 13,000; Turks, Syrians, with British assistance led by Sydney Smith. French failure to take the fortress thwarts the French conquest of Syria.

Alkmaar, 2 Oct 1799. Netherlands. French resistance to Anglo-Russian invasion force. French defeat.
French, Dutch (Brune), 30,000; British, Russians (Duke of York), 30,000. Allies force the French to evacuate the town, but are then besieged in turn. The Convention of Alkmaar follows (18 Oct).

Amberg, 24 Aug 1796. Bavaria. German campaign. French defeat.
French (Jourdan), 45,000; Austrians (Archduke Charles), 48,000. German counter-attack to drive the French out of S Germany which they have invaded. The French are driven back towards the Rhine.

Arcole, or **Arcola,** 15–17 Nov 1796. Italian campaign.
French (Bonaparte), 20,000; Austrians (Alvintzi), 17,000. Important battle which prevents the junction of Austrian armies during the siege of Mantua. 4,500 French, 7,000 Austrian losses.

Bassano, Sept 1796. Italian campaign.
French (Bonaparte), 22,000; 8 Austrians (Würmser), 20,000. Part of operations relating to the siege of Mantua.

Bergen-op-Zoom, 19 Sept 1799. Netherlands. French resistance to Anglo-Russian invasion force. Stalemate.
French, Dutch (Vandamme), 35,000; British, Russians (York), 35,000. Prior to the battle of Alkmaar.

Borghetto, 30 May 1796 (Or 'PASSAGE OF THE MINCIO'). Italian campaign.
French (Bonaparte), 28,000; Austrians (Beaulieu), 19,000. The French force a passage across the Mincio river, driving the Austrians back to the last redoubt in N Italy at Mantua.

Caldiero, 12 Nov 1796. Italian campaign. French defeat.
French (Bonaparte), 30,000; two Austrian armies (Alvintzi, Davidovitch), 37,000. French forced back from Mantua towards Verona.

Caliano, 5 Sept 1796. Italian campaign.
French (Bonaparte), 34,000; Austrians (Davidovitch), 20,000. Engagement during the siege of Mantua. Austrians driven out of Caliano and into the Alps.

Camperdown, 11 Oct 1797. Naval battle 7 miles off the Dutch coast. Dutch defeat, British victory.
British (Duncan), 16 warships; Dutch 18 warships. The British prevent the Dutch from coming to the aid of the French in Ireland. Five Dutch ships lost.

Cape Saint-Vincent, 14 Feb 1797. Naval battle. British victory.
British (Jervis), 15 warships; Spanish (de Cordova), 27 warships. Fought to prevent the Spanish fleet coming to the aid of the French.

Cassano, 27 Apr 1799. Italian campaign. French defeat.
French (Moreau), 30,000; Austrians, Russians (Suvorov), 65,000. The Austro-Russian force continues to drive the French out of the Italian peninsula. After the battle, Suvorov enters Milan and Turin and the French fall back on Genoa.

Castiglione, 5 Aug 1796. Italian campaign.
French (Bonaparte, Masséna), 30,000; Austrians (Wurmser), 24,000. Engagement during the siege of Mantua. Heavy Austrian casualties. Austria retreats into the Tyrol.

Dego, 14–15 Apr 1796. Italian campaign.
French (Bonaparte, with Masséna), 17,000; Austrians, Piedmontese, 5,000. The Austro-Piedmontese garrison is forced out.

'First of June', see USHANT.

Fleurus, 26 June 1794. Belgian frontier, near Charleroi.
French (Jourdan), 73,000; Austrians, Dutch (Saxe-Coburg), 52,000. Outstanding French victory inflicted on Allied troops coming to relieve Charleroi. The Allies fall back on Brussels, and the road into Belgium opens for the French.

Hondschoote, 6–8 Sept 1793. Near Dunkirk.
French (Houchard), 42,000; Allies under Freytag (British, Hanoverians, Dutch, Austrians), 13,000. The French effectively raise the siege of Dunkirk.

Imola, 3 Feb 1797. Italian campaign.
French, Italians (Victor), 8,000; Papal troops (Colli), 4,000. Comic-opera battle which forces the Pope to make the Peace of Tolentino with Bonaparte (19 Feb).

Jemappes, 6 Nov 1792. Belgian frontier, near Mons.
French (Dumouriez), 40,000; Austrians (Duke Albert of Saxe-Teschen), 13,000.
The French force the Austrians back and advance to take Brussels (16 Nov).

The Lahn, see NEUWIED.

Loano, 23–5 Nov 1795. Italy.
French (Schérer, Masséna); Austrians, Piedmontese. This French victory is not
followed up, as attention is still focused on Germany.

Lodi, 10 May 1796. Italian campaign.
French (Bonaparte), 30,000; Austrians (Beaulieu), 10,000. Famous French victory
inflicted on the rearguard of a retreating Austro-Piedmontese force.

Lonato, 3 Aug 1796. Italian campaign.
French (Bonaparte), 47,000; Austrians (Quasdonovitch), 18,000. Engagement
relating to the siege of Mantua.

Magnano, 5 Apr 1799. Italy. French defeat.
French (Schérer), 53,000; Austrians (Kray), 52,000. The French advance into
Italy is temporarily checked.

Malborghetto, 23 Mar 1797. Italian campaign.
French (Masséna), 41,000; Austrians (Archduke Charles), 33,000. French
advancing towards Vienna. Prelude to the Peace Preliminaries of Leoben (18 Apr).

Mantua (siege of), late May 1796–2 Feb 1797. The French siege of the Austrian
garrison here is a key operation in Bonaparte's Italian campaigns. Successive
Austrian attempts to lift the siege are thwarted in a series of battles, inc LONATO,
CASTIGLIONE, BASSANO, ARCOLA, RIVOLI, etc, before the garrison falls and the
Austrians fall back towards Vienna.

Marengo, 20 June 1799 (not to be confused with the more famous battle of
Marengo of 14 June 1800). Italy.
French (Moreau), 14,000; Austrians, Russians (Bellegarde), 20,000. Part of
indecisive manoeuvring in central Europe.

Medole, 5 Aug 1796. Italian campaign.
French (Bonaparte), 23,000; Austrians (Wurmser), 25,000. Part of operations
relating to the siege of Mantua.

Menin, 13 Sept 1793. Belgian frontier. French defeat.
French (Houchard), 40,000; Dutch, Austrians (Orange), 20,000. The Dutch are
routed, but the engagement with the Austrians goes against the French, and
Houchard, despite his brilliant earlier success at HONDSCHOOTE, is arrested and
guillotined.

Millesimo, 13 Apr 1796. Italian campaign.
French (Augereau), 10,000; Piedmontese (Colli), 6,000. The Piedmontese are
driven from their entrenchments.

Mondovi, 22 Apr 1796. Italian campaign.
French (Bonaparte), 45,000; Piedmontese (Colli), 25,000. Follow-up from French victory at Dego. It forces the Piedmontese out of the war (Armistice of Cherasco, 26 Apr).

Montenotte, 11–12 Apr 1796. Italian campaign.
French (Bonaparte), 40,000; Austrians, Piedmontese (Beaulieu), 55,000. Austrians driven from the field. Bonaparte's first victory in his first Italian campaign.

Mount Tabor, 17 Apr 1799. Syria. Egyptian campaign.
French (Bonaparte, Kléber), 4,500; Syrians (Pasha of Damascus), 35,000. French stave off Syrian attempts to force them to abandon the siege of Acre.

Neerwinden, 18 March 1793. Belgian frontier. French defeat.
French (Dumouriez), 45,000; Austrians (Saxe-Coburg), 40,000. Austrians holding back the French advance into Holland. French forced to retreat. Prelude to the defection of Dumouriez.

Neresheim, 11 Aug 1796. German campaign. Near Nordlingen. Indecisive.
French (Moreau), 50,000; Austrians (Charles), 48,000. Austrians fail to halt Moreau's advance into S Germany.

Neuwied (or 'Battle of the Lahn'), 18 Apr 1797. Holland.
French (Hoche), 80,000; Austrians (Werneck), 30,000. Hoche successful in forcing a way across the Rhine.

Nile (or Aboukir Bay), 1–2 Aug 1798. Naval defeat off Egyptian coast.
French (Brueys), 13 warships; British (Nelson), 13 warships. Destruction of the French expeditionary fleet, which has the effect of cutting off the French army from direct links to France.

Novi, 15 Aug 1799. Italy. French defeat.
French (Joubert), 35,000; Russians, Austrians (Suvorov), 50,000. Unsuccessful French attempt to retrieve their fortunes in Italy as the Allies reconquer the peninsula.

Passage of the Mincio, see BORGHETTO.

Pyramids, 21 July 1798. Egyptian campaign.
French (Bonaparte), 25,000; Egyptian Mamelukes (Murad Bey), 21,000. Crushing French victory which lays the foundations for the French occupation of Egypt.

Quiberon or **Quiberon Bay,** 16–21 July 1795. W France.
French (Hoche), 13,000; French *émigrés*, Chouans (d'Hervilly), 17,000. The expeditionary force is crushed, the pacification of the W being thereby assured.

Rivoli, 14–15 Jan 1797. Italian campaign.
French (Bonaparte), 20,000; Austrians (Alvintzi), 28,000. Final engagement in

operations relating to the siege of Mantua. The French occupy the city on 2 Feb.

Roveredo, 4 Sept 1796. Italian campaign.
French (Bonaparte), 30,000; Austrians (Davidovitch), 25,000. The Austrians are forced to retreat towards the Tyrol.

Stockach, 25–26 Mar 1799. Baden. German campaign. French defeat.
French (Jourdan), 35,000; Austrians (Charles), 60,000. Austrians attempting to force French out of S Germany. The French are driven back across the Rhine.

Toulon (siege of), 27 Aug–19 Dec 1793. Part of Federalist crisis.
French besieging force (Dugommier, with Bonaparte i/c artillery), 11,500. Inhabitants of Toulon assisted by the British navy. The city capitulates to Bonaparte's bombardment.

Tourcoing, 18 May 1794. Belgian frontier.
French (Pichegru), 82,000; Allies (Saxe-Coburg), 72,000. French victory which prepares the way for Fleurus.

Tournai, 22 May 1794. Belgian frontier. French defeat.
French (Pichegru), 62,000; Allies (Saxe-Coburg), 50,000. Check on French advance started at Tourcoing and completed at Fleurus.

Trebbia, 17–19 June 1799. N Italy. French defeat.
French (Macdonald), 25,000; Austrians, Russians (Suvorov), 30,000. Suvorov thwarts Macdonald's aim of combining his forces with Moreau's army of Italy.

Ushant (or **'First of June'**), 29 May–1 June 1794. Naval battle. French defeat.
French, 26 warships; British, 26 warships. Though formally a French defeat, the engagement allowed crucial grain convoys from America to get through to French ports.

Valmy, 20 Sept 1792. N France (dept of the Marne).
French (Dumouriez, Kellermann), 36,000; Prussians, Hessians, French *émigrés* (Brunswick), 34,000. No major engagement of forces, but a critical French victory which halts the Allied advance towards Paris. Brunswick retreats towards Germany.

Wattignies, 15–16 Oct 1793. Belgian frontier (dept of the Nord).
French (Jourdan), 50,000; Allies (Saxe-Coburg), 26,000. Victory allows the French to relieve the Maubeuge fortress. The Allies withdraw into winter quarters, thus lifting the threat to Paris.

Wurzburg, 3 Sept 1796. Bavaria. French defeat.
French (Jourdan), 40,000; Austrians (Archduke Charles), 45,000. Charles prevents Jourdan from making a junction with other French forces under Moreau. The French fall back on the Rhine.

Map 1   The battlefields of Revolutionary Europe.

Zurich.

(i) 4 June 1799. French (Masséna), 25,000; Austrians (Archduke Charles), 40,000. French defeat. Austrians endeavouring to force the French out of Switzerland. Masséna withdraws, and the Austrians occupy Zurich.

(ii) 25–30 Sept 1799. French (Masséna), 50,000; Austrians, Russians (Korsakov), 45,000. French victory over the Allied forces which were in superior positions. The Russians blame the Austrians and on 23 Oct Czar Paul withdraws his troops from W Europe.

VI. POLITICS

1. THE TOPOGRAPHY OF NATIONAL POLITICS AND GOVERNMENT

All locations in Paris unless otherwise stated.

The king
Versailles until 6 Oct 1789; the Tuileries palace in Paris from 6 Oct 1789 to 10 Aug 1792.

Estates General and National Constituent Assembly
Versailles. Opening session on 5 May 1789 with all three orders in the Salle des Etats, or Salle des Menus Plaisirs. The nobility and clergy then moved to separate chambers to verify their credentials, while the Third Estate (from 17 June, the Nat Ass.) continued in the Salle des Menus Plaisirs. All orders combined here from 27 June.

Constituent Assembly
Following their decision on 9 Oct 1789, the Ass. moved from Versailles to Paris on 19 Oct, and held its sessions provisionally in a room in the archbishop's palace. On 9 Nov, it was established in the Salle du Manège (riding-hall) of the Tuileries palace.

Legislative Assembly
Salle du Manège.

Convention
From 21 Sept 1792 to 9 May 1793, the Salle du Manège; from 10 May until 26 Oct 1795/4 brum IV, the Salle de Spectacle of the Tuileries palace.

Revolutionary Government
The main committees of government were located in the Tuileries palace. The CPS occupied the Pavillon de Flore (renamed Pavillon de l'Egalité), the CGS the Hôtel de Brienne, Place du Petit-Carrousel.

The Directory
The Luxembourg palace.

Conseil des Cinq-Cents
Tuileries palace.

Conseil des Anciens
Down to 21 Jan 1799/2 pluv VII, the Salle du Manège; from then until the *coup d'état* of 18 brum, the Palais-Bourbon.

2. COMPOSITION OF REPRESENTATIVE ASSEMBLIES, 1787–1799

First Assembly of Notables (Feb–May 1787) (*Egret 1962*)
14 prelates; 7 Princes of the Blood; 36 great nobles; 12 councillors of state; 37 magistrates of sovereign courts; 1 civil magistrate, Paris Châtelet; 12 deputies from the *pays d'états*; 25 heads of city governments = <u>144</u> (only two of whom were not nobles).

Second Assembly of Notables (Nov 1788)
13 prelates; 7 Princes of the Blood; 36 great nobles; 12 councillors of state; 38 magistrates of the sovereign courts; 1 civil magistrate, Paris Châtelet; 16 deputies from the *pays d'état*; 24 heads of city governments = <u>147</u>.

Estates-General (May–June 1789) (*Necheles 1974; Higonnet & Murphy 1975*)
First Estate (clergy): 192 (63.4%) parish priests; 51 (16.8%) bishops; 16 (5.3%) monks and abbots; 44 (14.5%) ecclesiastical functionaries = <u>303</u> (of whom 291 present).
Second Estate (nobility): 50 (17.7%) liberal aristocrats; 40 (14.2%) liberal provincial nobility; 77 (27.3%) conservative aristocracy; 115 (40.8%) conservative provincial nobility = <u>282</u> (of whom 270 present).
Third estate: <u>621</u> (of whom 578 present).

Constituent Assembly (July 1789–Sept 1791) (*Lemay 1977*)

Social composition:		(%)
Office-holders	315	48.6
Lawyers	151	23.3
Economic life (businessmen, merchants, etc)	90	13.9
Agriculture	40	6.2
Miscellaneous	52	8.0
TOTAL	648	

Legislative Assembly (Sept 1791–Sept 1792) (*Mitchell 1984*)

Political affiliation:		(%)
Feuillants	169	22.5
Jacobin Club	51	6.8
Other, unattached	530	70.7

Convention (Oct 1792–Oct 1795) (*Patrick 1972*)

(a) *Social composition:*		(%)
Clergy	55	7.3
Armed forces	36	4.8
Medicine	46	6.1
Men of letters	30	4.0
Academic	11	1.5
Clerks	3	0.4
Civil servants	51	6.8
Lawyers (official posts)	152	20.3
Lawyers (private practice)	205	27.4
Business	67	8.9
Artisans	6	0.8
Farmers	38	5.1
With private means	11	1.5
Unknown	38	5.1
TOTAL	749	
(b) *Political complexion:*		
Girondin inner group	58	7.7
Girondin supporters	120	16.0
Montagnards: Jacobin Club	142	19.0
Montagnards: supporters & regicides	160	21.4
Plain	250	33.4
Others	19	2.5
TOTAL	749	

Directorial Councils (following Year IV elections). (*Suratteau 1971*)

	Former Conventionnels		Newly Elected		Total	
		(%)		(%)		(%)
Royalists & counter-revs	41	9.0	48	21.5	89	13.1
Moderate royalists	—	—	69	30.9	69	10.2
Moderate constitutionalists	141	31.0	—	—	141	20.8
'Thermidorians'	197	43.3	45	20.2	242	35.7
Radicals, Jacobins	76	16.7	61	27.4	133	20.2
TOTAL	455		223		678	

Directorial Councils (year V elections, preceding Fructidor)

	Rump	%	Newly elected	%	Total	(%)
Royalists	150	32.1	180	69.2	330	45.3
Directorials	235	50.2	45	17.3	280	38.5
Radicals, Jacobins	33	7.0	35	13.5	68	9.3
Unknown, indeterminate	50	10.7	—		50	6.9
TOTAL	468		260		728	

Directorial Councils (Year V, following the Fructidor coup)

		(%)
Royalists & counter-revs	134	25.6
Thermidorians	271	51.7
Radicals, Jacobins	69	13.2
Unknown, indeterminate	50	9.5
TOTAL	524	

Directorial Councils (following Year VI elections)

Following elections which returned 10 royalists, 290 Directorials, 130 radicals or Jacobins and 14 of indeterminate opinion, the coup of Floréal cut back on elected representatives as follows:

	Elected	%	'Florealised'	%	Remaining	%
Royalists and counter-revs	115	14.3	9	7.8	106	15.3
Directorials	387	48.0	9	7.8	378	54.7
Radicals, Jacobins	175	21.7	84	72.4	91	13.2
Unknown, indeterminate	130	16.0	14	12.0	116	16.8
TOTAL	807		116		691	

3. POLITICAL GROUPS AND PARTIES

Amis du Loi, Amis du Roi, see CLUB MONARCHIQUE

Amis des Noirs ('Friends of the Blacks'). Pressure group demanding negro emancipation and the abolition of the slave-trade. Founded in Feb 1788 by Brissot, the society was patronised by Clavière, Mirabeau (briefly), Lafayette, Pétion, Condorcet, Grégoire, La Rochefoucauld, Carra, Siéyès, Bergasse, Lavoisier. Following the lead of the English abolitionists, they attached great importance to publicity and propaganda, at first in Brissot's *Patriote français*, then in the *cahiers* of 1789 and in petitions and addresses. They soon infiltrated the Jacobin network, and were well represented (Brissot, Condorcet, etc) in the Leg Ass. and Convtn. The cause outlived the Girondin leaders whose demise in 1793 caused the break-up of the society.

Anglomanes, see MONARCHIENS

Breton Club (*'Club Breton'*). The embryo of the Paris Jacobin Club owed its name to the fact that its founder-members were Third Estate deputies (Lanjuinais, Le Chapelier, Gleizen, etc) and some clerical members from Brittany. From 30 Apr, these met informally at Versailles to discuss matters of the day and prepare a common approach to parliamentary business. Soon an important nucleus of patriotic opinion, the club came to include Duport, d'Aiguillon, Siéyès, Barnave, the Lameth brothers, Bailly, Mirabeau, Pétion, Grégoire, Robespierre, La Révellière-Lépeaux. From mid Oct 1789 they changed name to the Club de la Révolution, and by Jan 1790 were known as the Club des Amis de la Constitution or Jacobin Club.

Brissotins, Buzotins, see GIRONDINS

Cercles constitutionnels. Moderate and liberal, anti-Clichyen (and usually anti-clerical) political clubs under the Directory based in Paris (about 40 branches) and the provinces (Blois, Vendôme, Le Mans, Auxerre, Strasbourg, Clermont-Ferrand, Riom, Périgueux, Toulouse, Marseille, Bordeaux, Lyon, etc). On the model of the Club de Salm in Paris, they rallied supporters of the regime and opponents of a royalist restoration. In practice they were often the rumps of former Jacobin societies. Originating in the early summer of 1797, they were closed down by the law of 23 July 1797/5 therm V, but the Fructidor coup of

Sept 1797 allowed their re-emergence. They were important in rallying provincial support for the Directory in the elections of Years VI and VII.

Cercle social (*'Confédération des Amis de la Vérité'*). Political club and publishing house, originating in Claude Fauchet's attempts to organise the political education of the Paris populace. At first élitist, it developed into a fraternal society in late 1790/early 1791, enjoyed a membership of 5,000 and started to build up a provincial network. It came under attack from the rival Jacobins. Leading members included Fauchet and Bonneville and a great deal of the *état-major* of the future Girondin movement (shorn of deputies from the Gironde), many of whom cut their political teeth in Parisian municipal politics from 1790: Brissot, Roland, Condorcet, Bancal des Issarts, Lanthénas, etc. Renowned for its republicanism, the club was closed after the Champ de Mars massacre, and the organisation expanded into a publishing operation. From 1790 it had published the *Bouche de fer.* and it now became the propaganda outlet for the Girondins – esp during Roland's tenure of the Ministry of the Interior in 1792. Besides the pro-Girondin *Sentinelle* and *Chronique du mois*, it also published the *Feuille villageoise*. Closed down when the Girondins fell in May–June 1793.

Clichyens, Clichiens. Supposed members of the parliamentary 'Club de Clichy' (a private house on the rue de Clichy) under the Directory. The term 'Clichyen' in fact referred more widely to 'moderates' though this term could include, depending on the political conjuncture, anti-Jacobins, crypto-royalists and constitutional monarchists. Down to 1797, they included moderate ex-Conventionnels like Boissy d'Anglas and Henri La Rivière and new deputies of moderate (Mathieu Dumas, Tronson du Coudray) and extremist (Imbert-Colomès) persuasion. The influx of new deputies after the Year V elections increased their numbers but reduced their cohesion, and moderates such as Dumas found themselves outflanked on the right by men like Gibert-Desmolières who nurtured links with the *émigrés*. Too anarchic to be an effective parliamentary caucus, they were breaking up even before the Fructidor coup, which saw many members either deported or exiled.

Club de l'Hôtel de Massiac (*'Société correspondante des Colons français'*). Pressure group of Saint-Domingue colonists based in Paris (Hôtel de Massiac, Place Louis XIV) who aimed to counteract the emancipationist propaganda of the Amis des Noirs. Founded 20 Aug 1789, they continued in existence until 1794. Annual subscription 48 liv in 1789, 240 liv by 1792. About 50 in number, they had links with merchant groups in the main ports (Nantes, Bordeaux, etc), with key political figures (Barnave, Théodore de Lameth, Arthur Dillon, Malouet, d'Eprémesnil, etc) and in the colonies themselves. From 1792 viewed as royalists and counter-revs, many were imprisoned under the Terror.

Club de la Réunion, see GIRONDINS

Club de la Révolution, see BRETON CLUB

Club de la Sainte-Chapelle. Caucus of middle-class, non-parliamentary moderates drawn from the Parisian electors (lawyers, doctors, merchants, municipal officials, etc), about 400 in number in 1791, who met from Sept 1791 until 1792 or 1793. At first moderate and anti-Girondin, by late 1792 they were viewed as reactionary.

Club des Allobroges. Expatriate political club formed in Paris, acting as a caucus for the annexation of Savoy and bringing together many of the numerous Savoyard workers in the capital and some Swiss. On 30 July 1792, the Leg Ass. permitted Doppet and other leaders of the club to form an Allobroge Legion of 2,000 men to fight on the SE front (a similar Belgian–Liégeois Legion had been formed in Apr, a Batavian Legion earlier in July). The Legion assisted Montesquiou in overrunning Savoy in Sept 1792; the club was successful in pushing the Convtn towards acceptance of annexation on 27 Nov.

Club des Amis de la Constitution, see JACOBINS

Club de Salm. A pro-Directory salon caucus, the archetype of the cercles constitutionnels, meeting from June 1797 in the Hôtel de Salm, rue de Lille, and then in the Hôtel de Montmorency. Its existence helped spawn numerous cercles constitutionnels in the provinces. Like them it focused supporters of the regime against a royalist restoration. Membership of the Club de Salm, however, was mainly parliamentary. Particularly prominent among members, who included Talleyrand, Siéyès, Marie-Jos Chénier, Tallien, Garat, Jourdan, Treilhard and Daunou, were Mme de Staël and Benjamin Constant. The 'Salmistes' or 'Salmigondis' countered royalist propaganda; issued the pro-Directorial newspaper, *L'Eclair*; lobbied for Talleyrand's appointment as Foreign Minister (16 July/5 therm); and helped prepare the Fructidor coup.

Club des Impartiaux. Parliamentary caucus of constitutional royalists, meeting from late 1789 to May 1790 in several locations in Paris. Leaders were Malouet and Mallet du Pan. They acted as a parliamentary caucus; issued propaganda (notably through the *Journal des Impartiaux*, Feb–Mar 1790); and attempted to foster support in the provinces.

Club de Valois. Orleanist pressure group and focus of patriotic sociability, which at times resembled an élitist dining club. Founded by Siéyès on 11 Feb 1789 – even before the EG had met – located in the Palais-Royal, it flourished down to 1791. It numbered about 500 in 1789–90, members being drawn from the robe and sword nobility, and the high bourgeoisie (Orléans, Lafayette, Talleyrand, Biron, Bergasse, Chamfort, Condorcet, the Lameth brothers, Custine, d'Antraigues, Fersen [*sic*], Narbonne, Hérault de Séchelles, etc).

Club du Manège (*'Réunion d'Amis de la Liberté et de l'Egalité'*). Founded 6 July 1799/18 mess VII, the club grouped neo-Jacobins and radical critics of the Directorial regime. It met in the Salle du Manège, the old meeting-place of the Convtn, and soon numbered over 3,000 individuals, including about 250 deputies in the councils. Members included Prieur de la Marne, Drouet, Bouchotte, Augereau, Félix Lepeletier, Audouin. Nostalgic reflections of the CPS and open support for Babeuf's views were soon voiced. After street fights with Parisian *muscadins* on 12 July/24 mess, they were evicted from the Salle du Manège and took refuge in the church of St Thomas Aquinas, rue du Bac. Their radical clarion calls, including the demand that *la patrie en danger* be declared, alarmed the Directors, and on 13 Aug/26 therm Police Minister Fouché closed down the club.

Club du Panthéon, see PANTHÉON CLUB

Club électoral, see ELECTORAL CLUB

Club monarchique (*'Club des Amis de la Constitution monarchique'*). Counter-rev propaganda machine and rallying-point which grew out of unofficial aristo-cratic clandestine gatherings in late 1790 and merged with the rightist strand from the Société de 1789. Often down to its dissolution in late 1792 the target for popular violence, it constantly moved location, and indeed after Varennes may not have had more than a mythical existence. Its leaders were Malouet and Clermont-Tonnerre, and at its height it counted perhaps 200 members drawn from the Ass., the clergy, nobility and upper bourgeoisie. Besides parliamentary activity, it sponsored counter-rev propaganda; fostered links with the *émigrés*; used charity to build up a popular following in Paris; and encouraged the foundation in the depts of clubs like the Amis de la Paix, Amis du Roi, etc.

Comité autrichien. Counter-rev court-based caucus. Shadowy, sporadic (and perhaps mythical?) existence, 1789–92. It was said to wish to subvert the Rev and restore absolutism by exploiting links with Austria, esp through Marie-Antoinette (*'l'Autrichienne'*), who was sometimes claimed to be its leader. Other alleged members included Montmorin and Bertrand de Moleville in 1790–1; Bertrand de Moleville, Besenval, Mercy-Argenteau, Fersen and Vaudreuil in 1791; Breteuil, Bouillé and perhaps Barnave and the Lameths in 1791–2.

Comité Valazé, see GIRONDINS

Conspiracy of Equals ('Conjuration des Egaux'), see EGAUX

Cordeliers (*'Société des Amis des Droits de l'Homme et du Citoyen'*). Orig-inating as the Society of the Cordeliers District, it became an independent political club on the rearrangement of Paris's internal administration in May 1790. It sat at first in the old Cordeliers monastery, but was ejected by the Commune in May 1791 and ended up in the Hôtel de Genlis, rue Dauphine. Like the Jacobins, it met four times weekly. 'A group of action and combat' (MATHIEZ), it was politically to the left of the Jacobins, and had an important role esp in the early days as a kind of democratic ombudsman, denouncing the misuse of power and righting individual as well as collective wrongs.

The membership originally was based on the Cordeliers district, but it spread to the whole capital in 1791. Admission was cheap (1 liv 4 sous) and monthly subscriptions low (2 sous), so that the membership (which included women) was large and wide. The leadership was predominantly middle class, and besides Danton and Desmoulins included many lawyers (Garran de Coulon, Pons de Verdun, Peyre), intellectuals, journalists and authors (Chaumette, Fréron, Bonneville, Robert, Momoro, Brune) and merchants and businessmen (Santerre, Legendre, Rossignol). Other leading members included Marat, Vincent, Paré and Fabre.

By 1791, the Cordeliers saw their functions as: the political education of the people, especially by the spread of fraternal societies; surveillance of the authorities; protection of popular leaders (through bodyguards, etc); and leadership of the democratic movement against aristocrats and reactionaries. They coordinated the popular critique of the new constitution in mid 1791; attacked the king after Varennes and were behind the organisation of the 'central committee' of fraternal societies which mobilised rpbcn opinion leading up to the Champ de Mars massacre; campaigned for admission of passive citizens into sectional assemblies; and helped to organise the *journée* of 10 Aug 1792.

After 1792, the Cordeliers' influence waned: many erstwhile leaders came to dominate the Jacobin Club, and sectional politics took up much of the attention of popular militants. Hébert and Vincent became the club's leaders, and the arrest and execution of the Hébertists in Mar 1794 destroyed it completely.

Dantonists. Name usually given to the group executed along with Danton on 5 Apr 1794 and associated with the desire to moderate the Terror in late 1793–early 1794, the so-called strategy of *indulgence*. In fact, many of those executed on 5 Apr were mere racketeers who had defrauded the government in various ways: Fabre d'Eglantine, Delaunay, Chabot (all implicated in the Compagnie des Indes swindle), plus Basire, d'Espagnac, the Frey brothers, Guzman and Diderichsen. Others were clearly Indulgents – Desmoulins, Delacroix, Philippeaux, Westermann, Fabre again – and had been or were Danton's associates and cronies. But Danton had no control and asserted no leadership over them and indeed since mid 1793 had put himself in the 'elder statesman' role in the Convtn. Associates of Danton to survive proscription – whose resentment towards the CPS came out at Thermidor – included Thuriot, Paré, Lecointre and Dubois-Crancé.

Egaux. Members or putative members of the radical conspiratorial group, the Conjuration des Egaux ('Conspiracy of Equals') organised by Gracchus Babeuf in 1795–6. On 30 March 1796/10 germ IV, Babeuf formed an Insurrectionary Committee to include Antonelle, Buonarroti, Debon, Darthé, Félix Lepeletier and Maréchal. A publicity campaign was launched, notably through Babeuf's *Tribun du peuple*, with agents for each of the 12 Parisian arrondissements; the newly formed Paris Police Legion was infiltrated; and links were established with ex-terrorists and ex-members of the Panthéon Club (Amar, Drouet, Lindet, etc). A mass following was never acquired, however, and an informer denounced the rev cell to the Directory. The Police Legion was disbanded (30 Apr/11 flor); Babeuf,

Buonarroti and others were arrested (10 May/21 flor); and a babouvist attempt to raise the military camp at Grenelle outside Paris failed (9–10 Sept/23–4 fruct). Many babouvists and left-wing radicals were either wiped out by the military commissions established after the Grenelle camp fiasco or else sent with Babeuf to be tried by the high court at Vendôme. Babeuf and Darthé received death sentences.

Some historians have seen Babeuf's conspiracy as an embryonically Leninist organisation, and highlight the communistic ideas (community of goods, services and labour, etc) preached by Babeuf in his *Tribun du peuple*.

Electoral Club (*'Club Electoral'*). Left-wing club grouping Parisian militants who had survived the spring and summer of 1794. Meeting from Aug 1794/fruct II, it tried unsuccessfully to rally the popular movement in the post-Thermidor atmosphere. Its leaders included Varlet, Legray, Crespin and Bodson, and its membership, which included Babeuf, numbered approx 400. Persecution by the CGS in Oct–Nov 1794 caused its demise.

Enragés. Loosely organised far-left grouping of activists in 1792–3 who emphasised social and economic aspects of the Terror. The most prominent in the group were Jacques Roux, Varlet, Leclerc and the two feminist radicals, Claire Lacombe and Pauline Léon. An *enragé* platform emerged in spring 1793; was manipulated by activists from the Commune such as Chaumette and Hébert; and contributed to the overthrow of the Girondins and the gradual acceptance of the Terror by the Convtn in the summer and autumn of 1793. Most of the *enragé* programme became law (death for hoarders, purges of aristocrats, state control of the grain trade, egalitarian economic policies, the *armée révolutionnaire*, etc). Yet individual *enragés* were persecuted: Robespierre denounced them, Roux was imprisoned and died, Leclerc was intimidated into silence, Varlet was gaoled and women's clubs were closed down. By Oct 1793 they were dead as a political force, though the Hébertists to a certain extent assumed their role as left critics of Rev Govt.

Feuillants (*'Société des Amis de la Constitution séante aux Feuillants'*). Club for constitutional royalists which was formed in July 1791 by a schism from the Jacobin Club after the flight to Varennes. Originating in private meetings and maintaining an élitist admissions policy, it developed a Jacobin-style organisation and prov network from Autumn 1791 and was in existence down to Aug 1792. In July 1791, they were said to number 365 deputies; later in 1791, 264 or perhaps 169; and in Aug 1792, 56. Their leaders effectively controlled the Constit Ass. in Aug–Sept 1791, and were influential in the early days of the Leg Ass.

The kernel of membership were the followers of the 'Triumvirate' (Barnave, Duport, Lameth) and those of Lafayette from the Société de 1789. Other members included Bailly, La Rochefoucauld, Vaublanc, Dumas and Pastoret. In the early days there were also some later radicals, such as Bazire, Gobel, Roederer, Reubell, Pache, La Révellière-Lépeaux, Châteauneuf-Randon and Dubois-Crancé. These filtered back to the Jacobins from late 1791, however, and the Feuillants' attempt to constitute themselves as a Jacobin-style club winning over the prov organisation of the Jacobins failed. Their influence waned, their major success in the Leg Ass. being the appointment of Narbonne as War Minister in Nov 1791. By early 1792 they were largely overtaken by events, and the term 'feuillant' began to be used indiscriminately to mean moderates or even reactionaries. Most of the leaders were arrested after the overthrow of the Girondins.

Girondins. Name given to the parliamentary group who supported a vigorously pro-war policy in the Leg Ass. and Jacobin Club, but who during the Convtn were expelled from the Jacobins and became increasingly critical of the emergency powers and centralising policies associated with the Montagnards. The main core of 'Girondins' (the term 'Girondin' was less favoured by contemporaries than 'Rolandins', 'Brissotins' or 'Buzotins') was purged from the Convtn after the *journée* of 2 June 1793.

Some historians – notably M. J. Sydenham (*1961*) – have doubted whether the 'Girondins' existed as a party. Certainly the group showed little sense of parliamentary discipline, while their identity is confused by the Montagnard practice of lumping them together with other political enemies. Some members of the group seem to have had little more than personal friendship in common, though in a period in which party links were in their infancy and indeed the whole justification for party formation seemed dubious, this friendship was inevitably thought to count.

There were a number of stages in the group's crystallisation:
(i) DOWN TO THE LEG ASS. The group originated in the partly overlapping circles of friends and political acquaintanceships of Brissot and Roland de la Platière and his wife. In his journalism but esp in his organisation of the emancipationist Amis des Noirs, Brissot from 1788 formed links with Clavière, Carra, Condorcet, Valady, Lanthénas, and from 1789 with Pétion and Buzot. In 1789 and 1790 he also frequented political salons and intervened in Parisian municipal politics where links were made with Bancal des Issarts, Manuel, Creuzé-Latouche and the Cercle social group. The Rolands's circle of friends included Bosc, Lanthénas and Champagneux; and when they moved to Paris in 1790 extended through Brissot to members of the Constit Ass. such as Grégoire, Servan, Buzot and Pétion.

From Feb to Sept 1791, Mme ROLAND'S 'FIRST' SALON, held *chez* the Rolands, Hôtel Britannique, rue Guénegaud, brought together three or four times a week individuals from these groups to discuss the questions of the day and elaborate a common strategy in the Ass. and the Jacobin Club.
(ii) THE LEG ASS. The circle of political acquaintanceship of Brissot and the Rolands extended considerably with the arrival in Paris of numerous new deputies. Close links were soon forged with the deputies of the Gironde dept, Ducos, Gensonné, Grangeneuve, Guadet and Vergniaud; with Kersaint; with Barbaroux (and his friends Deperret, Rebecquy, Duprat); with Dumouriez; and (through the

Jacobins) with Louvet. Many of the above met, from the Autumn of 1791 down to Sept 1792, in the so-called SALON OF VERGNIAUD (Vergniaud lodged with Ducos in the house of Mme Dodun, Place Vendôme). Discussion and preparation of political strategy in the Leg Ass. and Jacobin Club took place – notably the pro-war tactics associated with the group. Some ministerial plotting and wrangling also doubtless occurred which won Roland and his friends ministerial office in Mar 1792. From Mar to Sept, private meetings of the 'friends' also took place in the Ministry of the Interior. These groupings – and those from Aug 1792 down to Jan 1793 when Roland was again Minister of the Interior – are sometimes referred to as Mme ROLAND'S 'SECOND' SALON. Overlapping to some extent were the meetings of the rather shadowy CLUB DE LA REUNION (June–Oct 1792) which brought together deputies who were resentful of losing their former predominance at the Jacobin Club to Robespierre's influence and were more sympathetic to Brissot's positions. The group also tried to attract new members of the Convtn in Oct, but never achieved the status of full political organisation or counterweight to the Jacobin Club.

(iii) IN THE CONVTN. The group's need for organisation was all the greater in this period as most members either left or were expelled from the Jacobin Club.

Mme Roland's salon and the Réunion Club succeeded in attracting some of the new deputies into the Girondin orbit: notably Bergeoing, Boyer-Fronfrède, Pache (briefly), Savary, Vallée. The group as a whole was given greater consistency by the meetings in the salon of Valazé, in Valazé's dwelling on the rue d'Orléans-Saint-Honoré. Meetings of the so-called COMITE VALAZE had been going sporadically since Feb 1792, but they became more important from Dec. Girondin strategy over the king's trial, and esp the issue of the *appel au peuple* seems to have been devised here. The meetings, which brought together as many as 40–50 deputies, continued down to May and the salon became the headquarters of anti-Robespierrist sentiment. The group's attacks in the Convtn in the Spring of 1793 on the power of Paris looked increasingly shrill in the face of France's critical internal and external problems, and they lost much support from among the centrist deputies of the 'Plain'. The latter failed to prevent the purge of 22 deputies on the *journée* of 2 June and the subsequent proscription, arrest, execution and imprisonment of many more in the Summer and Autumn of 1793.

The Marxist tradition of rev scholarship associated with the writings of Jaurès, Lefebvre and Soboul, views the Girondins as the deputies of the upper middle class, more attached to private property and free trade than the Montagnards. Attempts to distinguish between Montagnards and Girondins on the basis of their social backgrounds have never been convincing, though it is certainly true that most of the upper middle class found little to support in the levelling social and economic policies associated with the Montagnards.

Estimates of the size of the Girondin group vary from 130 to 200 deputies, with a hard core calculated to consist of between 35 and 60. The difficulty of delineating the contours of the group can be seen in the table below, which shows attendance of 'deputies associated with Brissot' at the main political fora outlined above along with a number of other putative tests of 'Girondin' membership.

Some tests of membership of the Girondin 'Party' among members of the Convn (esp *Sydenham 1961*) are explained below and detailed in the following table.

(1) Known attendance at the salon of Vergniaud, 1791–2.
(2) Known attendance at the Réunion Club.
(3) Known attendance at the 'second' salon of Madame Roland, 1792–3.
(4) Known attendance at the salon of Valazé, 1792–3.
(5) Membership of the 'Commission of Twelve', May 1793.
(6) Deputies listed in petition from the Paris Commune, 15 Apr 1793.
(7) Deputies listed in petition presented to the Leg Ass. on 1 June 1793 by the sections, calling for their purge.
(8) Deputies placed under guard on the *journée* of 2 June 1793.
(9) Deputies named in a decree proposed by Saint-Just on 8 July 1793 as either traitors (T) or suspects (S).
(10) Deputies named in the decree of 28 July 1793 outlawing the Girondins as either traitors (T) or suspects (S); plus deputies proscribed before that date and not mentioned on 28 July (P).
(11) Deputies named by Amar, presenting a CGS report to the Convtn on 3 Oct 1793, as 'Girondins' (he also named the duc d'Orléans).
(12) Fate of 'Girondin' deputies in 1793: executed on 31 Oct after the 'show trial' of the Girondins (G); died in some other way such as suicide or execution by military commission (D); escaped and hid (E); imprisoned (P); continued to sit in the Convtn (C).
(13) Deputies reintegrated into the Convtn in 1794–5.

	(1)	(2)	(3)	(4)	(5)	(6)	(7)	(8)	(9)	(10)	(11)	(12)	(13)
Andrei	–	–	–	–	–	–	–	–	–	–	x	E	x
Antiboul	–	–	–	–	–	–	–	–	–	–	x	G	–
Bancal des Issarts	–	–	–	–	–	–	–	–	–	–	–	P	x
Barbaroux	–	–	x	x	–	x	x	x	T	T	–	D	–
Bergeoing	–	–	–	x	x	–	–	x	T	T	–	E	x
Bertrand la Hosdinière	–	–	–	–	x	–	–	x	–	–	–	P	x
Birotteau	–	–	–	–	–	x	x	x	T	P	–	D	–
Boilleau	–	–	–	–	x	–	–	x	–	S	x	G	–
Bonet	–	–	–	–	–	–	–	–	–	–	x	E	x
Boyer-Fonfrède	–	–	–	–	x	–	–	–	–	–	x	G	–
Bresson	–	–	–	–	–	–	–	–	–	–	x	P	x
Brissot	x	x	x	x	–	x	x	x	–	–	x	G	–
Buzot	–	–	x	x	–	x	x	x	T	T	–	D	–

	(1)	(2)	(3)	(4)	(5)	(6)	(7)	(8)	(9)	(10)	(11)	(12)	(13)
Carra	–	–	–	–	–	–	–	–	–	–	x	G	–
Chambon	–	–	–	x	–	x	x	x	–	T	x	D	–
Chasset	–	–	x	–	–	–	–	–	–	T	–	E	–
Condorcet	x	–	x	–	–	–	–	–	–	P	x	D	–
Couppé	–	–	–	–	–	–	–	–	–	P	–	E	x
Coustard	–	–	–	–	–	–	–	–	–	P	x	G	–
Cussy	–	–	–	–	–	–	–	–	–	S	x	D	–
Defermon	–	–	–	–	–	–	–	–	–	T	x	E	x
Delahaye	–	–	–	–	–	–	–	–	–	–	x	E	x
Deperret	–	–	x	x	–	–	–	–	–	–	x	G	–
Deverité	–	–	–	–	–	–	–	–	–	P	x	P	x
Doulcet	–	–	–	–	–	x	–	–	–	–	x	E	x
Duchastel	–	–	–	x	–	–	–	–	–	P	x	G	–
Ducos	x	x	–	–	–	–	x	–	–	–	x	G	–
Duprat	–	–	x	x	–	–	–	–	–	–	x	G	–
Dusaulx	–	–	–	–	–	x	–	–	–	–	–	P	x
Duval	–	–	–	–	–	–	–	–	–	–	x	E	x
Fauchet	–	x	–	–	–	x	–	–	–	S	x	G	–
Forest	–	–	–	–	–	–	–	–	–	P	–	P	x
Ganon	–	–	–	–	–	–	–	–	–	–	x	E	x
Gardien	–	–	–	–	x	–	–	x	S	S	x	G	–
Gensonné	x	x	x	x	–	x	x	x	S	S	x	G	–
Girard	–	–	–	x	–	–	–	–	–	–	–	P	x
Gomaire	–	–	–	x	–	–	x	–	–	P	–	P	x
Gorsas	–	–	x	–	x	–	x	x	T	T	–	D	–
Grangeneuve	–	x	–	–	x	–	x	x	–	S	x	D	–
Guadet	x	–	x	x	–	x	x	x	S	S	x	D	–
Hardy	–	–	–	–	–	x	–	–	–	–	x	E	x
Henry-La Rivière	–	–	–	–	–	x	–	x	–	T	x	E	x
Isnard	–	x	–	–	–	–	x	–	x	–	–	E	x
Kersaint	–	–	–	–	–	–	–	–	–	–	–	D	–
Kervélagan	–	–	–	x	–	–	x	–	–	T	–	E	–
Lacaze	–	–	–	x	–	–	–	–	–	–	x	E	x
Lanjuinais	–	–	–	–	–	x	x	x	T	T	x	E	x
Lanthénas	x	–	x	–	–	x	x	–	–	–	–	C	–
Lasource	–	x	–	–	–	x	x	x	–	S	x	G	–
Lehardy	–	–	–	x	–	x	x	x	–	–	x	G	–
Lesage	–	–	–	x	–	–	x	x	–	T	–	E	–
Lesterp-Beauvais	–	–	–	–	–	–	–	–	–	–	x	G	–
Lidon	–	–	x	–	–	x	x	x	–	T	x	D	–
Louvet	–	–	x	x	–	x	–	x	T	T	–	E	–
Magniez	–	–	–	–	–	–	–	–	–	P	–	P	x
Manuel	–	–	–	–	–	–	–	–	–	–	–	D	–

	(1)	(2)	(3)	(4)	(5)	(6)	(7)	(8)	(9)	(10)	(11)	(12)	(13)
Masuyer	–	–	–	–	–	–	–	–	–	P	x	G	–
Meillan	–	–	–	x	–	–	–	–	–	S	–	E	–
Michet	–	–	–	–	–	–	–	–	–	P	–	P	x
Minvielle	–	–	–	–	–	–	–	–	–	–	x	G	–
Mollevaut	–	–	–	x	x	–	–	x	S	S	x	E	x
Noël	–	–	–	–	–	–	–	–	–	–	x	G	–
Patrin	–	–	–	–	–	–	–	–	–	P	–	P	x
Pétion	–	–	x	x	–	x	x	x	T	T	–	D	–
Rabaut-St-Etienne	–	–	x	–	x	–	x	–	T	T	–	D	–
Rebecquy	–	–	–	–	–	–	–	–	–	–	–	D	–
Rouyer	–	–	–	–	–	–	–	–	–	–	x	E	x
Salle	–	–	–	x	–	x	x	x	T	T	–	D	–
Savary	–	–	–	–	–	–	–	–	–	–	x	P	x
Serre	–	–	–	–	–	–	–	–	–	P	–	P	x
Sillery	–	–	–	–	–	–	–	–	–	–	x	G	–
Valady	–	–	–	–	–	x	–	–	–	T	x	D	–
Valazé	–	x	x	–	–	x	–	x	–	S	x	D	–
Vallée	–	–	–	–	–	–	–	–	–	–	x	E	x
Vergniaud	x	x	–	–	–	x	x	x	S	S	x	G	–
Viger	–	–	–	x	–	–	x	–	–	P	x	G	–
Vitet	–	–	–	–	–	–	–	–	–	P	–	E	x

Hébertistes. Loose coalition centred around Hébert, editor of the *Père Duchesne* and leading activist in the Commune, which formed a left opposition to the Rev Govt from 2 June 1793 to Spring 1794. With the Paris Commune and sections as their base, with strong influence in the Ministry of War under Bouchotte and in the Cordeliers Club, they exploited *enragé* demands for radical social and economic legislation, together with agitation for the stepping-up of the Terror, a measure of direct democracy and dechristianising religious policies. Prominent allies of Hébert included Vincent, Ronsin, Momoro and Chaumette. Outmanœuvred by the CPS, which feared foreign infiltration, Hébert and his closest associates were arrested in Mar 1794, put on trial with a motley group of alleged participants in a 'foreign plot' (Proli, Pereira, Dubuisson, Desfieux, etc) and executed. The Commune was thereby neutralised politically and the *sans-culotte* movement weakened.

Indulgents, see DANTONISTS

Institut philanthropique. Royalist front organisation during the Directory which under the guise of charitable works established a royalist network throughout France. A veritable Chinese-boxes organisation, it comprised a pseudo-masonic organisation of *Amis de l'ordre*, whose commitment was to royalist electioneering and peaceful methods; and a hyper-secretive, more militaristic group, the *Fils légitimes*, committed to insurrectionary methods. After a shaky start, Despomelles and (with British finance provided through secret agent William Wickham) d'André had created 58 groups throughout France by mid 1797. The anti-royalist repression following the Fructidor coup broke up the network, though some members went even deeper underground, resurfacing in the fiascos of popular royalist insurrections in Aug 1799.

Jacobins. Members of the Jacobin clubs meeting throughout France from 1789 to 1794/5, which constituted the leading edge of extra-parliamentary political action for much of the period of their existence.

(i) THE PARIS JACOBIN CLUB. From its emergence out of the Breton Club of 1789 (see above) down to Sept 1792, known as the 'Société des Amis de la Constitution, séante aux Jacobins à Paris'; from 21 Sept 1792 onwards, the 'Société des Jacobins, Amis de la Liberté et l'Egalité). The name 'Jacobins' was first given mockingly, the society holding its meetings in the nationalised monastery of the Jacobin monks on the rue Saint-Honoré in Paris.

From the early sessions, the club acted as parliamentary pressure group for 'patriot' and 'radical' opinion, and in particular discussed and agreed a common line on business to be transacted in the Constit Ass. the following day. The aims of the society as stated in its earliest regulations (Feb 1790) were: (i) discussion of questions to be debated in the Ass.; (ii) the establishment and general acceptance of the constitution; (iii) correspondence with similar societies throughout France. Initially most members belonged to the Ass., though there was an admixture of non-deputies which grew stronger with time. From Oct 1790 sessions were opened to the public who sat in the *tribunes*. Openness was viewed as the best guarantee of the sincerity and unsubversiveness of their political intentions.

The club's form of business, like that of the myriad clubs in France which came to affiliate to it, was modelled on that of the Nat Ass. (debates, motions, amendments, committees, etc). Members were not, however, elected, but accepted on recommendation by existing members; only if there were any objections raised to a candidature was there a vote. The admission fee was at first 12 liv, with 24 liv as the annual subscription. This, and the expectation that all members would be active citizens, placed membership well beyond the reach of popular elements, who frequented the Cordeliers and fraternal societies. By and large, members in the early years were respectable middle-class and professional men, with a sprinkling of ex-nobles. By Feb 1790 there were over 1,000 members; by June 1791, 2,400.

From late 1789 the dominant strand of opinion in the club was represented by the 'Triumvirate' (Barnave, Duport, Lameth), though other individuals outside this faction – notably Robespierre, who was already gaining a reputation as 'the Incorruptible', Pétion ('the Virtuous'), the Cordeliers Danton and Desmoulins, Grégoire, Dubois-Crancé, Collot, Billaud-Varenne, Cloots and Carra – also won a following. Lafayette found himself ousted from a position of strength in the club, and from 1790 organised a break-away movement, the Société de 1789 (see below). The break-away club was increasingly viewed as moribund and reactionary.

The names of members elected to serve as Jacobin Club president give some idea of the political complexion of the club down to Varennes (the list is incomplete):

| Late 1789 | Le Chapelier |
| Late 1789 | Menou |

1790		*1791*	
8 Feb	d'Aiguillon	9, 31 Jan	Victor de Broglie
Late Mar	Robespierre	4 Feb	Reubell
3 June	Barnave	2, 30 Mar	Gaultier de Biauzat
23 July	Noailles	13, 29 Apr	Beauharnais
22 Sept	Dubois-Crancé	18 May	Goupil de Préfelne
10, 28 Oct	Duport	27 May	Prieur de la Marne
15 Nov	Chabroud	21 June	Bouche
30 Nov, 3 & 19 Dec	Mirabeau		

The flight to Varennes came close to destroying the club. Most deputies, finding the rpbcn sympathies of the club's members unsympathetic and rallying to the constitutional monarchist strategy propagated by the 'Triumvirate', left to form the Feuillants (see above). The continued presence of the popular Robespierre and Pétion in the Club – with Buzot, Grégoire, Prieur de la Marne, Roederer and Royer, the only deputies from the Constit Ass. not to defect to the Feuillants – retained the club much of its popular, extra-parliamentary following, both in Paris and the provinces. The Jacobin Club was no longer the prime focus for all patriotic deputies as it had been in 1789 and 1790, however, and when the Leg Ass. met in Sept 1791, fewer deputies subscribed to the Jacobin Club than rallied to the Feuillants. Membership fell from 2,400 before the schism to 1,200 in Nov 1791.

Among the keenest and most prominent members of the club were now Brissot and the so-called 'Girondins' (see above), and they won the club over to a pro-war, anti-'Austrian Committee' stance which immensely increased the Club's influence and prestige. The appointment of Jacobins Roland, Clavière and Servan to the 'patriot ministry' of March 1792 had a similar effect. Policies more radical than those of the Girondins were called for in the Leg Ass. and in the Jacobin Club by extreme left-wing deputies such as Merlin de Thionville, Chabot and Basire, while Robespierre, who was not a member of the Leg Ass., built up a strong personal following. Although Robespierre at first lost most of the debates with Brissot over the war (which he opposed), by Apr/May the club was slipping away from the Girondins towards the Robespierrists. Shifts in the club's political orientation are clear in the roster of club presidents:

1791		1792 (cont'd)	
24 July	Dufourny	17 Feb	Basire
3 Aug	Pétion	4 Mar	Thuriot
29 Aug	Roederer	18 Mar	Mailhe
3 Oct	Brissot	1 Apr	Vergniaud
19 Oct	Fauchet	17 Apr	Lasource
1 Nov	Condorcet	3 May	Lecointre
16 Nov	Couthon	17 May	Merlin de Thionville
2 Dec	Isnard	1 June	Chabot
22 Dec	Grangeneuve	17 June	Hérault de Séchelles
		2 July	Saladin
1792		16 July	Delaunay d'Angers
2 Jan	Antonelle	3 Aug	Maribon-Montaut
16 Jan	Guadet		
1 Feb	Broussonet		

By the time of the overthrow of the king in Aug 1792 (to which they contributed surprisingly little), Jacobins of all political hues were resigned to the advent of the Rpbc. The Sept Massacres and the powers assumed by the Paris Commune after 10 Aug produced a new rift among the Jacobins, however. The Girondins recoiled from the over-influential and over-sanguinary politics of the Commune now enthusiastically preached at the club. Following concerted Girondin attacks in the Ass. upon Robespierre, Danton, Marat and the Commune, Brissot was expelled from the club on 10 Oct and other Girondins either absented themselves or were expelled in their turn (e.g. 26 Nov, expulsion of Roland, Louvet, Lanthénas; 26 Dec, of Manuel; 11 Jan 1793 of Gensonné, Guadet and Vergniaud). Members were increasingly expected to vote for the Montagnard line in the Convtn and to give periodic justifications of their political conduct in a kind of purge, introduced in July 1791, known as the *scrutin épuratoire*.

From late 1792, the left dominated the club, though there were a number of different shades of opinion: moderate (Danton, Thuriot, Delaunay, etc), Robespierrist (Robespierre, Saint-Just, Couthon, etc), Maratist (Marat, Maure, Bentabole), ultra-rev (Billaud-Varenne, Collot-d'Herbois) or Hébertist (Hébert, Vincent, Ronsin, etc). The post of president alternated between these formations:

1792		1793	
19 Aug	Choudieu	1 Jan	Monestier
23 Sept	Pétion	4 Feb	Jullien de la Drôme
10 Oct	Danton	20 Feb	Billaud-Varenne
2 Nov	Jean Bon Saint-André	4 Mar	Collot-d'Herbois
17 Nov	Lepeletier	17 Mar	Lamarque
5 Dec	Dubois-Crancé	5 Apr	Marat
19 Dec	Saint-Just	22 Apr	Albitte
		8 May	Bentabole

<table>
<tr><td colspan="2">*1793 (cont'd)*</td><td colspan="2">*1794*</td></tr>
<tr><td>29 May</td><td>Bourdon de l'Oise</td><td>5 Jan/16 niv</td><td>Jay</td></tr>
<tr><td>16 June</td><td>David</td><td>18 Jan/29 niv</td><td>Reverchon</td></tr>
<tr><td>14 July</td><td>Simond</td><td>7 Feb/19 pluv</td><td>Thirion</td></tr>
<tr><td>7 Aug</td><td>Robespierre</td><td>26 Feb/8 vent</td><td>Lavicomterie</td></tr>
<tr><td>28 Aug</td><td>Simond</td><td>8 Mar/18 vent</td><td>Duval</td></tr>
<tr><td>4 Sept</td><td>Léonard Bourdon</td><td>26 Mar/6 germ</td><td>Legendre</td></tr>
<tr><td>18 Sept</td><td>Coupé de l'Oise</td><td>8 Apr/19 germ</td><td>Veau</td></tr>
<tr><td>4 Oct</td><td>Dubarran</td><td>22 Apr/3 flor</td><td>Lebas</td></tr>
<tr><td>23 Oct</td><td>Maribon-Montaut</td><td>10 May/21 flor</td><td>Vadier</td></tr>
<tr><td>11 Nov/21 brum</td><td>Cloots</td><td>22 May/3 prair</td><td>Voulland</td></tr>
<tr><td>1 Dec/11 frim</td><td>Fourcroy</td><td>4 June/16 prair</td><td>Fouché</td></tr>
<tr><td>6 Dec/26 frim</td><td>Bouquier</td><td>24 June/6 mess</td><td>Barère</td></tr>
<tr><td></td><td></td><td>21 July/3 therm</td><td>Elie Lacoste</td></tr>
</table>

The political complexion of the club is also evident in the list of those expelled: these included ex-nobles, bankers, speculators and foreigners from 12 Dec/22 frim (Daoust, Cloots, Duhem, etc); Guffroy, 3 Mar/13 vent; Fabre and Bourdon de l'Oise (?); Dubois-Crancé, 11 Jul/23 mess; Fouché, 13 July/25 mess; and Collot-d'Herbois and Billaud-Varenne, 25 July/8 therm. The social composition of membership was less upper middle class than formerly, though the absence of membership lists make exact comparison impossible.

Although pressure from the left through the club helped push the Convtn solidly towards acceptance of the need for 'terroristic' policies (price maximum, rev tribunal, laws against suspects, *armée révolutionnaire*, etc), by late 1793 faction-fighting within the club was getting out of hand. The Rev Govt's deactivation of the Commune in Spring 1794, and its purge of Hébertists (Mar) and Danton-ists (Apr) left the field free for Robespierre and his following. The former unruli-ness or debates in the club was replaced by a rather monochromatic subservience to the word of Robespierre and the Rev Govt. Much of the vitality and energy of the club had now gone and though it survived the overthrow of Robespierre at Thermidor and became the rallying-ground for those who wished to maintain the policies of the Terror it was never again a dominant force in opinion. The recrudescence of moderate and right-wing opinion put the Jacobins increasingly on the defensive. In particular the club was attacked by right-wing gangs of youths (the so-called *jeunesse dorée*). Following street brawls, the club was closed down permanently on 12 Nov 1794/22 brum II. Some Jacobin personnel remained loyal to the old policies of Year II under the Thermidorian and Direc-torial regimes, though their impact was muted. (See Club du Manège, Panthéon Club.)

(ii) THE PROV JACOBIN CLUBS. The rev cataclysm of 1789 threw up a wave of political associations which though quite novel did owe something to British and American precedents and to pre-rev masonic and literary societies. Meeting-places and fora for political discussion, drawing in most 'patriots' among local notables, clubs soon began to communicate among themselves. The prestige of the Parisian Jacobin Club and its links with the membership of the Nat Ass. made it a natural magnet for the sympathies of the prov clubs. From Feb 1790 inter-affiliation became one of the Paris Jacobins' main raisons-d'être.

There was initially a great deal of variety in the nomenclature, format, procedures and membership of the prov clubs. But the Paris Club was increasingly taken as the ideal to which most sought to approximate and, like them, they became 'friends of the Constitution' and resembled 'debating clubs with parliamentary organisation and parliamentary ambitions' (BRINTON). The clubs thus became major amplifiers of rev propaganda as well as seed-plots of would-be politicians. Besides stimulating the politicisation of the French nation, they also favoured, through their subscriptions to rev newspapers, the growth of the political press. They also engaged (at first with only limited success) in electioneering; became involved in economic lobbying and the protection of local interests; and through a policy of coordinated and collaborative petitioning, were able to keep up a barrage of pressure on the Nat Ass., orchestrated by the Paris Jacobins.

There was a vast growth in the Jacobin provincial network down to mid 1791, with the fastest period of growth coming in the Winter and Spring of 1790–1 (*Kennedy 1982*).

Number of cities with clubs affiliated to or in correspondence with the Paris Jacobins and its affiliates:

Pre 1790	23		
1790		*1791*	
Jan	20	Jan	349
Feb	23	Feb	427
Mar	32	Mar	543
Apr	48	Apr	650
May	66	May	745
June	91	June	833
July	113	July	921
Aug	137		
Sept	152		
Oct	177		
Nov	213		
Dec	276		

Not all provincial clubs belonged to the Jacobin network – the royalists for example tried to found local societies of *amis du roi* or *amis du loi*. A shock to the Jacobin network came, moreover, with the schism in July 1791 of the Feuillants, who campaigned to detach provincial clubs from the Paris Jacobins. They enjoyed only limited success, however: only 72 clubs declared for the Feuillants in the first fortnight after the break, and many of these returned to the Jacobin fold in the autumn.

In the early years, the social composition of members was, like the Paris Jacobins, respectably middle and upper-middle class. Membership was democratised from 1793 onwards, as the following table indicates (*Kennedy 1982; Brinton 1930*).

Social composition of membership of Jacobin Clubs, based on extant membership lists:

	1789–91 (sample of 13 clubs)	1793–5 (sample of 46 clubs)
	%	%
Clergy	6.7	1.6
Nobles	0.6	–
Rentiers	4.0	–
Farmers	1.1	9.6
Military	5.7	2.7
Lawyers	–	6.8
Liberal professions (minus lawyers for 1793–5)	13.5	6.9
Government employees and officials	16.7	6.7
Merchants and businessmen	12.1	8.2
Artisans and shopkeepers	38.6	45.0
Manual labourers	0.03	–
Miscellaneous	1.0	12.5

The democratisation of the movement stimulated its growth: at the height of Year II, there were perhaps 2,000 prov branches, containing 100,000 members. There were important changes too in the outlook and functions of the clubs. With the Feuillant and monarchical societies destroyed in 1792 and the Girondins proscribed in 1793, and with the drastic circumstances of civil and foreign war, the societies came to act as quasi-official cogs in the wheels of the Rev Govt. 'Reservoirs of patriots' (COLIN LUCAS) whose political fidelity was ensured through the *scrutin épuratoire* and close surveillance, they were consulted by reps *en mission*, while *comités de surveillance* and *armées révolutionnaires* were usually drawn from their ranks. Regular authorities worked in close collaboration with them, the poor came to rely on their involvement in welfare schemes and in food-supply problems, and the rich to fear their levelling instinct. Also important was their educational and propaganda role: by acting as auxiliary to other rev agencies, they served to explain and popularise the Rev Govt to the population at large and to offer a concrete embodiment of its mobilising will. As at Paris, however, the quasi-bureaucratisation of the clubs caused a falling off in their spontaneity and anarchic militancy. Thermidor, the closing of the Paris Jacobin Club in Nov 1794 and the White Terror were fatal blows for many clubs, all of which were prohibited by the law of 23 Aug 1795/6 fruct III.

Jeunesse dorée ('gilded youth'). Dandified vigilante gangs of youths organised after Thermidor, esp in Paris and in the cities of the SE. In Paris, they were drawn from the wealthier W and central sections; numbered between 2,000 and 3,000; and included large numbers of military 'draft-dodgers'. Their rallying-points were right-wing cafés like the Café de Chartres, and from here they set out on sorties involving mugging Jacobins and erstwhile sectional militants, street brawls and attacks on the Jacobin Club. One attack on the club led to its closure by the Convtn, 12 Nov 1794/22 brum III. Well connected with 'turncoat terrorists' like Fréron and Tallien, their attempt at military intervention against the faubourgs in the Prairial uprising ended in fiasco. Thereafter, they drifted to the right, and became suspect to the government. The Café de Chartres was closed down; stricter measures were introduced against draft-dodgers; and the involvement of the *jeunesse* in the royalist Vendémiaire rising led to their proscription.

Monarchiens (or **Anglomanes**). Moderate wing of the patriot movement which emerged in the Nat Ass. in July 1789 grouped round Mounier, Clermont-Tonnerre and Bergasse and including aristocrats like Lally-Tollendal and Virieu, which advocated an English-style constitution, including a bicameral legislature. They met in private houses, planned parliamentary strategy and cultivated links with the Necker ministry. They broke up in Oct 1789 when the attempt to introduce bicameralism had failed.

Montagnards. Name given to the left-wing deputies who at first in the Leg Ass. but esp in the Convtn sat on the benches high up to one side of the hall. The group was most clearly distinguishable as a result of its opposition to the Girondins in the Convtn, and by its utilisation of the Jacobin Club as a focus for policy discussion and strategic thinking. The group's radical policies dominated the Convtn from 2 June 1793 to the overthrow of Robespierre. The Rev Govt was in effect a Montagnard dictatorship. Although to most intents and purposes, a Montagnard was a deputy of the Convtn who attended the Paris Jacobin Club, some so-called Montagnards (e.g. Carnot) shunned the club. A recent estimate has put their number in the Convtn at 135, and listed them as follows (*Higonnet 1985*):

Albitte	Berlier	Bourbotte	Charbonnier	Dandenac
Amar	Bissy	Boutroue	Chasles	Dartigoëyte
Audouin	Bo	Cambon,	Châteauneuf-	David
Baille	Bordas-	Joseph	Randon	Delacroix,
Barbeau	Pardoux	Capmas	Chauvin	Charles
Barère	Borie	Carnot	Choudieu	Delaguelle
Bassal	Borie	Casabianca	Clauzel	Delaunay
Battelier	Cambort	Cassanyès	Couthon	Deleyre
Bayle	Bouillerot	Chambon-	Crassous	Deville
Beaugeard	Bouquier	Latour	Cusset	Deydier

Dubouchet	Goupilleau-	Lebas	Pérard	Taillefer
Duhem	Montaigu	Leblanc	Peyssard	Thirion
Dupuch	Goyre	Lejeune	Pinet	Vadier
Duquesnoy	Granet	Lepeletier	Piorry	Villetard
Duroy	Grosse-	Saint-	Pocholle	Voulland
Duval,	Durocher	Fargeau	Pressavin	
Charles	Guimberteau	Lesage-	Prieur de la	
Édouard	Guyardin	Senault	Marne	
Eschasseriaux	Guyton-	Levasseur,	Prieur de la	
Escudier	Morveau	Antoine	Côte-d'Or	
Espert	Hentz	Levasseur,	Prost	
Faure,	Huguet	René	Ricord	
Balthazar	Ichon	Lindet,	Robespierre,	
Fayau	Ingrand	Robert	Augustin	
Finot	Jacomin	Lindet,	Robespierre,	
Forestier	Jay	Thomas	Maximilien	
Fourcroy	Jean Bon	Loiseau	Romme	
Foussedoire	Saint-	Loncle	Roux	
Frécine	André	Louis	Roux-Fazillac	
Frémanger	Julien	Mallarmé	Ruamps	
Garnier,	Lacoste, Élie	Maure	Rühl	
Jacques	Laignelot	Milhaud	Saint-Just	
Garrau	Lanot	Millard	Saliceti	
Gaston	Laurens	Moltedo	Sautayra	
Gay-Vernon	Lavicomterie	Monestier	Soubrany	
Génissieu		Montégut	Souhait	
Goujon				

Panthéon Club (*'Club du Panthéon', 'Réunion des Amis de la République'*). Left-wing political society founded on 16 Nov 1795/25 brum IV by the printer Lebois, and meeting in a disaffected church on the butte Sainte-Geneviève. Largely composed of left rpbcns and ex-terrorists (Félix Lepeletier, Amar, Darthé, Buonarroti, Pache, Marchand), it numbered between 900 and 1,500 members at the beginning of 1796. Self-proclaimedly a counterbalance to 'aristocratic' groups (and tolerated as such by the Convtn) it was relatively moderate at first, but became increasingly radical, supporting Babeuf and advocating more extreme economic and financial policies. The Directory ordered its closure on 26 Feb 1796/7 vent V.

Rolandins, see GIRONDINS

Salon français. Aristocratic and counter-rev cabal meeting between Apr 1790 and early 1792. Based at first in the rue Royale, it moved to the Palais-Royal in May 1790. Its membership largely comprised aristocratic youths, many of whom were probably involved in the 'Conspiration des poignards'. Political intrigue and the organisation of the king's escape were its main aims. It faded in the post-Varennes atmosphere and as its ranks were reduced by emigration.

Sans-culottes. The 'popular movement' in Paris and, to a lesser extent, in prov cities, was said to comprise individuals who wore workmen's trousers rather than knee-breeches (*culottes*). From 1789 the political education provided by street action, plus the organisational structures of fraternal clubs and societies and, from mid 1792, sectional assemblies and the Commune, allowed the formation of a relatively autonomous political force drawn from a lower middle-class background than any of the political formations which had members in the Nat Ass. Most activists were artisans, shopkeepers, their journeymen and assistants, petty clerks and workers. The leadership of the Parisian movement and the general run of prov *sans-culottes* tended to be more middle class. The strike-force and the cannon-fodder of the main rev *journées*, *sans-culotte* militants by 1793 had evolved a broadly conceived political programme which included direct democracy and terror, and an economic programme, influenced strongly by the *enragés*, based on egalitarian policies, price-fixing, the right to work and to public assistance, etc. Their activities were canalised into support, at different times, for Maratist, *enragé* and Hébertist policies, and their effective alliance with the Montagnard deputies in the Convtn in the summer of 1793 was crucial in the launching of the Great Terror. From late 1793 to early 1794, however, the Rev Govt was deactivating the popular movement in Paris. The *sans-culottes* failed to rally in sufficient numbers to save Robespierre at Thermidor, and the rather aimless conduct of the vestiges of the popular movement in the *journées* of Germinal and Prairial (Apr–May 1795) led to its liquidation as a political force.

Société de citoyennes républicaines révolutionnaires. Women's popular society formed in Paris in May 1793 from female militants who had been active in the Cordeliers and other fraternal societies since 1790 and 1791. Presided over by Claire Lacombe and Pauline Léon, the society, besides urging specifically women's reforms such as better occupational training for young women, enjoyed close links with *enragé* leaders and followed a broadly *enragé* line. By Sept, the society numbered several hundreds of women, and members became involved in street battles with market-women over the wearing of the rev cockade (which a decree of the Convtn on 21 Sept made obligatory for women). On 30 Oct/9 brum, however, as part of its strategy of deactivating the *enragé* movement, all women's political societies were declared illegal.

Société de 1789, Club de 1789. Elitist, constitutional monarchist club-cum-salon and pressure group, in existence from Jan 1790 to Autumn 1791. Formed as a moderate, Fayettiste riposte to the Jacobin Club, the society distanced itself from the left and also from the hard-line royalists to the right. It activity often centred on banquets and dinners at which prov deputies were subjected to polite persuasion. It also encouraged affiliation of provincial clubs. Leaders included Lafayette, Bailly, Mirabeau, Roederer, Le Chapelier, Talleyrand, Siéyès; other members, André Chénier, Malouet, Condorcet, Guillotin, Roucher, Clavière, Liancourt, Rabaut Saint-Etienne, Duquesnoy, Brissot, Cérutti, Lavoisier, plus financiers, men of letters and the upper bourgeoisie. In 1790, membership stood at about 400. Admission was 40 liv, the subscription a further 60 liv. By early 1791, it was seen as increasingly reactionary. This led to some defections back to the Jacobins (Mirabeau, Brissot, Le Chapelier, etc), while others merged in mid 1791 into the Feuillants.

Société des Indigents. Parisian popular society, founded in Mar 1791 by Prudhomme (editor of the *Révolutions de Paris*) and based in the Quatre-Nations section. Membership was approx 300 in June 1791, drawn from the poorer classes, both men and women.

Société des Trente. Caucus and propaganda machine active in democratic organisation for the EG. First meeting in Nov 1788, it had a shadowy constitution based on the original membership of 12, and prided itself on being in the vanguard of the 'National' or 'Patriot' party. Adrien Duport, at whose house it often met, was a key figure, and other members included young parlementaires such as Lepeletier de Saint-Fargeau, liberal aristocrats inc Lafayette, Noailles, Lameth, La Tour-Maubourg, Talleyrand, d'Aiguillon, Biron and La Rochefoucauld and pamphleteers and publicists such as Condorcet, Target, Siéyès, Roederer, Lacretelle. The Swiss banker Clavière was also a member. Links were maintained with Orléans. The group published and distributed patriot pamphlets; liaised with like-minded groups in the provinces; issued model cahiers; and maintained influence at court, in the Paris parl and in the salons.

Société du Panthéon, see PANTHÉON CLUB

Société fraternelle des Halles (*'Club de la Section de Mauconseil'*). Parisian popular society founded in Jan 1791 by François Sergent and based in the Les Halles neighbourhood. Membership popular, both male and female; approx 400–500. Esp prominent in the Champ de Mars affair.

Société fraternelle des patriotes des deux sexes (or *'Société fraternelle des Jacobins'*). The first Parisian popular society, founded in Feb 1790 by schoolmaster Claude Dansard, who presided down to Mar 1791, and which was based from late 1790 in the library of the Jacobin monastery frequented by the Jacobin Club. Activity at first concentrated on civic and moral education; but from early 1791 this was supplanted by political education, organisation and (in conjunction with the Cordeliers, etc) agitation, notably for manhood suffrage. Membership lower middle class, male and female, with an admixture of intellectuals including some Jacobins. Subvention of 1 sou per session. 800–900 members in Feb–Apr 1791.

Société fraternelle du Palais-Cardinal or des Minimes. Parisian popular society founded in Jan 1791 by Tallien. At first located in the rue vieille du Temple, it moved to the Minimes monastery in the Place Royale. Membership was popular, male and female. Admission free. Approx 400 individuals at session in July 1791.

Théophilanthropes. Adherents of a kind of rationalist religion founded on 15 Jan 1797/26 niv V by the Parisian bookseller Chemin. Deist in a woolly way which allowed members of different faiths to belong, services orientated around edifying readings, sentimental music and meditation. Members included Bernardin Saint-Pierre, Hauy, Dupont de Nemours, Chénier, Servan, Paine, Creuzé-Latouche, some leftists such as David, Rossignol and Santerre, and the Director La Révellière-Lépeaux, who seems to have seen in the cult a potential state religion. By 1798 it was building up support in prov centres with a dechristianising past. The movement's political pretensions died with La Révellière-Lépeaux's exit from the Directory in 1799 and it was outlawed by Bonaparte.

4. SOME SIGNIFICANT VOTES AND ELECTORAL RESULTS

Tennis Court Oath, 20 June 1789.
Only one deputy (Martin Dauch, from Castelnaudary) voted against the resolution of the 'Nat Ass.' not to break up before a new constitution had been established.

Declaration of war, 20 Apr 1792.
Only seven deputies voted against the war: Théodore de Lameth, Jaucourt, Dumas, Gentil, Baert, Hua and Becquet.

Election to the PEC, 10 Aug 1792.
Voting figures were: Danton, 222; Monge, 154; Lebrun, 109, Grouvelle, 91. The first three were declared elected, with Grouvelle serving as secretary. They were complemented by three of the 'patriot ministry' of Mar–June 1793: Roland, Clavière and Servan.

Multiple election in the elections to the Convtn, 1792.
Carra, 7 depts; Condorcet, 5; Dubois-Crancé, 5; Paré, 4; Brissot, Siéyès, 3.

Vote of the Leg Ass. 26 Aug 1792, to accord honorary French citizenship to 'foreign philosophers and writers who had courageously maintained the cause of freedom'.

On the report of the Education Committee, the following were accorded this honour: Joseph Priestley, Jeremy Bentham, William Wilberforce, Thomas Clarkson, James Mackintosh, David Williams, Thomas Paine (British); Gorani (Italian); Anacharsis Cloots, Joachim-Heinrich Campe, Klopstock, Schiller (German); Pestalozzi (Swiss); Cornelius de Pauw (Dutch); Thaddeus Kosciusko (Polish); George Washington, Alexander Hamilton, James Madison (American).

Votes in the king's trial, 17 Jan 1793.

361 for death without conditions
26 for the 'Mailhe amendment' (= death, but with the reservation that a reprieve be considered if the majority voted the death penalty)
46 for death with conditions (e.g. only after the expulsion of all the Bourbons, when the constitution had been approved, when peace was established)
286 for imprisonment, detention, banishment
2 for imprisonment in irons.

Thus of 749 Conventionnels, 721 voted: 387 (53.7%) for death, and 334 (46.3%) against it.

Deputies who failed to secure election to the CPS, 7 Apr 1793. (For a list of the successful candidates, plus votes, see p. 90.)

La Révellière-Lépeaux	146 votes
Lasource	143
Isnard	141
Robert Lindet	122
Thuriot	103
Dubois-Crancé	96
Boyer-Fonfrède	86
Merlin de Douai	85
Cambacérès	62

Multiple election in the Year IV elections.
Lanjuinais, 39 depts; Henry La Rivière, 37; Boissy-d'Anglas, 36; Defermon, 16; Lesage de l'Eure-et-Loir, 12; Cambacérès, 11; Durand-Maillane, 10; Dussaulx, Pelet de la Lozère, Saladin, 9; Bailleul, Isnard, Louvet, Merlin de Douai, 6; Daunou, Pierret, Thibaudeau, 4; etc.

Multiple election in the Year V elections.
Volney, Laffon-Ladébat, Portalis, 2 depts.

Multiple election in the Year VI elections.
Monge, 4 depts; Chénier, Lamarque, 3; Baudin, Bergoeing, Chazal, Debry, Roger Ducos, Martinel, Tallien, Daunou, Génissieu, Barras, Robert Lindet, Siéyès, 2.

5. EMIGRATION AND COUNTER-REVOLUTION: CHRONOLOGY

16–17 July 1789 First wave of the emigration: Artois, Condé, Conti, the Polignacs, etc, leave France. Artois establishes himself at Turin and sets about devising means of freeing Louis XVI and of fomenting insurrection in the provinces.

14 July 1789 Following the dismissal of Necker and the appointment of a reactionary council of ministers, revolt in Paris and the capture of the Bastille thwart a royal coup aimed probably at the dissolution of the EG.

July–Sept 1789 'Emigration of fear' (nobles terrorised by the Great Fear, etc).

5–6 Oct 1789 The *journées* of 5–6 Oct provoke a new wave of emigration.

19 Feb 1790 Execution of the marquis de Favras who had plotted, probably with the help of the comte de Provence, to rescue the king.

28 Apr 1790 The Constit Ass. accepts that German princes with possessions inside France which have suffered as a result of the overthrow of the feudal system should be compensated for their losses. Louis XVI secretly urges these *princes possessionnés* to refuse to come to terms.

May–June 1790 Protestant/Catholic conflict in S France (notably the bloody *bagarre de Nimes*, 13–14 June 1790), partly fomented by the *émigrés*, whose abortive 'Languedoc Plan' is planned to involve counter-rev insurrections in the Midi.

18 Aug 1790 Camp de Jalès: counter-rev demonstration in the Vivarais (repeated sporadically down to 1796).

Oct 1790 Publication in London of Edmund Burke's *Reflections on the Revolution in France.*

26 Nov 1790 Breteuil appointed Louis XVI's secret envoy towards the courts of Europe.

Dec 1790 Louis XVI conveys disapproval of *émigré* plans to invade France from the SE.

22 Dec 1790 Any *émigré* occupying a governmental post to lose his salary if not back in a month.

19 Feb–Mar 1791 Political furore caused by the emigration of the king's aunts ('Mesdames') to Turin.

28 Feb 1791 'Chevaliers des poignards' affair: threat of Louis's abduction by a gang of young nobles.

15 June 1791   *Emigré* troop units begin to be formed, notably under Artois at Coblenz.

21 June 1791   Flight to Varennes provokes the closure of frontiers, as the Nat Ass. decrees the arrest of all travellers wishing to leave France. Escape to Belgium of the comte de Provence. 1791 becomes the 'year of military emigration', as large numbers of officers emigrate, esp after June.

9 July 1791   *Emigrés* who did not return to France within one month to pay a three-fold tax load for 1791 (coupled with a triple imposition on annuities from 1 Aug).

10 July 1791   Holy Roman Emperor Leopold II sends circular letter to fellow monarchs suggesting concerted action against France.

27 Aug 1791   Pillnitz Declaration: Leopold II and Frederick William II of Prussia threaten intervention on behalf of Louis XVI (but commit themselves to nothing).

25 Sept 1791   Penal Code: death penalty for persons taking up arms against France.

30 Sept 1791   Constit Ass. declares a political amnesty (inc repeal of all previous anti-*emigré* legislation).

14 Oct 1791   Declaration of Louis XVI calling for the return of his brothers from emigration.

20 Oct 1791   Brissot in the Leg Ass. demands military action to disperse the *emigré* troop formations on the frontiers.

31 Oct 1791   Decree stripping Provence of his rights to regency (vetoed by the king, 11 Nov).

9 Nov 1791   Law against the *emigrés*: death for conspirators, inc those in emigration; sequestration of their property, etc (vetoed by the king, 11 Nov).

29 Nov 1791   Leg Ass. requests the king take diplomatic action to secure the dispersal of *emigré* troop units.

2 Jan 1792   Decree of impeachment against Provence, Artois, Condé, Calonne, etc.

14 Jan 1792   Complicity with the *emigrés* to be equated with *lèse-nation*.

18 Jan 1792   Provence stripped of his rights to regency.

9 Feb 1792   Sequestration of *emigré* land decreed.

25 Mar 1792   French government requests that the Holy Roman Emperor should cease arming the *emigrés* and should disperse their formations.

8 Apr 1792   Law on emigration codifying and extending existing laws.

20 Apr 1792   Declaration of war. The *emigré* forces support (feebly and from the rear) the Allied invasion of France.

Apr–Sept 1792   Legislation against the refractory clergy (6 Apr, 27 May, 26 Aug, etc) makes 1792 the 'year of clerical emigration'.

May 1792   La Rouerie conspiracy in W France discovered (execution of some of the conspirators, 18 June 1792).

17 July 1792   *Emigré* land (under state sequestration since 9 Feb) to be sold off as nat lands. Further details provided in a law of 2 Sept.

15 Aug 1792   Families of *émigrés* put under permanent surveillance.

30 Aug 1792   Relatives of *émigrés* debarred from holding public office.

2–6 Sept 1792   'September Massacres' in Paris trigger off further waves of emigration.

20 Sept 1792   Emigration sufficient grounds for a divorce.

23 Oct 1792   All *émigrés* banished in perpetuity. Death as outlaws if captured in France.

24 Oct 1792   Sequestration and sale of the movable property of *émigrés*.

26 Nov 1792   Returned *émigrés* are to leave Paris within 24 hours, to leave France within a week.

Jan 1793   On hearing of the execution of Louis XVI, Provence and the *émigrés* declare Louis's imprisoned son 'Louis XVII'; Provence is to be regent during the minority.
Prussia disbands the ineffectual *émigré* armies of the Princes and of the duc de Bourbon. Only Condé's force remains under arms.

14 Feb 1793   Bounty of 100 liv for capturing an *émigré*.

10 Mar 1793   Outbreak of the Vendée revolt: W France in a state of open insurrection for most of 1793–4, tying up large numbers of troops.
Establishment of the Rev Tribunal: emigration comes within its jurisdiction.

19 Mar 1793   Death penalty without appeal for rebels captured under arms. Applied esp rigorously in civil war zones, this law will be responsible for far more deaths than the Rev Tribunal.

26 Mar 1793   Law on the disarming of suspects (ex-nobles, etc).

28 Mar 1793   Codification of the laws against *émigrés*: the latter are regarded as legally deceased.

5 Apr 1793   After failing to persuade his troops to march on Paris and seize power, Dumouriez, CinC on the N front, defects to the enemy.

May–June 1793   Moderate coup in Lyon (29 May), while the Parisian *journées* of 31 May–2 June spark off the Federalist revolt.

3 June 1793   Emigré land to be sold in small lots, so as to benefit poorer peasants.

12–13 July 1793   Massacre of royalist supporters at Jalès ends a threatened insurrection in the Vivarais.

1 Aug 1793   Scorched earth policy in the Vendée decreed, as the civil war in the W reaches an esp. brutal phase.

8 Aug 1793   As the Federalist revolt is gradually overcome, the siege of Lyon, where 'Federalists' make common cause with 'royalists', begins. In Toulon too, federalism merges with royalism, and the rebels hand over the port and the French Mediterranean fleet to the British (29 Aug).

6 Sept 1793   Death for strangers spying in France.

17 Sept 1793   Law of Suspects: definition of suspects widened.

Oct 1793–Jan 1794   Containment of counter-rev in France: Lyon (9 Oct), and Toulon (18 Dec) fall; Vendéan forces defeated repeatedly, following the fiasco of the sortie to Granville to meet up with the British fleet (Oct–Nov). Large popular emigration of individuals fleeing punitive measures for involvement in federalism and counter-rev.

7 Dec 1793/17 frim II   The property of parents whose children have emigrated may be confiscated by the state.

13 March 1794/23 vent II   New police laws prohibit ex-nobles from living in Paris, frontier towns and ports.

20 Apr 1794/1 flor II   Refractory priests equated with *émigrés*.

June 1794/mess   Provence in Verona.

2 Aug 1794/15 therm II   Law banning ex-nobles from public office.

3 Aug 1794/16 therm II   Repeal of law of previous day which banned ex-nobles from public office.

Autumn 1794   Post-Thermidor emptying of the prisons: many nobles and royalists freed.

15 Nov 1794/25 brum III   Codification of anti-*émigré* legislation: the Thermidorian Convtn maintains existing statutes.

Feb–May 1795   Pacification of W France: peace treaties with rebel leaders.

11 Jan 1795/22 niv III   Amnesty accorded to peasants and workers from Alsace who had emigrated in Spring–Summer 1794 to avoid the Terror.

24 June 1795/6 mess III   Following the death in Paris of 'Louis XVII', Provence proclaims himself Louis XVIII and issues the Declaration of Verona, committing the *émigrés* to a semi-integral return to the AR.

June–July 1795   Quiberon Bay landing by *émigrés*, with British aid, is repulsed.

Mid 1795   Successful British overtures through the spy William Wickham to Pichegru, commander of the Army of the Rhine-and-Moselle. Pichegru's flirtation with treason and royalism will lead to his dismissal in March 1796.

6 Sept 1795/20 fruct III   Amnesty to individuals who emigrated to avoid proscription following the Federalist revolt (notably individuals from Toulon).

19 Sept 1795/3 jc III   Confirmation of laws against *émigrés*.

5 Oct 1795/13 vendém IV   'Vendémiaire rising' in Paris: royalist protest, soon crushed.

25 Oct 1795/3 brum IV   'Law of 3 Brumaire': public office is denied to *émigrés* and their relatives; anti-clerical legislation of 1792 and 1793 reimplemented.

26 Oct 1795/4 brum IV   As Convtn dissolves, a political amnesty is proclaimed, but pointedly excludes *émigrés* and those involved in the Vendémiaire rising.

1796   Publication of Joseph de Maistre's *Considérations sur la France* and Bonald's *Théorie du pouvoir politique et religieux dans la société française*.

16–17 Apr 1796/27–8 germ IV   Councils decree the death penalty for persons advocating the restoration of the monarchy.

26 July 1796/8 therm IV   Louis XVIII retires to Blankenburg, in the estates of the Duke of Brunswick. He distances himself from constitutional royalists in France, despite the success of the latter's electoral strategy.

4 Dec 1796/14 frim V   Law of 3 Brumaire IV reaffirmed as regards *émigrés* and their families (the clauses of the law relating to refractory priests are withdrawn). Former leaders of Chouan and Vendéan rebels excluded from public office.

30 Jan 1797/11 pluv V   Arrest of the royalist conspirator Brotier and his counter-rev cell.

27 June 1797/9 mess V   Following elections in which constitutional royalists have been particularly successful, the royalist majority in the councils repeals the Law of 3 Brumaire IV.

5 Sept 1797/19 fruct V   *Coup d'état* of Fructidor: the Law of 3 Brumaire IV is reimplemented; and royalist sympathisers are drummed out of the councils and of all walks of public life.

29 Nov 1797/9 frim VI   Ex-nobles to be regarded as foreigners, and debarred from public office.

1797/8   Publication of abbé Barruel's *Mémoires pour servir à l'histoire du jacobinisme.*

18 Jan 1798/29 niv VI   As royalism is forced into non-legal channels following the Fructidor coup, the councils repress brigandage by establishing special military commissions with jurisdiction over criminal outrages.

23 Feb 1798/5 vent VI   Former leaders of rebels against the state debarred from public office and voting rights.

13 March 1798/23 vent VI   Louis XVIII moves to Mitau, at the invitation of Czar Paul.

9 Nov 1798/19 brum VII   Individuals who received sentences *in absentia* following the Fructidor coup to be regarded as *émigrés* unless they return to be punished.

12 July 1799/24 mess VII   'Law of Hostages' confers collective responsibility on relatives of *émigrés* for treasonable acts committed in civil war conditions; the authorities may use relatives as 'hostages' in the event of counter-rev activity. (The law is little utilised.)

Summer–Autumn 1799   Largely abortive and fragmented counter-rev rising in S and W France: royalist insurrection in the Haute-Garonne is crushed (20 Aug); chouannerie recrudescent in the W.

6. THE *ÉMIGRÉS* (GREER 1951; VIDALENC 1963)

Number
Approx 130–150,000.

Volume of legislation relating to émigrés

1791	13	IV	34
1792 (before 10 Aug)	8	V	10
1792 (after 10 Aug)	30	VI	18
1793 (Jan–Sept)	51	VII	12
II	50	VIII	5
III	87		

Chronology of emigration (sample: 36 departments)
1789–92 31.4%   1793–9 68.6%

Social and gender analysis (sample: 97,545 *émigrés*, of whom 14,256 [14.6%] were women)

	No.	% of total	(women	as % of group)
Clergy	24,596	25.2	252	1.0
Nobility	16,431	16.8	2,506	15.3
Third Estate	56,518	58.0	11,498	20.3
of whom				
Upper middle class	10,792	11.1	1,525	14.1
Lower middle class	6,012	6.2	1,135	18.9
Working class	13,953	14.3	2,886	20.7
Peasants	18,910	19.4	4,687	24.8
Indeterminate	6,851	7.0	1,265	18.5

The military emigration (approx 10% of the total emigration according to a sample of 97,545 emigrés)

Noble officers	5,695	58.4%
Bourgeois officers	1,818	18.6%
Soldiers, sailors	2,237	23.0%
TOTAL	9,750	

Geographical analysis (sample: 129,099 *émigrés*)

	No. of depts	No. & % of émigrés	
Less than 500 *émigrés*	17	5,302	4.1
500–1000	26	17,727	13.7
1,000–2,000	27	38,604	29.9
2,000–3,000	10	22,566	17.5
Over 3,000 *émigrés*	7	44,900	34.8

7. THE POLITICAL PHYSIOGNOMY OF REVOLUTIONARY FRANCE

KEY (1) = Population in 1791 (*Archives parlementaires XXVI*)

(2) = Political orientation (L = Left, 1789–99; LR = Left, 1789–94, Right, 1795–9; R = Right, 1789–99; RL = Right, 1789–94, Left 1795–9) (*Hunt 1984*)

(3) = Major political options in the Rev decade: C = area of chouannerie; F = region where the Federalist revolt was most long-lasting; I = depts invaded by or threatened by foreign invasion; R = depts outside the Vendée area where popular royalism most marked; V = depts involved in the Vendée revolt and its repression

(4) = Proportion of clergy swearing the oath for the Civ Constn, 1791 (figures for Summer where known; otherwise Spring) (*Tackett 1986*)

(5) = Number of place-name changes involving rev names (esp 1792–5) (*Figuères 1901*)

(6) = Number of *armées révolutionnaires*, 1793–4 (*Cobb 1961, 1963*)

(7) = Results of plebiscite of 1793 concerning the Constitution of 1793 (A = fewer yes-votes than other votes; B = twice the average number of votes cast against the constitution, in favour but with amendments, or abstentions; C = above average for the same categories; X = unanimity or near-unanimity in favour of the constitution (*Baticle 1909–10*)

(8) = Number of *émigrés* (*Greer 1951*)

(9) = Number of capital executions under the Terror (*Greer 1935*)

(10) = Results of plebiscite of Year III on the constitution: x = sizeable opposition recorded; O = elections not properly held because of civil disturbances (*Lajusan 1911*)

(11) = Results of the Year IV elections: CR = royalist or counter-rev; R = right-wing; I = uncommitted or divided; L = left-wing; J = Jacobin; blank = unreliable results (*Suratteau 1971*)

(12) = Results of the Year V elections: CR = counter-rev depts where the results were annulled; R = right-wing; D = divided; I = undecided; L = left-wing; J = Jacobin (*Suratteau 1971*)

(13) = Results of the Year VI elections: G = strong pro-government majority; J = strong Jacobin majority; GJ = pro-government majority, and substantial Jacobin minority; D = divided (*Suratteau 1971*)

(Note: for full list of departments, see below VII, 6).

	(1)	(2)	(3)	(4)	(5)	(6)	(7)	(8)	(9)	(10)	(11)	(12)	(13)
Ain	307,756	LR	F	84	28		B	660	6		R	CR	GJ
Aisne	407,904	R		77	47			1,128	5	x		I	G
Allier	267,126	L		86	46	1		340	4	x	R	I	J
B-Alpes	168,937	L		87	33	9	B	510	NIL		I	I	GJ
H-Alpes	120,485	RL		89	47	2	A	105	NIL		L	D	J
Alpes-M		LR	I		4		X	3,000	9		R	R	GJ
Ardèche	289,671	R	R	49	86		C	451	20	x	CR	CR	J
Ardennes	247,612	L	I	66	35			1,201	12		J	L	G
Ariège	197,889	L		65	9	1		480	4	x	J	CR	J
Aube	228,885	L		64	39	1		728	NIL	x	R	CR	D
Aude	239,642	L		58	8		B	759	1	x	L	I	D
Aveyron	371,835	LR	R	24	31	1	B	597	36		CR	CR	G
B-du-Rh	466,045	LR	FR	49	15	4	X	5,125	409	x	CR	CR	J
Calvds	391,332	R	FC	37	23		X	2,080	7		R	CR	G
Cantal	239,972	R	R	54	11	1	B	709	11	x		I	G
Charente	339,789	LR		70	8		X	633	3		R	CR	GJ
Char-Inf	438,042	L	V	62	142		C	1,335	107		L	L	G
Cher	207,541	R		77	39	1		239	6	x	R	CR	G
Corrèze	269,767	L		47	52		C	807	9	x	L	D	J
Corse	247,776		I	92	NIL			43	NIL			J	D
Cte-d'Or	342,986	LR		62	90			1,781	28			CR	D
Ctes-Nd	523,880	R	FC	23	24		B	2,575	32	O		CR	G
Creuse	238,352	L		75	17			280	3		J	L	G
Dordgne	438,343	L		68	35		C	2,000	21		L	CR	J
Doubs	219,642	LR	I	24	11			1,930	75	x	R	I	J
Drôme	246,687	RL		84	22	1		632	2	x	D	D	G
Eure	385,206	R	F	60	25	1		1,112	4	x	R	CR	GJ
Eure-L	256,656	R		85	29	1	X	760	1	x	CR	CR	G
Finstre	285,730	R	FC	19	9	1	B	2,086	80	O		I	GJ
Gard	313,464	R	F	28	88		X	638	136	x		I	D
Ht-Gne	456,555	L		40	49	2		1,157	45	x	J	J	J
Gers	315,854	L		36	71		C	611	12	x	L	J	GJ
Gironde	497,391	LR	FR	55	18	1	B	1,186	299		R	CR	G
Hérault	290,126	R		44	36	2		659	36		R	CR	GJ
I-Vilaine	519,619	R	VFC	17	18		B	2,072	509		R	CR	G
Indre	229,768	R		84	61		X	277	4	x	I	R	GA
Indre-L	272,925	LR		58	42	1		551	22	x	CR	CR	GJ
Isère	365,380	L		82	45	2		632	3		R	I	G
Jura	280,200	RL	F	45	24		A	910	2		I	D	GJ
Landes	257,387	LR	I	35	16	1		586	31		R	I	J
Loir-Cher	200,277	LR		64	58			385	3	x	CR	R	J
Ht-Loire	216,250	LR	R	43	78	1	X	271	52	x	CR	CR	G
Loire-Inf	331,270	R	V	22	20	1	C	1,750	3,548	O	I	CR	G
Loiret	285,775	R		91	16	1	X	520	4	x	CR	CR	G
Lot	443,667	R		42	17	2	B	569	13		CR	CR	GJ
Lot-Gne	411,808	L		77	11	1	B	1,610	5		L	L	GJ

	(1)	(2)	(3)	(4)	(5)	(6)	(7)	(8)	(9)	(10)	(11)	(12)	(13)
Lozère	142,110	R	R	16	16		C	338	87	O	CR	R	G
Mne-Lre	455,500	RL	VC	39	33		X	1,643	1,886	O	L	I	GJ
Manche	463,320	R	F	49	22			2,005	61		I	CR	G
Marne	348,885	LR		69	127	1	X	1,040	7	x	R	CR	GJ
Ht-Mne	223,010	LR		61	11			759	2	x	R	I	G
Mayenne	323,607	R	FC	26	17			3,253	495	O	I	CR	G
Meurthe	321,161	RL	I	45	41		X	1,544	10	x	I	L	G
Meuse	268,108	R	I	80	6			1,640	14	x	I	I	G
Morbihan	281,565	R	VC	9	8	1	B	1,353	37			CR	G
Moselle	328,365	LR	I	32	9	1		3,827	45	x	CR	CR	GJ
Nièvre	235,699	L		66	36	2	X	344	2	x		I	J
Nord	447,910	L	I	15	21	1	X	2,635	157		J	CR	D
Oise	348,972	LR		79	62			732	12	x	R	CR	G
Orne	381,760	R	V	44	36			1,870	187		R	CR	G
Pas-Cal	532,739	R	I	17	76		X	2,260	392		CR	CR	D
Puy-Dôme	516,593	L	R	41	41	1		840	17	x	J	CR	J
Ht-Pyr	188,690	L		77	10	1	B	391	5	x	L	D	J
B-Pyr	188,389	R	I	40	21	1		449	50	x	R	R	J
Pyr-Or	114,158	R	I	29	6		X	3,854	48	x	–	I	G
B-Rhin	415,080	LR	I	9	3	1	X	20,510	54	x	CR	CR	G
Ht-Rhin	283,252	R		40	4	1		2,746	12		L	CR	G
Rh-Loire	591,306	R	FR	83	96								
(Rhône)								332	1,880		CR	CR	D
(Loire)								105	87		R	CR	J
Hte-Saône	264,111	R		35	13			889	NIL		R	CR	G
Sne-Lre	442,600	LR		61	136	1		1,052	6		R	CR	D
Sarthe	347,837	L	VC	?	30			1,090	225		J	CR	J
Seine	647,472	–		66	28	1	X	2,069	2,639	x	CR	CR	J
Seine-Inf	536,400	R	V	49	58		X	2,038	9		R	CR	G
Sne-Mne	296,467	R		69	48		B	623	NIL	x	CR	CR	D
Sne-Oise	471,612	R		81	64		C	1,598	5	x	CR	CR	GJ
D-Sèvres	259,122	L	V	77	12			1,200	103		D	L	G
Somme	407,352	L		59	10		X	1,286	2	x	CR	CR	G
Tarn	289,148	L	R	16	21	1	B	846	9		L	CR	G
Var	275,472	LR	FR	90	13			5,331	309		CR	CR	GJ
Vaucluse		LR	F	–	13	1		1,275	442	x	CR	CR	GJ
Vendée	305,610	L	V	33	84			1,142	1,616	O	L	L	G
Vienne	257,953	L		65	12		X	1,710	33		D	D	GJ
Ht-Vienne	266,910	RL		65	25	1		1,165	13		J	J	J
Vosges	289,054	RL		63	26			567	10		L	J	G
Yonne	364,969	LR		85	33		C	472	2		CR	CR	G

VII. ADMINISTRATION, JUSTICE
AND FINANCE

1. ADMINISTRATION, JUSTICE AND POLICE: CHRONOLOGY

22 June 1787   Prov assemblies introduced by Loménie de Brienne into all *pays d'élection*:

- each parish to have a municipality composed of *curé*, seigneur and members elected from among those inhabitants paying 30 liv in taxes; inhabitants paying 10 liv in taxes are eligible to vote
- *élection* and prov assemblies at higher levels
- one prov ass. in each généralité
- election from 1790: in the interim, half of prov assemblies to be designated by the king, and the other half coopted
- the number of members from the Third Estate in prov assemblies to be equal to the numbers from the other two orders combined.

8 May 1788   'May Edicts': abolition of Parls (reversed Aug), abolition of torture, etc.

Mid 1789   'Municipal Revolution'. Overthrow of AR municipal government in major urban centres. The rev in local government is complemented by the diffusion of the Nat Guard.

28 July 1789   Establishment of a 'Search Committee' (*Comité des recherches*) to investigate crimes of *lèse-nation* (from 21 Oct 1789 to 25 Oct 1790, these are referred to the Paris Châtelet court).

4– 5 Aug 1789   'Night of 4 Aug': destruction of venal office, prov and municipal privilege, etc.

10–13 Aug 1789   Municipalities empowered to call in regular troops and the *maréchaussée* when public order is threatened.

26 Aug 1789   Declaration of the Rights of Man: implies the complete overhaul of the judicial system.

10 Oct 1789   Committee chaired by Thouret reports on interim changes in criminal procedures: publicity for all judicial procedures, including sentencing; judges to operate alongside selected *notables*; accused to appear before a judge within 24 hours; rights of defence counsels extended; abolition of all forms of torture.

21 Oct 1789   Martial law decree: the right of local authorities to declare martial law and call in troops when public order is threatened is confirmed and codified.

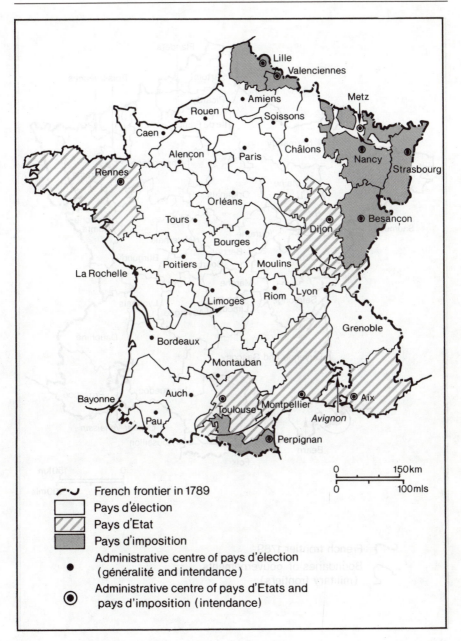

Map 2   The administrative regions of Ancien Régime France.

207

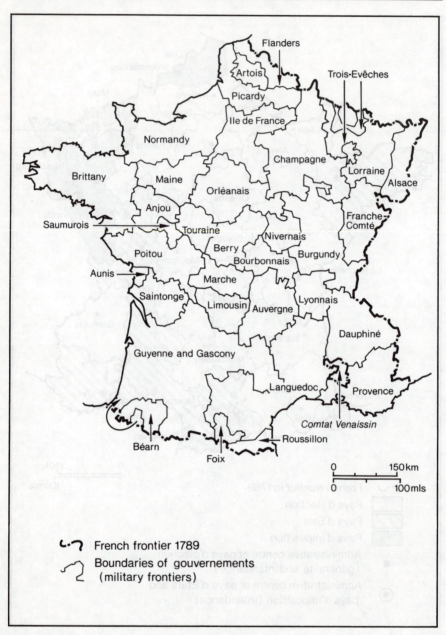

French frontier 1789
Boundaries of gouvernements
(military frontiers)

Map 3   The provinces of Ancien Régime France.

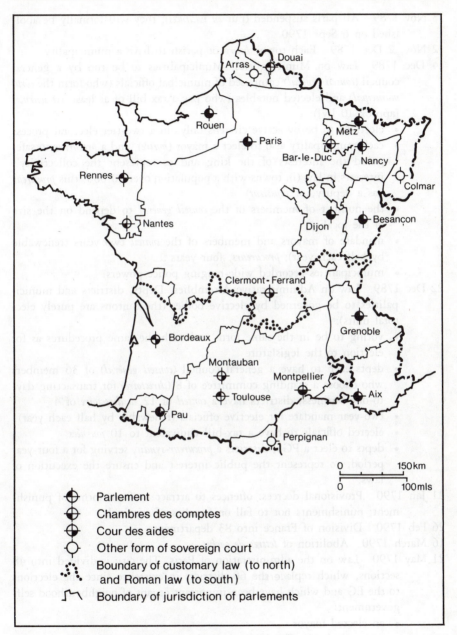

Map 4   Judicial organisation of Ancien Régime France.

3 Nov 1789   All parls suspended (put *en vacances*); they will formally be abolished on 6 Sept 1790.

12 Nov, 2 Dec 1789   Each town, *bourg* or parish to have a municipality.

14 Dec 1789   Law on Municipalities. Municipalities to be run by a general council (*conseil général*) composed of municipal officials (who form the *corps municipal*) and elected notables (who pay a tax-bill of at least 10 *journées* [approx 10 liv]):

- elections to be by active citizens only, in a two-tier electoral process
- each municipality also to elect a mayor (*maire*), and a *procureur* to safeguard the interests of the king and to represent the collectivity's interests in law (in towns with a population over 10,000, this *procureur* has a deputy, or *substitut*)
- the number of members of the *conseil général* to depend on the size of the locality
- mandate of mayors and members of the *conseil* two years (renewable by half each year); *procureurs,* four years
- municipalities accorded wide-ranging police powers.

22 Dec 1789   Law on Administrative Assemblies. Depts, districts and municipalities to be governed by elective bodies (the cantons are purely electoral units):

- voting to be in the same form and with the same procedures as for election to the legislature
- depts each to have a general council (*conseil général*) of 36 members who choose a standing committee of 8 (*directoire*) for transacting day-to-day business; districts have a *conseil* of 12, a *directoire* of 4
- two-year mandate for elective officials (renewable by half each year)
- elected officials to have a tax-bill equivalent to 10 *journées*
- depts to elect a PGS, districts a *procureur-syndic,* serving for a four-year period, to represent the public interest and ensure the execution of laws.

21 Jan 1790   Provisional decrees: offences to attract uniform forms of punishment; punishments not to fall on families of criminals.

26 Feb 1790   Division of France into 83 departments.

16 March 1790   Abolition of *lettres de cachet*.

21 May 1790   Law on the administration of Paris. The city is divided into 48 sections, which replace the 60 districts in existence since the elections to the EG and which have been important organs of neighbourhood self-government:

- an elected mayor
- mayor and 16 officials form the *bureau administratif* which transacts essential business
- 32 other elected officials form the *corps municipal*
- the above officials plus 96 elected notables (2 per section) form the *conseil général* (144 members in all)

- two-year mandate (renewable by half each year)
- each of the 48 sections has a police commissioner (*commissaire de police*) elected for two years. These are assisted by 16 citizen-deputies (*commissaires de section*) in each section.

16–24 Aug 1790 Decree on judicial organisation (following protracted debates since March):

- JPs on the English model introduced: one per canton, elected for two years by active citizens; to try cases up to the value of 50 liv, and cases on appeal up to 100 liv
- tribunal of five judges in districts, elected from among lawyers and judges over 30 years old with 5 years legal experience: for cases up to 1,000 liv, and for cases on appeal from other districts and from JPs
- judges for commercial tribunals elected by all traders and merchants
- 'family tribunals' for family-related cases
- the principle established that all cases should go to conciliation and arbitration before reaching the courts; cantonal *bureaux de paix* of six citizens chosen for two years to effect conciliation.

6 Sept 1790 Suppression of all AR courts, including the parls.

12 Oct 1790 Law on criminal procedure: criminal courts at district level; appointment of public prosecutors, etc.

22–4 Dec 1790, 16 Jan and 16 Feb 1791 Suppression of the *maréchaussée*, and its replacement as state police force by the Gendarmerie Nationale.

20 Jan 1791 Criminal courts established: one per dept, staffed by three judges drawn from among district judges, plus a public prosecutor serving for six years and a president, both elected by active citizens.

15 March 1791 Decree on local government: organisation and procedures.

19–22 July 1791 Law on municipal police: organisation and procedures.

26 July 1791 Law on 'seditious meetings' (= meetings of 15 individuals opposing the execution of a law or judgment).

3 Sept 1791 Constitution of 1791: emphasis on the separation of powers: e.g. judicial office-holders are disqualified from holding legislative or executive posts.

16–19 Sept 1791 Decree on the organisation of criminal justice: trial by jury; a district court judge appointed *directeur du jury* to investigate any case coming before it; the accused then passes before a *jury d'accusation* (12 citizens drawn from among active citizens), to see if there is a case to answer; the case can then go on to the dept criminal court, where the public prosecutor assumes charge of the prosecution.

21 Sept 1791 Law on the police of Paris.

22 Sept 1791 The system of *commissaires de police* established in Paris in May 1790 may be extended to provincial cities 'where adjudged necessary' (only the largest cities take any action).

25 Sept 1791 Penal Code: 'imaginary crimes' (heresy, magic, blasphemy, etc) erased from the list of crimes; uniform punishments for the same offence; scale of punishments, ranging from death by public decapitation to forced labour up to 24 years (*fers*), solitary confinement (*reclusion*), detention, deportation, loss of civil status and the stocks (*carcan*); the practice of branding is abolished.

28 Sept 1791 Law on police in the countryside.

25 Nov 1791 Creation of a *Comité de surveillance* in the Leg Ass., to investigate *lèse-nation* (its powers will be extended after the outbreak of war on 10 Apr 1792).

20–25 Mar 1792 The guillotine is accepted as the means of public execution. (It will be used for the first time on 25 Apr.)

4 July 1792 Law on *la patrie en danger:* when the Leg Ass. declares the fatherland to be in danger, municipalities are allowed emergency powers including wide-ranging rights of surveillance.

11 July 1792 *La patrie en danger* is declared and the law of 4 July put into execution.

9–10 Aug 1792 Overthrow of the Paris Commune: establishment of the Commune insurrectionnelle.

11 Aug 1792 Following the overthrow of the king, municipalities are entrusted with responsibility for the repression of acts threatening the security of the state.

Commune insurrectionnelle suspends the *directoire* of the dept of Paris. The Leg Ass. creates a new, provisional *directoire,* but under pressure allows the Commune to prevail. (The Commune will remain a power in the land through to Sept/Oct.)

17 Aug 1792 'Extraordinary Tribunal' established to try individuals for counter-rev offences committed on 10 Aug. (It achieves little, and is disbanded, 29 Nov.)

Aug–Oct 1792 Spontaneous and semi-legal purges of judicial, dept, district and municipal administrations throughout France, and the introduction of good 'patriots'.

27 Aug 1792 Deliberations of administrative bodies to be in public (except for security matters).

2 Sept 1792 Leg Ass. decrees: *Conseil général* of the Commune to be 288 members; the powers which the latter has assumed since 10 Aug are confirmed.

14 Sept 1792 No municipality is to have authority outside its constituency (an act directed against the presumptions of the Paris Commune).

22 Sept 1792 Convtn confirms the judicial and administrative purges which have taken place throughout France since 10 Aug. Judicial office opened to all citizens regardless of legal experience. New elections are called for local office, etc.

2 Oct 1792 Establishment of a CGS: this will control police activity throughout the Terror and for some time after, notably through the *comités de surveillance* established at local level on 21 Mar 1793.

29 Oct 1792 Election to administrative bodies to be by manhood suffrage.

24 Nov 1792 Elections decreed for the Commune. (These are held on 28–29 Nov and result in a Montagnard victory. The new Commune sits from 2 Dec.)

5 Feb 1793 All state functionaries must produce a valid *certificat de civisme*.

Mar–Sept 1793 Main apparatus of the Terror erected (e.g. creation of Rev Tribunal, 10 Mar).

21, 26 Mar 1793 Municipalities allowed to deliver *certificats de civisme* and to disarm ex-nobles, priests and suspects.

From 2 June 1793 'Federalist Crisis': numerous dept *directoires* throughout France protest at the *journée* of 2 June and the purge of Girondin deputies. This is followed by administrative purges, normally performed by reps *en mission,* with Montagnard nominees assuming office.

23 June 1793 Abolition of the hated martial law provisions of 21 Oct 1789.

15 Aug 1793 All state functionaries are obliged to take the 'Liberty–Equality' oath.

4 Dec 1793/14 frim II 'Law of 14 Frimaire' on rev govt: powers of depts reduced; districts are promoted to the major role in the surveillance of rev legislation; *agents nationaux* introduced at district and municipal level; purges to be conducted of all administrative bodies by reps *en mission.* A new wave of reps is sent out to enforce this law on 29 Dec/9 niv.

22 Dec 1793/2 niv II No property qualification for membership of juries.

7 Jan 1794/18 niv II Law on police and general security: districts may appoint to vacant JP posts during the Rev Govt.

16 Apr 1794/27 germ II Law on rev police: creation of the CPS's Police Bureau.

10 June 1794/22 prair II 'Law of 22 Prairial': streamlining of the Rev Tribunal.

27 July 1794/9 therm II Wholesale repression of personnel of the Paris Commune in the wake of the overthrow of Robespierre: nearly 100 members of the Commune follow Robespierre to the scaffold.

1 Aug 1794/14 therm II Repeal of the Law of 22 Prairial.

10 Aug, 28 Dec 1794/23 therm II, 8 niv III Reorganisation and reduction of the powers of the Rev Tribunal.

24 Aug 1794/7 fruct III Reorganisation of the committees of government: local administrative bodies report to the Legislation Committee, not the CGS.

31 Aug 1794/14 fruct II Law on the Paris Commune: the Commune's powers are shared out between *ad hoc* committees and the administrative commissions which have since Apr 1794 replaced the ministries.

28 Sept 1794/7 vendém III Committee of Legislation is allowed to designate replacements on the *directoire* of the Paris dept and other dept administrations.

19 Feb 1795/1 vent III   The *directoires* of dept administrations to comprise five members; the *conseils généraux* of districts prohibited from holding permanent sessions.

11 March 1795/21 vent III   *Commissaires de police* in Paris and prov cities to be appointed by the CGS and not elected.

14 Mar 1795/24 vent III   Legislation Committee may appoint administrators and municipal officials, etc.

10 Apr 1795/21 germ III   Following the Germinal *journées* (1–2 Apr), a public order law effectively reintroduces martial law provisions.

17 Apr 1795/28 germ III   Law of 14 Frimaire II on rev govt repealed: powers of depts prior to 1792 restored; they are to have a PGS (though no *conseil général*) and to report to the Legislation Committee; they exercise control over districts, which now have a *procureur-syndic* instead of an *agent national*. Municipalities also lose their *agents nationaux*.

31 May 1795/12 prair III   Abolition of the Rev Tribunal.

27 June 1795/9 mess III   The Paris Nat Guard and Gendarmerie division are merged into a single Police Legion (*Légion de Police générale*) (disbanded following babouvist infiltration on 30 Apr 1796/11 flor IV).

22 Aug 1795/5 fruct III   Constitution of Year III: complete reorganisation of local authorities, with elections by property franchise:

- *departments: directoires* to comprise five elected members, renewable by one-fifth each year, and responsible to the government; a *commissaire*, appointed by the Directory, is attached to each department (a kind of embryonic prefect with powers to ensure the enforcement of legislation)
- *districts:* abolished
- *cantons* (given some administrative functions for the first time): an elected president, and a *commissaire* of the Directory
- *municipalities:* no municipalities in communes with less than 5,000 inhabitants, local authority passing instead to an *agent municipal* and *adjoint* elected by the inhabitants; communes with a population up to 100,000 have an administration of between five and nine elected officials; in communes over 100,000, municipal powers are split between constituencies of between 30,000 and 50,000 inhabitants, with a *bureau central* performing any necessary coordination. The larger communes have a Directorial *commissaire* attached to them. All mandates are for two years
- Paris is divided into 12 municipal *arrondissements*, each with its own mayor. Coordination takes place through a *bureau central*
- some changes in judicial organisation.

11 Oct 1795/19 vendém IV   Municipalities take over from the CGS the right to appoint *commissaires de police* (from 1800, this power will be assumed by the central government through the system of prefects established by the law of 17 Feb 1800/28 pluv VIII).

Establishment of *commissions de police* in designated prov cities; and of coordinating police committees in Paris and the largest cities.

Winding down of the Paris sections, prior to the new constitution coming into effect.

25 Oct 1795/3 brum IV   Revised code of punishments: based on 1791 provisions, with some modifications.

26 Oct 1795/4 brum IV   Amnesty law for all individuals accused of crimes of a political nature (with the exception of those involved in the 13 vendém *journée,* deported priests and counterfeiters of assignats).

12 Dec 1795/22 frim IV   Directory may appoint to vacant judicial posts.

16 Dec 1795/25 frim IV   Directors may designate communal *agents municipaux* and *adjoints* in communes with a population less than 5,000.

2 Jan 1796/12 niv IV   Creation of a Police Minister (*Ministre de Police générale*).

12 Jan/22 niv–30 Mar 1796/10 germ IV   Directory institutes large numbers of personnel changes in local government.

29 Feb 1796/9 vent IV   Abolition of family courts.

19 Apr 1797/30 germ IV   Reform of judicial organisation.

From 4 Sept 1797/18 fruct V   Fructidorian purges of local government.

18 Jan 1798/29 niv VI   Military commissions created to deal with brigandage.

17 Apr 1798/28 germ VI   Reorganisation of the gendarmerie, whose ranks have been severely depleted by successive waves of incorporation into the army.

2. THE 'MUNICIPAL REVOLUTION', 1789

Overthrow of AR forms of municipal government in most major urban centres. Power passed either to a rev committee or was shared between a committee and delegates of the former municipality. The new bodies maintained order through some form of 'bourgeois militia' (later, Nat Guard). The earliest major example was at Marseille in Feb 1789, though most other change-overs occurred in the wake of the political crisis of July 1789. The Constit Ass. introduced the elective system and regulated forms of local government from Dec 1789.

The 'Municipal Rev' in 30 major cities (*Hunt 1976*):

   (i) *Cities where committees assumed power*

Clermont-Ferrand	Lille
Grenoble	Toulouse

   (ii) *Cities with power-sharing arrangements*

Angers	Orléans
Brest	Paris
Caen	Poitiers
Dijon	Rennes
Marseille	Rouen
Metz	Strasbourg
Montauban	Tours
Nantes	Troyes

   (iii) *Cities unaffected*

Amiens	Montpellier
Besançon	Nancy
Bordeaux	Nîmes
Limoges	Reims
Lyon	Toulon

3. MAYORS OF PARIS, 1789–1794

Bailly, 15 July 1789–19 Sept 1791
Appointed in the first instance by the Nat Ass. Elected 2 Aug 1790 by 12,550 out of approx 14,000 votes. Resigned.

Pétion, 19 Nov 1791–18 Oct 1792
Voting 1791: Pétion, 6,708; Lafayette, 3,123; d'André, 77; etc. Suspended from his post 6 July 1792 by the *directoire* of the dept of Paris for his alleged incompetence in handling popular disturbances on the *journée* of 20 June. Restored by the Leg Ass. following pressure from the Paris Commune, 13 July. Re-elected 9 Oct 1792, Pétion preferred to take up a place as deputy in the Convtn.

Chambon de Montaux, 1 Dec 1792–4 Feb 1793
Voting: Chambon, 3,682; Lhuillier, 2,491; etc. Resigned.

Pache, 15 Feb 1793–10 May 1794/21 flor II
Voting: Pache, 11,881; Roederer, 1,118; Roland, 494; etc (15,191 votes cast). Dismissed by CPS.

Fleuriot-Lescot, 10 May/21 flor II–27 July 1794/9 therm II
CPS nomination. A victim of the *journée* of 9 Thermidor.

4. THE PARIS DISTRICTS, 1789–90

Created as electoral divisions by the royal regulation of 13 Apr 1789. The districts became an integral part of municipal government until their suppression by the decree of 21 May 1790 which created a new network of agencies of local government, the sections.

1. Saint-André-des-Arts
2. Cordeliers
3. Carmes Déchaussés
4. Prémontrés
5. Saint-Honoré
6. Saint-Roch
7. Jacobins Saint-Honoré
8. Saint-Philippe-du-Roule
9. Abbaye de Saint-Germain
10. Petits-Augustins
11. Jacobins-Saint-Dominique
12. Théatins
13. Saint-Louis en l'Isle
14. Saint-Nicolas-du-Chardonnet
15. Saint-Victor
16. Blancs-Manteaux
17. Capucins du Marais
18. Enfants-Rouges
19. Pères-de-Nazareth
20. Saint-Etienne-du-Mont
21. Val-de-Grâce
22. Saint-Marcel
23. Saint-Nicolas-des-Champs
24. Sainte-Elisabeth
25. Filles-Dieu
26. Saint-Laurent
27. Barnabites
28. Notre-Dame
29. Saint-Séverin
30. Saint-Germain-de-l'Auxerrois
31. Oratoire
32. Feuillants
33. Capucins Saint-Honoré
34. Saint-Eustache
35. Petits-Pères
36. Filles-Saint-Thomas
37. Capucins-Chaussée-d'Antin
38. Mathurins
39. Sorbonne
40. Saint-Jacques-du-Haut-Pas
41. Petit-Saint-Antoine
42. Minimes de la Place Royale
43. Madeleine-de-Traisnel
44. Sainte-Marguerite
45. Grands-Augustins
46. Saint-Jacques-l'Hôpital
47. Bonne-Nouvelle
48. Saint-Lazare
49. Saint-Jean-en-Grève
50. Saint-Gervais
51. Saint-Louis-la-Culture
52. Enfants-Trouvés
53. Saint-Merry
54. Sépulcre
55. Saint-Martin-des-Champs
56. Pères-Récollets
57. Saint-Jacques-la-Boucherie
58. Saint-Leu
59. Saint-Magloire
60. Saint-Joseph

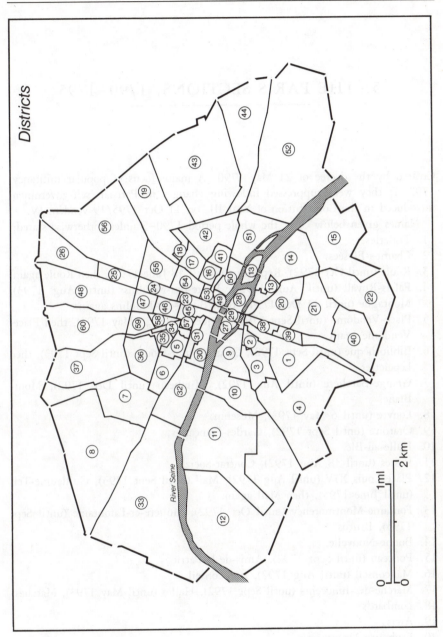

Map 5(a)   Districts of Paris, 1789–90.

5. THE PARIS SECTIONS, 1790–1795

Created by the decree of 21 May 1790. A major focus of popular militancy, 1792–4, they were suppressed following changes in Parisian self-government introduced in the Constitution of Year III, on 11 Oct 1795/19 vendém IV.

Names given below cover the whole period 1790–5 unless otherwise stated.
1. Tuileries.
2. Champs-Elysées.
3. Roule (until Oct 1792), République (until 18 June 1795), then Roule again.
4. Palais-Royal (until Aug 1792), Butte-des-Moulins (until Aug 1793), Montagne (until 11 Dec 1794), then Butte-des-Moulins again.
5. Place-Vendôme (until Sept 1792), Piques (until 23 May 1795), then Place-Vendôme again.
6. Bibliothèque (until Sept 1792), Quatre-Vingt-Douze (until Sept 1793), then Lepeletier.
7. Grange-Batelière (until Aug 1792), Mirabeau (until Dec 1792), Mont-Blanc.
8. Louvre (until 6 May 1793), Muséum.
9. Oratoire (until Sept 1792), Gardes-Françaises.
10. Halle-au-Blé.
11. Postes (until 18 Aug 1792), Contrat-Social.
12. Place Louis XIV (until Aug 1792), Mail (until Sept 1793), Guillaume-Tell (until June 1795), then Mail again.
13. Fontaine-Montmorency (until Oct 1792), Molière-et-Lafontaine (until Sept 1793), Brutus.
14. Bonne-Nouvelle.
15. Ponceau (until Sept 1792), Amis-de-la-Patrie.
16. Mauconseil (until Aug 1792), Bon-conseil.
17. Marché-des-Innocents (until Sept 1792), Halles (until May 1793), Marchés.
18. Lombards.
19. Arcis.
20. Faubourg-Montmartre.
21. Rue Poissonnière, or Faubourg Possoinnière.
22. Bondy.
23. Temple.
24. Popincourt.

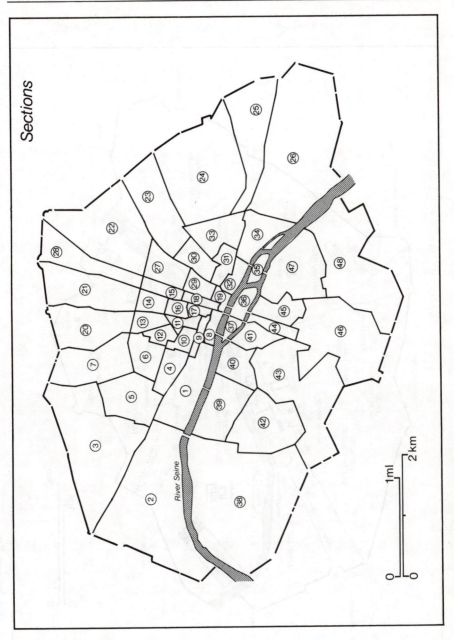

Sections

River Seine

1 ml
2 km

Map 5(b) Sections of Paris, 1790–95.

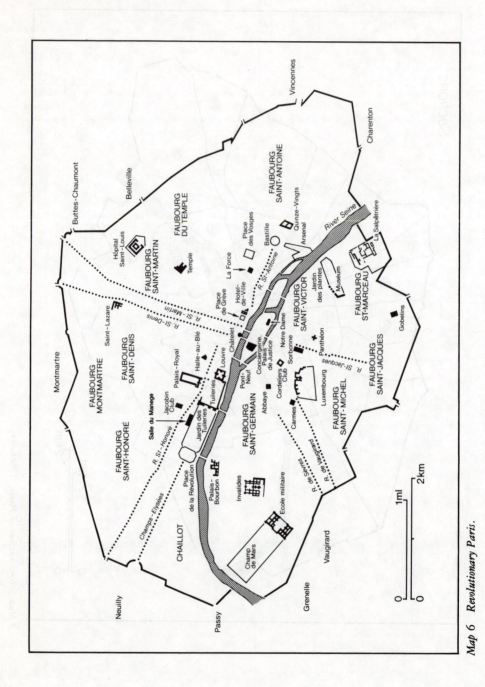

Map 6 Revolutionary Paris.

25. Rue de Montreuil.
26. Quinze-Vingts.
27. Gravilliers.
28. Faubourg-Saint-Denis (until Jan 1793), Faubourg-du-Nord.
29. Beaubourg (until Sept 1792), Réunion.
30. Enfants-Rouges (until Sept 1792), Marais (until June 1793), Homme-Armé.
31. Roi-de-Sicile (until Aug 1792), Droits-de-l'Homme.
32. Hôtel-de-Ville (until 21 Aug 1792), Maison-Commune (until Sept 1794), Fidélité.
33. Place-Royale (until Aug 1792), Fédérés (until 4 July 1793), Indivisibilité.
34. Arsenal.
35. Ile-Saint-Louis (until Nov 1792), Fraternité.
36. Notre-Dame or Ile (until Aug 1792), Cité (until 11 Nov 1793), Raison (until 25 Nov 1793 [*sic*]), then Cité again.
37. Henri IV (until 14 Aug 1792), Pont-Neuf (until 7 Sept 1793), Révolutionnaire (until 30 Nov 1794), then Pont-Neuf again.
38. Invalides.
39. Fontaine-de-Grenelle.
40. Quatre-Nations (until Apr 1793), Unité.
41. Théâtre-français (until Aug 1792), Marseille (until Aug 1793), Marseille-et-Marat (until Jan 1794), Marat (until Feb 1795), then Théâtre-Français again.
42. Croix-Rouge (until 3 Oct 1793), Bonnet-Rouge (until March 1795), Bonnet-de-la-Liberté (until May 1795), Ouest.
43. Luxembourg (until Oct 1793), Mutius-Scaevola (until May 1795), then Luxembourg again.
44. Thermes-de-Julien (until 8 Sept 1792), Beaurepaire (until 8 Feb 1794), Chalier (until Jan 1795), then Thermes-de-Julien again.
45. Sainte-Geneviève (until Aug 1792), Panthéon-Français.
46. Observatoire.
47. Jardin-des-Plantes (until Aug 1792), Sans-Culottes (until 28 Feb 1794), then Jardin-des-Plantes again.
48. Gobelins (until Aug 1792), Finistère.

6. DEPARTMENTS AND DISTRICTS

The name of the *chef-lieu* of each dept is given first, in **bold italic** type.

Ain. ***Bourg,*** Belley, Châtillon-sur-Chalaronne, Gex, Montluel, Nantua, Pont-de-Vaux, Saint-Rambert, Trévoux.

Aisne. ***Laon,*** Château-Thierry, Chauny, Saint-Quentin, Soissons, Vervins.

Allier. ***Moulins,*** Cérilly, Cusset, Le Donjon, Gannat, Montluçon, Montmarault.

Basses-Alpes. ***Digne,*** Barcelonnette, Castellane, Forcalquier, Sisteron.

Hautes-Alpes. ***Gap,*** Briançon, Embrun, Sèvres.

Alpes-Maritimes (created 4 Feb 1793). ***Nice,*** Menton, Puget-Théniers.

Ardèche. ***Privas,*** Coiron, Mezenc, Tanargue.

Ardennes. ***Charleville,*** Grandpré, Rethel, Rocroy, Sedan, Vouziers.

Ariège. ***Foix,*** Mirepoix, Saint-Girons, Tarascon-sur-Ariège.

Aube. ***Troyes,*** Arcis-sur-Aube, Bar-sur-Aube, Bar-sur-Seine, Evry, Nogent-sur-Seine.

Aude. ***Carcassonne,*** Castelnaudary, La Grasse, Limoux, Narbonne, Quillan.

Aveyron. ***Rodez,*** Aubin, Millau, Mur-de-Barrez, Saint-Affrique, Saint-Geniez, Sauveterre, Sévérac-le-Château, Villefranche-de-Rouergue.

Bec-d'Ambès, see GIRONDE.

Bouches-du-Rhône. ***Aix-en-Provence,*** Arles, Marseille, Salon, Tarascon (see also VAUCLUSE).

Calvados. ***Caen,*** Bayeux, Falaise, Lisieux, Pont-l'Evêque, Vire.

Cantal. ***Aurillac,*** Mauriac, Murat, Saint-Flour.

Charente. ***Angoulême,*** Barbezieux, Cognac, Confolens, La Rochefoucauld, Ruffec.

Charente-Inférieure. ***Saintes,*** Marennes, Montlieu, Pons, Rochefort, La Rochelle, Saint-Jean-d'Angély.

Cher. ***Bourges,*** Aubigny, Châteaumeillant, Saint-Amand, Sancerre, Sancoins, Vierzon.

Corrèze. ***Tulle,*** Brive, Ussel, Uzerche.

Corse. ***Bastia,*** Ajaccio, Cervione, Corte, L'Ile-Rousse, Oletta, Porta, Tallano, Vico (from 11 Aug 1793 until 19 Aug 1811, Corsica was split into two depts: GOLO: ***Bastia,*** Calvi, Corti; and LIAMONE: ***Ajaccio,*** Sartène, Vico)

Côte-d'Or. ***Dijon,*** Arnay-le-Duc, Beaune, Châtillon-sur-Seine, Is-sur-Tille, Saint-Jean-de-Losne, Semur-en-Auxois.

Côtes-du-Nord. *Saint-Brieuc,* Broons, Dinan, Guingamp, Lamballe, Lannion, Loudéac, Pontrieux, Rostrenen.

Creuse. *Guéret,* Aubusson, Bourganeuf, Boussac, Evaux, Felletin, La Souterraine.

Dordogne. *Périgueux,* Belvès, Bergerac, Excideuil, Montignac, Mussidan, Nontron, Ribérac, Sarlat.

Doubs. *Besançon,* Baume-les-Dames, Ornans, Pontarlier, Quingey, Saint-Hippolyte.

Drôme. *Valence,* Crest, Die, Louvèze (transferred to the dept of the Vaucluse on 25 June 1793 as the district of Carpentras), Montélimar, Nyons, Romans.

Eure. *Evreux,* Les Andelys, Bernay, Louviers, Pont-Audemer, Verneuil-sur-Avre.

Eure-et-Loir. *Chartres,* Châteaudun, Châteauneuf-en-Thymerais, Dreux, Janville, Nogent-le-Rotrou.

Finistère. *Quimper,* Brest, Carhaix, Châteaulin, Landerneau, Lesneven, Morlaix, Pont-Croix, Quimperlé.

Gard. *Nîmes,* Alès, Beaucaire, Pont-Saint-Esprit, Saint-Hippolyte-du-Fort, Sommières, Uzès, Le Vigan.

Haute-Garonne. *Toulouse,* Castelsarrasin, Grenade-sur-Garonne, Muret, Revel, Rieux, Saint-Gaudens, Villefranche-de-Lauragais.

Ger. *Auch,* Condom, L'Isle-Jourdain, Lectoure, Mirande, Nogaro.

Gironde (from 2 Nov 1793/12 brum II to 14 Apr 1795/25 germ III known as Bec-d'Ambès. *Bordeaux,* Bazas, Bourg, Cadillac, Lesparre, Libourne, La Réole.

Golo, see CORSE.

Hérault. *Montpellier,* Béziers, Lodève, Saint-Pons.

Ille-et-Vilaine. *Rennes,* Bain-de-Bretagne, Dol, Fougères, La-Guerche-de-Bretagne, Montfort-sur-Meu, Redon, Saint-Malo, Vitré.

Indre. *Châteauroux,* Argenton-sur-Creuse, Le Blanc, La Châtre, Issoudun.

Indre-et-Loire. *Tours,* Amboise, Châteaurenault, Chinon, Langeais, Loches, Preuilly-sur-Claise.

Isère. *Grenoble,* La-Tour-du-Pin, Saint-Marcellin, Vienne.

Jura. *Lons-le-Saulnier,* Arbois, Dole-du-Jura, Orgelet, Poligny, Saint-Claude-sur-Bienne.

Landes. *Mont-de-Marsan,* Dax, Saint-Sever, Tartas.

Liamone, see CORSE.

Loir-et-Cher. *Blois,* Mer, Mondoubleau, Romorantin, Saint-Aignan-sur-Cher, Vendôme.

Loire (prior to 19 Nov 1793/29 brum II, combined with the **Rhône** as **Rhône-et-Loire.** *Feurs,* Montbrison, Roanne, Saint-Etienne.

Haute-Loire. *Le Puy,* Brioude, Monistrol-sur-Loire.

Loire-Inférieure. *Nantes,* Ancenis, Blain, Châteaubriant, Clisson, Guérande, Machecoul, Paimboeuf, Savenay.

Loiret. *Orléans,* Beaugency, Boiscommun, Gien, Montargis, Neuville-aux-Bois, Pithiviers.

Lot. *Cahors,* Figeac, Gourdon, Lauzerte, Montauban, Saint-Céré.

Lot-et-Garonne. *Agen,* Casteljaloux, Lauzun, Marmande, Monflanquin, Nérac, Tonneins, Valence-d'Agen, Villeneuve-sur-Lot.

Lozère. *Mende,* Florac, Langogne, Marvejols, Meyrueis, Saint-Chély-d'Apcher, Villefort.

Maine-et-Loire. *Angers,* Baugé, Châteauneuf-sur-Sarthe, Cholet, Saint-Florent-le-Vieil, Saumur, Segré, Vihiers.

Manche. *Coutances,* Avranches, Carentan, Cherbourg, Mortain, Saint-Lô, Valognes.

Marne. *Châlons-sur-Marne,* Epernay, Reims, Sainte-Menehould, Sézanne, Vitry-le-François.

Haute-Marne. *Chaumont,* Bourbonne-les-Bains, Bourmont, Joinville, Langres, Saint-Dizier.

Mayenne. *Laval,* Château-Gontier, Craon, Ernée, Evron, Lassay, Mayenne, Villaines-la-Juhel.

Meurthe. *Nancy,* Blâmont, Château-Salins, Dieuze, Lunéville, Pont-à-Mousson, Sarrebourg, Toul, Vézelise.

Meuse. *Bar-le-Duc,* Clermont-en-Argonne, Commercy, Etain, Gondrecourt, Montmédy, Saint-Mihiel, Verdun.

Mont-Blanc (created 27 Nov 1792). *Chambéry,* Annecy, Carouge, Cluses, Moûtiers, Saint-Jean-de-Maurienne, Thonon-les-Bains.

Morbihan. *Vannes,* Auray, Le Faouët, Hennebont, Josselin, Ploërmel, Pontivy, La Roche-Bernard, Rochefort-en-Terre.

Moselle. *Metz,* Bitche, Boulay-Moselle, Briey, Longwy, Morhange, Sarreguemines, Sarrelouis, Thionville.

Nièvre. *Nevers,* La Charité, Château-Chinon, Clamecy, Corbigny, Cosne, Decize, Moulins-Engilbert, Saint-Pierre-le-Moûtier.

Nord. *Douai,* Avesnes, Bergues, Cambrai, Hazebrouck, Lille, Le Quesnoy, Valenciennes.

Oise. *Beauvais,* Breteuil-sur-Noye, Chaumont-en-Vexin, Clermont, Compiègne, Crépy-en-Valois, Grandvilliers, Noyon, Senlis.

Orne. *Alençon,* Argentan, Bellême, Domfront, Laigle, Mortagne-au-Perche.

Paris, see SEINE.

Pas-de-Calais. *Arras,* Bapaume, Béthune, Boulogne-sur-Mer, Calais, Montreuil-sur-Mer, Saint-Omer, Saint-Pol-sur-Ternoise.

Puy-de-Dôme. *Clermont-Ferrand,* Ambert, Besse-en-Chandesse, Billom, Issoire, Montaigut-en-Combraille, Riom, Thiers.

Basses-Pyrénées. *Pau,* Mauléon, Oloron-Sainte-Marie, Orthez, Saint-Palais, Ustaritz.

Hautes-Pyrénées. *Tarbes,* Argelès-Gazost, Bagnères-de-Bigorre, La Barthe-de-Neste, Vic-en-Bigorre.

Pyrénées-Orientales. *Perpignan,* Céret, Prades.

Bas-Rhin. *Strasbourg,* Benfeld, Haguenau, Wissembourg.

Haut-Rhin. *Colmar,* Altkirch, Belfort.

Rhône (created 19 Nov 1793/29 brum II; formerly part of the Rhône-et-Loire). *Lyon,* Saint-Genis-Laval, Villefranche-sur-Saône.

Rhône-et-Loire (Lyon), see LOIRE, RHONE.

Haute-Saône. *Vesoul,* Champlitte, Gray, Jussey, Lure, Luxeuil-les-Bains.

Saône-et-Loire. *Mâcon,* Autun, Bourbon-Lancy, Chalon-sur-Saône, Charolles, Louhans, Marcigny.

Sarthe. *Le Mans,* Château-du-Loir, Fresnay-sur-Sarthe, La Ferté-Bernard, La Flèche, Sablé-sur-Sarthe, Saint-Calais, Sillé-le-Guillaume.

Seine (created by the Constitution of Year III [22 Aug 1795/5 fruct II]; formerly the dept of Paris). *Paris,* Saint-Denis, Sceaux.

Seine-et-Marne. *Melun,* Meaux, Nemours, Provins, Rozoy-en-Brie.

Seine-et-Oise. *Versailles,* Corbeil, Dourdan, Étampes, Gonesse, Mantes, Montfort-l'Amaury, Pontoise, Saint-Germain-en-Laye.

Seine-Inférieure. *Rouen,* Cany-Barville, Caudebec-en-Caux, Dieppe, Gournay-en-Bray, Montivilliers, Neufchâtel-en-Bray.

Deux-Sèvres. *Niort,* Bressuire, Melle-sur-Beronne, Parthenay, Saint-Maixent, Thouars.

Somme. *Amiens,* Abbeville, Doullens, Montdidier, Péronne.

Tarn. *Castres-sur-Agout* (from 17 Nov 1797/27 brum VI, *Albi*), Albi, Gaillac, Lacaune, Lavaur.

[**Tarn-et-Garonne:** the present-day dept of this name was created in 1808 from parts of the depts of the Lot-et-Garonne, Lot, Aveyron, Gers and Haute-Garonne.]

Var. *Toulon* (from 28 Apr 1797/9 flor V, *Draguignan*), Barjols, Brignoles, Draguignan, Fréjus, Grasse, Hyères, Saint-Maximin-la-Sainte-Baume, Saint-Paul-du-Var.

Vaucluse (created 25 June 1793 by amalgamating part of the Bouches-du-Rhône with the district of Louvèze, or Carpentras, from the Drôme). *Avignon,* Apt, Carpentras, Orange.

Vendée. *Fontenay-le-Comte,* Challans, La Châtaigneraie, Montaigu, La Roche-sur-Yon, Les Sables-d'Olonne.

Vienne. *Poitiers,* Châtellerault, Civray, Loudun, Lusignan, Montmorillon.

Haute-Vienne. *Limoges,* Bellac, Le Dorat, Saint-Junien, Saint-Léonard-de-Noblat, Saint-Yrieix.

Vosges. *Epinal,* Bruyères, Darney, Lamarche, Mirecourt, Neufchâteau, Rambervilliers, Remiremont, Saint-Dié.

Yonne. *Auxerre,* Avallon, Joigny, Saint-Fargeau, Saint-Florentin, Sens, Tonnerre.

Lys
1795
Escaut
1795
Deux-Nèthes
1795
Meuse Inf.
1795
Roër
1797
Dyle
1795
Jemmapes
1793-5
Ourthe
1795
Pas-de-Calais
Nord
Sambre-et-Meuse
1797
Rhin-et-Moselle
1797
Forêts
1795
Sarre
1797
Mont-Tonnerre
1797
Somme
Aisne
Ardennes
Seine-Inf.
Oise
Manche
Calvados
Eure
Paris
Moselle
Marne
Meuse
Meurthe
Bas-Rhin
Finistère
Côtes-du-Nord
Orne
Seine-et-Oise
Seine-et-Marne
Ille-et-Vilaine
Mayenne
Eure-et-Loir
Aube
Haute Marne
Vosges
Morbihan
Sarthe
Loiret
Yonne
Haute Saône
Haut-Rhin
Loire-Inf.
Maine-et-Loire
Loir-et-Cher
Indre-et-Loire
Côte d'Or
Doubs
Nièvre
Cher
Mont-Terrible
1793
Vendée
Indre
Jura
Saône-et-Loire
Deux-Sèvres
Vienne
Allier
Léman
1798
Charente Inf.
Creuse
Ain
Rhône
1793
Hte. Vienne
Charente
Loire
1793
Puy-de-Dôme
Mont-Blanc
1792
Corrèze
Isère
Dordogne
Cantal
Haute Loire
Gironde
Hautes Alpes
Ardèche
Drôme
Alpes Maritimes
1793
Lot-et-Garonne
Lot
Lozère
Aveyron
Landes
Vaucluse
1793
Gard
Basses Alpes
Gers
Tarn
Hte. Garonne
Hérault
Var
Basses Pyrénées
Hautes Pyrénées
Ariège
Aude
Bouches-du-Rhône
Pyrénées Orientales
0
150 km
0
100 mls
Departmental frontier
Frontier areas annexed 1790-9
Fôrets
1795
Name of department and date of establishment (if after 1790)

Map 7 The departmental framework, 1790–9.

'ANNEXED DEPARTMENTS' (*DÉPARTMENTS RÉUNIS*), WITH *CHEF-LIEU*

Dyle (created 1 Oct 1795/9 vendém IV). *Brussels.*
Escaut (as Dyle). *Ghent.*
Forêts (as Dyle). *Luxembourg.*
Jemappes (2 Mar 1793, 1 Oct 1795/9 vendém IV). *Mons.*
Léman (25 Aug 1798/8 fruct VI). *Geneva.*
Lys (as Dyle). *Bruges.*
Meuse-Inférieure (as Dyle). *Maestricht.*
Mont-Terrible (23 Mar 1793). *Delemont.*
Mont-Tonnerre (4 Nov 1797/14 brum VI). *Mainz.*
Deux-Nèthes (as Dyle). *Antwerp.*
Ourthe (as Dyle). *Liège.*
Rhin-et-Moselle (as Mont-Tonnerre). *Coblenz.*
Roer (as Mont-Tonnerre). *Aix-la-Chapelle.*
Sambre-et-Meuse (as Mont-Tonnerre). *Namur.*
Sarre (as Mont-Tonnerre). *Trier.*

7. GOVERNMENT INCOME AND EXPENDITURE IN THE EIGHTEENTH CENTURY: FOUR PEACE YEARS (*MORINEAU 1980*)

Figures in millions of livres.

	1726	%	1751	%	1775	%	1788	%	% increase, 1726–88
Income									
Royal domain	1.5	0.8	5.6	2.2	9.4	2.5	51.2	10.8	3413
Clergy	1.8	1.0	14.3	5.5	3.0	0.8	–	–	–
Dons gratuits (pays d'état, etc)	5.7	3.2	8.0	3.1	23.9	6.3	20.6	4.4	361
Direct taxes	79.9	44.1	109.0	42.2	150.7	40.0	163.0	34.6	204
Indirect taxes	88.6	49.0	116.6	45.1	183.9	48.8	219.3	46.5	248
Other	3.5	1.9	5.0	1.9	6.3	1.6	17.5	3.7	500
	181.0		258.5		377.2		471.6		261
Expenditure									
Royal Household	31.0	17.0	26.0	10.1	43.0	10.5	42.0	6.6	135
Foreign affairs	4.3	2.3	22.8	8.9	11.8	2.9	14.4	2.3	335
War	57.0	31.3	76.9	30.0	90.6	22.0	107.1	16.9	188
Navy	8.0	4.4	28.8	11.2	33.2	8.1	51.8	8.2	648
Public works	2.0	1.1	6.4	2.5	5.4	1.3	14.9	2.4	745
Charity	–		–		–		19.0	3.0	–
Pensions, etc	14.0	7.7	18.9	7.4	33.0	8.0	47.8	7.6	341
Servicing the debt	61.0	33.5	71.8	28.1	154.4	37.5	261.1	41.2	428
Other	5.0	2.7	4.7	1.8	40.0	9.7	75.0	11.8	–
	182.3		256.3		411.4		633.1		347

Dunkirk

Pays exempt

Pays de Quart-bouillon

Paris

Pays de salines

Pays exempt

Lorient

Pays de grand gabelle

Pays rédimés

Pays de petite gabelle

Bayonne

Marseille

Pays exempt

Pays exempts

0   150km

0   100mls

〜〉 Frontier in 1789

Jurisdiction of the "Cinq Grosses Fermes"

Provinces réputées étrangères

Provinces de l'étranger effectif

● Port enjoying extensive trading privileges

Map 8   Indirect taxation in Ancien Régime France.

231

8. FINANCES: CHRONOLOGY

20 Aug 1786 To stave off impending state bankruptcy, Controller-General Calonne proposes a number of key structural reforms, inc a new tax imposable on all landowners. The resistance of the privileged classes to the programme outlined by Calonne and later reiterated by Loménie de Brienne provokes the 'Noble Revolt' (1787–8).

16 Aug 1788 *De facto* state bankruptcy obliges the king to dismiss the reformist ministry of Brienne and agree to the convocation of the EG to find some way out of the state's financial impasse.

5 May 1789 Meeting of the EG.

15 June 1789 The Third Estate, which rejects cooperation with the other orders under unfavourable terms, refuses to assent to a government loan.

17 June 1789 The new 'Nat Ass.' declares all taxes illegal on the grounds that they have not had national assent; but provisionally agrees to the continuation of existing taxes, thus reassuring state creditors.

23 June 1789 *Séance royale*, in which Louis XVI outlines his financial programme: suppression of pecuniary privilege; EG will vote taxes; nat accounts are to be presented annually to the EG.

4 Aug 1789 'Night of 4 Aug': suppression of financial privilege, venality of office, etc.

26 Aug 1789 Declaration of the Rights of Man: principle of financial equality.

Aug–Oct 1789 Provisional financial measures:
- *9 Aug:* loan of 30 million liv at 4.5 per cent
- *27 Aug:* further loan of 80 million liv at 5 per cent
- *26 Sept:* provisional continuation of old taxes, now payable by formerly privileged groups
- *6 Oct: contribution patriotique:* one-off, never-to-be-repeated income tax on all persons with income over 400 liv; levied at the rate of 25 per cent of income, but payable annually in thirds, 1790–2.

7 Sept 1789 Reduction in the price of salt, and abolition of obligatory purchasing.

2 Nov 1789 Ecclesiastical property placed at the disposal of the nation. Assignats will be issued (from 19 Dec), guaranteed by 'nat lands', as bonds which may be used to purchase this property.

19, 21 Jan 1790 Establishment of a *Caisse de l'extraordinaire* to receive revenue from the *contribution patriotique* and income from the sale of nat lands. 400 million liv of assignats, bearing 5 per cent interest, are issued.

21 Mar 1790   Abolition of the *gabelle*.

 1 Apr 1790   Publication of the *Livre rouge*, the register of royal pensions. Public opinion is appalled at the extravagance it reveals.

17 Apr 1790   Assignat accepted as a form of currency: it now bears interest at 3 per cent.

 9 May 1790   Crown lands nationalised.

 9 July 1790   All 'nat lands' may be placed on sale.

12 Sept 1790   Enforced quotation for the assignat (to offset tendency towards depreciation).

29 Sept 1790   Assignats to bear no interest.

 8 Oct 1790   Assignat notes down to 50 liv denominations to be printed.

23 Nov 1790   New land-tax (the *contribution foncière*) introduced. Estimated annual return of 210 million liv.

13 Dec 1790   Abolition of AR stamp tax.

13 Jan 1791   New tax on movable wealth created (the *contribution mobilière*), payable by active citizens. Estimated annual return of 60 million liv.

12 Feb 1791   State monopoly of cultivation, distribution and sale of tobacco abolished.

19 Feb 1791   Abolition of *octrois* (municipal tolls).

 2 Mar 1791   New tax on the practice of trades and professions (the *patente*). Estimated annual return of 12 million liv (in fact, only brings in 0.8 million liv in 1791).

29 Mar, 5 Aug 1791   State assumes financial responsibility for any debts incurred by local authorities in connection with their new obligations.

23 Sept 1791   Manufacture of saltpetre and gunpowder maintained as a state monopoly.

 9 Feb 1792   Sequestration of *émigré* lands; a further law of 17 July establishes that they may be put up for sale like church lands.

15 Dec 1792   Law establishing rev administration in all conquered territories (abolition of feudalism, nationalisation of church lands, etc).

 9 Mar 1793   Principle of a tax on wealth agreed.

12 Mar 1793   Abolition of the *patente*: commercial income to be assessed as part of the *contribution mobilière*.

18 Mar 1793   Pronouncement in favour of a wealth tax to finance the war effort (triggers off local wealth taxes in many depts, following the lead of the Hérault on 19 Apr).

11 Apr 1793   Forced quotation for the assignat.

20 May, 22 June and 3 Sept 1793   Forced loan on the rich: levied on persons with over 1,500 liv income; reimbursable after the war.

Summer–Autumn 1793   Numerous local taxes on the wealthy introduced by semi-autonomous reps *en mission*.

24 Aug 1793   Cambon of the Finance Committee gets the Convtn to decree the

establishment of the *Grand Livre de la Dette Nationale*, a consolidated register of the state's AR and Rev debts.

5 Sept 1793   Death penalty for undermining the assignat.

29 Sept 1793   'General Maximum': establishment of a directed economy, buttressed by Terror.

4 Dec 1793/14 frim II   'Law of 14 Frimaire II': levying of forced loans forbidden.

10 May 1794/21 flor II   Abolition of the *contribution mobilière*, and reorganisation of the basis of assessment of the *contribution foncière*.

24 Dec 1794/4 niv III   Suppression of the Maximum and trade controls, triggering off a fresh bout of depreciation of assignats.

3 Apr 1795/14 germ III   Cambon forced off the Finance Committee, which he has chaired throughout the Terror.

21 June 1795/3 mess III   Sliding scale introduced for use of assignats in payments.

20 July 1795/2 therm III   Half the land-tax to be paid in grains.

25 July 1795/7 therm III   *Contribution mobilière* reintroduced.

10 Dec 1795/19 frim IV   Forced loan on the 25 per cent wealthiest inhabitants of each department (little implemented).

19 Feb 1796/30 pluv IV   Assignat printing-presses formally broken as assignats are progressively withdrawn.

18 Mar 1796/28 vent IV   Creation of a new paper money, the *mandat territorial*, which collapses almost immediately.

17 July 1796/29 mess IV   Abolition of the compulsory quotation for the *mandat territorial*.

23 Aug 1796/6 fruct IV   Re-establishment of the *patente*.

4 Sept 1796/18 fruct IV   As the *mandat* depreciates fast, Belgian church lands are put on sale.

4 Feb 1797/16 pluv V   Withdrawal of the *mandat territorial* from circulation.

6 June 1797/18 prair V   Revised version of the land-tax introduced.

2 Aug 1797/14 therm V   Revised version of the tax on movable wealth.

10 Sept 1797/24 fruct V   Principle of indirect taxation accepted: *droit de passe* established.

30 Sept 1797/9 vendém VI   'Bankruptcy of the Two-Thirds'. Forced reduction in the size of the Nat Debt from 250 to 83 million liv. One-third of value is inscribed in the *Grand Livre*; two-thirds are reimbursed in (soon totally valueless) bonds.
Stamp tax on paper, documents, etc.

12 Nov 1797/22 brum VI   Creation of Direct Tax Agency under the Minister of Finances to organise the collection of taxes.

24 Nov 1797/4 frim VI   Tax on doors and windows.

18 Oct 1798/27 vendém VII   *Octroi* introduced at Paris (and extended to other cities by a series of laws from 1 Dec/11 frim).

22 Nov 1798/22 brum VII   Tax on tobacco.

23 Nov 1798/3 frim VII   Taxes to be paid in cash, not grain.

12 Dec 1798/22 frim VII   Registration tax introduced.

27 June and 18 Oct 1799/9 mess and 19 therm VII   Forced loan of 100 million
    liv decreed (little implemented).

9. CURRENCY

The AR currency was the *livre*. Since 1667, the livre tournois had been the national unit of currency, although local variations existed (e.g. the livre of Lorraine, worth about two-thirds of the livre tournois). The main denominations were:

louis	= 24 liv
écu	= 3 liv
livre	= 20 sous
sou (or sol)	= 12 deniers

The term 'franc' was sometimes used as a variant of liv, and this became more current in the Rev, especially after the Convtn introduced the metric system on 7 Apr 1795/18 germ II. Each franc comprised 100 centimes.

In 1789, a pound sterling exchanged for between 22 and 23 liv.

10. THE ASSIGNAT: CASH VALUE, 1789–1796

In exchange for 100 liv cash

	1789	1790	1791	1792	1793	1794	1795	1796
Jan	–	96	91	72	51	40	18	0.5
Feb	–	95	91	61	52	41	17	0.4
Mar	–	94	90	59	51	36	14	0.3
Apr	–	94	89	58	43	36	10	–
May	–	94	85	58	52	34	8	–
June	–	95	85	57	36	30	6	–
July	–	95	87	61	23	34	3	–
Aug	–	92	79	61	22	31	3	–
Sept	98	91	82	72	27	28	2	–
Oct	97	91	84	71	28	28	2	–
Nov	96	90	82	73	33	24	1	–
Dec	95	92	77	72	48	20	0.7	–

VIII. RELIGION AND IDEAS

1. RELIGION: CHRONOLOGY

19 Nov 1787   Edict of Toleration for France's 700,000 Protestants (passed by the Paris parl, 29 Jan 1788).

June 1788   The Ass. of the Clergy joins the 'Noble Revolt' by offering as its *don gratuit* only 1.8 million liv (instead of the 8 millions requested by the government).

June 1789   Clerical deputies lead a drift towards the Third Estate prior to the declaration of the Nat Ass.

4–11 Aug 1789   Abolition of 'feudalism': inc abolition of the tithe, priests' fee income, annates and ecclesiastical privilege.

26 Aug 1789   Declaration of the Rights of Man: religious toleration.

28 Oct 1789   Suspension of the taking of monastic vows.

2 Nov 1789   Church property nationalised (sales begin on 19 Dec): in return, the state will provide for the costs of public worship, the salaries of the clergy and public assistance.

24 Dec 1789   Protestants are no longer debarred from public office.

13 Feb 1790   Abolition of monastic vows and suppression of religious orders with solemn vows and others not dedicated to teaching or charitable work. Monks are free to leave their monasteries and will receive state pensions. Remaining monks will be regrouped, while nuns may remain *in situ*. (Fuller details are announced 8 Oct 1790.)

23 Feb 1790   Parish priests are to read new laws from the pulpit and explain them to the faithful.

13 Apr 1790   Rejecting a motion put by Dom Gerle that catholicism should be the sole state religion, the Ass. merely affirms its attachment to catholicism.

29 May 1790   Religious Committee introduces the Civil Constitution of the Clergy. Grégoire, Camus and Treilhard esp prominent in debates.

11 June 1790   The papal city of Avignon votes to be incorporated into France.

June 1790   *Bagarre de Nîmes:* violent Catholic–Protestant clashes in the S city and the Cévennes.

12 July 1790   Civil Constitution of the Clergy. Its main provisions are:
New ecclesiastical organisation
- one bishop per department (i.e. 83 instead of 136)

- 10 metropolitans, and these (not the Pope) will consecrate new bishops
- rationalisation of parishes
- abolition of cathedral chapters
- bishops are assisted by a set number of vicars episcopal

New system of appointment
- bishops elected in dept electoral assemblies of taxpayers (which may include non-Catholics) from among priests who have served 15 years in the diocese
- parish priests (*curés*) elected in district electoral assemblies from assistant priests (*vicaires*) who have served five years in the diocese
- assistant priests are chosen by *curés* from locally trained priests, vicars episcopal by the bishop
- all parish priests, as state functionaries, are to swear an oath of 'fidelity to the nation, the law, the king and the constitution' prior to assuming office

New system of ecclesiastical self-government
- creation of metropolitan and diocesan synods which all diocesan clergy may attend
- bishops are to be counselled by a standing committee composed of their vicars episcopal (12–16 in number) and seminary priests (up to four); all members of the committee are irremovable

New career structure
- the clergy is henceforth salaried by the state
- scale of stipends for bishops from 50,000 liv for Paris down to 12,000 liv for most dioceses
- vicars episcopal get between 2,000 and 5,000 liv
- *curés* get from 6,000 liv (Paris) to a minimum of 1,200 liv, *vicaires* from 700 to 1,200 liv
- all ecclesiastical functionaries are to be permanently resident
- none may hold secular office, but they may vote.

14 July 1790   *Fête de la Fédération* in Paris: Talleyrand, still bishop of Autun, holds a mass on the main altar erected on the Champ de Mars.

24 Aug 1790   Louis XVI sanctions the Civ Constn.

30 Oct 1790   16 bishops and 94 priests from the Constit Ass. assert that the Civ Constn requires papal endorsement.

2 Nov 1790   Suspension of the law of 23 Feb, following incidents in which priests have commented unfavourably on new laws.

27 Nov 1790   Decree on the oath required of state functionaries by the Civ Constn. Individuals who fail to take the oath will be adjudged to have resigned their positions.

26 Dec 1790   King sanctions the law of 27 Nov: the law will be promulgated

on 2 Jan 1791; ecclesiastical deputies in the Constit Ass. are to take the oath by 4 Jan (though most will refuse).

7 Jan 1791   Relaxation in some qualifications for office outlined in the Civ Constn: e.g. *curés* may be drawn from among priests from other dioceses.

5 Feb 1791   The oath is extended to preachers (on 15 Apr, it will be extended to hospital and prison chaplains).

24 Feb 1791   Talleyrand consecrates the first batch of constitutional bishops, who have been elected since 5 Feb. Fifty-five of the new constitutional bishops will be ex-*curés*.

10 March, 13 Apr 1791   Pope attacks the Civ Constn and the Rev in general. Breakdown in diplomatic relations ensue.

Spring 1791   Growing dissension as numerous priests refuse the civic oath (becoming 'refractory' or 'non-juring' clergy), and are replaced. Only seven of the 136 AR bishops take the oath.

18 Apr 1791   Louis XVI prevented by a Parisian crowd from going to Saint-Cloud allegedly to receive mass from a refractory priest.

7 May 1791   Constit Ass. affirms that refractory priests *may* hold religious services.

20 June 1791   Refractory clergy are deprived of their pensions.

27 Sept 1791   Jews may be active citizens.

29 Nov 1791   Following a report concerning socio-religious disturbances in the Vendée, the Ass. decrees:
- all priests (not just state functionaries) are to take an oath of allegiance within a week
- refractories against this oath are to be stripped of their right to a pension, placed under municipal surveillance and may be exiled from their homes in areas affected by religious dissension or imprisoned for up to two years for provoking disturbances. They are also deprived of their right to use religious buildings, which are henceforth to be monopolised by the constitutional clergy. (The king vetoes this decree on 19 Dec, but it is enforced in many depts).

6 Apr 1792   Suppression of religious dress.

27 May 1792   Refractory clerics may be deported on the request of 20 active citizens from a canton. (Vetoed by the king, 19 June, but again widely enforced.)

26 June 1792   Every commune is to erect an *autel de la patrie*.

Aug–Sept 1792   Flurry of legislation in the context of the developing political crisis and the overthrow of Louis XVI, helping to trigger off a massive ecclesiastical emigration:
- *3 Aug:* religious houses to be evacuated and alienated
- *4 Aug:* suppression of most female religious orders; all houses at present occupied by monks and nuns are to be evacuated and sold off
- *10 Aug and after:* attacks on and harassment of refractory clerics, esp

through the enforcement of the laws of 29 Nov 1791 and 27 May 1792
- *14–15 Aug:* a new oath (the so-called 'Liberty-Equality' oath) is required of all ecclesiastics and state functionaries (finalised 3 Sept)
- *16 Aug:* Paris Commune prohibits religious processions and services in public
- *18 Aug:* suppression of all religious communities, including nursing and educational orders and lay confraternities. Prohibition of the wearing of ecclesiastical dress except for constitutional clergy within their own parishes
- *26 Aug:* deportation for priests who fail to take the oath and whose removal is requested by six citizens
- *2–6 Sept:* Sept Massacres in Paris: assassination of three ex-bishops and over 200 priests
- *10 Sept:* requisitioning of church silver is permitted for the war effort.

20 Sept 1792 Laicisation of the *état-civil* (registration of births, marriages and deaths).

Spring–Summer 1793 Further drift towards anti-clericalism stimulated by war, political crisis and the clerico-royalist rising in the Vendée (10 Mar):
- *13 Mar:* death for priests compromised in the disturbances
- *28 Mar:* deported priests found in France may be referred to a military jury and executed within 24 hours
- *21 Apr:* refractory clerics and priests accused of *incivisme* by six citizens are to be deported to Guiana
- *18 July:* episcopal palaces are to be sold off
- *19 July:* bishops opposing the marriage of priests are threatened with deportation (reaffirmed on 12 Aug)
- *23 July, 3 Aug:* church bells are to be melted down for cannon
- *10 Aug:* first civic festival totally without religious trappings
- *26 Aug:* deportation from France of all priests who have not taken the civic oath
- *17 Sept:* married priests who are harassed by their congregations are to have their salaries paid by the commune involved. On the same day, the Law of Suspects permits increased surveillance of religious personnel
- *18 Sept:* reduction in the salaries of constitutional bishops
- *26 Sept:* Fouché, rep *en mission* in Nevers launches a dechristianisation campaign which will spread throughout the provinces and in Paris in late 1793.

5, 24 Oct, 24 Nov 1793 Convtn accepts the principle of reform of the calendar, and the introduction of a Rev Calendar.

5 Nov 1793/15 brum II Convtn approves a list of civic festivals.

10 Nov 1793/20 brum II As the dechristianisation campaign gets under way

in Paris, and following the renunciation of their priesthood (7 Nov) by Gobel, archbishop of Paris, and 12 of his cathedral priests, the Festival of Reason is celebrated in Paris, with Notre-Dame renamed the 'Temple of Reason'.

15 Nov 1793/25 brum II Married refractory priests are only to be deported if three citizens accuse them of *incivisme*.

Presbyteries in communes in which no form of religion is observed are to be converted to charitable or educational use.

21 Nov 1793/1 frim II Robespierre in the Jacobin Club attacks atheism (i.e. dechristianisation).

22 Nov 1793/2 frim II Priests who abdicate are to receive a pension of between 800 and 1,200 liv.

23 Nov 1793/3 frim II Paris Commune orders the closure of all churches.

Nov 1793–May 1794 Anti-clerical repression in Nantes, including the *noyades*.

6 Dec 1793/16 frim II In the face of the dechristianisation campaign in Paris (led by the Commune and the Hébertists) and the provinces (led by radical reps *en mission*), the Convtn, prompted by Cambon, Danton and Robespierre, reaffirms the principle of freedom of worship.

12 Mar 1794/22 vent II Refractories are treated as *émigrés*, and their property confiscated.

7 May 1794/18 flor II Robespierre in the Convtn attacks atheism. Decree recognising the existence of a Supreme Being and the immortality of the soul. A programme of rev festivals is agreed upon. The principle of freedom of worship is again reaffirmed.

8 June 1794/20 prair II Festival of the Supreme Being in Paris, staged by David and presided over by Robespierre.

18 Sept 1794/2 jc II Convtn accepts the proposal of Cambon of the Finance Committee that the state should suspend payment of the salaries of priests and the cost of public worship.

Autumn 1794 Post-Thermidor clearing of the prisons brings the release of many refractory and suspect priests.

17 Nov 1794/27 brum III Decree on education: religion is banished from schools and replaced by moral education and civic training.

21 Feb 1795/3 vent III Formal separation of church and state: state renounces any financial liability for public worship. Freedom proclaimed for all religions. (Paradoxically, this law will have the effect of reopening many churches and stimulating the revival of Catholic worship in the following months.)

Spring 1795 Hoche's pacification of W France involves the recognition of greater freedom there for the practice of catholicism.

30 May 1795/11 prair III Citizens are allowed use of church buildings, under the general surveillance of municipal authorities. Where necessary a rota is established (e.g. among refractory and constitutional clergy). All priests are to swear an oath of submission to the laws of the Rpbc.

31 May 1795/12 prair III   Priests who have emigrated voluntarily may claim back their confiscated property.

6 Sept 1795/20 fruct III   Elderly and infirm priests who have been sentenced to deportation have their penalty commuted to life banishment.

29 Sept 1795/7 vendém IV   Law codifying dispositions regarding public worship: penalties for individuals disrupting public worship; all forms of worship placed under the surveillance of the authorities; wearing of religious dress prohibited; no religious meetings in private houses to number more than 10 individuals; all individuals conducting public worship are to swear an oath of submission to the laws of the Rpbc.

25 Oct 1795/3 brum IV   Following clerical and royalist involvement in the Vendémiaire rising (5 Oct/13 vendém), and in the wake of the return of many ecclesiastical *émigrés*, the Convtn, on the eve of its dissolution, reimplements legislation of 1792 and 1793 relating to refractory priests. The latter are also excluded from the general political amnesty proclaimed the following day (26 Oct/4 brum) as the Convtn breaks up.

Autumn 1795   Reconstitution of the Constitutional Church by Grégoire and others (now increasingly calling itself the 'Gallican Church').

Spring 1796–early 1797   Following the discovery of the Babeuf plot, the regime moves to the right, and more conciliatory religious policies emerge:

- *31 May 1796/12 prair IV:* priests who have emigrated voluntarily are allowed to claim back their confiscated property
- *23 June 1796/5 mess IV:* armistice with the Papal States
- *29 June 1796/11 mess IV:* nuns who have not taken the 'Liberty–Equality' oath of Sept 1792 are allowed to claim their pensions (These provisions are extended to elderly refractory priests on 5 Sept/19 fruct.)
- *4 Dec 1796/14 frim V:* the clauses of the law of 3 brum IV (25 Oct) regarding refractories are repealed. Many priests are subsequently released from gaol.
- *19 Feb 1797/1 vent V:* Peace of Tolentino with the Pope: the latter cedes territory to France, but makes no religious concessions.

Summer 1797   Cult of Theophilanthropy, encouraged by Director La Révellière-Lépeaux, is organised in Paris and elsewhere. The leaders secure use of churches for theophilanthropist worship in rota with Catholics.

15 Aug 1797/28 therm V   Meeting of the first nat council of the 'Gallican' (i.e. Constitutional) Church.

24 Aug 1797/7 fruct V   Legislation of 1792 and 1793 regarding refractory priests is formally repealed. The way is opened to the return of refractory priests.

5 Sept 1797/19 fruct V   Following the *coup d'état* of 18 Fructidor, a new campaign against the refractory clergy is launched:

- the law of 7 fruct V is revoked, and all anti-refractory legislation of 1792–3 is reimplemented

- exile of deputies formerly supporting a conciliatory religious policy (Pastoret, Portalis, etc)
- all individuals whose names are on the *émigré* lists are to leave France within a fortnight on pain of death
- Directors are empowered to deport individuals for disturbing order (over 1,500 priests are deported in Year VI)
- new civic oath imposed: 'hatred of royalty and anarchy'.

15 Sept 1797/29 fruct V   The councils will no longer meet on *décadis*, and will observe all nat festivals.

15 Feb 1798/27 pluv VI   The French in Italy overthrow papal government and proclaim a Roman Rpbc. The Pope falls prisoner to the French.

3 Apr 1798/14 germ VI   La Révellière-Lépeaux urges the observance of the decadal cult. Use of the Rev Calendar is made obligatory.

6 July 1798/18 mess VI   Domiciliary visits to hunt out refractory priests are permitted. A bounty of 100 liv is offered for every priest captured.

4 Aug & 30 Aug 1798/17 therm and 13 fruct VI   Wearing the national cockade and the 'citizen' mode of address are made compulsory. In addition, Minister of the Interior François de Neufchâteau organises a series of nat festivals throughout 1798–9.

Oct–Nov 1798   Application of the 'Jourdan Law' on conscription in Belgium leads to a popular insurrection, supported by the Belgian clergy. In the repression that follows, over 7,000 priests will be sentenced to deportation.

29 Aug 1799/12 fruct VII   Pope Pius VI dies a French prisoner at Valence. His successor, Pius VII, will negotiate a Concordat with Bonaparte in 1801.

2. THE CLERGY AND THE REVOLUTION

Dons gratuits made by the Ass. of the Clergy in the reign of Louis XVI (in millions of liv) (*Marion 1914–31*):

1775, 16;   1780, 30;   1782, 16;   1785, 18;   1788, 1.8.

Strength in 1789 (*Langlois & Tackett 1980; Lebrun 1980*):

Parish clergy (*curés, vicaires*)	59,500
Other secular clergy (male)	28,500
Regular clergy (male)	26,500
Female orders	55,000
TOTAL	169,500

Takers of the Civil Constitution oath, 1791 (*Tackett 1986*):

Secular clergy	26,542 (52.2%)
Regular clergy	1,081 (41.9%)
TOTAL	27,623

Abdications (i.e. renunciations of priesthood) (*Lebrun 1980*): Approx 30,000

Marriages (*Lebrun 1980*): Approx 6,000

Executed under the Terror (*Greer 1935*): 920 known victims of rev justice

Emigrated (*Greer 1951*):

		No.	%
(a)	Upper clergy	2,298	9.3
	Lower clergy	18,493	75.2
	Unknown	3,805	15.5
	TOTAL	24,596	
(b)	Secular	18,688	76.0
	Regular	2,103	8.5
	Unknown	3,805	15.5
	TOTAL	24,596	

Recent research (*Lebrun 1980*) suggests that the real total of ecclesiastical *émigrés* may be between 30,000 and 40,000. Whichever total is accepted, it would appear that between 15 and 25 per cent of the ecclesiastical order emigrated during the Rev. This is the largest proportion for any major social or professional group, and can only be compared with the nobility: 16,431 known *émigrés* from this order comprise only about 5 per cent of the nobility if we assume its global size in 1789 was 300,000, about 15 per cent if we accept some recent estimates of the size of the nobility at 110,000–120,000 (*Chaussinand-Nogaret 1985*).

State of the episcopacy of the Constitutional Church in Year V:
44 in place, of whom 41 had been elected in 1790–1.
Of the 42 others elected in 1791:

• 9 married
• 6 resigned
• 6 had not resumed functions
• 8 executed
• 13 death from other causes.

248

3. THE RELIGIOUS CULT OF THE REVOLUTION

REVOLUTIONARY SYMBOLS

Cockade, tricolore (a rev emblem from 17 July 1789, a nat one from 21 Oct 1790), *bonnet rouge* or *bonnet phrygien*, tree of liberty, *autel de la patrie*, carmagnole, trousers (i.e. no breeches [*culottes*]), mountain, fasces, pike, carpenter's level, eye, compass, etc.

REVOLUTIONARY FESTIVALS

(a) Approved by the Convtn, 7 May 1794/18 flor II

Anniversaries of 14 July 1789, 10 Aug 1792, 21 Jan 1793, 31 May 1793. Decadal festivals commemorating the Supreme Being and Nature; Humanity; the French People; Benefactors of Humanity; Martyrs of Liberty; Liberty and Equality; the Rpbc; Freedom of the World; Love of Fatherland; Hatred of Tyrants and Traitors; Truth; Justice; Modesty; Glory and Immortality; Friendship; Frugality; Courage; Good Faith; Heroism; Disinterestedness; Stoicism; Love; Conjugal Love; Paternal Love; Maternal Tenderness; Filial Piety; Childhood; Youth; the Virile Age; Old Age; Misfortune; Agriculture; Industry; Ancestors; Posterity; Happiness.

(b) Approved by the Convtn, 25 Oct 1795/3 brum IV

Youth, Old Age, Spouses, Gratitude, Agriculture, Foundation of the Rpbc (1 vendém), Liberty (9–10 therm).

(c) Later changes

From 14 Jan 1796/24 niv IV, commemoration of 21 Jan 1793 (execution of Louis XVI); from 28 July 1796/10 therm IV, plus commemorations of 14 July 1789 (fall of the Bastille) and 10 Aug 1792 (overthrow of the king).

249

THE 'MARTYRS OF LIBERTY'

Marat, the assassinated Conventionnel Lepeletier de Saint-Fargeau and the Lyonnais militant Chalier (executed by moderates in June 1793) were the original 'martyrs' whose cult enjoyed success among rev militants from Autumn 1793. In Spring 1794, the names of the Bara and Viala, youths who had died fighting bravely for the Rpbc, were often added. The cult died out soon after Thermidor.

INDIVIDUALS VOTED THE 'HONOURS OF THE PANTHÉON'

(In accordance with the decree of 4 Apr 1791 regarding the honouring of great men. On 25 Oct 1795/3 brum IV, the Convtn decreed that the honours of the Panthéon could only be awarded 10 years after an individual's death.)

Mirabeau (vote 4 Apr 1791; ceremony of burial, 5 Apr)

Voltaire (vote 30 May 1791; ceremony of transfer of ashes, 11 July 1791)

Beaurepaire (Verdun commander who committed suicide rather than surrender: vote 12 Sept 1792; ceremony Oct 1792)

Lepeletier de Saint-Fargeau (vote 21 Jan 1793)

Descartes (vote 2 Oct 1793)

Joseph Sauveur (rpbcn official killed by the Vendéan rebels:?)

Fabre de l'Hérault (conventionnel killed in battle: vote 12 Jan 1794/23 niv II)

Haxo, Moulin (generals: vote 28 Apr 1794/9 flor II)

Dagobert (general: vote 30 Apr 1794/11 flor II)

Bara (vote 28 Dec 1794/8 niv II and 7 May 1794/18 flor II)

Viala (vote 7 May 1794/18 flor II)

Marat (ceremony 24 Sept 1794/3 vendém III) (*sic*)

Rousseau (ceremony 11 Oct 1794/20 vendém III).

REVOLUTIONARY NAMING

The practice of renaming places and individuals in accordance with the spirit of the Rev was esp widespread in 1793–4. It had its roots in the abolition of feudalism (4 Aug 1789), the ending of noble titles (19 June 1790), the overthrow of the king (10 Aug 1792) and the growth of the dechristianisation movement (1793–4). For anti-feudal reasons, for example, Fontenay-le-Comte renamed itself Fontenay-le-Peuple; for anti-monarchical reasons, Roiville was renamed Peuple-ville; and for religious reasons, Saint-Flour became Mont-Flour. The practice was given the endorsement of the Convtn in late 1793 by the adoption of the Rev Calendar, and by the decision to rename major Federalist centres (on 12 Oct,

250

Lyon became Ville-, later Commune-Affranchie; Marseille was subsequently renamed Ville-sans-Nom; Toulon, Port-Montagne; the dept of the Gironde, Bec-d'Ambès; the depth of the Vendée, Vengé).

The main elements in adoptive names tended to be: (a) nature, esp as laid down in the Rev Calendar; (b) heroes of antiquity; (c) heroes and great men of the Enlightenment and the Rev; and (d) resonant rev terms (e.g. Montagne, Ami). Among well-known figures with 'rev' forenames one notes 'Gracchus' Babeuf, 'Anacharsis' Cloots, 'Anaxagoras' Chaumette and 'Pervenche' (= periwinkle) Doppet. Representative rev place-name changes were 'Fort-d'Hercule' (Monaco), 'Berceau-de-la-Liberté' (Versailles), 'Havre-Marat' (Le Havre), 'Fort-Peletier' (Aigues-Mortes), 'Montagne-Charente' (Angoulême), 'Dun-sur-Loir' (Châteaudun) and 'Rocher-de-la-Liberté' (Saint-Lô). One notes also the new dignity of 'Guignes-Libre' (formerly Guignes-la-Putain). Among recorded rev forenames, the following is a representative sample: Blé (= grain)-Cicero; Solon-Cumin (= caraway); Abricot-Viala; Myrthe (= myrtle)-Voltaire; Socrate-Safran (= saffron); Chanvre (= hemp)-Bacchus; Fleurus-Céleri; Newton-Zinc; Ami-Salpêtre (= saltpetre); Colin-Champignon (= mushroom); Houille (= coal); and Térence-Thlaspy (= penny-cress); while one sympathises with one Fumier (= manure) Laguille.

The use of 'dechristianised' and rev names died out from 1795.

4. SOCIOLOGY OF THE ENLIGHTENMENT

Authors active in 1784 (Roche 1978)

	(%)
Nobility	13.5
Clergy	32.2
Medicine	11.6
Teachers	5.8
Law, administration	10.4
Non-noble army officers	2.8
Savants, artists, journalists	6.7
Bourgeois	5.5
Others	11.5

Members of academies and masonic lodges (Roche 1978)

	Academies (%)	Masonic lodges (%)
Clergy		
Bishops	2.0	NIL
Canons, vicars-general, etc	10.8	1.2
Parish clergy	6.2	1.7
Regulars	3.2	1.1
TOTAL	22.2	4.0
Nobility		
Provincial	5.9	3.2
Royal service	4.9	0.8
Office	19.2	2.9
Army	8.4	9.9
Other	1.6	1.4
TOTAL	40.0	18.2
Third estate		
Medicine	10.8	4.3
Law, administration	19.3	25.7
Industry, business	2.9	21.5
Artisans, shopkeepers	–	9.2
Miscellaneous	4.8	14.0
Unknown	–	3.7
TOTAL	37.8	78.4

5. THE PHYSIOGNOMY OF THE ENLIGHTENMENT IN URBAN FRANCE

KEY:
(1) Population in 1789 (*Roche 1978; Higonnet 1985*)
(2) Major administrative centre
(3) Major economic centre (trade, manufacturing)
(4) University city (0 = college of medicine only)
(5) Society of Agriculture in 1789
(6) Academy: date of foundation (*Roche 1978*)
(7) Number of masonic lodges in the eighteenth century (*Le Bihan 1967*)
(8) Established theatre: date of foundation (*Roche 1978*)
(9) Number of bookshops (*Histoire de l'édition 1984; Almanach royal, 1789*)
(10) Number of printers (*Ibid*)
(11) Number of subscriptions to the *Encyclopédie* (*Darnton 1979*)
(12) News-sheet (*Affiches*): date of foundation (*Feyel 1984*)

	(1)	(2)	(3)	(4)	(5)	(6)	(7)	(8)	(9)	(10)	(11)	(12)
PARIS	524,186	x	x	x	x	1660	?	—	—	—	575	—
Aix	24,492	x	—	x	x	—	13	1757	2	4	6	1769
Amiens	43,492	—	x	0	—	1745	4	1778	3	2	59	1770
Angers	27,596	x	—	x	x	1695	6	x	3	4	109	1773
Arles	24,700	—	—	—	—	1667	1	—	1	1	NIL	—
Avignon	24,238	x	x	x	—	—	8	—	—	20	55	1768
Arras	20,410	x	—	—	—	1737	5	—	3	2	?	1788
Bayonne	20,000	—	x	—	—	—	4	1777	2	2	?	—
Besançon	20,228	x	—	x	—	1752	6	1775	12	4	338	1766
Bordeaux	82,602	x	x	x	—	1713	22	1735	12	6	356	1758
Brest	33,852	—	x	—	—	1752	10	x	1	1	20	—
Caen	31,902	—	x	x	x	1705	9	x	10	4	221	1786
Clermont	31,590	x	—	0	x	1750	7	—	2	2	13	1779
Dijon	21,298	x	—	x	—	1740	4	1787	7	4	152	1770
Dunkirk	28,548	—	x	—	—	—	9	x	4	2	?	—
Grenoble	24,830	x	—	0	—	1771	6	1765	1	4	80	1774
Lille	70,000	—	x	0	—	—	7	—	7	5	28	1761
Limoges	32,856	—	x	0	x	—	4	1786	2	4	3	1775
Lyon	138,684	x	x	0	x	1700	33	x	30	12	1,079	1750
Le Mans	21,866	—	—	0	x	—	4	—	5	2	?	1771
Marseille	76,222	x	x	0	—	1725	17	x	10	4	228	1760

	(1)	(2)	(3)	(4)	(5)	(6)	(7)	(8)	(9)	(10)	(11)	(12)
Metz	46,332	x	–	–	–	1757	17	1738	10	2	22	1765
Montauban	23,920	–	x	0	x	1744	7	1773	2	2	105	1777
Montpellier	33,202	x	x	x	–	1706	19	1752	7	2	169	1770
Nancy	33,432	x	–	x	–	1750	7	1707	17	10	121	–
Nantes	64,994	–	x	x	–	–	14	1749	6	5	38	1757
Nîmes	48,360	–	x	0	–	1682	11	1739	5	2	212	1786
Orléans	35,594	–	x	0	x	1784	5	–	7	4	52	1764
Reims	30,602	–	x	x	–	–	4	1773	8	2	24	1772
Rennes	20,000	x	–	0	–	–	4	–	6	5	218	1784
Rouen	64,722	x	x	0	x	1742	15	1774	30	10	125	1762
Strasbourg	41,922	x	x	x	–	–	15	x	7	5	16	1731
Toulon	30,160	–	x	–	–	–	9	1765	2	1	22	–
Toulouse	55,068	x	–	x	–	1695	17	–	15	10	451	1759
Tours	31,772	–	x	–	x	–	9	–	5	3	65	1768
Troyes	30,706	–	x	0	–	–	2	–	3	3	53	1782
Versailles	44,200	x	–	–	–	–	18	–	6	0	5	–

6. FREEDOMS OF THE INDIVIDUAL: CIVIL STATUS, THE PRESS, EXPRESSION, ASSOCIATION

20 Nov 1787, 4 May 1788   The government uses *lettres de cachet* to try to silence political opposition in the Paris parl during the Pre-Rev crisis. The parl protests loudly at the deployment of 'arbitrary power'.

5 July 1788   Royal edict invites opinions concerning the holding of the EG: establishment of *de facto* press freedom (confirmed in the *Résultat du conseil* of 27 Dec).

Late 1788–May 1789   Massive wave of political pamphleteering, despite some harassment from the courts, inc the Paris parl. Calls for press freedom from Mirabeau (*Sur la liberté de la presse*), Condorcet (*Lettre d'un gentil-homme à MM. du Tiers Etat*), Target (*Lettre sur les Etats Généraux*), etc.

19 May 1789   Following an episode in which Mirabeau is legally pursued for printing an account of the EG, newspapers are permitted to print a verbatim record of debates.

May–July 1789   Despite attempts by the courts to restrict freedom of expression, virtually total press freedom is achieved (and will last down to Aug 1792).

4 Aug 1789   'Night of 4 Aug': abolition of the feudal system, inc personal servitude.

26 Aug 1789   Declaration of the Rights of Man: inc freedom of opinion and expression.

Autumn 1789/Spring 1790   Further (unsuccessful) attempts to restrict press freedom.

14 Dec 1789   Law on municipalities: only active citizens (in the depts) are permitted to organise collective petitions or to gather in associations. (Extended to Paris, 21 May.)

24 Dec 1789   Protestants no longer debarred from public office.

28 Jan 1790   Citizenship granted to Jews from S France.

15 Mar 1790   Abolition of feudal honorific distinctions (acts of homage, primogeniture on feudal and seigneurial lands, etc).

16 Mar 1790   Abolition of *lettres de cachet*.

19 June 1790   Abolition of noble titles: no family crests or liveries.

31 July 1790   Following extremist radical journalism from Marat, etc, the Constit Ass. decrees that journalists calling for the overthrow of the constitution will be prosecuted by the Châtelet court (repealed on 2 Aug).

6 Aug 1790   Abolition of the *droit d'aubaine* (monarch's right to claim the estate of foreigners dying on French soil).

13 Nov 1790   The right enjoyed by societies to hold meetings and establish societies is reaffirmed.

13–19 Jan 1791   Freedom of theatrical performance (though under municipal surveillance).

Law on copyright, the so-called 'Declaration of the Rights of Genius' (LAKANAL): a work is the property of its author; it falls into the public domain five years (from 19 July 1793, 10 years) after his death.

8 Apr 1791   Law on the right of succession: the abolition of primogeniture is reaffirmed.

1 May 1791   Soldiers are permitted to attend political clubs.

9 May 1791   The wall-sticking of anonymous newspapers is forbidden.

15 May 1791   Coloured men born of free parents in the colonies are accorded equality with whites; but slavery is maintained.

18 May 1791   Petitioning may not be delegated: collective petitioning is thus made illegal.

July–Sept 1791   Post-Champ de Mars reaction against democratic politics,

- *19–22 July:* law on municipal police: all clubs are to make declarations to the municipality
- *31 July:* persons who provoke murder, pillage, arson, civil disobedience, etc, are to be arrested
- *23 Aug:* press law: jury trials for libels, preaching disobedience to the law, defiance of the public authorities, etc. (These dispositions are incorporated into the 1791 Constitution, Sept 1791, but never fully implemented)
- *29–30 Sept:* on the eve of dissolution, the Constit Ass. declares that clubs have no formal right to existence, to petition or to send delegations. Formal prohibition of collective petitioning. (In fact, neither law is implemented.)

30 July 1791   Suppression of orders of chivalry (though military decorations are provisionally maintained).

27 Sept 1791   All Jews may become active citizens.

28 Sept 1791   Suppression of slavery within France.

4 Apr 1792   Political rights accorded mulattos and free blacks in the colonies.

28 June 1792   Lafayette is unsuccessful in his attempt to persuade the Leg Ass. to defuse the impending political crisis by closing down Jacobin clubs.

12 Aug 1792   Following the overthrow of the king (10 Aug), the Paris Commune muzzles the royalist and aristocratic press: pro-royalist newspapers are closed down (Aug–Sept).

Aug 1792/Jan 1793   Minister of the Interior Roland subventions the Girondin press.

20 Sept 1792   Laicisation of the *état civil*: lay registration of births, marriages and deaths. Law on divorce. Marriage law.

4 Dec 1792   Death penalty for advocating the re-establishment of the monarchy.

16 Dec 1792   Death penalty for threatening the unity and integrity of the Rpbc.

7 Mar 1793   Restriction of the right to make a will, so as to protect the rights of children.

9–10 Mar 1793   Parisian mobs attack and destroy the printing-presses of Girondin newspapers.

12 Mar 1793   Reaffirmation of freedom of theatrical performance.

18 Mar 1793   Death penalty for advocating the *loi agraire.*

29 Mar 1793   Law on seditious writings: death penalty (meted out by the Rev Tribunal) for proposing the dissolution of the Convtn, the re-establishment of the monarchy and for attacks on popular sovereignty.

13 Apr 1793   Death penalty for advocating peace on terms disadvantageous to France.

Late May 1793   Disappearance of the Girondin press.

13 June 1793   Following Federalist repression of clubs, the Convtn decrees that local authorities are not to trouble the meetings of clubs. (On 25 July, a penalty of 10 years in irons is fixed for this offence.)

24 June 1793   'Constitution of 1793': individual freedom and freedom of expression are maintained. (The constitution is never enforced.)

19 July 1793   Two copies of every book printed in France are to be deposited in the Bibliothèque Nationale.

2 Aug 1793   Law on the theatre: designated theatres are to stage performances of patriotic pieces on a regular basis; theatres staging plays which tend to deprave public spirit or reawaken royalist sentiment are to be closed down. (The Théâtre-Francais is closed under the provisions of this law on 3 Sept.)

17 Sept 1793   Law of Suspects: 'supporters of tyranny and federalism' are adjudged suspects.

30 Oct 1793/9 brum II   All female clubs and popular societies are closed down. All meetings of clubs are to be open to the public.

2 Nov 1793/12 brum II   Law on illegitimacy gives illegitimate children equal rights: supporters of the law claim there are 'no more bastards in France'.

6 Dec 1793/16 frim   In the face of the growth of the dechristianisation movement in Paris and the provinces, the Convtn reaffirms the principle of freedom of worship.

28 Dec 1793/8 niv II   Speeding up of divorce procedure in family courts.

4 Feb 1794/16 pluv II   Decree abolishing slavery in French colonies.

23 Apr 1794/4 flor II   Desertion for six months regarded as sufficient grounds for divorce.

14 May 1794/25 flor II   Theatrical censorship introduced.

23 Aug 1794/6 fruct II   Decree condemning the adoption of 'rev' forenames ('Brutus', 'Gracchus', 'Jonquille', etc).

16 Oct 1794/25 vendém III   As the Thermidorian reaction gets under way,

collective petitioning and similar federative activity are prohibited.

12 Nov 1794/22 brum III   Closure of the Paris Jacobin Club.

10 Apr 1795/21 germ III   Disarming of ex-terrorists.

1 May 1795/12 flor III   'Chénier Law': despite a right-wing move to re-establish press freedom, the law of 29 Mar 1793 on seditious writings is reaffirmed, though it is altered so that it remains an offence to humiliate the deputies; and the penalty is banishment, not death.

22 Aug 1795/5 fruct III   'Constitution of Year III': total press freedom affirmed; but with the proviso that this may be restricted on the authority of the Directors for a year. No clubs with political objectives allowed; no collective petitioning; etc.

23 Aug 1795/6 fruct III   Suppression of all clubs and popular societies.

5 Oct 1795/13 vendém IV   'Vendémiaire rising' in Paris: followed by attacks on and closure of many royalist newspapers.

8 Oct 1795/17 vendém IV   Suppression of sectional assemblies: *de facto* end of the freedom of association.

25 Dec 1795/5 niv V   Newspaper vendors are only permitted to shout the titles of newspapers.

8 Jan 1796/18 niv IV   Theatre managements are to ensure that 'rpbcn' music is played prior to performances and during intervals.

16 Feb 1796/25 pluv IV   Law of 2 Aug 1793 on the theatre is repromulgated.

26 Feb 1796/7 vent IV   Closure of the neo-Jacobin Panthéon Club and other Jacobin societies.

16–17 Apr 1796/27–8 germ IV   Death penalty for proposing dissolution of the assembly, the re-establishment of the monarchy, the 1791 or 1793 Constitutions, attacks on property, etc. All newspapers and journals must contain the name of the author and printer.

24 June 1796/6 mess IV   Rise in postal rates (aimed at restricting the press).

2 Aug 1796/15 therm IV   Law on bastardy is attenuated.

25 July 1797/7 therm V   Following the appearance of political societies (cercles constitutionnels, etc), all political societies are formally suppressed.

4–5 Sept 1797/18–19 fruct V   The Fructidorian coup changes the political atmosphere:
  - arrest of authors and printers of right-wing newspapers
  - law of 7 therm V forbidding political societies is repealed, though the law of 27 germ IV on seditious opinions is upheld
  - 8 Sept/22 fruct   Directors invoke emergency powers grounded in the constitution to muzzle the press for a year. (Dozens of newspapers will be closed down 1797–9.)

30 Sept and 4 Oct 1797/9 and 13 vendém VI   Stamp tax on paper introduced.

14 March 1798/24 vent VI   Prohibition of collective petitioning: any club engaging in the practice will be closed down.

26 Aug 1798/9 fruct VI   Prolongation of the year's restriction on press freedom, introduced 8 Sept 1797.

25 May 1799/6 prair VII   Increased stamp tax.

22 July 1799/4 therm VII   The Directors' policing powers over the press are removed.

 2 Sept 1799/16 fruct VII   The Directors utilise their constitutional powers for suppressing sedition to close down royalist newspapers and deport their journalists.

13 Aug 1799/26 therm VII   Police Minister Fouché closes down the Club du Manège.

7. THE REVOLUTION AND LITERARY PRODUCTION

New books, 1780–8, and 1794–9 (Estivals 1965)

1780	466	1794	371
1781	425	1795	308
1782	754	1796	240
1783	1,005	1797	345
1784	937	1798	475
1785	831	1799	815
1786	1,224		
1787	1,238		
1788	1,166		

(NOTE: pre-Rev figures are estimates, post-1794 figures are based on the *dépôt légal* system)

Publication of novels, 1787–1799 (Martin et al. 1977)

	New	Reissues	Total		New	Reissues	Total
1787	69	94	163	1794	16	62	78
1788	99	117	216	1795	41	90	131
1789	101	86	187	1796	54	90	144
1790	55	68	123	1797	73	124	197
1791	42	61	103	1798	96	118	214
1792	38	102	140	1799	174	107	281
1793	20	95	115				

Genres of new novels (Martin et al. 1977)

KEY
(1) Sentimental intrigues, pastoral love-stories
(2) *Galanterie, libertinage*
(3) Pornography
(4) Romanesque tales, mysteries
(5) Travels
(6) Depiction and critique of mores
(7) Political and court intrigue, war

(8) Historical and pseudo-historical elements
(9) Chivalry, troubadour genre
(10) Fairy-tales, supernatural elements, legends, the Bible
(11) Allegory
(12) Philosophical themes and ideas, utopias
(13) Didactic and pedagogic works, novels with educational themes
(14) Moralising works, edifying tales, religious morals.
(NOTE: more than one element appears in many novels)

	(1)	(2)	(3)	(4)	(5)	(6)	(7)	(8)	(9)	(10)	(11)	(12)	(13)	(14)
1787	18	9	2	20	9	14	2	2	–	1	–	4	6	4
1788	47	12	2	18	19	18	5	1	1	2	–	3	4	5
1789	40	5	3	16	24	21	9	7	2	7	5	7	8	8
1790	15	4	3	9	9	11	4	1	1	3	2	4	3	2
1791	7	2	2	7	8	4	3	2	–	–	2	3	2	1
1792	9	5	5	8	4	6	4	1	1	–	1	1	1	–
1793	7	2	3	2	2	–	–	1	–	–	1	1	–	2
1794	8	1	–	3	2	2	–	–	–	–	–	1	1	–
1795	13	3	1	10	8	4	2	1	1	1	1	2	7	1
1796	23	6	1	11	5	12	1	1	1	3	1	3	3	4
1797	29	7	1	28	9	12	–	5	1	2	–	4	6	4
1798	31	9	2	41	14	17	2	4	–	3	–	5	5	8
1799	56	20	3	60	19	28	4	7	2	12	–	5	13	17

Political songs, 1789–1800 (Brécy 1981)

1789	116	1795	137
1790	261	1796	126
1791	308	1797	147
1792	325	1798	77
1793	590	1799	90
1794	701	1800	25

New newspapers, 1789–1800 (Walter and Martin 1936–43)
(Paris-based figures which underestimate the provincial press)

	1789	1790	1791	1792	1793	1794 II	1795 III	1796 IV	1797 V	1798 VI	1799 VII	VIII
Niv	–	–	–	–	–	7	9	5	12	5	1	2
Jan	3	32	28	19	14	–	–	–	–	–	–	–
Pluv	–	–	–	–	–	3	6	7	9	4	1	–
Feb	1	23	18	8	2	–	–	–	–	–	–	–
Vent	–	–	–	–	–	8	8	3	6	7	2	–
Mar	–	26	14	3	7	–	–	–	–	–	–	–
Germ	–	–	–	–	–	6	5	8	9	9	2	–
Apr	7	26	14	11	4	–	–	–	–	–	–	–

	1789	1790	1791	1792	1793	1794 II	1795 III	1796 IV	1797 V	1798 VI	1799 VII	VIII
Flor	–	–	–	–	–	4	5	4	4	2	1	–
May	17	26	9	12	5	–	–	–	–	–	–	–
Prair	–	–	–	–	–	1	4	4	15	1	2	–
June	–	17	14	8	9	–	–	–	–	–	–	–
Mess	–	–	–	–	–	4	4	–	7	1	11	–
July	29	21	14	7	11	–	–	–	–	–	–	–
Therm	–	–	–	–	–	5	4	3	11	3	5	–
Aug	26	22	10	8	2	–	–	–	–	–	–	–
Fruct/jc	–	–	–	–	–	11	6	8	40	3	7	–
Sept	19	18	9	17	5	–	–	–	–	–	–	–
						II	III	IV	V	VI	VII	VIII
Vendém	–	–	–	–	1	13	6	9	15	7	7	–
Oct	24	12	10	12	6	–	–	–	–	–	–	–
Brum	–	–	–	–	5	7	6	3	8	–	2	–
Nov	21	14	5	11	–	–	–	–	–	–	–	–
Frim	–	–	–	–	5	6	3	6	3	3	3	–
Dec	15	14	5	11	–	–	–	–	–	–	–	–
UNKNOWN	12	25	8	7	1	2	5	3	5	4	1	1
TOTAL	174	226	158	134	78	–	–	–	–	–	–	–
	1789	1790	1791	1792	1793*							
	–	–	–	–	–	66*	77	57	131	61	42	14
						II	III	IV	V	VI	VII	VIII

*17 items from 1793/II counted in *both* the 1793 and Year II totals.

8. SOME SIGNIFICANT PUBLICATION AND LITERARY DATES

(i) = work directly influenced by, or influencing, the Rev
(ii) = work reflecting taste in France and Europe at large

1787   (ii) Louvet de Couvray, *Les Amours du chevalier Faublas* (to 1790)
Bernardin de Saint-Pierre, *Paul et Virginie*
Goethe, *Iphigenia auf Tauris*
Schiller, *Don Carlos*
Mozart, *Don Giovanni*.

1788   (i) Mirabeau, *De la Monarchie prussienne sous Frédéric le Grand*
Saint-Simon, *Mémoires* (1st edn)
  (ii) Restif de la Bretonne, *Les Nuits de Paris* (to 1794)
Mercier, *Tableau de Paris* (12 vols)
Mme de Staël, *Lettre sur J. J. Rousseau*
Barthélemy, *Voyage du jeune Anacharsis en Grèce*
Goethe, *Egmont*
Kant, *Critique of Practical Reason*
Jeremy Bentham, *Introduction to the Principle of Morality*
First appearance of *The Times* (*Daily Register* since 1785)
Death of Buffon, Gainsborough, C. P. E. Bach.

1789   (i) Siéyès, *Qu'est-ce que le Tiers Etat?*
Malouet, *Considérations sur le gouvernement*
Marie–Joseph Chénier, *Charles IX*
Foundation of the *Journal des débats* and the *Moniteur*
  (ii) Lavoisier, *Traité de chimie*
William Blake, *Songs of Innocence*
Gilbert White, *Natural History of Selborne*
Mozart, *Cosi fan tutte*
Death of Holbach.

1790   (i) Edmund Burke, *Reflections on the Revolution in France*
André Chénier, *Avis au peuple français*
Sénac de Meilhan, *Des principes et des causes de la Révolution*
Radischev, *Journey from St Petersburg to Moscow*
  (ii) Kant, *Critique of Judgement*
Death of Adam Smith.

1791   (i) Th. Paine, *The Rights of Man* (part I)
         Cloots, *L'Orateur du genre humain*
         André Chénier, *Le Serment du Jeu de Paume*
         Collot-d'Herbois, *Almanach du père Gérard*
         Olympe de Gouges, *Déclaration des droits de la femme*
       (ii) Volney, *Les Ruines, ou Méditations sur les révolutions des empires*
         Bernardin de Saint-Pierre, *La Chaumière indienne*
         Sade, *Justine*
         Boswell, *Life of Johnson*
         Mozart, *The Magic Flute*
         Foundation of *The Observer*
         Death of Mozart, John Wesley

1792   (i) Th. Paine, *The Rights of Man* (part II)
         Marat, *Les Chaînes de l'esclavage* (trans. from English)
         Cloots, *La République universelle*
         Rouget de l'Isle, 'La Marseillaise'
         Arthur Young, *Travels in France . . . in 1787, 1788 and 1789*
         Mary Wollstonecraft, *Vindication of the Rights of Women*
       (ii) Florian, *Fables*
         Beaumarchais, *La Mère coupable.*

1793   (i) Mallet du Pan, *Considérations sur la nature de la Révolution en France*
         Sylvain Maréchal, *Jugement dernier des rois*
         Cloots, *Base constitutionnelle de la république du genre humain*
         Marie–Joseph Chénier, *C. Gracchus*
         Sade, *La Philosophie dans le boudoir*
         William Godwin, *The Inquiry Concerning Political Justice.*

1794   (i) Marie–Joseph Chénier, Méhul, *Le Chant du départ*
         Xavier de Maistre, *Voyage autour de ma chambre*
         Coleridge, *The Death of Robespierre*
         Th. Paine, *The Age of Reason*
         William Godwin, *Caleb Williams*
         Schiller, *Letters Concerning the Aesthetic Education of Mankind*
       (ii) Legendre, *Eléments de géometrie*
         William Blake, *Songs of experience*
         Erasmus Darwin, *Zoomania, or the Laws of Organic Life*
         Anne Radcliffe, *The Mysteries of Udolpho*
         Death of Gibbon.

1795   (i) Condorcet, *Esquisse d'un tableau du progrès de l'esprit humain*
         (posthumous)
         Chamfort, *Œuvres* (posthumous)
         Hannah More, *Cheap Repository Tracts* (to 1798)
       (ii) Goethe, *Wilhelm Meisters Lehrjahre*
         Jean-Paul, *Hesperus*
         Lewis, *The Monk.*

1796   (i) Jos de Maistre, *Considérations sur la France*
        Bonald, *Théorie du pouvoir politique et religieux*
        Benjamin Constant, *De la Force du gouvernement actuel de la France*
       (ii) Restif de la Bretonne, *M. Nicolas*
        Sade, *Juliette*
        Fichte, *Principles of natural law*
        Fanny Burney, *Camilla.*
1797   (i) Barruel, *Mémoires pour servir à l'histoire du jacobinisme*
        Chateaubriand, *Essai . . . sur les révolutions*
        Sénac de Meilhan, *L'Emigré*
        Holderlin, *Hyperion*
        Goethe, *Hermann & Dorothea*
       (ii) Diderot, *Jacques le fataliste* (posthumous)
        Lagrange, *Théorie des fonctions analytiques*
        Lamarck, *Mémoires de physique*
        Schelling, *Philosophy of Nature*
        Death of Burke.
1798   (ii) Pinel, *Nosographie philosophique, ou la Méthode de l'analyse appliquée à la médecine*
        Wordsworth, Coleridge, *Lyrical Ballads*
        Malthus, *Essay on the Principle of Population*
        Edward Jenner, *Inquiry into the Causes and Effects of the Variolae Vaccinal*
        Death of Casanova.
1799   (ii) Senancour, *Rêveries sur la nature primitive de l'homme*
        Monge, *Traité de géometrie descriptive*
        Schiller, *Wallenstein*
        Death of Beaumarchais, George Washington.

9. SOME REVOLUTIONARY AND COUNTER-REVOLUTIONARY NEWSPAPERS

Les Actes des Apôtres, Nov 1789–Oct 1791. Director: Peltier. Contributors: Bergasse, Montlosier, Rivarol, Suleau, Mirabeau-Tonneau. Counter-rev, witty, vitriolic, it was often the object of popular demonstrations in Paris. Appeared two or three times a week and sold at 6 sous.

L'Ami des citoyens, Aug 1791–Jan 1793; Aug 1794–18 Feb 1795. Director: Tallien (Méhée de la Touche from late 1794). Political information for 'the least educated citizens'; with trade, agriculture and science from late 1794, by which time it had developed into a Thermidorian newspaper. Weekly until Jan 1793, more irregular until late 1794, then daily. At least 4,500 subscriptions in Apr 1792, less thereafter.

L'Ami des lois, July 1794–1800. Director: Poultier, deputy in Convtn for Pas-de-Calais. Daily. Denounced as anarchist and incendiary under the Directory.

L'Ami du peuple, ou le Publiciste parisien (various wordings), 12 Sept 1789–14 July 1794. The mouthpiece of Marat, widely read in the clubs. Specialised in denouncing conspiracy, uncovering plots and calling for popular violence. Daily at first, then appearing more irregularly. Posthumous imitations included Leclerc's *Ami du peuple,* 20 July–15 Sept 1793; and that of Chasles, then Lebois, Sept 1794–Oct 1797.

L'Ami du roi, 1 June 1790–4 May 1792. Director: abbé Royou. Violently counter-rev, with aristocratic, *émigré* and popular readership. Persecuted by Leg Ass. in July 1791, then May 1792 at the same time as Marat's *Ami du peuple.* 3,000 subscriptions in Sept 1790, 5,700 in May 1791.

Annales patriotiques et littéraires (slight changes in title), 3 Oct 1789–12 Dec 1797. Directors: Mercier and Carra from 1789 until June 1793 (when Carra, who was purged as a Girondin, was claiming subcriptions from 1,200 popular societies and a potential readership of a million); Mercier and Salaville from Dec 1794 to Sept 1797. Popular and influential, esp among provincial Jacobin clubs. By the late 1790s, it was critical of the Directory.

La Bouche de fer, Jan 1790–28 July 1791. Directors: Fauchet and Bonneville. Contributors inc Cloots, Condorcet, Paine, Etta Palm. Organ of the Cercle social, it eschewed political reportage, preferring articles of wider social and cultural interest. Thrice weekly.

Bulletin de l'Assemblée Nationale, 7 July 1789–Dec 1789, then irregularly until Aug 1791. Director: Maret (until he joined the *Moniteur* in early 1790). The earliest attempt at parliamentary reportage.

Chronique de Paris, 24 Aug 1789–25 Aug 1793. Directors: Millin, Noel. Contributors inc Condorcet (political reportage), Ducos, Cloots, Manuel, Rabaut Saint-Etienne. At first identified with a constitutional monarchist position, it became a Girondin organ from 1791. Its presses were ransacked in the disturbances of 9–10 March 1793. It never recovered from the *journées* of 31 May and 2 June.

Chronique du mois (various titles), Nov 1791–July 1793. Director: Bonneville. Contributors inc Clavière, Condorcet, Mercier, Broussonet, Brissot, Garran de Coulon, Lanthénas, Dussaulx, Collot-d'Herbois. From the Cercle social presses, it was increasingly identified with the Girondins. Monthly.

Courrier de l'Europe, 1776–Dec 1792. Director: Swinton. Editors inc Brissot, Montlosier. Appeared twice weekly from London. An important model for early rev newspapers.

Courrier de Provence, July 1789–Sept 1791. Successor to the *Lettres du comte de Mirabeau à ses commettants* which Mirabeau had brought out from 10 May to 24 July 1789. Collaborators included Chamfort, Clavière, Dumont, Lamourette. Thrice weekly.

Courrier des 83 départements (various titles), 5 July 1789–31 May 1793. Editor: Gorsas. Increasingly identified with the Girondins, it appeared daily. Its presses were ransacked, 9–10 Mar 1793. Thrice weekly.

Le Défenseur de la Constitution, 17 May 1792–20 Aug 1792. Editor: Robespierre. Twice weekly. Precursor of *Lettres à ses commettants de Maximilien Robespierre.*

La Feuille villageoise, 30 Sept 1790–2 Aug 1795. Directors: Cérutti, Rabaut Saint-Etienne, Grouvelle, Guinguené. Contributors inc Boncerf, François de Neufchâteau, Lanthénas. It offered summaries of legislation and accounts of public affairs, and was highly important in propagating the ideas of the Rev in the countryside. Over 15,000 subscriptions in 1790.

Gazette de France (various titles), 1631–1914. The first French newspaper. Director from 1786 to 1791 was Pankoucke. Editors from 1789 inc Peuchet, Dubois-Fontanille, Fallet, Chamfort. Daily from 1 May 1792.

Gazette de Paris, 1 Oct 1789–10 Aug 1792. Director: de Rozoi. Royalist daily, esp informative on counter-rev feelings and activities. Its offices were sacked on 10 Aug 1792 and its director executed. 4,000 subscriptions in Jan 1791, 2,300 in June 1792.

Journal de la liberté de la presse, see *le Tribun du peuple*

Journal de la Montagne, June 1793–Nov 1794. Directors: Laveaux, Valcour Rousseau. A Montagnard daily, the successor to the *Journal des Amis de la Constitution* and the *Journal des débats de la Société des Amis de la Constitution.*

Journal de la Société de 1789 (from 21 Aug 1790, *Mémoires de la Société de 1789*), 5 June 1790–15 Sept 1790. Directors inc Condorcet, Kersaint. Contributors inc André Chénier, Dupont de Nemours, Hassenfratz, La Rochefoucauld.

Journal de Paris (various titles), 1777–1811. Director: Corancez, with Roederer from 1795. The first French daily newspaper, it had semi-official status early in the Rev. Garat, then Condorcet in charge of parliamentary reporting in 1789. It was seen as increasingly counter-rev after André Chénier joined the reporting team in Oct 1791. Its offices were ransacked on 11–12 Aug 1792, and it suspended publication until Oct 1792. Mercier a contributor in the late 1790s, when it became pro-Bonaparte.

Journal des Amis de la Constitution, see *Journal des débats de la Société des Amis de la Constitution*

Journal des débats de la Société des Amis de la Constitution, 1 June 1791–14 Dec 1793. The orthodox Jacobin journal included correspondence as well as accounts of debates from Jan 1792. Disowned by the Jacobins, its role was assumed from June 1793 by the *Journal de la Montagne.*

Journal des débats et décrets, 1 Sept 1789–Apr 1797; then June 1797–1944. Editors in early 1790s inc Lacretelle, Louvet. Politically neutral parliamentary reportage. Famous only from the Consulate.

Journal des défenseurs de la patrie, 12 Apr 1796–1800. Director: Lavallée. Daily, specialising in military news and reportage.

Journal des Etats généraux (then *Journal de l'Assemblée Nationale,* etc) 27 Apr 1789–Aug 1792. Director: Hodey. Parliamentary reportage from the time of the EG.

Journal des hommes libres, ou le Républicain (various titles), 2 Nov 1792–1800. Director: Duval. Contributors inc Félix Lepeletier, Antonelle. Daily. By the late 1790s a fierce left-wing critic of the Directory.

Journal du club des Cordeliers, 28 June 1791–10 Aug 1791. Editors: Sintiès, Momoro. The official organ of the Cordeliers appeared four times each week but was broken up in the repression following the Champ de Mars.

Journal général de la Cour et de la Ville (various titles), Sept 1789–10 Aug 1792. Directors: Brune (until Dec 1789) and Gautier de Syonnet. It appeared in two forms, one for street sales ('édition de colportage') which was known as 'le petit Gautier', which offered crude counter-rev opinions and was widely read. Daily. 6,000–10,000 subscriptions.

Journal politique national, 12 July 1789–May 1790. Director: abbé Sabatier de Castres, then Rivarol. Right-wing political and general commentary. Popular. Appeared thrice weekly.

Lettres à ses commettants de Maximilien Robespierre, Oct 1792–25 Apr 1793. Robespierre's mouthpiece, successor of *le Défenseur de la Constitution.* Weekly. Aimed at a provincial readership.

Lettres du comte de Mirabeau à ses commettants, see *le Courrier de Provence*

Le Logographe, 27 Apr 1791–17 Aug 1792. Owned by the 'Triumvirate' (Lameth, Barnave, Duport). Director: Hodey. Weighty and serious political reportage. The *armoire de fer* showed that the journal was secretly financed by the court. It appeared daily and followed a constitutional monarchist line. Suppressed by the Convtn.

Mercure britannique, Aug 1798–Mar 1800. Director: Mallet du Pan. Royalist. Published in London, it appeared twice a month.

Mercure de France (various titles), 1672–1820. Directors: Mallet du Pan from 1784 to 1792, then Marmontel (1792), La Harpe and Chamfort (until 1793); Lenoir-Laroche (with Cabanis, Destutt de Tracy) from Apr 1796. Contributors inc Marie–Joseph Chénier, François de Neuchâteau, Lalande, Lebrun, Pankoucke. Appeared once a week, often more.

Le Moniteur universel, ou Gazette nationale, 25 Nov 1789–1865 (when it became the *Journal officiel*). Director: Pankoucke The Hansard of the rev assemblies, it was politically moderate and authoritative. Owed much to the hyper-accurate parliamentary reporting of Maret from early 1790 to Sept 1791. Subscriptions, 8,500 in 1792. It became the official organ of the government from 1800.

L'Orateur du peuple, 23 May 1790–Sept 1792, then 11 Sept 1794–12 Aug 1795. Director: Fréron. Popular sensationalist daily. Radical in the early years (Fréron offered space in his columns to Marat), after Thermidor the newspaper became the official journal of the *jeunesse dorée,* and 'the Thermidorian newspaper par excellence' (GODECHOT).

Le Patriote français, 6 May 1789–2 June 1793. Director: Brissot. Contributors inc Pétion, Grégoire, Condorcet, Paine, Clavière, Lanthénas, Kersaint, Bosc d'Antic. A well-informed daily for the Girondin cause. Its presses were threatened in demonstrations on the *journée* of 9–10 Mar 1793.

Le Père Duchesne, or *Le Père Duchène* Sept 1790–Dec 1790, then Jan 1791–Mar 1794. The personal mouthpiece of Hébert, it offered a popular and scatalogical political commentary on the times. It died with its proprietor. Much imitated, there were nearly 200 journals with some reference in their titles to the Père Duchène, among them the *Père Duchêne* of Lebois, which appeared between June and Nov 1799.

Petit Gautier, see *Journal général de la Cour, etc*

Le Point du jour, ou Résultat de ce qui s'est passé la veille à l'Assemblée Nationale, 19 June 1789–21 Oct 1791. Director: Barère. Parliamentary reportage. Daily.

Le Républicain, see *Journal des hommes libres*

Les Révolutions de France et de Brabant, 28 Nov 1789–18 July 1791, then Oct–Dec 1792. Directors: Desmoulins at first, with Merlin de Thionville in 1792. Popular and radical weekly.

Les Révolutions de Paris, 12 July 1789–24 Feb 1794. Director: Prudhomme. Contributors inc (esp) Loustalot, Chaumette, Maréchal, Fabre d'Eglantine. The most independent of the early newspapers, it appeared weekly, had possibly 200,000 readers and was widely imitated.

Rougyff, ou le Frank en vedette, 20 July 1793–May 1794. Director: Guffroy. Violent attempt to emulate Marat. It appeared twice or thrice a week and was widely circulated in the armies.

Le Sentinelle, May–July 1792, then 24 June 1795–3 May 1798. Director: Louvet; from 1797 Baudin and Daunou. Subsidised by the Roland ministry in 1792, Louvet claimed to produce 20,000 copies of each number.

Le Tribun du peuple, ou le Défenseur des droits de l'homme, 5 Oct 1794–24 Apr 1796. Director: Gracchus Babeuf. Continuation of the *Journal de la liberté de la presse,* 3 Sept 1794–1 Oct 1794. Where the latter had been anti-Robespierrist, the *Tribun du peuple* was radical, communistic and neo-Jacobin. Daily. Average print run, 2,000.

La Tribune des patriotes, 30 Apr–May 1792. Directors: Desmoulins and Fréron. Sequel to the *Révolutions de France et de Brabant,* only four numbers appeared.

Le Vieux Cordelier, 25 Nov 1793–24 Feb 1794. Director: Desmoulins. Organ of the policy of *indulgence,* it died with its director after only seven issues.

10. EDUCATION: CHRONOLOGY

4 Aug 1789   Abolition of tithes and seigneurial dues in the 'Night of 4 Aug' has serious financial implications for many educational establishments.

22 Dec 1789   Law on local government places public education under the surveillance of dept authorities.

13 Feb 1790   Educational and charitable congregations are exempted the provisions of the law abolishing the making of vows.

28 Oct 1790   Property of educational institutions exempted sale as nat lands.

19 Feb 1791   Abolition of *octrois* (municipal tolls) further compromises the income of many schools.

22 Mar 1791   Schoolteachers (laymen and clerics) are to take the oath of allegiance associated with the Civ Constn. Resultant defection of many teachers.

10–19 Sept 1791   Talleyrand, on behalf of the Education Committee, introduces plans for the reorganisation of education. (Like all other educational reports down to mid 1793, this will not be implemented.)

26 Sept 1791   Provisional maintenance of institutions of higher education (universities, etc), pending the formulation of comprehensive educational plans. (As many institutions have been hard hit by the abolition of tithes, *octrois*, etc, this involves a state commitment to expenditure.)

23 Oct 1791   Professors of colleges who are members of ecclesiastical communities are maintained in post.

7 Feb 1792   Schools maintained in the enjoyment of their revenues.

20–21 Apr 1792   Condorcet introduces (never-to-be-implemented) plans for the comprehensive reorganisation of public education.

29 May 1792   Credits of 200,000 liv set aside for education.

18 Aug 1792   Disbandment of religious communities dedicated to either charitable or educational purposes. But individual members may continue in post, provided they take the 'Liberty–Equality' oath.

25 Nov 1792   Suspension of all nominations and replacements to academies.

14 Feb 1793   Adjournment of sale of nat lands used for educational purposes. Prohibition of teachers taking fees for pupils: establishment of the principle of free education.

8 Mar 1793   The sale of all nat lands owned by educational establishments is permitted, except for the buildings in use. State agrees to pay masters and mistresses a fixed wage.

30 May 1793   Law on primary educations: every commune with between 400 and 1,500 inhabitants is to have at least one primary school. Basic salary for schoolmasters of 1,200 liv.

18 June 1793   Establishment of the *Muséum d'histoire naturelle* (which assumes many of the functions of the defunct Jardin du Roi) for teaching of and research in the natural sciences. Staff includes Fourcroy, Daubenton, Jussieu, Geoffroy de Saint-Hilaire, Lamarck, Lacépède.

24 June 1793   Constitution of 1793 (never implemented) stipulates that education is a civic right.

13 July 1793   Robespierre introduces in the Convtn the radical plans of the assassinated conventionnel, Lepeletier de Saint-Fargeau, for educational reform (including the institution of obligatory state boarding schools).

8 Aug 1793   Abolition of academies (whose property is nationalised).

15–16 Sept 1793   Abolition of AR universities (though in practice, these are provisionally maintained).

8 Nov 1793/18 brum II   Creation of a national institution for music (the Conservatoire) (reorganised 3 Aug 1795/16 therm III)

19 Dec 1793/29 frim II   'Bouquier Law' on primary schooling:
- establishment of the principle of obligatory primary schooling (poorly implemented)
- any private individual may open a school, under municipal surveillance
- the syllabus includes, besides the three 'R's, the Rights of Man, the Constitution and heroic and virtuous actions.

27 Jan 1794/8 pluv II   All depts are to open public libraries.

2 Feb 1794/14 pluv II   Creation of the 'Ecole des Armes': for several months, district authorities are invited to send two citizens to Paris for short courses in the manufacture of gunpowder and cannon.

22 Feb 1794/4 vent II   Law on primary education:
- education free for children between 6 and 13
- teachers must take the oath and have a valid *certificat de civisme*.

1 June 1794/13 prair II   Creation of the short-lived 'Ecole de Mars' at Paris, a rpbcn military academy (closed in Oct).

28 Sept 1794/7 vendém III   Establishment of the Ecole Centrale des travaux publics (from Sept 1795, the Ecole polytechnique) for the teaching of engineering. Staff includes Lagrange, Monge, Berthollet, Guyton-Morveau.

10 Oct 1794/19 vendém III   Establishment of the Conservatoire des arts et métiers, for research and training in technical subjects.

30 Oct 1794/9 brum III   Establishment of three *écoles normales*, for training of teachers (closed down 19 May 1795/30 flor III).

17 Nov 1794/27 brum III   Law on primary education:
- no obligation to attend primary schools

- salaries of schoolmasters fixed at 1,200 liv (schoolmistresses, 1,000 liv)
- syllabus to include the three 'R's, the Constitution, the Rights of Man, heroic and virtuous actions and songs, rpbcn morality, the French language, the geography and history of a free people, natural phenomena, etc
- teaching is to be in French
- pupils will visit hospitals and workshops, and help in the fields
- manual labour is included in the syllabus.

4 Dec 1794/14 frim III   Establishment of three medical schools (*écoles de santé*), at Paris, Montpellier and Strasbourg, to train physicians.

25 Feb 1795/7 vent III   Law on secondary education. Establishment of *écoles centrales* in the depts for secondary and (in the continued absence of the universities, which this law effectively suppresses) higher education:

- one school per 300,000 head of population (roughly one per department)
- entry restricted to boys
- syllabus to include maths, physics, natural history, scientific method, political economy and legislation, history, hygiene, arts and crafts, ancient and modern languages, etc
- teaching in French
- each school to possess a library, a natural history collection, a chemistry laboratory, etc
- scholarships to be provided for children from poorer homes
- teachers appointed by a dept 'education jury' on the basis of a competitive examination
- salaries of staff set at 2,000 liv, plus a capitation fee on students
- private individuals are free to create 'free colleges' which may compete with the *écoles centrales* and provide secondary education for both boys and girls

25 June 1795/7 mess III   Establishment of the Bureau des longitudes for promoting and coordinating research in astronomy and meteorology.

13 July 1795/25 mess III   Former Collège du Roi reorganised as the Collège de France.

25–26 Oct 1795/3–4 brum IV   'Daunou Law' (25 Oct) on all levels of education (with additional clauses on primary education on 26 Oct):

- schoolteachers are not to be salaried (and are thus expected to derive their income from school fees)
- one primary school per canton (*not* per commune)
- separate primary schools are to be provided for girls
- girls at primary level are to be taught the three 'R's, rpbcn morality and training in useful skills
- scholarships are to be provided in the *écoles centrales*

273

- pupils leaving the Ecole polytechnique are to proceed to specialised schools under the Ministry of the Interior for artillery, military engineering, mines, civil engineering (*ponts et chaussées*), etc
- establishment of the Institut (which assumes many of the functions of AR academies) to promote and coordinate higher research.

13 July 1796/25 mess IV   Property of AR colleges is affected to the *écoles centrales*.

11 Sept 1797/25 fruct V   Sale of educational buildings as nat lands suspended.

17 Nov 1797/27 brum VI   Candidates for public place to show prior attendance at state schools, or else attendance of their children there.

5 Feb 1798/17 pluv VI   Municipalities empowered to make unannounced visits to private schools (which since the Fructidor coup of Sept 1797 have been under closer municipal surveillance) to check on observance of the *décadi*, educational standards, physical hygiene, etc.

IX. SOCIETY AND THE ECONOMY

1. THE DEVELOPMENT OF THE FRENCH ECONOMY IN THE EIGHTEENTH CENTURY

Agricultural prices: +62% (periods 1725–35, 1775–89)

Land rents: +142% (periods 1730–9, 1780–9)

Tithes: in kind, +10 to 20% (periods 1730–9, 1780–9)

       in cash, +35% (*idem*)

Nominal wages: +26% (periods 1726–41, 1771–89)

Real wages: −15 to −25% over eighteenth century

Agricultural production: +25 to 40% (1700–9, 1780–9)

Industrial production: +409% (1700–9, 1780–9)

Trade: Europe, +400%

      Colonies, +1,000%

      TOTAL, +500%

(NOTE: As F. Crouzet (1985) has pointed out, the overall performance of the economy compares favourably with Britain's over the same period. However, global figures such as the above disguise or occlude regional disparities; the differential pace of development (prices speeded up in the last decades of the AR, growth slowed down); structural weaknesses (lack of factor endowment, technological backwardness compared with Britain, etc); and lopsidedness of the economy overall (a booming overseas trade sector contrasted with a more sluggish agricultural sector, esp in the Midi.)

2. THE STRUCTURE OF SOCIETY AT THE END OF THE ANCIEN RÉGIME, ACCORDING TO THE ABBÉ EXPILLY
(1780)

Social group	Number	(%)
1. Clergy	200,000	0.8
2. Nobility		
• heads of family	18,200	
• women, children	59,890	
TOTAL	78,090	0.3
3. Soldiers	300,000	
• women, children	50,000	
TOTAL	350,000	1.5
4. Judicial & financial officials	60,000	
• women, children	240,000	
TOTAL	300,000	1.2
5. University professors, lawyers, doctors, surgeons, apothecaries	25,000	
• women, children	70,000	
TOTAL	95,000	0.4
6. Bourgeois, financiers, businessmen, merchants, artisans	1,020,000	
• women, children	3,060,000	
TOTAL	4,080,000	16.9
7. Sailors, seafarers	70,000	
• women, children	210,000	
TOTAL	280,000	1.2
8. River-folk	10,000	
• women, children	30,000	
TOTAL	40,000	0.2
9. Big farmers, peasants with livestock	426,000	
• women, children	1,704,000	
TOTAL	2,130,000	8.8
10. Wine-growers & workers	1,000,000	
• women, children	3,500,000	
TOTAL	4,500,000	18.7
11. Wage-earners, day-labourers	2,500,000	
• women, children	7,500,000	
TOTAL	10,000,000	41.4

Social group	Number	(%)
12. Servants		
• men, boys	1,026,000	
• women, girls	928,000	
TOTAL	1,954,000	8.1
13. Children 15 years old and under	122,110	0.5
GRAND TOTAL	24,129,200	

3. SOCIAL COMPOSITION OF SOME ANCIEN RÉGIME CITIES

(a) Paris, 1749 (Based on 2,165 marriage contracts) (Furet & Daumard 1961)

	No.	(%)
Army	25	1.1
Royal service	156	7.2
Lawyers, notaries	38	1.8
Health professions	33	1.5
Liberal professions, arts	72	3.3
Jewellers, goldsmiths	85	3.9
Food trades	245	11.3
Building, furnishing	223	10.3
Clothes (inc wigmakers)	303	14.0
Cloth trade	40	1.9
Transport, horse trades, etc	47	2.2
Servants	364	16.8
No profession	240	11.1
Other	294	13.6

(b) Some provincial cities
(Based on CAPITATION records) (Roche 1978)

	Clergy	(%)	Nobility	(%)	Liberal Professions, Administration	(%)	Bourgeoisie Living on Rentes	(%)	Business, Industry	(%)	Artisans, Wage-Earners, Servants	(%)	Total	Population in 1789
Arles (1789)	189	3.9	71	1.5	263	5.4	87	1.8	118	2.4	4,140	85.0	4,868	24,700
Bordeaux (1777)	1,136	15.5	185	2.5	302	4.2	–	–	455	6.2	5,244	71.6	7,322	82,602
Caen (1789)	112	2.5	200	4.5	247	5.6	512	11.5	50	1.1	3,326	74.8	4,447	31,902
Dijon (1789–90)	120	4.5	270	10.1	435	16.3	242	9.1	94	3.1	1,508	56.5	2,669	21,298
Grenoble (1789)	500	11.6	265	6.2	385	8.9	550	12.7	31	0.8	2,575	59.8	4,306	24,830
Montauban (1790)	270	6.6	154	3.8	188	4.5	118	2.9	380	9.3	2,980	72.9	4,090	23,920
Pau (1790)	50	2.2	147	6.3	202	8.7	17	0.7	9	0.4	1,901	81.7	2,326	8,500
Rouen (1789)	513	5.3	400	4.1	600	6.2	–	–	256	2.6	7,961	81.8	9,730	64,722

4. SOCIAL COMPOSITION OF THE ADMINISTRATIVE ÉLITE AT THE END OF THE ANCIEN RÉGIME

Proportion of nobles in high public office (Edelstein 1982)

Ministers of State	85.7% (Necker the only commoner out of 7)
Royal council	
• councillors of state	75.5% (37 out of 49)
• masters of requests	84.1% (58 out of 67)
TOTAL	80.5% (95 out of 118)
High diplomats	89.7% (35 out of 39)
Intendants	100.0%
Military governors	100.0%
Archbishops, bishops	100.0%
Army officers	*c.* 80%–95% (of whom the 11 marshals of France 100% noble)
Parlement of Paris	*c.* 90%

Social origin of individuals ennobled, 1774–89 (Bien 1974)

	Commoners		Nobles				Total	
			2nd generation		3rd + generation			
	No.	(%)	No.	(%)	No.	(%)	No.	(%)
Lettres de noblesse	270	100.0	–	–	–	–	270	8.0
Purchase of post of								
secrétaire du roi	878	99.4	5	0.6	–	–	883	26.0
Municipal office	100	100.0	–	–	–	–	100	2.9
Bureau des finances	539	94.9	12	2.1	17	3.0	568	16.8
Cours des Aides, etc	391	66.4	84	14.3	114	19.3	589	17.4
Parlements	129	19.0	83	12.2	468	68.8	680	20.1
Other sovereign								
courts	106	87.6	8	6.6	7	5.8	121	3.6
Royal								
administration	64	36.0	39	21.9	75	42.1	178	5.2
TOTAL	2,477	73.1	231	6.8	681	20.1	3,389	

5. SOCIOLOGY OF LANDOWNERSHIP
(*LEFEBVRE 1963; VOVELLE 1984; LEFEBVRE 1924; FORSTER 1960; SOBOUL 1958; TILLY 1964; BOIS 1960; POITRINEAU 1965*)

Approximate proportions of the land held by the main social groups in 1789

Church	6–10%
Nobility	20–25%
Bourgeoisie	20–30%
Peasantry	40–45%

Some regional examples in 1789 (all figures are percentages)

Location	Nobility	Clergy	Bourgeoisie	Peasantry	Common land
Dept. Nord (208 localities)	22.0	22.4	17.2	31.9	6.5
Artois (Pas-de-Calais: 27 localities)	31.8	19.8	9.0	37.7	1.7
Laon region (Aisne: 51 localities)	30.1	20.5	19.4	30.0	–
Beauce/Gâtinais (15 localities)	42.7	5.3	12.2	39.8	–
Upper Maine (10 localities)	22.0	14.0	51.5	12.5	–
Mauges, W France (15 localities)	59.8	5.1	27.6	17.2	–
District of Bar-le-Duc (Meuse)	25	16	15	28	
Burgundy (Côte-d'Or: 18 localities)	35	11	20	33	–
AR *élection* of Brive (Corrèze: 37 localities)	16.8	0.8	26.7	54.8	–
AR *élection* of Tulle (Corrèze: 81 localities)	14.7	3.7	25.8	55.5	–

Location	Nobility	Clergy	Bourgeoisie	Peasantry	Common land
Auvergne (34 localities)	15.0	0.8	18.3	64.3	1.6
AR Toulouse diocese (78 localities)	44.4	6.5	25.2	22.5	1.2
District Saint-Gaudens (Haute-Garonne)	15.8	2.1	38.4	29.1	14.9
Montpellier region (Hérault: 12 localities)	15.2	5.8	20.1	37.2	21.7

Peasant share in the purchase of national lands (biens nationaux) (as % of surface area: most other purchasers can be taken as 'bourgeois')

Dept Nord	52
District Saint-Omer (Pas-de-Calais)	19.3
District Laon (Aisne)	57.1
Districts Versailles, Mantes, Dourdan (Seine-et-Oise)	13.5
Canton Vire (Calvados)	16.3
Canton Pontfarcy (Sarthe)	56.2
District Strasbourg	44
Canton Epinal (Vosges)	35–40
Canton Sens (Yonne)	40
Côte-d'Or (4 districts)	56.1–72.8
Nièvre (2 districts)	51.2, 62.7
District Toulouse (Haute-Garonne)	15.2
District Tarascon (Bouches-du-Rhône)	45.7

(NOTE: These figures constitute only a very rough guide to the scale of land transfers in the rev decade. Land of identical extent might have had different productivity levels. Figures for surface area often differ from those for purchasers: e.g. in the district of Toulouse, 15.2% of the land went to peasants, yet peasants made up over two-thirds of total purchasers. Also, land often changed hands subsequently, or was purchased through 'front-men' by *émigré* owners. For the dept of the Nord, where 52% of land purchased went to peasants, and where the clergy had owned 22.4% of land in 1789, the peasant share of the land rose from 31.9% in 1789 to 42.1% in 1802, that of the bourgeoisie rose from 17.2% to 28.8%, while that of the nobility shrank from 22.0% to 12.8%)

6. WEATHER AND HARVESTS,
1785–1799

Year	State of harvest	Comment on weather	Other observations
1785	Fair	Cold winter, 1784–5, dry summer	
1786	Bad in W France	Second dry summer running, ruining forage crops	Shortage of forage crops forces peasants to sell off livestock
1787	Poor Failure of silk harvest	Rainy autumn, mild winter, hot summer	Disruption caused by free trade in grain
1788	Appalling	Rainy spring, freak hailstorm in July	Continuing disruption, 1788–9
1789	Good Poor wine harvest	Hard winter, with bad frosts 1788–9	Distribution problems caused by peasant disturbances, late 1789–early 1790
1790	Good		
1791	Poor	Warm summer, heavy autumn rain and hailstorms	Prices rise from late 1791
1792	?	—	Major distribution problems caused by war mobilisation, grain regulations, etc
1793	? Poor wine harvest	Dry summer	High prices caused by problems of distribution rather than production
1794	?	Late autumn downpours, 1794	As 1793
1795	Poor	Appalling winters, 1794–5, 1795–6	Virtual famine conditions in many parts of France, worsened by agricultural under-production, assignat depreciation, post-Year II deregulation of the economy, etc

284

Year	State of harvest	Comment on weather	Other observations
1796	Excellent	–	Prices plummet in 1797, to the satisfaction of consumers, but to the distress of farmers
1797	Excellent	–	–
1798	Very good	Hot summer causes loss of forage crops, wine glut	Wine-growers and peasants losing their livestock suffer
1799	Poor	–	Prices rising, late 1799

7. THE PRICE OF WHEAT, 1770–1799
(*LABROUSSE ET AL. 1970*)

National average price of a hectolitre of wheat

1770	18.8	1786	14.1
1771	18.2	1787	14.2
1772	16.7	1788	16.1
1773	16.4	1789	21.9
1774	14.6	1790	19.5
1775	15.9	1791	16.2
1776	12.9	1792	22.1
1777	13.4	1793	–
1778	14.7	1794	–
1779	13.6	1795	–
1780	12.6	1796	–
1781	13.5	1797	19.5
1782	15.3	1798	17.1
1783	15.0	1799	16.2
1784	15.3		
1785	14.8		

8. THE REVOLUTION AND POPULATION CHANGE (*POPULATION, 1975*)

Population growth in the eighteenth century

	Size (*millions*)	Rate of growth (%)		Size (*millions*)	Rate of growth (%)
1700	21.5	–	1760	25.7	4.9
1710	22.6	5.1	1770	26.6	3.5
1720	22.6	NIL	1780	27.6	3.8
1730	23.8	5.3	1790	28.1	1.8
1740	24.6	3.4	(1795)	(28.1)	(NIL)
1750	24.5	−0.4	1800	29.1	3.6

Illegitimacy, infant mortality, life expectancy, 1740–1809

	Illegitimacy (%)	Infant mortality (‰)	Life expectancy at birth (yrs)
1740–9	1.2	232	28.6
1750–9	1.4	–	–
1760–9	1.6	–	–
1770–9	1.8	–	–
1780–9	2.2	252	28.5
1790–9	2.7	229	31.0
1800–9	4.2	195	34.9

Births, marriages and deaths, 1787–1799 (in thousands)

	Births	Marriages	Deaths
1787	1,084	240	907
1788	1,074	231	907
1789	1,046	215	871
1790	1,048	219	866
1791	1,008	245	934
1792	1,032	251	961
1793	1,017	325	880
1794	1,073	323	1,090

	Births	*Marriages*	*Deaths*
1795	1,025	238	824
1796	1,004	244	749
1797	1,066	269	730
1798	1,064	?	702
1799	1,047	?	709

Rates of births, marriages and deaths (per ‰), 1785–1797

	Births	*Marriages*	*Deaths*
1785–9	38.8	8.6	35.5
1790–4	37.1	9.8	37.1
1795–7	36.6	8.8	29.5

Age pyramid, 1785–1800 (in ‰)

Ages	*1785*	*1790*	*1795*	*1800*
0–19	401.5	401	403	410
20–59	513	514	509.5	500.5
60+	85.5	85	87.5	89

Losses in war

	1792–4	203,000
	1795–9	235,000
TOTAL		438,000

9. PEASANTS AND THE LAND: CHRONOLOGY

Spring 1789   Peasant uprisings: notably in Provence and the Dauphiné in the S, in Hainaut, the Cambrésis and Picardy in the N and in the Paris–Versailles region.

Mar–Apr 1789   Peasant involvement in preparations for the EG: attendance at primary assemblies; election of delegates to *bailliage* assemblies; drawing up of *cahiers des doléances*. The multi-tiered election procedures mean, however, that no out-and-out peasant is elected to the EG.

July–Aug 1789   Violent peasant uprisings in Franche-Comté, Alsace, Hainaut and the Mâconnais, the combined result of political agitation and very high prices.

Mid July–early Aug 1789   The 'Great Fear': peasant mobilisation caused by the political deadlock and by panic fears of counter-rev: attacks on châteaux, etc.

4 Aug 1789   The 'Night of 4 Aug' witnesses the 'complete abolition of feudalism'.

5–11 Aug 1789   Laws enshrining the 'abolition of feudalism' backtrack on the intoxicated generosity of the 4 Aug session:
- outright abolition of mortmain and practices relating to personal servitude
- consequently, France's 1.5 million serfs are emancipated
- abolition of hunting rights, and of exclusive rights to own rabbit-warrens, dovecotes, etc
- abolition of seigneurial justice
- abolition of tithes (though they are to continue to be paid until alternative arrangements are made for public worship, poor relief, etc)
- abolition of *banalités*
- rights allegedly having a firm contractual and propertied basis (including *champart* and *cens*) are maintained, but are to be redeemable
- drawing up the small print of the abolition of feudalism is placed in the hands of a 'Feudal Committee' chaired by Merlin de Douai
  (Louis XVI initially refuses to sanction these measures, which are only officially promulgated 3 Nov.)

2 Nov 1789   Nationalisation of church lands (sales authorised from 19 Dec).

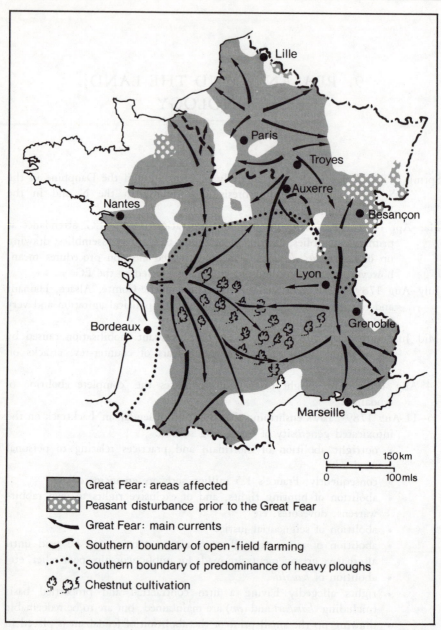

Lille

Paris

Troyes

Auxerre

Nantes

Besançon

Lyon

Bordeaux

Grenoble

Marseille

| 0 | | 150 km |
| 0 | | 100 mls |

■ Great Fear: areas affected

▨ Peasant disturbance prior to the Great Fear

➤ Great Fear: main currents

〜 Southern boundary of open-field farming

⋯ Southern boundary of predominance of heavy ploughs

🌳 Chestnut cultivation

Map 9   The Great Fear and rural France.

Dec 1789–Jan 1790   Peasant disturbances over payment of tithes, seigneurial dues, etc, esp in Brittany, Maine, Quercy, Périgord, Lorraine, etc.

19 Dec 1789, 9 Mar 1790   Nationalisation of royal domain lands.

15 March 1790   Law on the abolition of feudalism (following the report of Merlin de Douai's Feudal Committee): a crucial distinction is maintained between rights grounded in violence and usurpation (abolished), and rights alleged to have originated in a contractual concession of land (redeemable):

- abolition of personal servitude and 'feudal' honorific distinctions (homage, primogeniture, etc)
- abolition of *triages* (forcible enclosure of common lands, with one-third going to the seigneur), and suppression of those performed since 1760
- abolition *without indemnity* of mortmain, seigneurial *corvées*, seigneurial tolls, fair and market rights, *banvin*, etc
- redeemable seigneurial rights are to be viewed as a concession of property unless the tenant can prove the contrary; and in cases where titles have been burnt or lost, prior enjoyment over 30 years is adjudged sufficient legal proof
- redemption is to be on an individual basis and to cover rights *en bloc* (including, for example, adventitious *droits casuels* such as *lods et ventes*).

9 Apr 1790   Following the agreed sale of a bloc of nat lands to the Paris municipality, regulations are agreed for the sale of such property to all communes.

3 May 1790   Regulations regarding the mode of redemption of seigneurial rights:

- redemption is to be performed on an individual and contractual basis between peasant and seigneur
- rights are to be redeemed at 20–25 times their annual value
- rights are to continue to be paid until full reimbursement.

14–17 May 1790   Regulations for the sale of nat lands: property is to be auctioned, at prices between 12 and 30 times the annual value; it is to be subdivided where possible; sales are to take place in the district capital; an interest charge of 5 per cent is charged; payments must be complete in 12 instalments.

18 June, 3 Aug 1790, 11 Mar 1791   Peasants are enjoined provisionally to continue paying tithes (widely ignored).

18 June 1790   Nat lands placed under the surveillance of municipalities.

9 July 1790   All nat lands are put up for sale. District and dept authorities are to oversee sales.

28 Oct 1790   Closer control of the sales of nat lands. Lands of a charitable or educational nature are provisionally exempted sale.

3 Nov 1790   Changes introduced in the mode of sale for nat lands: the law of 14–17 May 1790 is altered in ways which disadvantage the small

buyer: subdivision of land is discouraged; buyers have only four and a half years to pay in full; etc.

23 Nov 1790   New land-tax, the *contribution foncière*, is introduced.

Nov 1790–Feb 1791   Peasant disturbances in N, in SW (Charentais, Quercy, Périgord, Agenais) and in Brittany (where it links up with religious discontent over the Civ Constn).

13 Apr 1791   Maintenance of existing collective and customary practice in regard to uncultivated land (*terres vaines*).

5 June 1791   Abolition of the *contrainte de sole* (forced rotation of crops, widely practised among peasant communities).

20 July 1791   *Loi Le Chapelier* forbidding workers' associations and strikes is extended to agricultural workers and servants.

28 Sept 1791   Rural Code introduced, codifying earlier legislation. Individuals are free to enclose their own land, but no regulations are introduced to enforce communal enclosures.

Late 1791–early 1792   Attacks on grain convoys and similar peasant disturbances in N (esp in the Beauce) and Centre; counter-rev peasant disturbances in the W (Vendée, Deux-Sèvres, etc).

Feb–Apr 1792   Violently anti-seigneurial disturbances in the Midi (Provence, Languedoc, Auvergne, Limousin).

18 June 1792   Adventitious seigneurial dues (*droits casuels*) are abolished without indemnity, save where the original title deed is intact. (In the latter case, they may be redeemed.)

17 July 1792   *Emigré* land (placed under state sequestration from 9 Feb) to be sold off alongside church lands.

14 Aug 1792   Law hastily passed in the heat of the moment following the overthrow of Louis XVI stating that all common land is to be split among inhabitants (never implemented; suspended 11 Oct).

20, 25 Aug 1792   Abolition of all feudal and seigneurial dues which cannot be justified by the original title deed. (Where deeds exist, the dues may still be redeemed.)

28 Aug 1792   Formal dissolution of all acts of *triage* performed since 1669, when the law on *triage* was introduced.

Nov–Dec 1792   Serious peasant disturbances, with outbreaks of price-fixing, in the Beauce region (Sarthe, Eure-et-Loir, Loir-et-Cher, Indre-et-Loire).

10 Mar 1793   Lands formerly exempted sale as nat lands (e.g. college lands) placed on sale.
Outbreak of the Vendée rebellion: provoked by state demands for army conscripts, the rebellion will develop into a dangerous peasant counter-rev in W France.

18 Mar 1793   Death penalty for advocating the *loi agraire* (communal share-out of private property).

4 Apr 1793   Big domains among nat lands to be split prior to sale.

24 Apr 1793   In the name of individual rights, associations of peasants are

debarred from bidding collectively for nat lands.

4 May 1793   Grain price maximum established. The beginning of state regulation of agriculture, 1792–4, which will be deeply resented by the peasantry and lead to deliberate under-production in agriculture in 1795–6.

3 June 1793   *Emigré* lands are to be sold off in small lots. Family heads owning
less than an *arpent* of land are granted the lease of an additional *arpent*,
taken from nat lands.

10 June 1793   Royal domain lands to be sold off.
Law on common lands: these *may* (i.e. there is to be no compulsion, as
the law of 14 Aug 1792 had urged) be divided up on the request of a
third of inhabitants.

July 1793   Peasant disturbances in the Seine-et-Marne and the Gers.

17 July 1793   All former seigneurial dues are suppressed without indemnity.
All seigneurial title deeds are to be publicly burnt.

21 July 1793   Regulations regarding the division of *émigré* lands among more
impoverished heads of households in villages (little implemented).

11 Sept 1793   Grain maximum established.

13 Sept 1793   Modification of regulations of 3 June regarding sale of *émigré*
lands: poorer heads of households are given a bond worth 500 liv with
which nat lands may be purchased. Conditions of sale are made easier
for the poorer peasants: no interest is charged, and they may pay in 20
instalments.

29 Sept 1793   General Maximum introduced.

22 Oct 1793   Landlords are forbidden to add on to their leases the value of lost
tithes and seigneurial dues (widely ignored).

22 Nov and 24 Dec 1793/2 frim, 4 niv II   Regulations of the law of 3 June
1793 regarding the sale in small lots of *émigré* lands are extended to all
forms of nat lands.

26 Feb, 3 Mar 1794/8, 13 vent II   'Laws of Ventôse': property of suspects is
to be made available to indigents (never properly implemented).

24 Dec 1794/4 niv III   Following widespread evasion over preceding months,
the Maximum is abolished and all state regulation of the economy lifted.

31 May 1795/12 prair III   Law on sales of nat lands: auctions may be bypassed
if an individual agrees to pay, within a period of three months, 75 times
the 1790 income (in real terms, this is equivalent only to 4 times: the
law enables fortunes to be made overnight).

20 July 1795/2 therm III   Leases are to be paid half in grain, half in specie
(formerly, they had tended to be paid in devalued assignats).

18 Mar 1796/28 vent IV   Individuals offering the newly created *mandats territoriaux* may bypass auctions of nat lands and purchase at between 18 and
22 times the 1790 income.

9 June 1796/21 prair IV   Suspension of the law of 10 June 1793 relating to
common lands.

6 Sept 1796/20 fruct IV   Sale of nat lands without auctions abolished.

6 Nov 1796/16 brum V   Law on sales of nat lands: auction sales are reinstated; they take place in the departmental capital (which disadvantages most peasants); and sales must be paid half in notes, half in specie.

1797–9   Minister of the Interior François de Neufchâteau encourages the establishment of local agricultural societies, and issues a great deal of agrarian information and propaganda.

17 Oct, 17 Nov 1798/26 vendém, 27 brum VII   Minor adjustments made to regulations regarding the sale of nat lands. Full payment must be made in specie.

10. THE SOCIAL PHYSIOGNOMY OF REVOLUTIONARY FRANCE

KEY (see above, VII. 6, for a full list of departments)

 (1) Population in 1791 (*Archives parlementaires XXVI*)

 (2) Population in 1806 (*Le Mée 1971*)

 (3) Proportion of population in 1810 in localities of 2,000 inhabitants and over (*Le Mée 1971*)

 (4) Population density (per square league) (*Herbin de Halle 1803*)

 (5) Proportion of indigents, according to the inquiry of the Mendicity Committee of the Constit Ass. in 1790–1 (*Bloch & Tuetey 1911*)

 (6) Proportion of beggars and vagrants, according to the same inquiry

 (7) *Contribution mobilière* in 1791 (in millions of liv) (*Archives parlementaires* **XXVI**)

 (8) *Contribution foncière* (in millions of liv) (*Archives parlementaires XXVI*)

 (9) *Contribution foncière* (in millions of liv) (*Archives parlementaires XXVI*)

(10) Value of agricultural yield per hectare in 1812 (in liv) (*Chaptal 1819*)

(11) Significant presence of industry in 1789 (A = calicoes; B = coal; C = cotton; D = ceramics; M = metalworks; P = major port, with [esp colonial] processing industries; S = silk; T = other textiles; blank space indicates no significant presence of industry)

(12) Literacy levels (0 = 0–9%; 1 = 10–19%; 2 = 20–9%; 3 = 30–9%; 4 = 40–9%; 5 = 50–9%; 6 = 60–9%; 7 = 70–9%; 8 = 80–9%. National average = 37%) (*Fleury & Valmary 1957*)

(13) General political orientation in the Rev (L = Left 1792–8; LR = Left 1792–4, Right 1795–8; R = Right 1792–8; RL = Right 1792–4, Left 1795–8) (*Hunt 1984*)

	(1)	(2)	(3)	(4)	(5)	(6)	(7)	(8)	(9)	(10)	(11)	(12)	(13)
Ain	307,756	304,468	7.8	985			0.3	1.5	1.4	26	T	1	LR
Aisne	407,904	442,726	12.4	1,136	11.8	0.6	1.0	4.8	4.3	36	CT	5	R
Allier	267,126	260,046	12.4	747			0.4	2.0	1.9	15	CT	1	L
Alpes-B	168,937	146,994	14.9	376	13.4	1.1	0.2	0.9	0.8	6		3	L
Alpes-H	120,485	124,771	9.8	471	10.6	0.4	0.2	0.7	0.6	6		5	RL
Alpes-M	—	131,266	34.9	544			—	1.2	0.6	—		—	LR
Ardèche	289,671	290,801	8.9	895			0.3	1.2	1.1	19	T	1	R
Ardennes	247,612	275,792	12.5	953			0.5	2.6	2.3	17	M	7	L
Ariège	197,889	222,936	10.3	785			0.2	0.8	0.7	15	MT	1	L
Aube	228,885	238,819	20.0	789			0.6	2.7	2.2	21	C	4	R
Aude	239,642	240,993	18.1	698			0.6	2.6	2.4	23	CMT	2	L
Aveyron	371,835	331,373	10.4	692			0.7	3.2	2.8	15	T	2	LR
B-du-Rh	466,045	293,235	67.7	1,074			0.9	2.2	1.8	27	APT	1	LR
Calvados	391,332	505,420	18.9	1,668			1.2	5.7	5.1	55	BT	8	R
Cantal	239,972	251,436	8.8	807			0.6	2.7	2.0	15		2	R
Charente	339,789	327,052	7.0	1,124	6.3	0.5	0.6	2.7	2.4	27		1	LR
Char-Inf	438,042	405,592	16.4	1,133	7.4	0.3	0.7	3.7	3.2	30	PT	4	L
Cher	207,541	228,158	15.4	592			0.4	1.6	1.4	13	T	1	R
Corrèze	269,767	254,271	6.6	815	7.1		0.4	1.9	1.5	13	M	2	L
Corse	247,776	177,582	12.0	—			0.1	0.2	—	—		—	—
Côte-d'Or	342,986	355,436	15.9	781	9.1	0.8	0.7	3.4	3.2	25	CMT	3	LR
Cts-Nd	523,880	516,428	6.8	1,416			0.4	2.2	2.0	23	T	1	R
Creuse	238,352	226,283	4.4	751	8.7	0.2	0.4	1.5	1.1	10	T	1	L
Dordogne	438,343	424,113	4.8	910	5.3	0.2	0.6	2.8	2.6	21	M	1	L
Doubs	219,642	226,093	15.7	908	13.4	0.6	0.3	1.4	1.3	21	M	8	LR

Drôme	246,687	253,372	15.5	757	10.6	0.8	0.4	1.7	1.6	18	CT	2	RI
Eure	385,206	421,344	11.2	1,354			1.0	5.0	4.4	40	CT	7	R
Eure-L	256,656	266,008	12.3	866	13.4	0.7	0.9	3.9	3.3	31	MT	4	R
Finstre	285,730	452,895	12.1	1,383			0.7	1.7	1.6	20	T	2	R
Gard	313,464	322,144	39.6	1,058			0.5	2.3	2.1	26	BST	3	R
Ht-Grne	456,555	367,551	19.4	1,159	10.6	0.6	0.6	2.7	2.3	22	AP	2	L
Gers	315,854	286,493	7.8	861			1.3	4.0	3.9	32	ACT	1	LR
Gironde	497,391	514,462	21.4	968			0.8	3.5	3.0	27	CMPT	2	R
Hérault	290,126	299,882	41.5	921			0.5	2.6	2.3	26		2	R
I-Vilaine	519,619	508,192	14.1	1,408	18.3	1.2							
Indre	229,768	204,721	17.9	591			0.3	1.4	1.4	12	MT	1	R
Indre-L	272,925	275,292	14.6	747			0.6	2.4	2.3	21	CMS	1	LR
Isère	365,380	471,660	9.8	1,543			0.7	3.2	2.8	24	CMT	2	L
Jura	280,200	300,395	12.9	1,132	9.6	1.1	0.4	1.7	1.6	27	M	4	RL
Landes	257,387	240,146	7.8	489			0.3	1.3	0.9	6	M	0	IR
Loir-Cher	200,277	213,482	18.7	662	10.6	0.5	0.6	2.3	2.1	24	CT	2	IR
Loire-H	216,250	268,202	12.3	975			0.4	1.6	1.3	19	ACMPT	2	LR
Loire-Inf	331,270	407,827	21.2	1,047			1.0	2.0	1.9	24	T	1	R
Loiret	285,775	285,315	24.4	1,204	11.8	0.7	0.7	3.2	2.9	17		2	R
Lot	443,667	268,149	10.3	1,060			0.6	3.0	2.7	19			
Lot-Gne	411,808	326,127	20.4	1,274	18.3	2.5	0.7	3.2	3.0	35	AM	1	L
Lozère	142,110	143,247	7.8	579			0.2	0.8	0.7	11	T	3	R
Mne-Loire	455,500	404,134	15.2	1,016	15.5	0.4	0.9	3.9	3.6	29	CT	1	RL
Manche	463,320	581,429	11.4	1,663	15.5	0.6	1.1	5.1	4.6	41	T	8	R
Marne	348,885	311,017	21.6	766	8.7	1.7	0.9	4.2	3.4	20	CT	7	LR
Ht-Marne	223,010	237,785	13.1	715	6.3	0.3	0.5	2.4	2.1	17	M	5	LR
Mayenne	323,607	332,253	11.2	1,234	18.3	1.1	0.7	3.0	2.7	25	CMT	2	R
Meurthe	321,161	365,810	20.1	1,103			0.3	2.3	2.1	24	CM	8	RL
Meuse	268,108	284,703	14.7	867	6.7	0.2	0.4	2.2	2.0	22	M	8	R
Morbihan	281,565	403,423	12.5	1,297			0.4	1.9	1.7	20	PT	0	R

	(1)	(2)	(3)	(4)	(5)	(6)	(7)	(8)	(9)	(10)	(11)	(12)	(13)
Moselle	328,365	385,958	16.7	1,079	9.6	0.6	0.4	2.5	2.3	26	CM	0	IR
Nièvre	235,699	241,739	11.6	713	6.9	0.6	0.4	1.9	1.8	17	CDMT	4	L
Nord	447,910	839,533	34.3	2,786	18.3	0.9	1.1	5.2	4.7	70	BCMT	5	L
Oise	348,972	372,676	10.7	1,238	11.8	0.6	1.1	4.9	4.5	40	AT	5	IR
Orne	381,760	424,669	9.0	1,284			0.8	3.6	3.1	29	MT	5	R
Pas-Cal	532,739	570,338	23.9	1,726	18.3	1.0	0.5	3.3	3.3	45	T	3	R
Puy-Dôme	516,593	542,834	19.8	1,393			0.9	3.8	3.0	24	T	2	L
Pyr-Ht	188,690	198,763	11.8	879	11.8	0.6	0.1	0.7	0.7	14	MT	2	L
Pyr-Bass	188,389	382,575	12.4	994			0.2	1.0	1.0	17	MT	4	R
Pyr-Or	114,158	126,692	21.3	555			0.2	0.9	0.8	16	M	2	R
Rhin-Ht	283,252	336,940	22.0	1,344			0.4	1.9	1.8	37	ACM		R
Rhin-Bas	415,080	500,926	29.8	1,660			0.5	2.4	2.4	42	CM		LR
Rh-Loire	591,306	658,033	26.2	1,879			1.9	6.3	5.6	39	ABMST	3	R
Sne-Hte	264,111	299,054	8.7	1,223	8.7	0.6	0.4	1.8	1.7	32	M	4	R
Sne-Lre	442,600	471,236	11.0	1,031	9.1	0.5	0.8	3.7	3.5	30	BCM	1	LR
Sarthe	347,837	410,380	13.2	1,265	16.7	1.0	0.9	3.8	3.5	28	T	2	L
Seine	647,472	671,937	89.3	26,165			8.2	12.6	12.3	216	ACT		
Seine-I	536,400	643,093	29.1	1,800			2.4	7.0	6.7	68	ACMPT	5	R
Seine-Mne	296,467	304,263	16.0	995	13.4	0.8	1.2	5.5	4.8	40	C	5	R
Sne-Oise	471,612	431,072	20.6	1,502	8.0	0.7	1.6	7.3	6.6	51	CT	5	R
D-Sèvres	259,122	254,105	9.8	795	11.8	1.7	0.6	2.6	2.3	24	CT	1	L
Somme	407,352	494,642	17.3	1,490			1.2	5.6	4.8	45	ACT	5	R
Tarn	289,148	296,228	17.5	1,012			0.6	2.6	2.3	25	BT	1	L
Tar-Gne		230,514	23.5							39	T		
Var	275,472	283,260	41.0	712	9.6	0.2	0.4	1.8	1.7	27	P	1	LR
Vaucluse	–	205,833	41.4	1,639						30	T	1	LR
Vendée	305,610	268,444	5.7	725	13.4	1.2	0.6	2.6	2.3	20	T	1	L
Vienne	257,953	252,351	15.4	729	13.4	1.2	0.3	1.7	1.6	15	CT	1	L
Ht-Vienne	266,910	241,986	17.4	902	8.7	0.3	0.4	1.8	1.5	13	CDM	0	RL
Vosges	289,054	333,925	11.5	1,044	11.8	0.9	0.3	1.6	1.5	19	CM	8	RL
Yonne	364,969	326,548	15.4	909	9.6	0.4	0.6	3.0	2.6	21	C	3	LR

11. THE SOCIAL PHYSIOGNOMY OF REVOLUTIONARY PARIS

KEY (see above VII, 5 for a full list of section names)
 (1) Proportion of active citizens eligible to stand for public office (active citizens paid tax equivalent to 3 days' labour, those eligible for public office, 10 days) (*Reinhard 1971*)
 (2) Active citizens in 1791 (*Rudé 1959*)
 (3) Indigents, Oct 1791 (*1* = 450–900;   *2* = 1,000–1,800;   *3* = 2,000–3,100;   *4* = 3,600–7,000) (*Reinhard 1971*)
 (4) Wage-earners in employment in 1791 (*Braesch 1912*)
 (5) Employers in 1791 (*Braesch 1912*)
 (6) Number of workers per employer in 1791 (based on *4, 5*)
 (7) Population in 1792 (*Rudé 1959*)
 (8) Number of indigents, Apr 1794 (*Soboul 1958a*)
 (9) Aid to indigents, June 1794–June 1796 (*1* = less than 2,000 liv;   *2* = 2,000–5,000 liv;   *3* = 5,000–10,000 liv; *4* = 10,000–15,000 liv;   *5* = 15,000–25,000 liv;   *6* = 25,000–50,000 liv;   *7* = over 50,000 liv (*Reinhard 1971*)
(10) Population in 1795 (*Rudé 1959*)
(11) Number of indigents under the Directory (*1* = less than 600;   *2* = 800–1,200;   *3* = 1,300–2,000;   *4* = 2,000–3,000;   *5* = 3,000–5,000;   *6* = over 5,000) (*Reinhard 1971*)
(12) Proportion of indigents under the Directory (*1* = 20–40%;   *2* = 42–55%;   *3* = 60–70%;   *4* = over 70%) (*Reinhard 1971*)
(13) Population density in 1800: inhabitants per 4,000 sq. metres (*Rudé 1959*)

	(1)	(2)	(3)	(4)	(5)	(6)	(7)	(8)	(9)	(10)	(11)	(12)	(13)
1. Tuil	71.8	1,654	2	646	40	16.2	12,600	508	1	15,148	1	3	74
2. Ch-El	55.0	873	3	—	—	—	8,000	977	3	8,000	3	2	11
3. Roule	55.4	1,289	3	1,497	106	14.1	12,850	1,365	6	11,377	3	4	23
4. Pal-R	70.0	2,395	4	1,334	92	14.5	20,400	1,008	3	16,719	3	3	251
5. Pl-V	69.9	1,030	2	—	—	—	14,000	784	3	13,428	3	3	75
6. Bibl	77.2	1,517	2	782	46	17.0	12,987	510	1	9,930	1	3	147
7. Gr-B	67.6	856	3	1,197	55	21.8	11,570	1,031	4	10,920	3	3	39
8. Louv	58.5	2,023	3	1,094	61	17.9	11,800	522	3	22,691	3	4	259
9. Orat	67.0	1,902	2	1,677	77	21.8	6,612	365	1	12,846	2	2	444
10. H-Blé	62.5	1,870	1	621	37	16.8	7,011	200	1	11,640	2	2	294
11. Post	58.8	1,809	2	—	—	—	9,869	900	6	12,567	3	3	330
12. L XIV	72.6	1,394	1	969	71	13.6	13,000	370	1	9,500	3	1	266
13. F-Mcy	69.4	1,087	1	298	29	10.2	12,472	355	1	9,424	2	1	224
14. B-Nv	50.8	1,607	3	2,367	129	18.1	9,950	1,807	6	14,860	3	4	360
15. Pceau	46.7	1,607	2	5,288	242	21.6	13,645	521	4	16,648	3	1	360
16. Mcsl	54.8	1,708	3	1,866	115	16.2	11,000	642	2	13,818	3	3	388
17. M-Inn	50.1	1,072	3	1,705	61	28.0	14,722	502	4	13,146	3	3	555
18. Lomb	44.9	2,504	2	1,421	110	12.9	12,550	561	2	14,811	3	1	438
19. Arcs	46.0	1,753	3	—	—	—	12,000	855	5	11,600	3	1	580
20. FbgM	58.2	687	4	1,242	78	15.9	13,800	1,567	5	10,104	4	3	51
21. R-Pss	63.8	834	3	1,517	97	15.7	12,000	1,847	3	8,435	2	4	43
22. Bndy	45.6	1,439	3	—	—	—	13,315	1,856	5	12,404	4	3	32
23. Temp	53.1	1,662	3	1,273	99	12.9	25,000	1,340	5	11,988	4	1	48
24. R-Pop	48.1	1,268	3	1,358	84	16.2	13,747	3,930	5	10,933	5	4	17
25. R-Mtl	40.1	1,478	4	1,330	84	15.8	15,000	4,211	6	13,479	5	4	45

26. Q-Vts	46.6	1,958	4	1,831	141	13.0	12,550	6,601	5	18,283	5	4	27
27. Grav	40.4	3,305	2	4,699	339	13.9	11,000	1,616	3	24,774	5	1	364
28. FSt Ds	40.1	1,330	2	3,217	101	31.9	13,840	1,938	4	11,630	4	4	62
29. Bbrg	50.2	2,285	2	2,958	166	17.8	11,015	1,219	3	16,320	4	1	315
30. Enf-R	59.6	1,784	1	1,015	102	10.0	8,974	358	3	10,481	2	1	132
31. RSic	54.0	1,811	1	1,028	67	15.3	10,500	1,265	5	12,321	3	1	239
32. Hde V	43.2	1,729	3	—	—	—	11,230	4,258	3	12,231	5	2	304
33. Pol-R	58.6	1,883	2	1,172	75	15.6	14,500	955	3	11,836	4	4	123
34. Asnl	52.1	1,407	3	890	58	15.3	21,000	845	5	10,246	4	1	82
35. I-St L	54.3	1,032	2	305	28	10.9	5,257	1,180	1	4,862	2	2	204
36. N-D	44.4	1,657	3	—	—	—	11,780	767	7	11,402	4	2	310
37. H IV	65.8	883	3	459	54	8.5	3,581	158	5	5,126	1	2	297
38. Inv	35.2	1,100	2	767	30	25.6	11,000	1,662	2	10,401	4	4	17
39. F-Gr	49.9	2,100	1	985	71	13.9	10,878	792	1	12,554	2	4	86
40. Q-Nat	48.5	3,900	4	2,310	164	14.1	21,516	1,401	2	21,601	3	3	204
41. Th-F	62.5	2,600	2	2,207	105	21.0	16,600	846	1	14,400	3	2	275
42. Cx-R	47.5	1,551	3	1,669	118	14.1	17,600	2,037	3	16,744	4	4	67
43. Lux	51.7	2,100	4	1,061	84	12.6	17,000	773	4	17,633	3	3	52
44. Th-J	55.2	2,000	2	1,139	72	15.8	14,490	1,246	5	12,394	3	3	325
45. St Gen	52.4	2,762	4	2,136	129	16.6	22,645	2,630	7	24,977	5	4	320
46. Obs	64.9	1,700	2	1,133	55	20.6	19,907	2,803	5	13,193	5	4	32
47. J-Pl	51.9	2,178	4	1,695	66	25.7	16,000	3,946	5	15,185	5	4	60
48. Gob	61.0	1,200	4	613	38	16.1	12,741	4,951	3	11,775	5	4	35
	54.4	82,270	—	62,743	3,776		635,504	72,781	—	636,772	—	—	—

12. TRADE AND INDUSTRY:
CHRONOLOGY

26 Sept 1786   Anglo-French ('Eden') Trade Treaty: reduction of duty on English manufactured goods entering France and on French wines and spirits entering Britain. The treaty seems to worsen the crisis of French industry, already in recession and soon to be hit by a slump in home demand consequent on the agrarian crisis of 1788–9.

17 June 1787   Brienne introduces free trade in grain.

28 Nov 1788   Necker introduces new regulations on the grain trade.

4 Aug 1789   'Night of 4 Aug' seems to attack the corporative organisation of trade and manufacturing, though these are not made specific targets in the ensuing legislation. Abolition of prov and municipal privileges.

29 Aug 1789   Free trade in grain declared (reiterated 18 Sept, and maintained 1789–90 despite fierce popular agitation), and grain exports prohibited.

15 Mar 1790   Seigneurial tolls (*péages*) are abolished, though municipal tolls (*octrois*) are maintained.

21 Mar 1790   Suppression of the *gabelle*, the hated salt-tax.

3 Apr 1790   Suppression of the privileges of the Compagnie des Indes: the East Indies trade is opened to all comers.

8 May 1790   Accepting the need for uniform weights and measures, the Ass. asks the Academy of Sciences to propose a nat system (its committee includes Borda, Monge, Lagrange, Laplace, Condorcet).

16 Aug 1790   Reorganisation of commercial justice: establishment of *tribunaux de commerce*.

31 Oct–5 Nov 1790   Abolition of *traites* and all other internal customs dues. France thus becomes an internally unified customs area.

31 Dec 1790   Law on industrial patents (*brevets d'invention*) which are made the property of the inventor for an agreed period of time before they revert to the public domain (amended 14 May 1791).

18 Jan 1791   Trade with Senegal opened to all comers.

19 Feb 1791   Abolition of municipal tolls (*octrois*).

2 Mar 1791   *Loi d'Allarde:* suppression of AR corporations (with certain exceptions, the object of specific legislation in ensuing months, e.g. pharmacists on 14 Apr, goldsmiths on 31 Mar–3 Apr) and all state privileges formerly granted industry.
New (moderately protectionist) customs tariff introduced.

18 Mar 1791   Introduction of a more liberal colonial tariff. The *Exclusif* (the obligation of colonies to trade only with the mother country) is, however, maintained.

27 Mar 1791   Landowners with exploitable minerals below their land-surface are accorded rights of property over mining.

3 Apr–2 May 1791   Abolition of the old Compagnie des Indes.

17 June 1791   *Loi Le Chapelier:* against the background of severe working-class agitation by Parisian carpenters and other workers, the Constit Ass. agrees to the proposal of the Breton deputy, Le Chapelier, that groups of workers should not be covered by the rights of assembly: workers' associations and coalitions are suppressed and strike action forbidden (this law remains on the statute-book until 1864).

20 July 1791   *Loi Le Chapelier* extended to agricultural workers and servants.

22 July 1791   Marseille is deprived of its AR monopoly of the Levantine trade.

27 Sept–16 Oct 1791   Suppression of the AR factory inspectorate and the old system of industrial regulation.

Jan–Feb 1792   Demonstrations and riots in Paris over shortage of sugar and other colonial products.

3 Mar 1792   Assassination of Simonneau, the mayor of Etampes, who had refused to give in to popular demands for fixing the price of bread.

6 May 1792   Moderate deputies accord Simonneau a state funeral to underline their commitment to free trade and the rule of law.

28 May 1792   Robespierre abandons economic liberalism and supports price-fixing.

Autumn 1792   Temporary suspension in free trade in grain:
- *3 Sept:* amnesty accorded individuals arrested for agitating over the price of grain
- *4 Sept:* requisitioning for the needs of the army permitted
- *9–16 Sept:* civil authorities allowed to requisition for grain
- *8 Dec:* the Convtn repeals the Sept legislation of the Leg Ass.: free trade in grain is again proclaimed, though grain exports are again forbidden.

16 Nov 1792   The Executive Council declares freedom of navigation on the river Scheldt. This contravenes the Treaty of Munster (1648) and predisposes Britain towards war.

3 Feb 1793   Paris sections demonstrate against rising prices.

25 Feb 1793   Pillaging of wholesale groceries in Paris. Continuation of disturbances in Mar–Apr, encouraged by the political agitation of the *enragés*.

1 Mar 1793   Trade with Britain is forbidden, and privateering permitted. Foreign trade goes into a slump (war, assignat depreciation, etc) which will last throughout the period of the Convtn.

4 May 1793   Grain price maximum established, following furious debates in the Convtn. Requisitions are permitted if markets are not being properly supplied (though the law is unevenly applied).

27 June 1793 Closure of the Paris *Bourse* (stock exchange).

1–5 July 1793 Dept administrations are permitted to make forcible purchases of grain from private individuals.

26 July 1793 Law on hoarding: death penalty for hoarders; *commissaires aux accaparements* are to verify and monitor the grain trade.

1 Aug 1793 Decision to adopt a decimal system of measurement.

9 Aug 1793 Establishment of a public granary (*grenier d'abondance*) in each district (unevenly applied).

24 Aug 1793 Abolition of joint-stock companies, insurance companies, etc.

Autumn 1793 Reps *en mission* have wide-ranging powers to regulate the economic life of the provinces and ensure that towns and armies are properly provisioned in all necessities.

19 Aug 1793 Dept administrations are authorised to fix maximum prices for firewood and coal.

11 Sept 1793 Grain maximum: a maximum price for grain is to be fixed for the whole of France, though at levels varying with local circumstances. Districts are given wide-ranging powers to requisition.

21 Sept 1793 Navigation Act: overseas trade is to be conducted in French vessels only (this law is inoperable because of the war; its unintentional effect will be to make the import of foodstuffs virtually impossible).

29 Sept 1793 Law of the General Maximum: state regulation of the nat economy:
  • confirms price maximum declared on 11 Sept
  • price levels agreed at 1790 levels plus one-third for prices, and plus one-half for wages
  • municipalities are to enforce the law
  • no allowance is made for transport costs.

5 Oct 1793 Rev Calendar decreed: economic life is fixed on a 10-day rather than a 7-day basis.

9 Oct 1793 Manufactured goods from Britain, its colonies and other Allied powers are prohibited entry into France.

27 Oct 1793 Establishment of a National Food Commission (the Commission des subsistances) to run the nat economy under the Maximum.

12 Dec 1793/22 frim II CPS regulations on arms manufacturing: severe stipulations regarding workers' strikes and associations.

10 Feb 1794/22 pluv II The Commission des subsistances is split into two, the 'Commission de l'agriculture et des arts' and the 'Commission du commerce et des approvisionnements'.

26 Feb 1794/3 vent II General fixing of price levels, under the aegis of the Maximum:
  • nat price levels are to be set
  • prices again fixed at 1790 levels plus one-third, wages plus one-half
  • profit margins now allowed of 5 per cent for wholesalers, 10 per cent for retailers.

27 Feb 1794/4 vent II   Suppression of the AR commercial privileges of free ports (Marseille, Dunkirk, etc).

1 Apr 1794/12 germ II   Suppression of the *commissaires aux accaparements* established on 26 July 1793.

23 July 1794/5 therm II   Paris Commune publishes a wage maximum, to be enforced under the provisions of the General Maximum for the first time: it denotes a fall in wage-levels, and will lose Robespierre potential street support on 9 Thermidor.

7 Sept 1794/21 fruct II   The Maximum is maintained for the rest of Year III (though in fact it is soon falling into abeyance).

17 Oct 1794/26 vendém III   Manufacturers are permitted to import necessary raw materials.

9 Nov 1794/19 brum III   Grain price maxima are set at district rather than national level.

15 Nov 1794/25 brum III   Ports are permitted to trade freely with neutrals. The Navigation Act of 21 Sept 1793 is thus repealed.

26 Nov 1794/6 frim III   Freedom granted to import non-prohibited merchandise

24 Dec 1794/4 niv III   Suppression of the Maximum and associated regulation. Opening up of foreign trade.

6 Jan 1795/17 niv III   As the remnants of the Food Commission are abolished, a special commission is established to supervise army supply. Military provisioning from henceforward will be in the hands of private contractors.

7 Apr 1795/18 germ III   Introduction of the metric system.

1795–6   Trade improves, esp as France concludes peace treaties with Spain, Holland, Prussia, etc.

29 Sept 1795/7 vendém IV   Though price-fixing is still abolished, other economic regulations (e.g. regarding obligation to trade in markets) remain in force.

Nov–Dec 1795   Paris is hit by a number of strikes (assignat workers, typographers, etc)

21 Nov 1795/30 brum IV   Repeal of the law of 24 Aug 1793 which abolished joint-stock companies.

2 Sept 1796/16 fruct V   In a measure typical of a repressive policy towards workers in evidence throughout the period of the Directory, paper-workers are forbidden to leave their work without giving 40 days' notice.

9 June 1797/21 prair V   Free trade in grain proclaimed.

18 Jan 1798/29 niv VI   Law permitting the seizure of foreign vessels discovered to be transporting British goods.

18–21 Sept 1798/2–5 jc VI   Industrial exhibition organised ir Paris by Minister of the Interior François de Neufchâteau.

Late 1798–99   Generalisation of municipal tolls throughout France to bolster municipal and charitable finances (e.g. for Paris on 18 Oct 1798/27 vendém VII, for Bordeaux on 12 May 1799/23 flor VII, etc).

13. THE STRUCTURE OF
FOREIGN TRADE, 1776, 1792
(LEVASSEUR 1903; MORINEAU 1977)

All figures (here in in millions of liv) are subject to the highest degree of caution.
Strict comparability of all regions is unfortunately impossible.

	Exports		Imports		Surplus(+)/ Deficit(−)	
	1776	1792	1776	1792	1776	1792
Britain	10.9	30	13.2	28	−	+
Holland	38.3	68	22.1	13.5	+	+
Austrian Netherlands (1776)	22		10.7		+	
Austria (1792)		34		10		+
Germany, inc Hanseatic Towns in 1792	28.9	80	8.6	?	+	?
Switzerland	9.7	26	7.6	4	+	+
Denmark, Baltic, Sweden (1776)	46.1		15.5		+	
Russia (1776)	3.2		4.4		−	
N Europe (1792)		22		5		+
Milan, Tuscany (1792)		14		6.5		+
Sardinia	6.2	9.5	5.6	13	+	−
Portugal, Rome, Venice (1792)		9		4		+
Naples	3	7	7.2	17	−	−
Rest of Italy (1776)	24.4		29.9		−	
Portugal (1776)	4.4		3.9		+	
Spain	44.5	26	35.5	39	+	−
Levant	22.2	21	28.3	42	−	−
Colonies	61.5	4(?)	172.2	19	−	−

14. POOR RELIEF: CHRONOLOGY

4 Aug 1789 'Night of 4 Aug': abolition of many of the major sources of income of existing charitable institutions (tithes, seigneurial dues, etc).

2 Nov 1789 Nationalisation of church lands includes the theoretical appropriation of property of hospitals, though in practice these are exempted from sale. The state assumes responsibility for reorganising poor relief.

14 Dec 1789 Law on municipal government accords municipalities oversight of charitable institutions.

Dec 1789 Reopening of charity workshops (*ateliers de charité*) in Paris, which had been closed down on 31 Aug.

2 Feb 1790 First meeting of the Mendicity Committee of the Constit Ass., chaired by the liberal duc de La Rochefoucauld-Liancourt. It will make far-ranging and ambitious recommendations for the reorganisation of poor relief in a series of reports down to Sept 1791. Little constructive, however, will be done before 1793.

15 Feb 1790 The religious congregations which run many hospitals and charitable institutions are specifically excluded from the law prohibiting perpetual vows and reorganising regular orders.

19 Feb 1790 Abolition of municipal tolls (*octrois*) deals another blow to hospital income.

30 May 1790 Reorganisation of *ateliers de charité* in Paris. Depts are encouraged to establish similar workshops.

31 Aug 1790 Further reorganisation of the Paris *ateliers de charité*, whose unpopularity with middle-class opinion will soon lead to their closure.

16 Dec 1790 Emergency grant of cash (15 million liv) to the beleaguered charitable institutions (additional grants of 4 millions will be made on 29 Mar 1791, and 3 millions on 25 July 1791. This system of periodic and insufficient state grants will continue throughout the 1790s.)

Spring 1791 Application of the Civ Constn oath leads to the retirement or dismissal of many members of nursing communities attached to charitable institutions.

24 Mar 1791 Generous law on invalidity pensions for retired soldiers.

18 Aug 1792 Religious congregations, both charitable and educational, are dissolved. Nursing sisters may, however, remain at their posts, without religious dress and in a personal capacity.

26 Nov 1792, 6 June 1793   Laws reorganising and extending the system of pensions for the dependants of fighting soldiers.

19 Mar 1793   Law on public assistance: the main principles are established: state aid is to be distributed according to prices and population in each dept; work is to be provided for the able-bodied, home relief wherever possible for other varieties of the needy; and almsgiving is prohibited.

28 June 1793   Law on public assistance: state aid is to be given through district 'agencies' to children, to the aged and (for the first time in French history) to unmarried mothers. Abandoned children are to be received in hospitals until they are 12 years old, when they are to be apprenticed out.

15 Oct 1793/24 vendém II   Law on begging: begging and almsgiving are prohibited; departmental *maisons de répression* are to be established, to set beggars to work.

23 Oct 1793   All former religious sisters working in charitable institutions are to take the 'Liberty–Equality' oath, or else be replaced by female patriots. Growing anti-clericalism at nat and local level sees the withdrawal of many nursing sisters.

Late 1793   Some of the more radical reps *en mission* introduce radical policies, with a measure of social redistribution.

9 Feb 1794/21 pluv II   Further law on pensions for soldiers' dependants.

21 Feb 1794/3 vent II   Law on the running of military hospitals.

11 May 1794/22 flor II   Law establishing the *Grand Livre de Bienfaisance Nationale*, a register of state pensions benefiting the needy in rural areas.

4 June 1794/16 prair II   Generous and humane law on pensions for war widows.

11 July 1794/23 mess II   Nationalisation of hospital property (occasioned by the need for resources for the war effort rather than by prior agreement on a plan for poor relief).

8 Apr 1795/19 germ III   Suppression of all private societies, including charitable bodies such as the *Société de Charité maternelle*.

27 Aug 1795/9 fruct III   Suspension of the sale of hospital property under the provisions of the Law of 23 Messidor II.

23 Oct 1795/2 brum IV   The Law of 23 Messidor II is repealed: hospital property is 'denationalised', as the state cuts back on its financial commitments, runs down the pension schemes introduced under the Terror and encourages the revival of private charity.

1795–6   With no real state support, following the losses sustained since 1789, and faced with semi-famine conditions in the wake of the bad winter of 1795, most existing hospitals are in appalling condition, with high morbidity and mortality.

7 Oct 1796/16 vendém V   Law entrusting the administration of hospitals to a single administrative board of five individuals in each commune, chosen by and responsible to the municipality.

27 Nov 1796/7 frim V Law establishing *bureaux de bienfaisance* in every commune for the provision of home relief: to be financed by restored AR patrimony, private charity and a 'theatre tax' (*droit des pauvres*), from which hospitals are also to benefit. The pension schemes adumbrated by the laws of 19 Mar and 28 June 1793 and 22 flor II are officially closed, and military welfare schemes also run down.

17 Dec 1796/27 frim V Law officially recognising the state's responsibility to provide for abandoned children: they are to be accepted without charge in the nation's hospitals.

17 Jan 1797/29 pluv V Hospitals released from obligation to pay debts incurred before 1794.

 4 July 1797/16 mess VII Personnel on the hospital administration boards are placed under supervision of the Minister of the Interior, thus prefiguring the tight prefectoral control instituted after 1800.

1797–9 Congregations of nursing sisters are reintroduced into many charitable institutions on a personal basis. In 1800, the old congregations such as the Daughters of Charity (*Filles de la Charité*), will be allowed to reform.

18 Oct 1798/27 vendém VII Creation of an *octroi* (municipal toll) for Paris, proceeds from which will help finance the city's charitable institutions. Similar laws follow for most major cities down to 1800–1.

15. THE METRIC SYSTEM

Weights and measures varied in every respect throughout France under the AR. The Constit Ass. determined to rationalise them, and appointed a commission of the Academy of Sciences to work on the matter in May 1790. It was agreed to base the new measures in nature. Hence, for example, the decision to make the common unit of length (the metre) one-ten-millionth part of the quadrant of the circumference of the globe, measured from the North Pole to the Equator through Paris. The work, slow and complex anyway, was interrupted by political instability. On 7 Apr 1795/18 germ III, the nomenclature and provisional measures were adopted. The basic measures, and their main AR equivalents, were as follows:

Weight

AR: livre (pound) poids de marc = 2 marcs

marc = 8 onces

once = 8 gros

Rev: 1 livre poids de marc = 489.6 grams

Linear measures

AR: perche de l'arpent de Paris = 3 toises

toise = 6 pieds

pied = 12 pouces

pouce = 12 lignes

Rev: 1 perche de l'arpent de Paris = 5.9 metres

1 toise = 1.95 metres

Distance

AR lieue (league) commune: petite lieue, or lieue de poste

(Petite lieue = 2,000 toises)

Rev: lieue commune = 4.5 kilometres

petite lieue = 3.9 kilometres

Surface area

AR: arpent de Paris = 100 perches

Rev: arpent de Paris = 34.2 ares

Dry capacity

AR: sétier = 2 mines
    mine = 2 minots
    minot = 3 boisseaux

Rev: sétier = 156.1 litres
  boisseau = 13 litres

Liquid capacity

AR: muid = 36 sétiers
    sétier = 4 quartes
    quarte = 2 pintes
    pinte = 2 chopines
Rev: muid = 268.2 litres
    pinte = 0.93 litres

X. BIOGRAPHIES

Aelders (baronne d'), see PALM

Agra (bishop of), see FOLLEVILLE

Aiguillon (Armand-Desiré Duplessis-Richelieu, duc d'), 1761–1800. A cavalry colonel before 1789, and one of the biggest landowners in France, d'A. was elected to the EG by the nobility of Agen; joined the Third Estate on 25 June 1789; and was prominent in renouncing privileges on 4 Aug 1789. A left-wing royalist, he was a member of the Breton, then the Jacobin Club. He rejoined the army in 1791, but his views had shifted to the right and in Sept 1792 he emigrated.

Alba, see LASOURCE

Albert de Rions (Fs-Hector), 1728–1802. Of ancient Provençal noble lineage, A. de R. pursued a naval career under the AR. He came to prominence when as commander at Toulon he crossed swords with local patriots in 1789. In Dec 1790 he resigned his commission and joined Condé's forces. He returned to France after Brumaire.

Albitte (Ant-L), 1761–1812. A lawyer from Dieppe, A. was a radical deputy in the Leg Ass. and Convtn, specialising in military matters. *En mission* in 1793, he participated in the repression of the Federalist revolt in the SE, and was a radical, dechristianising deputy in the Ain and Mont-Blanc. Compromised in the Prairial *journées*, he went into hiding, but was amnestied in 1795. He supported Brumaire, and re-entered military administration.

Allarde (P-Leroy, baron d'), 1752–1809. A liberal noble in the EG and Constit Ass., d'A. was the author of the *Loi d'Allarde* (2 Mar 1791) suppressing corporations. He emigrated to the USA in 1792, returning to France under Napoleon.

Amar (J-B-André), 1755–1816. Lawyer in the Grenoble parl and *trésorier de France*, A. was prominent in local politics before being elected to the Convtn. He sat with the Montagnards and distinguished himself by his violent attacks on the king. An energetic rep *en mission* (Ain, Isère), he denounced and contributed to the sentencing of the Girondins in Oct 1793. A member of the CGS from June 1793, he reported to the Convtn on the Compagnie des Indes scandal, and on the indictment of the Hébertists and Dantonists. He distrusted Robespierre and plotted Thermidor. Arrested and tried after Thermidor along with Vadier, Collot and Billaud-Varenne, he was sentenced to life imprisonment. Freed in the 1795 amnesty, he was subsequently arrested as a babouvist. Exiled from Paris, he returned to Grenoble and private life.

André or **Dandré** (Ant-Balthazar-Jos, baron d') 1759–1825. Councillor in the parl of Aix, elected by the nobility of Provence to the EG, d'A. was active in the Constit Ass. where he followed a constitutional royalist line. He emigrated in 1792, first to Germany, then to Britain, and became a secret agent of the British, hatching counter-rev plots. Based in Switzerland from 1795 then returning to France, he became a key figure in the constitutional royalist movement prior to the 1797 elections. Obliged to flee after Fructidor, he returned to France and to high office in 1815.

Anselme (Jq-Bernard-Modeste d'), 1740–1814. A career soldier under the AR, A. was prominent in the French seizure of Nice in Sept 1792. Replaced for failing to control his troops, he was imprisoned in Feb 1793 and, though released after Thermidor, did not resume his military career.

Antonelle (P-Ant, marquis d'), 1747–1817. After an unsuccessful military career, A. returned to his native Arles, became mayor in 1790 and was elected to the Leg Ass. and joined the Jacobins. He sat on the Rev Tribunal in 1793, but his radical views were regarded as too extreme and he was arrested in Nov 1793. Freed after Thermidor, he contributed to the *Journal des hommes libres*, was implicated in the Babeuf plot and put under house arrest. His election to the C500 was annulled (twice), and he retired into obscurity.

Antraigues (L-Emmanuel-Henry-Alexandre de Launai, comte d'), 1753–1812. Of ancient Vivarais noble stock, d'A. had a varied Pre-Rev career as soldier, *philosophe* and politician, before being elected to the EG by the nobility of the Vivarais. His political activity was soon eclipsed by his royalist pamphleteering and clandestine counter-rev plotting. After emigrating, he established clandestine links with Pichegru under the Directory, but was arrested in Trieste by Napoleon in 1797. After his release, he maintained his espionage contacts, travelling round Europe before ending his life in Britain the victim of an assassin.

Armonville (J-B), 1756–1808. A weaver from Reims, A. was one of only two working-class deputies in the Convtn, which he attended in workman's clothes and where he made a reputation as a Jacobin and a Maratist. Suspect after Thermidor and linked with Babeuf, he was imprisoned on two occasions, and retired from public life.

Artois (Ch-Ph, comte d'; from 1824 to 1830 Charles X, King of France), 1757–1836. *Bon viveur* turned hyper-reactionary, the youngest brother of Louis XVI, A. was a notorious hate-figure in 1789 and was suspected of involvement in the *pacte de famine*. He emigrated on 16–17 July 1789 and settled in Turin where with Condé and Calonne he directed the émigrés and intrigued in foreign courts. From July 1791 he was based in Coblenz with his elder brother, Provence, and fought in France once war broke out. In Oct–Nov 1795 he led a British-backed expedition to the island of Yeu off the coast of Brittany, but failed in his intention of linking with Charette. He retired to Edinburgh, then to London, returning to France in 1814.

Aubert-Dubayet (J-B-Annibal), 1757–97. Son of a French officer in Louisiana, A.-D. was in the army until 1785. He was elected by the Isere to the Leg Ass., where he pursued an independent line. In 1792 he rejoined the army, fighting on the Rhine and in W France before being imprisoned during the Terror.

Released after Thermidor, he was commander of the Army of the Cherbourg Coasts, before being appointed War Minister in Nov 1795. He resigned in Feb 1796 and was sent as ambassador to Constantinople, where he died of a fever.

Augereau (P-Fs-Ch), 1757–1816. Son of a servant, A. had a turbulent military career under the AR, serving in the Prussian and Neapolitan as well as the French army. He rejoined the army as a volunteer in 1792, fought bravely in W France and in the Pyrenees and was promoted general in Dec 1793. From 1795 he fought in Italy where he was a crucial support to Bonaparte. Back in Paris, he played a key role in the Fructidor coup, and was nearly made Director. Elected to the C500 in 1799, he supported Bonaparte after Brumaire. He returned to the army and fought in many of Napoleon's campaigns.

Babeuf (Fs-Noël, or 'Gracchus'), 1760–guill 27 May 1797. Of modest family background, this early proponent of communism served as feudal clerk and surveyor in the 1780s in Picardy. He led a chequered career in the early 1790s, winning a reputation as an agitator and a radical pamphleteer in Paris and in his home dept of the Somme. In 1793–4, he worked for the Paris Food Commission. At first he welcomed Thermidor, but was soon attacking the Convtn then the Directory in his *Journal de la liberté de la presse*, which in Oct 1794 changed its name to the *Tribun du peuple*. Gaoled in late 1794, he returned to politics and from Nov 1795 helped organise the Panthéon Club until its closure in Feb 1796. From Mar 1796 he organised the insurrectionary committee of the so-called 'Conspiracy of Equals' and prepared a *coup d'état*, but he was arrested along with the alleged *Egaux* on 10 May 1796. The high court at Vendôme sentenced him to death and, after attempting to commit suicide in his cell, he was executed.

Baco de la Chapelle (René-Gaston), 1751–1800. Son of a Nantes businessman, B. pursued a legal career in Brittany where he was prominent in leading opposition to the crown in the Pre-Rev. Elected to the EG and a founder member of the Breton Club, he made little impression and returned to private life in Nantes. He helped organise rpbcn opposition in the Vendée, but was unable to avoid imprisonment as a Girondin supporter. Released after Thermidor, he served obscurely in the C500, and then entered colonial administration, dying in the W Indies.

Bailleul (Jq-Ch), 1762–1843. Son of a Norman farmer, B. became a lawyer in the Paris parl in the 1780s. Elected to the Convtn, he proved a moderate but energetic Girondin. Imprisoned in Oct 1793, he was released following Thermidor, returned to the Convtn, and sat on the right. A diligent supporter of the Directory in the C500, he became a tax official under Napoleon.

Bailly (J-Sylvain), 1736–guill 12 Nov 1793. Son of Court painter Jq-B Bailly, B.'s reputation as an astronomer and savant won him first place in the Parisian elections to the EG, and in June 1789 he became president of the Third Estate, a position he held at the Tennis Court Oath session of 20 June. Elected first president of the Constit Ass., which appointed him mayor of Paris, he presided over the formation of the Nat Guard and welcomed Louis XVI to the capital on 17 July. His lack of political experience won him few friends and his surviving credit was ruined by his involvement in the massacre of the Champ de Mars on 17 July 1791. He resigned as mayor in Sept and tried to lie low in the provinces. In 1793, however, he was arrested, brought back to Paris and guillotined on the Champ de Mars.

Bancal des Issarts (J-Henri), 1750–1826. Son of a Languedoc manufacturer, B. studied law in Lyon before settling in Paris as a notary in 1783. He was an early member of the Amis des Noirs and worked as publicist and pamphleteer for Brissot. Elected to the Convtn, he sat as a Girondin and voted for the banishment of the king. In Apr 1793, Dumouriez handed him and other representatives of the Convtn to the enemy. Exchanged for Louis XVI's daughter in Dec 1795, he served briefly in the C500, then retired in 1797 into private life.

Bara (Fs-Jos), 1780–battle 7 Dec 1793. This son of a Norman gamekeeper, though too young to fight, joined the rpbcn forces in the Vendée as a servant. He died heroically in a rebel ambush, and his death became a symbol of rev patriotism, exploited by Robespierre. He was accorded the honours of the Panthéon on 28 Dec 1793.

Barbaroux (Ch-J-Marie), 1767–guill 25 June 1794. From a well-off Marseille merchant family who trained him as a lawyer, B. became involved in local Marseille politics from 1789. In July 1792 he accompanied the Marseille *fédérés* to Paris; helped plan the overthrow of the king; and was elected to the Convtn. A radical in Marseille, he became a Girondin and a moderate in Paris, opposing the power of the Jacobins and the Commune and voting the *appel au peuple*. Arrested on 2 June 1793, he escaped, fleeing to Normandy where he failed to raise an army against Paris. He hid in the Bordelais for eight months. Fearing capture, he attempted to commit suicide, but failed and was brought to Bordeaux where he was guillotined.

Barbé-Marbois (Fs), 1745–1837. Son of a merchant from Metz, B.-M. served as tutor to the children of future Navy Minister Castries in the 1770s, and through his good offices became a diplomat. Intendant in Saint-Domingue in 1789, he returned to France in 1790 and played a behind-the-scenes role in negotiations with the *princes possessionnés*. He lay low during the Terror, and when elected to the C Anciens in 1795 was denounced as a royalist agent. Deported at Fructidor, he returned to France and continued his political career under Napoleon.

Barentin (Ch-L-Fs de Paule de), 1738–1819. A distinguished Parisian magistrate, B. was a member of the Ass. of Notables in 1787; protested against the May Edicts in 1788; and succeeded Lamoignon as Garde des Sceaux in Sept 1788. He soon fell out with Necker, and from the first day of the meeting of the EG, when he read an uninspired speech to the assembled deputies, had a reputation as a reactionary. He resigned as Garde des Sceaux after the fall of the Bastille, and emigrated in 1790, returning to France and to high office in 1814.

Barère or **Barère de Vieuzac** (Bertrand de), 1755–1841. Originally from Tarbes, B. was carving himself a brilliant legal and academic career in Toulouse on the eve of the Rev. Elected to the EG by the Third Estate of Bigorre, he was a moderate in the early years, though Varennes helped radicalise him. He edited a journal in Paris, the *Point du jour*; was elected to the Convtn by the Hautes-Pyrénées; voted for the king's death; and was increasingly identified with the Montagnards. A great committeeman and highly competent spokesman, he served continuously on the CGD and CPS from 4 Jan 1793 to beyond Thermidor. He attacked Robespierre at Thermidor, but was tried along with Collot, Billaud-Varenne and Vadier and sentenced to deportation in May 1795. He escaped, however, and lay low until Brumaire. He was to serve Napoleon in undistinguished fashion.

Barnave (Ant-P-Jos-Marie), 1761–guill 29 Nov 1793. An educated Grenoblois barrister involved in the Pre-Rev in the Dauphiné along with Mounier, B. was at once prominent in the Jacobin Club and in the Constit Ass., where from late 1789 he formed the 'Triumvirate' with Lameth and Adrien Duport. His radicalism waned as time went on, and he switched to active support of the king after accompanying the royal party back to Paris from Varennes. A Feuillant, increasingly overtaken by events, he returned to the Dauphiné in early 1792. Arrested in Aug 1792, he wrote his celebrated *Introduction à la Révolution française* in prison.

Barras (J-Nic-Paul-Fs, vicomte de), 1755–1829. Scion of an ancient Provençal noble family, B. was an army officer and led a disreputable life in the last years of the AR, but became involved in rev politics from 1789. He represented the Var in the Convtn. *En mission* with Fréron in the Midi, he was responsible for the brutal repression of counter-rev in Marseille and the capture of Toulon. By early 1794, he felt threatened by Robespierre, conspired against him and as acting commander of the pro-Convtn forces in Paris played a key role on the *journée* of 9 Thermidor. He became prominent in the Thermidorian Convtn, crushing the Vendémiaire rising with Bonaparte's help and, elected to the C500, became a Director. Unscrupulous, corrupt, he had a fine political flair, and was the only Director to remain in place from the inception of the regime until its end. He was esp prominent in the organisation and execution of the Fructidor coup. After Brumaire, Bonaparte forced him out of politics and even, from 1810, into exile.

Barruel (Augustin, abbé), 1741–1820. A Jesuit in his early days, the abbé B. had acquired a reputation under the AR as a religious polemicist. His *Patriote véridique* in 1789 anticipated his more famous *Mémoires pour servir à l'histoire du jacobinisme*, written in Britain in 1797, where he popularised the argument that the Rev had originated in a conspiracy by *philosophes* and freemasons.

Barthélemy (Fs), 1747–1830. A diplomat under the AR, B. continued in this profession under the Rev: in particular he negotiated peace with Spain and Prussia in 1795. In May 1797 Clichyen influence secured him the post of Director in place of Letourneur, but Barras had him arrested as a royalist and deported to Guiana in the Fructidor coup. He returned from the New World in the late 1790s and continued his political and diplomatic career under Napoleon and the Bourbons.

Basire or **Bazire** (Claude), 1764–guill 5 Apr 1794. A wastrel from a solid bourgeois family in Dijon, B. was prominent in local politics before being elected to the Leg Ass. and Convtn. He became noted (along with Chabot and Merlin de Thionville) as an ultra-left deputy. He was elected to the CGS in February 1793. Dubious contacts (including those with Etta Palm who became his mistress) increased distrust of him in the Convtn, and his involvement in the Compagnie des Indes scandal finished him politically. He was arrested in Jan 1794 and executed with the Dantonists.

Batz (J-P, baron de), 1754–1822. A Gascon adventurer under the AR with masonic links and a reputation for financial wheeling and dealing, B. proved a fervent royalist in the EG. Although he emigrated in 1792, he returned under false passports on a number of occasions, including a plot to rescue Louis XVI from the scaffold. Involved in the scandal of the Compagnie des Indes, and with links in the Convtn that seemed to put substance in the idea of a 'foreign plot', he continued in counter-rev espionage throughout the 1790s. He returned to France under Napoleon.

Baudin 'des Ardennes' (P-Ch-L), 1748–99. A political moderate, originally a postmaster from Sedan, who served in the Leg Ass., Convtn and C Anciens, B.'s most significant political act was getting the Convtn to pass a general political amnesty on the last day of its sessions.

Baudot (Marc-Ant), 1765–1837. A doctor from the Charolais, B. entered nat politics as a *suppléant* to the Convtn in July 1792. An enthusiast for the war effort, he was away from Paris most of 1793 and early 1794 *en mission*, notably in the SW, where he helped put down the Federalist revolt, and in Alsace, where he initiated radical and dechristianising policies, but fell out with Saint-Just and Lebas. Threatened as a former terrorist, he emigrated in late 1794, but returned in the late 1790s and resumed his medical practice in Charolles.

Bayle (Moïse), 1760–1815. Originally from Languedoc, B. was PGS of the Bouches-du-Rhône and mayor of Marseille before being elected to the Convtn. He opposed the federalism of his compatriots and was elected to the CGS. He managed to avoid arrest after Thermidor and passed into the police bureaucracy, then oblivion.

Bazire, see BASIRE

Beauharnais (Alexandre-Fs-Marie, vicomte de), 1760–guill 23 July 1794. A career soldier who had been married to the future Empress Josephine from 1779 until 1783, B. was elected by the Blois nobility to the EG where he proved a liberal, rallying to the Third Estate in June and making a mark on the 'Night of 4 Aug'. He served with the Armies of the North and the Rhine in 1793, but resigned in Aug 1793. He passed before the Rev Tribunal and was executed days before Thermidor.

Beauharnais (Josephine, vicomtesse de), see TASCHER DE LA PAGERIE

Beaumarchais (P-Augustin Caron de), 1732–99. The author of the *Mariage de Figaro* (1784) had let success spoil him. By the late 1780s and early 1790s, he was mainly involved in financial wheeling and dealing and as an unsuccessful impresario. His *Mère coupable* (1792) was a flop and the leftward trend of the Rev forced him into emigration.

Bénézech (P), 1749–1802. From a family of Languedoc magistrates and administrators, B. established himself in Paris in the late 1780s. His gifts as an administrator kept him out of political trouble, notably during the Terror when he organised the manufacture of armaments. A resourceful Minister of the Interior from Nov 1795, he resigned when compromised by links with the right. Under Napoleon, he served as prefect in Saint-Domingue, where he died of yellow fever.

Bentabole (P-L), 1756–98. Son of a military administrator in Alsace, B. was a lawyer who was PGS for the Bas-Rhin before being elected to the Convtn. A Jacobin, he mimicked Marat and violently attacked the Girondins. Sent *en mission* on several occasions in 1793, he fell in love with an heiress, moved from left-wing to right-wing politics and was prominent among the Thermidorians and as deputy in the C500 until 1798.

Bergasse (Nic), 1750–1832. Son of a Lyon merchant, B. renounced an ecclesiastical career to study law. By the late 1780s he was a renowned barrister in Paris, and he became involved in the Pre-Rev and was elected by Lyon to the EG. An energetic deputy, he was associated with Mounier and Lally-Tollendal in the attempt to make the new constitution bicameral. He withdrew from the Ass. after the *journées* of 5–6 Oct 1789, becoming a counter-rev pamphleteer, polemicist and, possibly, secret counsellor to Louis XVI. He served in the latter's defence during his trial. Imprisoned under the Terror he was released in Jan 1795 and returned to private life.

Bernadotte (J-B-Jules), 1763–1844. Son of a magistrate at Pau, B. abandoned a legal career for service in the Royale-Marine. The Rev unblocked his promotion chances and by 1794 he was a general in the Army of the Sambre-and-Meuse under Jourdan. From 1796 he served in Italy and somewhat unwillingly entered Bonaparte's political orbit. He was briefly ambassador in Vienna in 1798, then War Minister, but resumed his military career under Napoleon, and ended his life as king of Sweden.

Bernard 'de Saintes' (André-Ant), 1751–1818. Son of a notary from the Saint-onge, B. was a lawyer prominent in local politics before being elected to the Leg Ass. and Convtn. A Montagnard with Hébertist links, he served briefly on the CGS and was a fierce rep *en mission* in E France (where, notably, he oversaw the annexation of Montbéliard in Oct 1793), returning to Paris in Apr 1794. Imprisoned after the Prairial rising, but amnestied in 1795, he returned to law and administration at Saintes.

Bernier (Et-Alexandre-J-B-Marie), 1762–1806. The 'Talleyrand of the Vendée' (G. WALTER). A parish priest in Anjou in 1790, B. refused the Civ Constn, and in June 1793 joined the Vendéan rebels. Prominent on the battlefield, he was also a skilled negotiator, coming to terms with the Rpbc in 1795. From 1796 he was commander of the Vendée rebels, and played a leading part during the Consulate in negotiating a peace in the Vendée and also the Concordat with the Pope. In 1802 he became bishop of Orléans.

Bernis (Fs-Joachim de Pierre, cardinal de), 1715–94. B. had enjoyed a brilliant ecclesiastical and political career under Louis XV, and in 1789 was French ambassador in Rome. He refused the Civ Constn; declined to return to France when summoned; and welcomed members of the royal family and *émigrés* in Rome.

Berthier (L-Alexandre), 1753–1815. Son of a military cartographer, B. was an officer in the army under the AR and became major-general in the Paris Nat Guard in 1789. He volunteered in 1791, served in the N and the W and by June 1796 was a general in the Army of Italy. Commander of the Army of Italy in Dec 1797, he seized Rome and organised the Roman Rpbc. He was subsequently attached to the Armies of England and the Orient; cooperated in the Brumaire coup; and served Napoleon as a soldier and as War Minister.

Berthollet (Claude-L), 1748–1822. By training a doctor, this chemist of renown and ally of Lavoisier was involved in the reform of technical and higher education during the Rev, esp 1792–4.

Bertier de Sauvigny (L-Benigne-Fs de), 1737–assass 22 July 1789. An enlightened intendant of Paris since 1776, B. de S. was compromised by organising food supplies for the soldiers surrounding Paris in July 1789. Brought to Paris to be tried, he was seized by rioters and assassinated along with his father-in-law Foulon.

Bertrand de Moleville (Ant-Fs, comte de), 1744–1818. Intendant of Brittany whose role in attempting to deal with the 'Noble Revolt' had led to his resignation in 1788, B. de M. served as Navy Minister from Oct 1791 to March 1792. A full-blooded reactionary, he then acted as the king's spy on the Jacobins. He fled to Britain in Aug 1792 to avoid arrest, returning to France in 1814.

Besenval (P-Jos-Victor, baron de), 1721–94. CinC of the Interior in 1781 and a favourite of Marie-Antoinette, B. played an uncharacteristically lethargic part in deploying troops in and around Paris in July 1789. He retired, lay low and died in bed.

Beurnonville (P Riel de), 1752–1821. An infantry colonel in 1789, B. remained in the army in the early 1790s and fought in the N. Briefly War Minister (Feb–Mar 1793), he returned to the front and denounced Dumouriez. The latter arrested him and handed him over to the enemy in Apr 1793, but he returned to France and to the army in Dec 1795. He pursued a military and diplomatic career under Napoleon.

Billaud-Varenne (Jq-Nic), 1756–1819. Oratorian schoolmaster turned lawyer with literary pretensions, B.-V. pursued politics mainly through the Jacobins and Cordeliers in the early 1790s; was substitute to the *procureur* of the Commune insurrectionnelle in 1792; and was elected to the Convtn for Paris. He proved an extreme left-winger, and was elected on to the CPS under *sans-culotte* pressure on 6 Sept 1793. Threatened by Robespierre, he was one of the Thermidorian conspirators. Arrested and tried after Thermidor with Collot-d'Herbois, Vadier and Barère, he was deported to Guiana. He stayed in the New World and died a farmer in Saint-Domingue.

Biron (Armand-L de Gontaut, duc de), 1747–guill 31 Dec 1793. As duc de Lauzun (till 1788) B. pursued the life of a dissipated aristocrat and soldier. Elected to the EG by the nobility of Quercy, he came out as an Orleanist, and won some good commands in 1792–3. In the Vendée, however, he quarrelled with Rossignol and was dismissed for moderation in July 1793. In Dec, he went before the Rev Tribunal.

Bo (J-B-Jérôme), 1743–1814. This Rouerguat doctor was elected by the Aveyron to the Leg Ass. and Convtn and proved prominent in the reform of poor relief and education. A capable organiser and man of action, he was often sent *en mission*: in 1793 in the Aveyron and the Tarn, with the Army of the Ardennes and in the Marne; in 1794 in the depts of Lot, Cantal, Tarn, Aveyron and Lozère and at Nantes; and in 1795 with the Army of the Pyrenees. Briefly imprisoned in 1795, he entered the bureaucracy before returning to private practice in Fontainebleau in 1809.

Boisgelin de Cucé (Jean de Dieu-Raymond de), 1732–1804. Archbishop of Aix since 1770, B. sat in the Ass. of Notables in 1787 and then in the EG. He seemed a major political figure in the Autumn of 1789, but opposed the Constit Ass.'s ecclesiastical reforms, refused the Civ Constn and emigrated in 1792. He returned in 1801, was made Archbishop of Tours in 1802 and Cardinal in 1803.

Boisset (Jos-Ant), 1748–1813. A lawyer from Montélimar, B. was elected by the Drôme to the Convtn, where he voted for the king's death and was sent *en mission* in S France. After Thermidor *en mission* in the E and at Lyon, he harrassed terrorists. He also sat on the C Anciens but abandoned politics after Brumaire.

Boissy d'Anglas (Fs-Ant de), 1756–1826. A Protestant lawyer and man of letters from the Ardèche, B. d'A. was trying to make his way in Paris in 1789. He represented the Ardèche (for which he served as PGS in 1791–2) in the EG, Constit Ass. and Convtn, where he sat with the Plain and supported imprisonment rather than death for Louis XVI. His active political career only started after Thermidor: he was a member of the CPS; showed sang-froid as president of the Convtn during the Prairial uprising; helped draw up the Constitution of Year III; and in the C500 was viewed as a Clichyen. After Fructidor he fled to England, but he returned after Brumaire and continued a distinguished parliamentary career.

Bonald (L-Gabriel-Ambroise, vicomte de), 1754–1840. The reactionary ideologue had served as king's musketeer and in 1789 was mayor of Millau. He abandoned politics over the Civ Constn and joined Condé's army, though he soon reentered France under an alias.

Bonaparte (Lucien), 1775–1840. At first a supporter of Paoli in Corsica, this younger brother of Napoleon came to France and pursued a career in military administration and Jacobin politics during the Terror. Elected for Liamone (Corsica) to the C500 he acted as his brother's eyes and ears in Parisian politics, esp during the Egyptian campaign. He played a key role in the preparation and organisation of Brumaire. Though rewarded with the Ministry of the Interior, he was dissatisfied and never really profited from the Empire, preferring to live in semi-retirement in Italy.

Bonaparte (Napoléon; from 1804 to 1815, emperor), 1769–1821. Son of a Corsican lawyer, Bonaparte (or Buonaparte, as he often still spelled his name) trained in the Paris Ecole militaire and in 1785 was seconded to a crack artillery regiment. He was involved in Corsican politics in the early 1790s, but sprang to nat prominence in Dec 1793 when he commanded the artillery in the siege of Toulon. Viewed as a Jacobin general (he had joined the Jacobin Club of Valence as early as 1791, and was friendly with Augustin Robespierre), he was briefly imprisoned in Aug 1794. He aided Barras in repressing the Vendémiaire rising in Paris in Oct 1795 'with a whiff of grapeshot' (for which he was dubbed 'General Vendémiaire') and was appointed commander of the Army of the Interior. In Mar 1796 he married Joséphine de Beauharnais, and was immediately sent to take over from Schérer as commander of the Army of Italy. Throughout 1796 and 1797 he enjoyed a series of brilliant victories which climaxed in the Peace of Campo-Formio with the Austrians in Oct 1797. Appointed commander of the Army of England, in Mar 1798 he was switched to the new Army of the Orient. His Egyptian campaign was not crowned with success, and in Oct 1799 he returned to France and instigated the coup of 18 Brumaire which brought him to power as First Consul.

Bonneville (Nic), 1760–1828. Son of an attorney from Evreux, B. was pursuing a literary career in Paris when the Rev broke out. In Dec 1790 he founded, along with Fauchet, the Cercle social, and edited the journal, the *Bouche de fer*. Linked with the Girondins, he was imprisoned under the Terror. Released after Thermidor, he was to die a poor bookseller in the Latin Quarter.

Bonnier d'Alco (Ange-L-Ant), 1750–assass 19 Apr 1799. A wealthy *robin* from Montpellier, B. d'A. was prominent in local politics before being elected to the Leg Ass. and Convtn, where he sat among the Plain. Under the Directory, he was used as a diplomat and in Apr 1799 was French representative at the Congress of Rastadt where he was assassinated, possibly by Austrian troops.

Botherel (René-J, comte de), 1745–1805. This key figure in the Chouan movement had served as a soldier under the AR before becoming the last *procureur-syndic* of the Estates of Brittany. At first involved in the Breton Pre-Rev, he was associated with the La Rouërie conspiracy and then became link-man between the Chouans, the *émigrés* and the British government in the late 1790s.

Bouchotte (J-B-Noël), 1754–1840. A career soldier from Metz who had only reached the rank of captain in 1789 after over 20 years of service, B. welcomed the Rev, and on Dumouriez's defection distinguished himself on the N front. Elected War Minister, 4 Apr 1793, he enlarged and 'sansculottised' military administration, and ensured the implementation of key military reforms. Attacked by the Girondins and Dantonists, he was given strong support by the CPS. When ministries were abolished in Apr 1794, he returned to the army. Arrested in June 1794, he was amnestied the following year. Under the Directory he dabbled in neo-Jacobin politics, but supported Bonaparte at Brumaire and retired on a military pension.

Bouillé (Fs-Claude-Amour, marquis de), 1739–1800. Distinguished career soldier and fervent royalist, B. achieved political notoriety by repressing army mutinies at Metz and then at Nancy (Aug 1790). From mid 1790 he was devising ways of freeing Louis XVI. He planned and almost succeeded in freeing him in the flight to Varennes, at which juncture he emigrated, joining the army of the princes and fighting alongside the Duke of York in 1793 before emigrating to Britain, where he died.

Boulanger (Servan-Beaudouin), 1756–guill 29 July 1794. A Paris jewellery-worker in Paris since 1773, B. joined the Nat Guard in 1789, the regular army in 1793 and in the autumn of 1793 was appointed to the Paris *armée révolutionnaire*. He fought for Robespierre at Thermidor, and was executed two days later.

Boulay 'de la Meurthe' (Ant-Jq-Claude-Jos), 1761–1840. A lawyer by training, B. was elected to the C500, where he expressed strong opinions against the *émigrés*, the nobility, the non-juring clergy, etc, and supported the Fructidor coup. By 1799, however, he was evolving towards the right and he welcomed

Brumaire. He was to have a distinguished political and administrative career under Napoleon.

Bourbon (L-Henri-Jos, duc de; from 1818 prince de Condé), 1756–1830. Governor of Franche-Comté in 1789, B. was, along with his father the prince de Condé, among the first *émigrés*. He fought against the Rpbc in 1793 and was involved in the Yeu expedition in 1795. He lived in London until 1814.

Bourbotte (P), 1763–guill 17 June 1795. A lackey under the AR, B. represented the Yonne in the Convtn, where he sat among the Montagnards. He was involved in the pacification of the W, and was responsible for the massacre of Vendéan prisoners on the island of Noirmoutier in Jan 1794. Implicated in the Prairial rising, he was imprisoned and, after an unsuccessful suicide attempt, guillotined. A 'martyr of Prairial'.

Bourdon 'de l'Oise' (Fs-Louis), 1758–dep 1798. Attorney in the Paris parl and leader of the *basoche* in the Pre-Rev period, B. was unsuccessful in his early rev career and was only elected to the Convtn as a result of a confusion over names. At first attracted to the Girondins, he moved unsteadily (he was a heavy drinker) towards the Montagne, and was active in the *journée* of 31 May 1793. *En mission* on a number of occasions in 1793, notably in the W, he fulfilled his functions poorly and was suspected of corruption. He conspired against Robespierre at Thermidor. Viewed as a Clichyen in the C500, he was deported following Fructidor.

Bourdon (Léonard), 1754–1807. A lawyer from Alençon, Léonard B. spent the early years of the Rev in Parisian sectional politics. Elected to the Convtn, he favoured Hébert and was distrusted by Robespierre for suspected corruption and excesses of rev zeal (notably while he was *en mission* at Orléans). A conspirator against Robespierre at Thermidor, his past caught up with him and he was imprisoned. Amnestied in 1795, he tried to re-enter politics. In 1798, the Directors made him consul at Hamburg. He spent his last years as a military administrator.

Boyer-Fonfrède (J-B), 1765–guill 31 Oct 1793. Son of a wealthy Bordeaux businessman, B.-F. was prominent in local politics in the early years of the Rev. Elected to the Convtn for the Gironde, he tried to mend the quarrel with the Montagnards, but stood by his compatriots in the crisis of 1793, for which he was executed with them.

Bréard or **Bréard-Duplessis** (J-Jq), 1751–1840. Son of a colonial administrator, B. was a lawyer who was elected to the Leg Ass. where he proved a radical and energetic deputy. He sat on the CGD, then the CPS from April to June 1793. He opposed Robespierre at Thermidor, and was elected to the CPS again after his fall. A member of the C Anciens until 1798, he pursued a career in bureaucracy under Napoleon.

Breteuil (L-Auguste Le Tonnelier, baron de), 1730–1807. Diplomat, then, from 1783, Minister of the Royal Household with special responsibility for Paris. The progenitor of numerous enlightened reforms (regulation of *lettres de cachet*, hospital and prison improvement, etc), B. fell out with Calonne and resigned. Reactionary even in 1787, he was chosen to supervise the royal coup against Paris in July 1789. He emigrated directly after this. In Nov 1790, Louis XVI appointed him plenipotentiary for negotiations with foreign powers. He returned to France in 1802 and died in obscurity.

Brienne or **Loménie de Brienne** (Et-Ch de), 1727–94. Careerist cleric, friend of the *philosophes* and, though allegedly an atheist, archbishop of Toulouse since 1763, B. was a highly competent administrator in the Turgot mould. The main opponent of Calonne at the Ass. of Notables in 1787, he became the king's principal minister after Calonne's fall and adopted most of his predecessor's reform programme. In Jan 1788 he had himself appointed archbishop of Sens and in May introduced the notorious May Edicts. This reform package provoked the opposition of the nobility and in Aug 1788 Brienne resigned. He obtained a cardinal's hat in recompense and spent the next two years in Italy, but returned in 1790 to accept the Civ Constn and to hope for greater things. In Nov 1793, however, he was arrested and he died shortly afterwards under house arrest.

Brissot or **Brissot de Warville** (Jq-P), 1754–guill 31 Oct 1793. A brilliant school career led this son of a Chartres caterer to try to make a literary career for himself in Paris. He was not successful, being imprisoned for debts and even serving as a police spy to make ends meet. Things improved in 1788 when he formed the Société des Amis des Noirs, which brought him into contact with many of the future Girondins. In the early years of the Rev, he was best known for his journalism (in his *Patriote français*) and for his part in Parisian municipal politics. Paris elected him to the Leg Ass., where he pressed for war along with the other Girondins. In the Convtn his views became less left-wing. He attacked the Commune over the Sept Massacres; voted the *appel au peuple*; and was arrested in the *journées* of 31 May–2 June 1793.

Broglie (Victor-Fs, duc de), 1718–1804. A brilliant career soldier with strongly royalist sympathies, B. was recalled by Louis XVI to command troops round Paris, then appointed War Minister on 12 July 1789. He resigned following the fall of the Bastille and emigrated. He commanded *émigré* forces in 1793, but retired in 1797 and died in Germany.

Brotier or **Brottier** (André-Ch), 1751–dep 12 Sept 1798. A cleric, maths teacher and journalist under the AR, B. was arrested during the Terror because of his links with the abbé Maury. On his release he became involved in royalist polemics and conspiracy. Imprisoned briefly for his alleged role in the Vendémiaire rising, he was arrested in Jan 1797 along with Duverne de Presle for allegedly recruiting for the royalist cause, and sentenced to deportation.

Bruix (Et-Eustache), 1759–1805. A career naval officer who had served in the W Indies in the 1780s, B. was put in charge of the Irish expedition in 1796. From Apr 1798 to July 1799 he was a capable Navy Minister. He supported the Brumaire coup and was made an admiral by Napoleon.

Brune (Guillaume-Marie-Anne), 1763–1815. Son of a lawyer from Brive, B. worked in a Paris printing-house in the 1780s, when he became acquainted with Bonneville, Danton and Desmoulins. A Cordelier and a journalist in the early years of the Rev, his career was transformed when, in 1791, he volunteered for the army. He commanded the rpbcn force at the 'battle' of Pacy-sur-Eure against the Federalists in 1793. Particularly reliable for internal repression, he aided Barras in putting down the Vendémiaire rising in Paris; helped in the pacification of the Vendée and the Midi; and crushed the Babouvist Grenelle Camp incident. After 1796, he served in Italy, Switzerland and Holland, but though his career continued under Napoleon he never achieved the highest posts.

Buonarroti (Filippo Michele), 1761–1837. Of ancient though impoverished Florentine noble ancestry, B. served the French forces in Italy on various administrative and propaganda missions after the outbreak of war. Arrested following Thermidor, he met Babeuf in prison, and following his release collaborated with him in the Panthéon Club and then in the Babeuf plot. Sentenced to deportation by the Vendôme High Court, he in fact languished in prison until the Consulate. Prominent in Italian secret societies in the early nineteenth century, his celebrated work, the *Conspiration pour l'égalité dite de Babeuf*, was published in 1828.

Buzot (Fs-Nic-Léonard), 1760–suic 18 June 1794. Son of a magistrate from Evreux, a lawyer himself, B. was elected to the EG. A Jacobin and, after Varennes, a rpbcn, he was elected to the Convtn. He fell in love with Madame Roland, fell out with Robespierre and was soon viewed as a Girondin, and voted the *appel au peuple*. Opposed to the growing power of the Commune and of the Rev Govt, he fled arrest on the *journée* of 2 June 1793, though he failed to rally military support in Normandy. On the run in the Bordelais for eight months, he escaped arrest only by committing suicide.

Cabanis (P-J-Georges), 1757–1808. The 'idéologue' of the late 1790s was born in Brive and followed a literary and scientific career prior to the Rev. An enthusiast for 1789, and Mirabeau's friend and physician, he was a key figure in the reform of Parisian hospitals and the establishment of the Paris Medical School. In 1798 he was elected to the C500 for the Seine, and was involved in the Brumaire coup, though he was subsequently to become suspect to Napoleon and forced out of public life.

Cabarrus (Thérèse, from 1794 Madame Tallien; from 1805 comtesse de Caraman and princesse de Chimay), 1773–1835. Daughter of a Spanish finance minister who married a councillor in the Paris parl, Madame Tallien was allegedly in prison when Tallien, *en mission* in Bordeaux, encountered her. She came into her own in the Thermidorian period when her salon became a notorious rallying-ground for the *jeunesse dorée*. When Tallien abandoned her, she moved abroad.

Cadoudal (Georges), 1771–1804. This Vendéan rebel chief was from a well-off Breton landowning family, and joined the Vendéan movement from Feb 1793. Arrested and imprisoned in June 1794, he escaped after Thermidor and formed a new rebel force; established links with London; and was involved in the Quiberon Bay expedition. Forced to come to terms, he emigrated to Britain, but returned from 1799 to 1800 and then again in 1803, when he was captured and executed.

Cahier de Gerville (Bon-Claude), 1751–96. Son of a wealthy businessman from Bayeux, C. was a lawyer in 1789 in Paris where his patriotic attitudes won him the post of assistant *procureur-syndic* to the Commune. He served as Minister of the Interior from 27 Nov 1791 to 15 Mar 1792 and retired to his home town on his dismissal.

Calonne (Ch-Alexandre de), 1734–1802. A distinguished intendant from the 1760s, C. had never lost the hostility of the parls for his handling of the Rennes parl crisis of 1765. Controller-General from 1783, his attempts at financial reform (1786–7) foundered on the opposition of the nobility and the legal establishment. Retiring to Britain in disgrace on the dissolution of the Ass. of Notables in Apr 1787, he approached Artois in mid 1789 and became virtual prime minister of the *émigrés*. Dropped unceremoniously by the princes in 1792, however, he returned to London.

Cambacérès (J-Jq-Régis de), 1753–1824. This scion of an influential *robin* family in Montpellier and future Arch-Chancellor of Napoleon was elected to the Convtn by the Hérault. A trimmer by nature, he lay low during the Terror. President of the CPS after Thermidor, he served on the C500 down to 1789. After the coup of Prairial Year VII he became Minister of Justice, and was to be chosen by Bonaparte as his second consul.

Cambon (P-Jos), 1756–1820. From a wealthy business family in Montpellier, Jos C. was prominent in local politics before being elected to the Leg Ass., then the Convtn. At first a member of the Plain who shared many of the positions of the Girondins, he moved towards the Montagnards in early 1793; voted for the king's death; served briefly on the CGD; and from 10 July 1793 as chairman of the Finance Committee played an immensely important part in financing the war effort. Conflict with Robespierre over financial policy led him to participate in the Thermidor coup. He remained on the Finance Committee down to Apr 1795, but was increasingly viewed as a terrorist. His involvement in the Prairial *journées* led him to take to hiding. Amnestied in 1795, he returned to Montpellier.

Camus (Armand-Gaston), 1740–1804. An erudite canon law specialist, C. was elected to the EG and played a major role in framing the Civ Constn. Elected to the Convtn, he sat on the CGD and was sent on a number of important missions. In Apr 1793 Dumouriez handed him and other representatives over to the enemy. He was returned to France in Dec 1795; sat on the C500; and began his influential reign as director of the national archives.

Canclaux (J-B-Camille de), 1740–1817. Career soldier and military theorist under the AR, C. served from 1792 in W France where he enjoyed much success until his dismissal in Sept 1793. After Thermidor he returned to the army as commander in the Vendée, aiding Hoche at Quiberon. After 1795 he served as ambassador in Naples. He supported Napoleon at Brumaire and continued a distinguished career under him.

Carnot (Lazare-Nic-Marguerite), 1753–1823. Son of a Burgundian notary, C. was trained at the Mézières military engineering college, and by 1783 was captain in the engineers. Elected to the Leg Ass., he joined the Jacobins, but tended to speak on technical and military matters. Given a number of key areas *en mission* from Aug 1792 in the N and S, in Aug 1793 he was elected to the CPS where he specialised in military matters. Only spared exile after Thermidor because he was seen as the 'organiser of victory' in Year II, he was elected to the C Anciens and then in Nov 1795 became a Director. His political opinions had moved to the right, and at Fructidor he fled to Switzerland and Germany, only returning after Brumaire. Napoleon's War Minister for a few months, he soon returned to private life.

Carra (J-L), 1742–guill 31 Oct 1793. Author, contributor to the *Encyclopédie* and polemicist, C. threw himself into journalism in 1789, founding with Mercier the *Annales patriotiques et littéraires*, a journal highly popular with the prov Jacobin clubs. Elected with acclaim to the Convtn, he was identified as a Jacobin, but his eccentric ideas (he had proposed the Duke of York for the French throne) and Girondin links made him suspect, and he was arrested and executed.

Carrier (J-B), 1756–guill 16 Dec 1794. Son of a well-off farmer from the Cantal, C. was an attorney in Aurillac in 1789. He won a reputation as a local patriot and was elected to the Convtn. A staunch Montagnard, he gained notoriety for the brutality of his treatment of Brittany and the Vendée during his period *en mission* there from Aug 1793 to Feb 1794 (notably the *noyades* of thousands in the estuary of the Loire). He was recalled by the CPS and after Thermidor defended himself before the Convtn (Nov 1794) before being sent before the Rev Tribunal.

Carteaux (J-B-Fs), 1751–1813. After an odd career as soldier and artist, C. became adc to Lafayette in the Paris Nat Guard in July 1789. He volunteered for the army, and by 1793 was one of the generals responsible for putting down the Federalist revolt in the Midi. Imprisoned in Dec 1793, he was released after

Thermidor and resumed his military career. He participated in the repression of the Vendémiaire rising, but his career stagnated and under Napoleon he entered the bureaucracy.

Castries (Armand-Ch-Augustin de la Croix, comte de), 1752–1842. This wealthy and liberal career soldier sat in the EG and moved increasingly to the right, eventually emigrating and fighting against the Rpbc.

Castries (Ch-Eugène-Gabriel, marquis de), 1727–1801. A long-serving career officer, C. was Navy Minister from 1780 to 1787, when the death of his patron Vergennes led to his dismissal. He was an early *émigré*; sat on the princes' council at Coblenz; commanded an *émigré* force against the Rpbc in 1792; and in the late 1790s served as an adviser to Louis XVIII.

Cathelineau (Jq), 1759–14 July 1793. A weaver on the outbreak of the Rev, C. became involved in the Vendée revolt by leading a conscription riot in March 1793. He was soon prominent among the rebel leaders and after taking Saumur in June 1793 was appointed generalissimo of the 'Royal and Catholic Army'. He died of the wounds he had sustained in attacking Nantes in July 1793.

Cazalès (Jq-Ant-Marie de), 1758–1805. From a family of *noblesse de cloche*, C. was a soldier in 1789 and, elected to the EG, was soon prominent as an eccentric right-winger. His attempts to join the *émigrés* were initially spurned, though he did fight against the Rpbc with *émigré* forces in 1793. Shortly after, he settled in England where he became a confidant of Burke and tried to suborn deputies in the Councils. He returned to France in 1803.

Cérutti (Jos-Ant-Joachim-Camille), 1738–92. A Milanese ex-Jesuit and polemicist, C. played a part in the Orleanist clique in 1787–8: served in Paris local government; was elected to the Leg Ass.; but died in Feb 1792. He is best known as the founder of the popular journal, the *Feuille villageoise*.

Chabot (Fs), 1756–guill 5 Apr 1794. Son of a cook, C. became a Capucin priest, if a dissolute one. He accepted the Civ Constn and became Grégoire's vicar-general in the Loir-et-Cher, which dept he represented in the Leg Ass. He was prominent on the far left and popularised the idea of a *comité autrichien*. In the Convtn, he served *en mission* and, from 21 Jan to Sept 1793, on the CGS. His marriage to the sister of the shadowy Austrian banker Junius Frey and his disreputable private life brought him enemies, and involvement in the Compagnie des Indes swindle completed his fall. Arrested in Nov 1793 he was executed along with the Dantonists.

Chalier (Marie-Jos), 1747–exctd July 1793. This 'martyr of liberty' was a Dominican novice in Lyon, then a travelling salesman in Italy and the Levant. He participated in the overthrow of the Bastille, then returned to Lyon and became prominent as a radical in local politics. After vicious factional struggles in the Spring of 1793, moderates provoked the Lyon rising on May 1793 in the course of which C. was arrested and executed.

Chambon de Montaux (Nic), 1748–1826. A doctor holding prestigious hospital appointments at the end of the AR, C. joined the Jacobins, was active in sectional politics and served as mayor of Paris from 1 Dec 1792 to 4 Feb 1793. Acknowledged to be politically impotent, he retired to Blois.

'Chamfort' (sobriquet of Sébastien-Roch NICOLAS), 1741–94. After an early flirtation with a career in the church, C. developed into a salon intellectual and celebrated wit. Linked with Mirabeau, he was a prominent Jacobin in 1790–1, and Roland appointed him director of the Bibliothèque Nationale in 1792. Under surveillance during the Terror, he in fact died during a surgical operation.

Champion de Cicé (Jérôme-Marie), 1735–1810. This liberal aristocrat, archbishop of Bordeaux from 1781, was elected by his clergy to the EG. Quick to rally to the Third Estate in June 1789 and reputed for his advanced views, he replaced Barentin as Garde des Sceaux on 4 Aug 1789. His opposition to the Civ Constn made his position untenable, however, and he resigned in Nov 1790 and emigrated in 1791. He was to return to France in 1802 and become archbishop of Aix.

Championnet (J-Et), 1762–1800. The illegitimate son of a postmaster, C. volunteered from the Valence Nat Guard; served with Hoche on the Rhine in 1793; and by Dec 1794 was a general. By 1798 he was commander of the Army of Rome, took Naples against Directorial orders and proclaimed the Parthenopean Rpbc. He was arrested over a dispute with civil commissary Faypoult, but released following the Prairial coup in 1799. Appointed commander of the Army of Italy, he was defeated by the Austrians at Genola in Nov 1799, then died in an epidemic.

Chappe (Claude), 1763–1805. The inventor of the telegraph, who presented his invention to the Leg Ass. in 1792, was championed by Romme. News of the taking of Le Quesnoy in Aug 1794 was the first major piece of information relayed by this method.

Chaptal (J-Ant-Claude), 1756–1832. Son of a wealthy landowner in the Lozère, C. was a brilliant medical student at Montpellier and Paris who moved into the industrial application of chemistry, establishing a major chemical works outside Montpellier just before the Rev. He was implicated in the Federalist revolt, but his abilities as an administrator saved him: he was entrusted with the collection of saltpetre. Professor in the Montpellier Medical School from 1794, he moved to Paris in 1799, serving as Napoleon's Minister of the Interior from 1801 to 1804.

Charette or **Charette de la Contrie** (Fs-Athanase), 1763–exctd 29 Feb 1796. A naval officer quick to emigrate in 1789, C. returned disillusioned from Coblenz and was drawn into the Vendée revolt. Prominent in military action during 1793, he was recognised as the Vendéans' commander. Affairs went badly, however, and in Feb 1795 he came to terms with the Rpbc in the Treaty of La Jaunaye. He was reactivated by the Quiberon Bay expedition but, harried by Hoche, he was captured and shot.

Charles X, see ARTOIS

Chartres (L-Ph, duc de; from Nov 1793, duc d'Orléans; from 1830 to 1848, Louis-Philippe, king of France), 1773–1850. The eldest son of the duc d'Orléans and, like his father, an active Jacobin in the early years of the Rev, C. served as adc to Dumouriez when war broke out and fought bravely. He followed his commander into emigration in Apr 1793.

Chasles (P-Jq-Michel), 1753–1826. Son of a carpenter from Chartres, and a canon of Tours cathedral in 1789, C. was royalist in the early days of the Rev, but accepted the Civ Constn. He evolved fast and, elected to the Convtn, supported the death penalty for Louis XVI, the proscription of the Girondins, etc. *En mission* with the Army of the North from Oct 1793 to Mar 1794, during which time he was wounded in battle, Chasles was linked with Amar and Vadier and distrusted Robespierre. A Thermidorian of the left, he was arrested after Thermidor. He was amnestied in 1795 and retired to near Chartres.

Chateaubriand (Fs-René, vicomte de), 1768–1848. Son of a Breton *hobereau*, the celebrated author was serving his apprenticeship in the literary salons of the capital when the Rev broke out. He visited the USA in 1791, returning to Europe in Jan 1792 to join the *émigré* army at Coblenz. Wounded in battle, he moved to London, but by 1800 was back in France and beginning his literary career.

Châteauneuf-Randon (Alexandre-Paul-Guérin de Tournel de), 1757–1827. Scion of an illustrious noble family from the Gévaudan, C.-R. was a soldier until 1788 when he threw himself into politics. *Suppléant* to the EG, he entered the Constit Ass. on 1 Sept 1789 and sat on the left. He rejoined the army in 1791, but was elected to the Convtn. A Montagnard, he was often *en mission* in the Midi. He returned to Paris after Thermidor, was elected to the CPS in Oct 1794, but returned to the army on the home front in 1795. He was briefly to serve as a prefect under Napoleon.

Chaumette (P-Gaspard, or 'Anaxagoras'), 1763–guill 13 Apr 1794. Son of a cobbler from Nevers, C. was a medical student in Paris in 1789. He soon became involved in sectional politics, becoming a Cordelier and writing for the *Révolutions de Paris*. A key member of the Commune insurrectionnelle in Aug 1792, he became the Commune's *procureur* in Dec and played a prominent part in the politics of the capital in 1793–4, esp the dechristianisation campaign. Robespierre regarded him as dangerous and he was arrested and tried shortly after Hébert.

Chauvelin (Bernard-Fs, marquis de), 1766–1832. Master of the King's Wardrobe in 1789, but supporter of the new ideas, C. was appointed ambassador to

London in 1792. He returned only to be imprisoned as a supporter of Dumouriez. Released after Thermidor, he pursued an administrative career under the Empire and Restoration.

Chénier (André-Marie de), 1762–guill 25 July 1794. Son of a diplomat, the poet C. was more moderate in politics than his brother Marie-Joseph. A member of the Société de 1789, then of the Feuillants and a telling counter-rev journalist, he was imprisoned under the Terror and executed two days before Thermidor. His poetry was published posthumously.

Chénier (Marie-Jos-Blaise de), 1764–1811. Man of letters and member of the Société de 1789 like his brother, Marie-Joseph C. subsequently pursued his career through the Jacobins. A member of the Convtn, and a key figure on its education committee, he sat with the Montagnards and voted for the king's death. He helped in the overthrow of Robespierre, and emerged as a Thermidorian of the right, attacking Collot-d'Herbois. A prominent member of the C500, he welcomed Brumaire, but ended his life an impoverished schoolteacher.

Choderlos de Laclos, see LACLOS

'Chouan', see COTTEREAU

Choudieu (P-René), 1761–1838. From a solid bourgeois background in Angers, C. had served as an army officer but was training as a lawyer in 1789, when he entered the Angers Nat Guard and joined the local Jacobins. He was elected to the Leg Ass. and Convtn. A Montagnard, he was sent *en mission* against the Vendéans in Mar 1793 and to the Army of the North in Feb 1794. Denounced as a terrorist after Thermidor, C. spent some time in prison, emerging in the amnesty of 1795. Arrested as a babouvist, though subsequently acquitted, he sought refuge in Belgium.

Clarke (Henry-Jq-Guillaume), 1765–1818. Of Irish aristocratic extraction, C. was captain in the army in 1789 and served on the Rhine in 1792–3. Arrested as a suspect under the Terror, he reappeared in 1795, was made a general and pursued a distinguished military and diplomatic career, esp under Napoleon.

Clavière (Et), 1735–suic 8 Dec 1793. Wealthy Genevan banker who was involved in the Genevan revolt of 1782 before coming to France to make a fortune out of speculation, C. was linked first with Mirabeau in opposition to Necker, then with Brissot through the Amis des Noirs. With Brissot's help, he became Finance Minister in March 1792 and though dismissed along with the Girondin ministers on 20 June 1792 was reinstated after 10 Aug. His Girondin links cost him dear, however: sectional militants had him arrested and imprisoned in June 1793, and he committed suicide in his cell.

Clermont-Tonnerre (Stanislas, comte de), 1757–assass 10 Aug 1792. Godson of Louis XV's queen, C.-T. had enjoyed a rather varied career under the AR and was a cavalry colonel in 1789. He was prominent among liberal nobles in the EG, and was president of the Constit Ass. in Aug 1789. He supported an absolute veto for the king and a bicameral legislature: in late 1789 he founded (with Malouet) the Club des Impartiaux. In 1792, he plotted with Malouet to save Louis XVI, and on the *journée* of 10 Aug 1792 was attacked by the Paris crowd and defenestrated.

Cloots or **Clootz** (baron J-B, from 1790 'Anacharsis'), 1755–guill 24 March 1794. An itinerant German nobleman interested in literature, C. settled in France in 1789 and became an enthusiastic rev. In his prolific radical journalism and in the Jacobin Club he popularised the idea of the Rev's cosmopolitan potential. On 26 Aug 1792 the Leg Ass. awarded him honorary French citizenship. The Oise elected him to the Convtn, where, however, Robespierre came to suspect him because of his foreign links and for his militant atheism. In Dec 1793 he was expelled from the Jacobins, then excluded from the Convtn and imprisoned. He was sent before the Rev Tribunal along with other supposed Hébertists.

Cochon 'de l'Apparent' (Ch), 1750–1825. A lawyer in Fontenay-le-Comte, C. was elected to the EG, initially as a *suppléant*, and then to the Convtn. A member of the Plain, he tended to favour the Montagnards, and voted the king's death. He was elected to the CPS after Thermidor and elected to the C Anciens. In Apr 1796 he was appointed Police Minister and played an important part in breaking up the Babeuf and Brotier plots. At Fructidor he was imprisoned, only to be released after Brumaire by Napoleon who made him a prefect.

Coffinhal (J-B), 1754–guill 6 Aug 1794. Attorney at the Châtelet in 1789, Coffinhal was prominent in the main *journées* of the early Rev; was a Jacobin; and in 1793 was made judge in, then vice-president of, the Rev Tribunal. He supported Robespierre at Thermidor and was executed for his pains.

Collot-d'Herbois (J-Marie), 1749–dep 8 June 1796. C. had pursued a theatrical career under the AR and in 1787 was resident dramatist and director of the Lyon theatre. He settled in Paris in 1789, joined the Jacobin Club and composed the highly popular *Almanach du père Gérard* (1791). A member of the Commune insurrectionnelle from 10 Aug 1792, he was elected to the Convtn by Paris. *En mission* in Nice (Dec 1792–Jan 1793), the Nièvre and Loiret (Mar 1793) and the Oise and the Aisne (Aug 1793), he was elected to the CPS on 6 Sept 1793 under *sans-culotte* pressure. Along with Fouché he was responsible for the repression (including the infamous *mitraillades*) in Lyon. On 20 May 1794 he was victim of the Ladmiral assassination attempt. Threatened by Robespierre, he was one of the architects of Thermidor. He left the CPS and was soon attacked for his terrorist past. Arraigned along with Barère, Billaud-Varenne and Vadier, he was deported to Guiana where he died.

Condé (L-Jos de Bourbon, prince de), 1736–1818. A Prince of the Blood with a distinguished military career behind him, C. spoke in favour of reform in the

Ass. of Notables in 1787. In 1789, however, he was among the first *émigrés*. From 1789 until 1791 he was based in Turin, and then moved to Worms where he organised the *émigré* army which he led in campaigns from 1792 to 1796. In 1797 he moved to Blankenburg with Louis XVIII and lived after 1801 in Britain before returning to France in 1814.

Condorcet (J-Ant-Nic de Caritat, marquis de), 1743–suic 29 March 1794. 'The last of the philosophes' (MICHELET) renounced a military career for literary and scientific pursuits. Liberal, anti-clerical, permanent secretary of the Academy of Sciences since 1785, C. joined the Société de 1789 in 1790, but soon progressed to membership of the Jacobin Club and rpbcn views. Elected by Paris to the Leg Ass. and by the Aisne to the Convtn, he made links with the Girondins, developed his interest in educational reform, and was responsible for the 'Girondin Constitution' debated in the Convtn from Feb 1793. Denounced in July 1793, he went into hiding but was soon arrested. In his cell he wrote his famous *Esquisse d'un tableau historique des progrès de l'esprit humain*, before committing suicide.

Constant (Benjamin, sobriquet of Benjamin de REBECQUE), 1767–1830. The author of *Adolphe* (1807) was born in Switzerland of French Huguenot extraction, and spent a bohemian youth travelling across Europe. In 1794 he became Madame de Staël's lover and came to Paris with her in 1795 to break into politics. The moderate rpbcn Cercle constitutionnel which he and Mme de Staël organised achieved a certain influence in Directorial circles. The two became notorious members of the liberal opposition under Napoleon.

Corday (Marie-Anne-Charlotte de), 1768–guill 17 July 1793. Charlotte C., the assassin of Marat (13 July 1793), was an educated woman from Caen whose brothers were *émigrés* and who identified with the Girondins. Tried by the Rev Tribunal on 17 July, she was executed on the same day.

Cottereau (J, alias 'Jean Chouan'), 1757–94. A salt-smuggler who under the AR had served time for killing an excise officer, C. formed a royalist band following a recruitment riot in Aug 1792. He fought with the Vendéans, but was ambushed in July 1794 and died of his wounds. His alias became synomymous with the cause he represented.

Couthon (Georges-Auguste), 1755–guill 28 July 1794. Son of a notary, lawyer in Clermont-Ferrand and consigned permanently to a wheelchair from 1789, C. was elected to the Leg Ass., joined the Jacobins and became friendly with Robespierre. Elected to the Convtn, he served *en mission* in the Loir-et-Cher (Nov 1792) and with the Army of the Alps (Aug 1793), and was also involved in the repression of Lyon (though he was rather lenient compared with Fouché and Collot-d'Herbois who succeeded him there). Elected to the CPS on 30 May 1793, C. became increasingly close to Robespierre and Saint-Just; was responsible for drawing up the Law of 22 Prairial II; and was executed as a Robespierrist on 10 Thermidor.

Creuzé-Latouche (Jq-Ant), 1749–1800. A magistrate in Châtellerault in 1789, C.-L. was most notable in the EG for his committee work. Elected to the Convtn, he was a moderate; voted the *appel au peuple*; and lay low during the Terror. A member of the CPS after Thermidor he played a part in the revision of the Constitution and was elected to the C Anciens, and then in 1798 to the C500. Under the Directory he was a close supporter of La Révellière-Lépeaux; a dedicated anti-Clichyen; and a prominent theophilanthropist.

Custine (Adam-Ph, comte de), 1740–guill 28 Aug 1793. A career soldier and fanatical follower of the precepts of Frederick the Great, C. was nevertheless among the liberal nobles in the EG to rally to the Third Estate in June 1789 and to support the 'Night of 4 Aug 1789'. He returned to the army in 1791 and from Sept 1792 had a number of commands on the northern front. He was recalled in July following defeats, imprisoned and executed.

Dampierre (Auguste-Marie-Henri de Picot, marquis de), 1756–battle 7 July 1793. Army officer, balloonist, admirer of Frederick the Great, friend of Orléans, D. was promoted fast in the Rev. He was notable at Jemappes, and by Mar 1793 was a general. He died in skirmishes around Valenciennes.

Danton (Georges-Jq), 1759–guill 5 Apr 1794. Trained as a lawyer like his father, D. was prominent from 1789 in the Cordeliers district and club, then from early 1791 in the Jacobin Club. Substitute to the *procureur* of the Paris Commune from Dec 1791, he was involved in the overthrow of Louis XVI. Appointed Minister of Justice in the PEC, he did not prevent the Sept Massacres, but he did rally the capital for the war effort. Elected by Paris to the Convtn, he soon fell out with the Girondins who hated him for his venality, his links with Dumouriez and for his complicity in the Sept Massacres. *En mission* in Belgium in late 1792/early 1793, member of the CPS from 6 Apr to 10 July 1793, he supported the institution of the Terror (Rev Tribunal, *armées révolutionnaires*, etc). He retired in ill health (Oct–Nov 1793) to his home at Arcis-sur-Aube, and when he returned attacked the dechristianisation movement and became associated with the campaign to slow down the Terror. Attacked as an *Indulgent*, he was arrested and executed.

Darthé (Augustin-Alexandre), 1769–guill 25 May 1797. Son of a surgeon, D. was still a law student when he became involved in the overthrow of the Bastille in 1789. By 1792 he was a zealous administrator in his native Pas-de-Calais, and as public prosecutor in the Rev Tribunals of Arras and Cambrai assisted Joseph Lebon in his mission in the Nord in 1794. Following a period of detention after Thermidor, he became a member of the Panthéon Club, became involved with Babeuf and was tried by the Vendôme high court and executed following an attempt to kill himself in his cell.

Dartigoëyte (P-Arnauld), 1763–1812. Son of a notary from SW France, D. was elected to the Convtn by the Landes. He was most remarked for his energetic and violent spells as rep *en mission* in the SW. He was recalled to Paris after Thermidor, imprisoned in Oct 1794 as a terrorist but amnestied in 1795, when he returned to private life.

Daunou (P-Claude-Fs), 1761–1840. Son of a Boulogne surgeon, D. was an Oratorian schoolmaster who in 1787 became a priest. He welcomed the Civ Constn, and became the vicar-general of Gobel, archbishop of Paris. Elected to the Convtn by the Pas-de-Calais, he opposed the death of the king and the expulsion of the Girondins, and was imprisoned in Oct 1793. Released after Thermidor, he was reinstated in the Convtn; became a member of the CPS; influenced the drafting of the Constitution of Year III; and served in the C500. Founder-member of the Institut, he was the main author of the law of 3 brum IV on education. In 1798, he was entrusted with organising the Roman Rpbc. His career continued under Napoleon.

David (Jq-L), 1748–1825. Already enjoying the reputation of a great artist before 1789, D. threw himself into the Rev with gusto, joining the Jacobin Club, painting the Tennis Court Oath and, from 1791, acting as director of the great rev and rpbcn festivals in Paris. Elected to the Convtn by Paris, he voted for the king's death; was instrumental in the abolition of much of the artistic and academic establishment of the AR; and in Sept 1793 was elected to the CGS. Identified as a Robespierrist, he endured several spells in prison after Thermidor, but in 1797 began his long relationship with Bonaparte.

Davout or **D'Avout** (L-Nic), 1770–1823. Son of a noble army officer, D. was trained in the Ecoles militaires of Auxerre and Paris, and was at the beginning of his career in 1789. He showed great intrepidity at the front and by 1793 was a general in the Army of the North. In 1798, he participated in the Egyptian campaign, embarking on an illustrious military career under Napoleon.

Davy de la Pailleterie, see 'DUMAS' ('Alexandre')

Debry or **De Bry** (Jean), 1760–1834. Son of a textiles manufacturer from Vervins, an attorney and freemason under the AR, D. served in local government in the Aisne before being elected to the Leg Ass. and Convtn, where he sat on the left. A prominent Thermidorian, he was elected to the C500 by the Orne and was present at Rastadt during the outrage of Apr 1799. He was to become a prefect under Napoleon.

Deforgues (Fs-L-Michel Chemin), 1759–1840. A Norman lawyer who served as Danton's secretary under the AR and followed him into politics. A member of the Commune insurrectionnelle and a leader in the Sept Massacres, D. held posts in the War Office and attached to the CPS before being chosen Foreign Minister in June 1793. Since France was at war with all of Europe, he had little to do. In Apr 1794, he was imprisoned as a Dantonist, but was freed after Thermidor. He was arrested again in 1795 for his part in the Sept Massacres, but was amnestied soon afterwards. The Directory used him in a number of diplomatic missions.

Delacroix or **Delacroix de Contaut** (Ch), 1741–1805. A high-ranking functionary in the department of the Controller-General under the AR, Delacroix was elected to the Convtn by the Marne and joined the Jacobin Club. After Thermidor, he turned reactionary; was elected to the C Anciens; served as Foreign Minister from Nov 1795 to July 1797, negotiating unsuccessfully with the British; was Dutch ambassador in 1797–8; and following Brumaire became a prefect.

Delacroix (Jq-Vincent), 1743–1832. Son of a royal bureaucrat, D. was a pamphleteer in the early years of the Rev. By 1792 he had swung from left to right, and he defended the king. He resumed his literary career in Year III after lying low during the Terror.

Delacroix or **Lacroix** (J-Fs), 1753–guill 5 Apr 1794. Son of a surgeon, D. was a lawyer and served as PGS for the Eure-et-Loir before going on to represent the dept in the Leg Ass. and Convtn, where he sat as a Montagnard. He was associated with Danton, notably while *en mission* with him in Belgium in early 1793, and sat on the CPS with him (Apr–July 1793). In Aug 1793 he was sent *en mission* to Normandy, but was recalled in Jan 1794, arrested and executed as a Dantonist.

Delaunay (Jos), 1752–guill 5 Apr 1794. A lawyer, D. was an ardent rev in his native Angers before being elected to the Leg Ass. and the Convtn, where he sat among the Montagnards while managing to maintain links with Roland and other Girondins. His political career was compromised by his involvement with Chabot and Fabre d'Eglantine, notably in the Compagnie des Indes scandal. He was denounced by Chabot to the CPS, and arrested with the Dantonists.

Delaunay (P-Marie), 1755–1814. A lawyer like his brother Joseph (see above), D. served as PGS in the Maine-et-Loire before being elected to the Convtn. Unlike his brother, he sat in the Plain, voted against the death of the king and was nearly implicated in the Federalist revolt. In the C500, he steered between royalism and neo-Jacobinism, before returning to his legal practice in Angers in 1797.

Delauney, see LAUNEY

Delescure, see LESCURE

Delessart, see LESSART

Desaix or **Des Aix** (L-Ch-Ant), 1768–battle 1800. Son of an Auvergnat noble, D. was a professional soldier under the AR, and continued in the army despite the fact that many of his relatives were *émigrés*. He was outstanding in the campaigns of 1793 and 1796–7 with the Army of the Rhine; went to Egypt in

1798; and won the battle of Marengo for Bonaparte in 1800, dying of wounds in the process.

Desault (P-Jos), 1744–96. From a peasant family in Franche-Comté, D. had trained as a surgeon in Paris, served in various Parisian hospitals and since 1788 was chief surgeon in the Paris Hôtel-Dieu, where he revolutionised clinical teaching methods. Arrested under the Terror but freed on the instances of his pupils, he was appointed professor of clinical surgery in the Paris Medical School in 1794. He numbered Corvisart, Laënnec and Bichat among his pupils.

Desfieux (Fs), 1755–guill 24 March 1794. A wine-merchant from Bordeaux, D. created a niche for himself in sectional and Jacobin politics in the capital. In Oct 1792, the Jacobins sent him *en mission* to the Army of the Pyrenees. Hostile to the Girondins, his alleged links with Proli, Pereira, Dubuisson and Batz seemed to make him part of the 'foreign plot', and he was arrested in Oct 1793 and eventually executed.

Desgenettes (René-Nic Dufriche de), 1762–1837. Son of a *robin* from Alençon, D. trained as a doctor. He joined the army medical services in 1790, became linked with Bonaparte, and laid the foundations for a brilliant medical career by his exemplary conduct in a plague epidemic during the Egyptian campaign.

Desmoulins (Lucie-Camille-Simplice), 1760–guill 5 Apr 1794. Son of a magistrate from the Aisne, Camille D. was a scholarship boy at the collège Louis-le-Grand in Paris, where Robespierre was a school-friend. His legal career in the 1780s was unremarkable, but in 1789 he proved a street-figure and pamphleteer of verve. From Nov 1789, he ran the *Révolutions de France et de Brabant*. A prominent Cordelier, linked with Danton and Fabre d'Eglantine, he joined the Jacobin Club in late 1791. After 10 August 1792, he served as Danton's secretary in the Ministry of Justice, and was elected by Paris to the Convtn, where he sat among the Montagnards, violently attacked the Girondins and voted the king's death. By Dec 1793, however, he began publishing the *Vieux Cordelier*, which called for a relaxation of the Terror. Taxed with 'indulgence', he was arrested in Mar 1794, tried with the Dantonists and executed.

Dillon (Arthur, comte), 1750–guill 13 Apr 1794. A professional soldier of Irish extraction, D. was governor of Tobago in 1789. Elected to the Constit Ass. by Martinique, he showed himself a reactionary over the slavery issue but otherwise a liberal. In 1791 he rejoined the army, fought at Valmy and in the N. In July 1793, however, he was arrested and subsequently executed.

Dillon (Théobald-Hyacinthe), 1745–battle 29 Apr 1792. A proprietary colonel in the army under the AR, Dillon served on the outbreak of war under Dumouriez in the N. He was killed by panicking troops under his command.

Dobsen (Claude-Emmanuel), 1743–1811. Son of an iron-merchant from Noyon, D. was a lawyer in the Marne when the Rev broke out. He served in local politics in 1790–1, but, linked with Robespierre, became increasingly prominent in Parisian politics. He played a part in organising the *journées* of Feb and March 1793, and esp those of 31 May and 2 June 1793. He was appointed to the Rev Tribunal, but was perhaps too moderate, and was replaced in May 1794. He survived Thermidor, and despite a number of political scrapes under the Directory, pursued a successful legal career under the Consulate and Empire.

Dolivier (P), 1746–1811. A radical priest under the AR and pamphleteer in 1788–9, D. was elected to the EG by the clergy of Etampes. He made his name in 1792 when, following the assassination of Simonneau, mayor of Etampes, in a grain riot, he attacked free trade in grain. His primitive communist ideas resembled those of the *enragés*, influenced Babeuf and prefigured socialism. He married in 1792, and became a schoolteacher under the Directory.

Doppet (Fs-Amédée or 'Pervenche'), 1753–99. Son of a candle-maker from Chambéry, D. had a varied career under the AR as physician, university teacher (at Turin), soldier, pamphleteer and novelist. He came to Paris in 1789 as the secretary of Aubert-Dubayet, joined the Jacobins and Cordeliers and founded the Club des Allobroges. When war broke out he formed the Légion des Allobroges, which was instrumental in the annexation of Savoy. He was soon a general, served at the siege of Lyon, then in the Pyrenees. Suspect after Thermidor, he remained in post until forced to resign by ill health in 1797.

Drouet (J-B), 1763–1824. The famous postmaster of Sainte-Menehould personally responsible for the capture of Louis XVI in the latter's flight to Varennes became a national hero overnight. He was *suppléant* to the Leg Ass., then elected to the Convtn. His opinions were radical and Maratist, but in Sept 1793 while *en mission* with the Army of the North he was captured by the enemy and imprisoned. He was released in an exchange of political prisoners in Dec 1795 and was allowed to sit in the C500. His Jacobin views were now somewhat *dépassé* and he made little impact. Though linked with Babeuf he was acquitted by the Vendôme high court. In 1799, he acted as commissary for the Directory in the Marne, and then helped organise the Club du Manège in Paris. Under Napoleon he became the sub-prefect of Sainte-Menehould.

Dubarran (Jos-Nic Barbeau), 1761–1816. A lawyer who had served as PGS to the Gers, D. represented the same department in the Convtn, where he sat with the Montagnards, and from Sept 1793 served on the CGS. Threatened with imprisonment after Thermidor for involvement in the Prairial rising, he retired to his home dept.

Dubois-Crancé (Edmond-L-Alexis), 1746–1814. Son of a military administrator, and king's Musketeer himself until 1775, D.-C. was elected to the EG by Vitry-le-François, and served on the Finance and Military Committees. He returned to military service in 1791, but was elected to the Convtn by the Ardennes. He was sent on various *missions* to the armies; sat on the CGD in early

1793; voted for the king's death; served alongside Couthon in putting down federalism in the Midi; and was influential in the implementation of major military reforms, including the *amalgame*. He was elected to the CPS in Dec 1794, though he made little impact. Member of the C500 till 1797, of the C Anciens till 1799, he served as War Minister from 14 Sept 1799 until Brumaire. He then retired from public life.

Dubuisson (P-Ulric), 1746–guill 23 May 1794. Dramatist and man of letters, D. was an enthusiastic Jacobin and sectional militant. In early 1793 he was appointed commissary to Dumouriez's army, and was subsequently under suspicion with Proli and Pereira for his shady part in Dumouriez's defection. Linked with Hérault de Séchelles, he was tried and executed as a Hébertist.

Ducos (J-Fs), 1765–guill 31 Oct 1793. Son of a wealthy Bordeaux businessman, D. was elected to the Leg Ass. and Convtn. Like other front-rank Girondins, he attacked the Montagnards over the king's trial, but eventually voted for the death sentence, not the *appel au peuple*. He survived the purge of Girondins in May–June 1793 largely through the good offices of Marat, but was arrested on 3 Oct 1793 and executed with other Girondins.

Ducos or **Roger Ducos** (P-Roger), 1747–1816. A lawyer from Dax, Roger D. represented the Landes in the Convtn. Though a Jacobin, he sat with the Plain and kept out of political in-fighting. He sat in the C Anciens from 1795 and presided during the Fructidor coup. He subsequently retired to his home town, but Barras brought him back as a Director following the Prairial coup in 1799. On 18 Brumaire he was to be appointed provisional consul. His political career continued under Napoleon.

Dufriche-Valazé, see VALAZÉ

'Dugommier' (sobriquet of Jq COQUILLE), 1738–battle 17 Nov 1794. Son of an *anobli*, D. was born in Guadeloupe, and became a professional soldier. He returned to France in 1791, was sent to S France and was prominent in the siege and capture of Toulon. A general, he was then transferred to the army of the E Pyrenees and though successful in driving the Spanish forces back was killed in action.

Duhem (P-Jos), 1758–1807. The son of a Lille weaver, D. was doctor attached to the city's hospital in 1789. Elected to the Leg Ass., then the Convtn, he sat on the left and was entrusted with a number of journeys *en mission* on the N front. A member of the CGS in Jan 1793, he fell out with Robespierre who had him expelled from the Jacobins in Dec 1793. After Thermidor, he was faithful to the left, defending Amar, Vadier, etc. Eventually he abandoned politics for a career as military physician.

'Dumas' ('Alexandre' – sobriquet of Thomas-Alexandre DAVY DE LA PAILLETERIE), 1762–1806. An illegitimate half-caste born in Saint-Domingue, Alexandre D.

entered the army in 1786. He served in numerous battle theatres, where his bravery led to speedy promotion. His advanced political views were not always popular, however, and he was briefly imprisoned 1799–1800 before being dismissed from the service definitively in 1802.

Dumas or **Mathieu-Dumas** (Gabriel-Mathieu), 1753–1837. Son of a Montpellier financier, Mathieu D. was a military engineer under the AR. Adc to Lafayette in the Paris Nat Guard, personally responsible for the detachment which brought the king back from Varennes, he was elected to the Leg Ass. A Feuillant, he was respected for his opinion on military matters. He went into hiding and then emigration in Aug 1792, only returning to public life after Thermidor. He was a Clichyen in the C Anciens but was expelled after Fructidor and left France. He returned after Brumaire, and enjoyed a military career through the Empire and Restoration.

Dumas (René-Fs), 1757–guill 28 July 1794. Son of an officer in the *maréchaussée*, René D. abandoned an ecclesiastical career for a legal practice at Lons-le-Saulnier, where he served as mayor in 1791. Robespierre invited him to Paris to become first vice-president (from 28 Sept 1793), then Hermann's successor as president (from 8 Apr 1794) of the Rev Tribunal. Ferociously devoted to the Robespierrist cause, he shared his master's fate and was executed on 10 Thermidor.

Dumolard (Jos-Vincent), 1766–1819. A lawyer in Grenoble in 1789, D. was elected to the Leg Ass., where he was the youngest of the deputies. Links with the Fayettistes made him flee in 1792 to the provinces, where he was arrested. Released after Thermidor, he was elected to the C500, where he was regarded as a Clichyen. This led to his imprisonment after Fructidor. Under Napoleon, he became a sub-prefect.

Dumont (André), 1764–1838. Son of a wealthy notary from Oisemont, near Abbeville, André D. led a frivolous career prior to the Rev, though he threw himself into local administration after 1789 and was elected to the Convtn. He sat with the Montagnards, and voted for the king's death. *En mission* with Chabot in the Somme from July 1793, he introduced radical and dechristianising policies before returning to Paris in Apr 1794. He was elected to the CGS directly after Thermidor and immediately denounced Lebon. A prominent Thermidorian, he was a member of the CPS after Dec 1794. Elected to the C500 in 1797 and attacked as a terrorist, his political career ended in the Prairial *journées*. He re-emerged under Napoleon, to serve as a sub-prefect.

Dumouriez (Ch-Fs du Périer), 1739–1823. Adventurous professional soldier before 1789, D. welcomed the Rev and after a successful spell in local politics in Cherbourg moved to Paris where he established links with Mirabeau and Lafayette and joined the Jacobins. In Mar 1792 he was appointed Foreign Minister, but resumed his military career when dismissed along with the Girondin ministry in June. Victor at Valmy and Jemappes, he was responsible for the French invasion of Belgium and Holland. Linked with the Girondins, he became increasingly disenchanted with rev politics. Following the forced evacuation of Belgium and his defeat at Neerwinden, he unsuccessfully attempted to lead his army on Paris, and emigrated in Apr 1793. Rejected by the *émigrés*, he travelled Europe widely and ended up in England after 1800.

Duplay (Maurice), 1736–1820. A carpenter from the Haute-Loire, Duplay had made his fortune in property in Paris. Pro-Jacobin from the early days, he admired Robespierre and from Oct 1791 the latter lodged with him. He served on the Rev Tribunal, and was arrested on 10 Thermidor but was subsequently freed.

Dupont de Nemours (P-Samuel), 1739–1817. Son of the king's watchmaker, D. de N. had made a reputation for himself under the AR as a physiocrat. Confidant of Calonne, secretary of the Ass. of Notables in 1787, he became an active Fayettiste in the Constit Ass. He lay low from 1792 and though arrested under the Terror was saved by Thermidor. Elected to the C Anciens in 1795, he was arrested after Fructidor. In 1799 he emigrated to the USA.

Duport (Adrien-J-Fs), 1759–98. Noble, freemason, mesmerist, councillor in the Paris parl and a founder-member of the Société des Trente, Adrien D. was prominent in the parl opposition during the Pre-Rev. Elected to the EG by the Paris nobility, he came to form (with Barnave and Lameth) the 'Triumvirate', which dominated the 'patriot' party in the Constit Ass. and the Jacobin Club. From mid 1791 he was aiming to end the Rev, and was crucial in winning the support of the Ass., after Varennes, for the fiction of the king's abduction. A prominent Feuillant, he was overtaken by events, and eventually emigrated. He was to die in Switzerland.

Duportail (Ant-J-L), 1743–1802. Career soldier under the AR, D. had fought in America alongside Lafayette, who was largely responsible for his elevation to the Ministry of War in Nov 1790. Attacked by royalists as well as by the popular movement, he resigned in Dec 1791 and rejoined the army. He fled arrest in late 1792, but stayed in Paris throughout the Terror in hiding. He revisited the USA, but died on the return journey.

Duport-Dutertre (Marguerite-L-Fs), 1754–guill 29 Nov 1793. A Parisian lawyer who entered municipal politics under the wing of Lafayette, D.-D. became Minister of Justice in Nov 1790. He was viewed as a Feuillant, however, and resigned in Mar 1792. Arrested in the wake of 10 Aug 1792, he was executed under the Terror.

Duquesnoy (Ernest-Fs-L), 1749–suic 16 June 1795. Soldier, then farmer in the Pas-de-Calais, D. was elected by his dept for the Leg Ass. and then the Convtn. He was entrusted with a number of important *missions* at the front in 1792–3. He was out of Paris at Thermidor, and remained on the left. Following his part in the Prairial *journées*, he was sentenced to death and, with Romme and Goujon, committed suicide on the way to the scaffold. A 'martyr of Prairial'.

Durand-Maillane (P-Toussaint), 1729–1814. Lawyer attached to the parl in Aix-en-Provence under the AR, D.-M. specialised in canon law, and in the Constit Ass. he was instrumental in the formulation of religious reforms including the Civ Constn. Elected to the Convtn by the Bouches-du-Rhône, he sat with the Plain and voted for the *appel au peuple* but otherwise lay low. He was elected to the C Anciens, but was excluded at Fructidor, temporarily imprisoned and then returned to private life.

Duroy (J-Michel), 1753–guill 17 June 1795. A lawyer from Bernay, D. was *suppléant* for the Eure to the Leg Ass. before being elected to the Convtn, where he sat among the Montagnards. He was prominent in the repression of federalism, serving *en mission* in Normandy in the summer of 1793. He remained a staunch Montagnard even after Thermidor, and was arrested and sentenced to death for his alleged role in instigating the Prairial uprising. After attempting to commit suicide with the other 'martyrs of Prairial', he was executed.

Dussaulx or **Dusaulx** (J), 1728–99. Soldier, then writer under the AR linked with philosophic circles, D. became involved in Parisian politics from 1789. He was *suppléant* for Paris in the Leg Ass. (and was called to sit in June 1792), then deputy in the Convtn. He was linked with the Girondins and voted for the *appel au peuple*. Imprisoned during the Terror, he returned to the Convtn after Thermidor, and was elected to the C Anciens, in which he served down to 1798.

Duval (Ch-Fs-Marie), 1750–1829. From a legal background in Brittany, D. served as radical deputy in the Leg Ass. and Convtn, where he became best known for his journalism, notably in his *Journal des hommes libres* which at one time received a subvention from the Ass. and remained true to democratic principles after Thermidor. A left-wing deputy in the C500, he retired from public life in 1798 and entered the bureaucracy.

Duval d'Eprémesnil, see EPRÉMESNIL

Duverne de Presle (Th-Laurent-Madeleine), 1763–1844. Career soldier in the marines, D. de P. initially welcomed the Rev, but was soon disillusioned and emigrated in 1791. He returned under an alias and seems to have acted as a royalist spy. After the unsuccessful Quiberon Bay venture, he helped promote constitutional royalism, with some success. He was moving towards more violent methods when, along with the abbé Brotier and other central figures in the royalist network, he was informed on and arrested in Jan 1797. He was deported to Guiana, returning to France under Napoleon.

Edgeworth (Henry Essex, abbé), 1743–1807. An Irish Catholic educated in Toulouse and Paris, E. was attached to the Missions étrangères at the beginning of the Rev, when Madame Elisabeth, the king's sister, took him as her confessor.

He acted as intermediary for the crown with the *émigrés*, and accompanied Louis XVI to the scaffold. He subsequently went into hiding, emigrated to England and spent the late 1790s performing various secret royalist missions.

Egalité, see ORLÉANS

Elbée (Maurice-Jos-L Gigost d'), 1762–exctd 3 Jan 1794. D'E. served in the French and Polish armies before returning to his estates in Anjou in 1783. He protested against the Civ Constn in 1791, emigrated, then returned to take part in the La Rouerie plot. In 1793 he joined the Vendéans, and was elected their commander in July 1793 following the death of **Cathelineau**. He was not suited to the task, however, suffered defeats and was arrested and shot.

Elisabeth (Philippine-Marie-Hélène, Madame), 1764–guill 10 May 1794. Sister of Louis XVI, Madame E. did not get on well with Marie-Antoinette and kept up close contact with the *émigrés*. The discovery of compromising correspondence with Artois led to her arrest and execution.

Emery (Jq-André), 1732–1811. A native of Gex, E. was superior-general of the Sulpicians in 1789. He opposed the Civ Constn, but tried to keep up a dialogue between priests of all persuasions. His conciliatory and irenic stand, which won him opposition from royalists, constitutional clergy and rpbcns (he was imprisoned from July 1793 to Oct 1794), paved the way for the Concordat.

Eprémesnil (J-Jq Duval d'), 1745–guill 23 Apr 1794. Vigorous defender of the rights of the parls in the closing decades of the AR, scourge of Turgot and Necker before becoming, during the Pre-Rev, the stern critic of Calonne and Brienne, d'E. was among the first councillors of the Paris parl to call for the meeting of the EG. He was imprisoned by *lettre de cachet* at the time of the May Edicts in 1788, but was released to popular acclaim in Sept. He urged that the EG meet in its 1614 form, however, and was soon overtaken by events. In the Constit Ass., to which he had been elected by the nobility of Paris *hors-les-murs*, he was viewed as a reactionary and as 'the most ardent defender of parlementary stupidity' (ROBESPIERRE). He was arrested under the Terror.

Espagnac (Marc-René-Marie d'Amarzit de Sahuguet, abbé d'), 1752–guill 5 Apr 1794. This worldly and wealthy priest enjoyed friendly contacts in financial circles and with Calonne and Orléans before 1789. He played a small part in the crisis of July 1789 as a Parisian elector; supported the Civ Constn; and made a fortune out of army contracting in 1792–3. His links with Dumouriez were his downfall, and he was eventually tried and executed with the Dantonists.

Evrard (Simone), 1764–1824. Daughter of a ship's carpenter, Simone E. from 1790 was Marat's mistress and then common-law wife. She defended his reputation after his assassination.

Expilly (L-Alexandre), 1742–guill 22 May 1794. This obscure Richerist priest from Brittany played an important part in the drafting of the Civ Constn. In Nov

1790 he became constitutional bishop of Finistère. Pro-Girondin, he was caught up in the Federalist revolt in 1793, however, and was executed at Brest.

Fabre (Claude-Dominique-Cosme), 1762–battle 20 Dec 1793. Like his father a councillor in the Chambre des Comptes of Montpellier, Claude F. was elected to the Convtn by the Hérault, and sat on the left. He was killed on the field of battle at Port Vendres when *en mission* with the Army of the E Pyrenees.

Fabre d'Eglantine (Ph-Fs-Nazaire), 1750–guill 5 Apr 1794. Son of a cloth merchant, F. was a lay teacher for the Doctrinaires before, in 1772, embarking on a theatrical career. He was based in Paris from 1787, and from 1790 was prominent in the Cordeliers and was linked with Danton and with Marat, whose penchant for radical journalism he shared. Elected by Paris to the Convtn he sat with the Montagnards; was elected to the CGD; and in Oct was responsible for the introduction of the Rev Calendar. His sordid financial dealing in military contracting and then in the Compagnie des Indes scandal was brought to the attention of Robespierre, who forced him out of the Jacobin Club in Dec 1793. He was arrested in Jan 1794 and executed with the Dantonists.

Faipoult or **Faypoult** (Guillaume-Ch), 1752–1817. From minor gentry stock from Champagne, F. had served in the engineering corps under the AR, and in 1789 joined the Paris Nat Guard and the Jacobin Club. Secretary to the Minister of the Interior in 1792–3, he lay low during the Terror, but re-emerged after Thermidor to serve as Finance Minister from Oct 1795, then as Plenipotentiary Minister attached to Genoa from Feb 1796. Effective here and in other Italian states to which he was attached in a similar capacity, he became a prefect under Napoleon.

Fauchet (Fs-Claude), 1744–guill 31 Oct 1793. In 1789, Claude F. was vicar-general at Bourges and enjoyed a reputation as a liberal preacher. He was elected to the Paris Commune in July 1789 and he welcomed the Civ Constn. He founded the Cercle social in 1790, and along with Bonneville edited the journal, the *Bouche de fer*. A Jacobin, in 1791 he was elected bishop of the Calvados, and was also elected to the Leg Ass., and later the Convtn. He was becoming more moderate in his views, however; was expelled from the Jacobins in Sept 1792; voted the *appel au peuple*; and from June 1793 was under virtual house arrest. He was imprisoned in July 1793 for allegedly inspiring Charlotte Corday and executed.

Favras (Thomas de Mahy, marquis de), 1744–executd 19 Feb 1790. F. had a rather turbulent military career under the AR, and in Feb 1790 was arrested and subsequently executed for allegedly conspiring to abduct the king and allow Provence, Favras's master, to become regent.

Faypoult, see FAIPOULT

Fersen (Axel, comte de), 1750–1810. A Swedish aristocrat who served as colonel of the Royal Swedish Regiment in the French army, F. was possibly the lover, certainly the confidant of Marie-Antoinette. He arranged the flight to Varennes, emigrating at the same time.

Fézensac, see MONTESQUIOU-FÉZENSAC

Flesselles (Jq de), 1721–assass 14 July 1789. The last (from Apr 1789) *prévôt des marchands* of Paris, F. tried to temporise with the rev crowds in mid July 1789. He paid for it with his life.

Fleuriot-Lescot (J-B-Edmond), 1750–guill 28 July 1794. F.-L. had spent his youth in Belgium but came to Paris to make a career as an architect. He became a Jacobin, a sectional militant and a member of the Commune insurrectionnelle in Aug 1792. Substitute of Fouquier-Tinville in the Rev Tribunal, in May 1794 the CPS made him mayor of Paris in place of Pache. He fought for Robespierre on 9 Thermidor, and was executed in consequence. The last mayor of rev Paris.

Folleville (abbé Guyot de, known as the 'bishop of AGRA'), 1760–guill 5 Feb 1794. A minor cleric in Brittany under the AR, F. passed himself off to the Vendéan rebels in 1793 as a bishop *in partibis infidelium* who had been secretly consecrated by the Pope. He was used by the Vendéan generals for prestige purposes, but was caught up in the defeat of the royalist movement in early 1794.

Fouché (Jos), 1763–1820. Son of a sea-captain from Nantes, F. served as a lay schoolteacher for the Oratorians under the AR, and was chosen as principal of the College of Nantes on the dissolution of the order in 1790. He was elected to the Convtn by the Loire-Inf, and was sent on a series of important *missions:* Nantes and the W, then the Aube in early 1793; the Nièvre in Aug and Sept (when he distinguished himself in leading a radical and dechristianising policy); and Lyon, with Collot-d'Herbois in Nov, where he organised the *mitraillades*. Recalled to Paris in Apr 1794, he felt threatened by Robespierre and plotted Thermidor. He found it difficult to stay in politics under the Thermidorian regime, but became a protégé of Barras who sent him as ambassador to the Cisalpine Rpbc in Sept 1798. He returned to Paris in 1799 and was made Police Minister, striking out to left and right. He welcomed Brumaire and continued his notorious public life under Napoleon.

Foulon (Jos-Fs), 1715–assass 22 July 1789. A distinguished administrator under the AR, F. was given a key role in organising military resistance to Paris in July 1789. Highly unpopular on account of his alleged remark that if the poor were hungry they should eat straw, he was assassinated by the crowds in Paris who mutilated his body prior to killing his father-in-law, Bertier de Sauvigny.

Fouquier-Tinville (Ant-Quentin), 1747–guill 7 May 1795. Son of a wealthy landowner from Picardy, F.-T. was making his way as a lawyer in Paris when the Rev broke out. An enthusiastic participant in the early rev *journées*, he was appointed to the Rev Tribunal from its creation in Mar 1793 and was made public prosecutor, a post in which he gained considerable notoriety. After Thermidor, he tried to claim he had only been following Robespierre's orders.

Fourcroy (Ant-Fs), 1755–1809. Son of a pharmacist, this distinguished scientist had qualified as a doctor in 1780 and developed interests in chemistry and politics. *Suppléant* to the Convtn, he was called to sit in the Ass. in July 1793 *vice* Marat. He was involved esp in the collection of saltpetre for the war effort; reform of medical education; and protection of various savants. Elected to the CPS after Thermidor, he was instrumental in the creation of the Ecole polytechnique, the medical schools, etc. A member of the C Anciens until 1798, he pursued his academic career under Napoleon.

Fournier 'l'Américain' (Claude), 1745–1823. Son of an Auvergnat weaver, F. emigrated to Saint-Domingue as a young man, made a fortune, lost it, then returned to France in 1785. Violent participant in many of the Parisian *journées* and a prominent Cordelier, he was discredited in Sept 1792 for allegedly having allowed prisoners in his custody to be massacred by a Versailles mob. Imprisoned in Apr 1794 for excessive violence, he was to continue his picaresque adventures in both the New World and the Old before dying a pauper.

François or **François de Neufchâteau** or **Neufchâteau** (Nic-L), 1750–1828. Son of a schoolteacher from Lorraine, F. had been something of a literary child prodigy. The administrative gifts to which he owed his career were refined in the W Indies in the 1780s and in the dept administration of the Vosges. He was elected to the Leg Ass., where he sat on the Legislation Committee, but refused a seat in the Convtn, fell out with the CPS over one of his plays and was imprisoned. An administrator in his native dept after Thermidor, he was called up to be Minister of the Interior in July 1797, a post he held with a brief interlude as Director down to June 1799. Highly enterprising and energetic, he encouraged economic growth and educational and technological innovation. He continued his administrative and technical career under Napoleon.

Fréron (L-Stanislas), 1765–1802. Son of the famous literary critic of the Enlightenment, F. inherited from his father the editorship of the *Année littéraire* in 1776, but lost control of it in 1781. From early 1790, he produced the Maratist *Orateur du peuple*, became a Cordelier and was a member of the Commune in 1792. Elected to the Convtn, where he voted for the death of the king, he only came to prominence after the fall of the Girondins. *En mission* with Barras in the SE from Sept 1793, his extravagantly violent repression of Toulon attracted much criticism and he was recalled by the CPS in Jan 1794. Threatened by Robespierre, he plotted Thermidor, and thereupon lurched violently into reactionary politics in his newspaper, in the Convtn, and, along with his so-called *jeunesse dorée*, in the streets. Instrumental in the closure of the Jacobin Club and the repression of the Prairial rising, he served as Directorial agent in the Midi during the White Terror. His past ruled him out from an active political career, however, and he entered the bureaucracy, eventually dying as sub-prefect of Saint-Domingue.

Frey (Junius: adopted name of Siegmund-Gottlob DOBROUJKA-SCHOENFELD), 1759–guill 5 Apr 1794. A Moravian Jew, and the wealthy son of a leading Austrian financier, Junius F. and his brother Emmanuel (1767–94) had made their fortune in military contracting for the Habsburgs before coming to Strasbourg in 1792 and becoming naturalised. They were soon in Paris, enriching themselves with speculating on nat lands and also infiltrating various political circles. In Oct 1793 they were denounced to the CPS as spies, and although they survived the accusation, further denunciations in Dec and the prevailing fear of a 'foreign plot' led to their arrest and execution.

Froment (Fs-Marie), 1756–1825. A local administrator in S France at the outbreak of the Rev, F. became a counter-rev agent, attempting in 1790 to raise revolt in Languedoc, an act for which the comte de Provence ennobled him. In the late 1790s he acted as royalist agent on a variety of secret missions throughout Europe.

Frotté (Marie-P-L de), 1766–1800. Army officer who emigrated to fight with Condé's forces in 1791, F. visited Englánd, where he was primed by Puisaye to prepare insurrection in Normandy from 1795. After a slow start, he and the Chouans under him made some headway before temporarily ending hostilities in 1796. He returned from Britain in the summer of 1799 to relaunch another counter-rev insurrection, but was unsuccessful again and was eventually shot by a military commission.

Garat (Dominique-Jos), 1749–1833. A lawyer from the Basse-Navarre who made his name under the AR as a contributor to the *Mercure de France* and as a minor literary celebrity, Garat was a member of the EG. He succeeded Danton as Minister of Justice in Oct 1792; condoned the Sept Massacres; and was Minister of the Interior from Mar to Aug 1793. A 'political eunuch' (Mme ROLAND), he was regarded as too insignificant to attack under the Terror. He re-emerged from private life to serve as ambassador to Naples in 1797–8 before being elected to the C Anciens. He welcomed Brumaire and was to have a distinguished administrative career under Napoleon.

Garran de Coulon (J-Ph), 1748–1816. A young attorney in Paris at the outbreak of the Rev, G. was an elector in 1789 and was elected to the Leg Ass. and the Convtn, where he spoke mainly on legal matters. Pro-Directory in the C500, he rallied to Brumaire and became an ardent Bonapartist.

Gasparin (Th-Augustin), 1750–11 Nov 1793. From a Protestant family in the Comtat Venaissin, G. was an army captain in 1789. He was instrumental in arranging the annexation of Avignon and was elected by the Bouches-du-Rhône to the Leg Ass. and the Convtn, where he sat among the Montagnards. Elected to the CPS in June 1793, he resigned in July to make way for Robespierre. *En mission* in S France, he played a role in the siege of Toulon, but died shortly afterwards.

Genlis (Stéphanie-Félicité Ducrest de Saint-Aubin, comtesse de), 1746–1830. Woman of letters who in the 1780s became the governess to the children of the duc de Chartres (from 1785 the duc d'Orléans), then the latter's mistress, Madame de G. had initially supported the Rev, but she was forced against her will into emigration with Orléans's widow in 1793. After travels throughout Europe in the 1790s, she returned to France and became a literary celebrity under Napoleon.

Gensonné (Armand), 1758–guill 31 Oct 1793. Son of a military surgeon, G. was a lawyer in Bordeaux in 1789. He was elected to the Leg Ass. and the Convtn, and became a leading member of the Girondin group. Though he denounced the *émigrés*, the ministers and the *Comité autrichien* in early 1792, in July and Aug he tried unsuccessfully to negotiate with the court. A violent critic of the Sept Massacres, the Paris Commune and the Montagnards, he was compromised by his friendship with Dumouriez. He was put under surveillance after the *journée* of 31 May 1793 and eventually executed with the other Girondins.

Gérard (Michel), 1737–1815. A peasant from the faubourgs of Rennes, 'Père' G. was elected to the EG and caused a minor sensation with his rustic dress and manners. He took little active part in the deliberations of the Constit Ass. and retired to private life in 1791.

Gerle (Christophe-Ant, dom), 1737–1801. A Carthusian monk elected by the clergy of Riom to the EG, G. rallied to the Third Estate on 20 June 1789 and sat on the left. The defeat of his motion on 12 Apr 1790 that catholicism should be declared the state religion pushed him to the right. His links first with the visionary Suzanne Labrousse, then with the prophetess Catherine Théot made him suspect, and he was imprisoned in 1794. Released after Thermidor, he became a minor administrative official in the Ministry of the Interior.

Gibert-Desmolières (J-L), 1747–dep 1799. A well-off bureaucrat in the final years of the AR and the beginning of the Rev, G.-D. was elected to the C500 in 1795. A leader of the Clichyen group, he was arrested and deported after Fructidor and died in Guiana.

Gobel (J-B-Jos), 1727–guill 13 Apr 1794. Suffragan since 1772 of the bishop of Basle with responsibility for the French part of the diocese, G. was an important figure in Alsatian affairs under the AR. Elected to the EG, he accepted the Civ Constn and was elected to the archbishopric of Paris in 1791. A member of the Jacobins, he was instrumental in persuading the government to occupy the principality of Basle in 1792. Linked with Hébert and Chaumette, he became involved with the dechristianising movement in the capital and in Nov 1793 publicly abjured his priesthood. He was arrested with Chaumette and executed as a Hébertist.

Gohier (L-Jérôme), 1746–1830. A Breton lawyer who became involved in the Pre-Rev defending the prerogatives of the Estates of Brittany, G. represented the Ille-et-Vilaine in the Leg Ass. In Oct 1792 he became secretary of the Minister of Justice, and served as Minister himself from 20 Mar 1793 to 1 Apr 1794. He then pursued his legal career, returning briefly as a Director in 1799 but retiring again into private life after Brumaire.

Gorsas (Ant-Jos), 1752–guill 7 Oct 1793. The schoolmaster son of a cobbler, G. had a taste for literature and was even put in the Bastille in 1788 for his satires. Active in the *journée* of 5 Oct 1789, he threw himself into journalism, editing the *Courrier des 83 départements*. He was elected to the Convtn, and though at first he condoned the Sept Massacres, he moved towards the Girondins, attacking the Commune and the Montagnards and voting the *appel au peuple*. On 9–10 Mar 1793, Parisian mobs threatened to destroy his printing-presses. On 2 June, he fled arrest and organised resistance in Normandy until the 'battle' of Pacy-sur-Eure. He then went into hiding, but was arrrested visiting his mistress in Paris and executed.

Gouges (Marie-Olympe de), 1755–guill 4 Nov 1793. A woman of letters remarked for her beauty and her interest in literature, Olympe de G. threw herself into campaigns for female emancipation and political rights from 1789. Her plea before the Ass. for a 'Declaration of the Rights of Women' (1791) was more than a little hopeful. Her sympathy for the condemned Louis XVI aroused suspicions, and in July 1793 she was arrested and passed before the Rev Tribunal.

Goujon (J-Marie-Claude-Alexandre), 1766–suic 17 June 1795. The son of an administrator in the postal service, G. had served as a sailor before becoming politically active in, then PGS of, the Seine-et-Oise. Elected as *suppléant* to the Convtn, he replaced Hérault de Séchelles in Apr 1794. An energetic Montagnard, he stayed true to his opinions after Thermidor. Implicated in the Prairial *journées*, and sentenced to death, he committed suicide on the way to the scaffold, thus becoming one of the 'martyrs of Prairial'.

Goupilleau 'de Fontenay' (J-F), 1753–1823. A notary at Montaigu, G. was elected to the EG, and later to the Convtn by the Vendée. For most of 1793 and 1794 he was away from Paris *en mission*, notably with the armies and in his home dept. Elected to the CGS after Thermidor, he supported Barras in putting down the Vendémiaire *journée*. He sat in the C Anciens until 1797, then became a bureaucrat.

Goupilleau 'de Montaigu' (Ph-Ch-Aimé), *c* 1760–1823. Cousin of Goupilleau de Fontenay, G. was a lawyer in Montaigu in 1789 and was elected to the Leg Ass. and the Convtn by the Vendée and served on the CGS from Oct 1792 until Jan 1793. *En mission* in the Vendée and then in S France, he rallied to the Thermidorians and served on the CGS again. He served on the C500 until 1797, then again in 1798–9. A staunch rpbcn, he was excluded from the legislature on 19 Brumaire.

Gouvion-Saint-Cyr (Laurent), 1764–1830. Son of a tanner from Toul, G.-S.-C. was an artist in Paris in 1789. He joined the Nat Guard and then in 1792 volunteered. He served with distinction on the Rhine from 1792 to 1797, becoming a general in Sept 1794. In 1798 he was appointed commander of the Army of Rome and helped organise the new Roman Rpbc. His career continued under Napoleon and the Restoration.

Grangeneuve (J-Ant Lafargue de), 1751–guill 21 Dec 1793. An attorney prominent in municipal politics in Bordeaux from 1789, G. was elected to the Leg Ass. and was prominent among the Girondins. Radical in the Leg Ass., he became more moderate in the Convtn. He fled arrest on 2 June 1793. He was ultimately discovered in the Guyenne and executed.

Grave (P-Marie, marquis de), 1755–1823. Career soldier under the AR, de G. was a fervent Orleanist and replaced Narbonne as War Minister in Mar 1792. He resigned in May, however, and emigrated, returning to France in 1804.

Grégoire (Henri-B, abbé), 1750–1831. Son of a tailor, abbé G. was *curé* in a Lorraine village in 1789 when he was elected to the EG. He was among the first members of the clerical order to join the Third Estate in June 1789; helped found the Breton Club; was prominent on the night of 4 Aug; and championed negro emancipation. He supported the Civ Constn, and was elected bishop of the Loir-et-Cher. Elected to the Convtn, he welcomed the Rpbc in Aug 1792, but on humanitarian grounds opposed the king's execution. He was also involved in the abolition of the slave-trade and in educational reform. Nat leader of the Constitutional Church, he managed to survive the Terror, and then served in the C500 until 1798. He worked hard in the late 1790s to reorganise the constitutional clergy, and was to refuse Napoleon's Concordat with the Pope in 1801.

Guadet (Marguerite-Elie), 1758–guill 15 June 1794. A lawyer from Bordeaux, G. was elected to the Leg Ass, where he became a Girondin leader, attacking the refractory priests and the *émigrés* and calling for war. In the Convtn, his shrill attacks worsened relations between Girondins and Montagnards. On 24 Apr 1793 he urged the Convtn to move from Paris to Versailles. He escaped arrest on 2 June by fleeing first to Normandy then to the Bordelais, where he was captured and executed.

Guffroy or **Guffroi** (Armand-Benoît-Jos), 1740–1801. A lawyer from Arras who served on the prov ass. of Artois in 1787, Guffroy was elected to the Convtn and assumed a modish ultra-rpbcn stance there and in his journal *Rougiff* (an anagram of his name). He served on the CGS from Sept 1793 to Mar 1794, by which time his views were arousing suspicion and he was expelled from the Jacobins. He turned reactionary after Thermidor and assailed Lebon and Duhem before the

Convtn. After failing to make a new career as a theophilanthropist, he passed into the bureaucracy of the Ministry of Justice.

Guillotin (Jos-Ignace), 1738–1814. A distinguished physician under the AR, G. was elected by Paris to the EG where he spoke in favour of the reform of medicine and of the penal system. In Mar 1792, he got the Leg Ass. to agree that all executions in future should be performed by a 'humane' contraption at that time called a 'Louison' or 'Louisette', but soon to be called a 'guillotine', the first use of which occurred on 25 Apr 1792. Imprisoned under the Terror, he returned to medical practice after Thermidor.

Guyton de Morveau (L-Bernard), 1737–1816. From a distinguished Burgundian legal family, G. de M. was *avocat-général* to the Dijon parl in 1789, but was as well known for his interest in science and esp in chemistry. After serving as PGS of the Côte-d'Or, he sat in the Leg Ass. and then the Convtn, where he was elected to the CGD and the CPS down to July 1793. After Thermidor, he served again on the CPS, was elected to the C500, but from 1797 left politics for academic life and scientific work, notably in the Ecole polytechnique.

Guzman (Andres Maria de), 1753–guill 5 Apr 1794. A naturalised Spaniard, G. was violently pro-rev from the early days. After serving as a volunteer in the army he returned to Paris and became linked with Hébert and Desfieux. A prominent member of the Commune, he played a key role in the organisation of the *journée* of 31 May 1793. In 1794 he was arrested and executed along with the Dantonists.

Hanriot or **Henriot** (Fs), 1761–guill 28 July 1794. Son of poor peasants from Nanterre, H. was a clerk with the *Ferme générale* in 1789, and soon became active in Parisian sectional politics. He rose within the ranks of the Paris Nat Guard; participated in the *journée* of 10 Aug 1792; was prominent in the Sept Massacres; and headed the armed forces of the sections during the *journée* of 31 May 1793. Commander of the Paris Nat Guard from 1793 with the rank of general, he was protected by Robespierre despite his Hébertist links. He remained loyal to Robespierre on 9 Thermidor, a fact for which he was executed the next day.

Hassenfratz (J-Henri), 1755–1827. An autodidact of humble origins, H. was director of Lavoisier's laboratory in the 1780s. Although a moderate in Parisian sectional politics, he was prominent in the *journées* of 10 Aug 1792 and 31 May 1793. Under the Terror, he worked in the military bureaucracy. Imprisoned for his part in the *journées* of Germinal and Prairial, he was amnestied, and became a professor in the Ecole des Mines and the Ecole polytechnique.

Haussmann (Nic), 1760–1846. Originally from the Colmar region, H. was a cloth merchant in Versailles in 1789. Involved at first in local politics in the Seine-et-Oise, he was elected to the Leg Ass. and the Convtn. He served *en mission* in 1793 and 1794 with a number of the armies, and after 1795 passed into the military bureaucracy.

Haüy (René-Just), 1743–1822. This son of a weaver had entered the church, but owed his fame to his writings as a mineralogist and crystallographer. He was a refractory priest, but avoided arrest by helping the bureaucracy in a technical capacity. In 1795 he was appointed to the Institut, and continued his scientific career.

Haxo (Nic), 1750–battle 20 Apr 1794. H. had served as a grenadier, but by 1789 was a magistrate in Saint-Dié. In 1791 he volunteered, and served with distinction on the Rhine and then in W France, where by Aug 1793 he was a general of brigade. He led the attack on the Vendéan rebels in Noirmoutier in Jan 1794, inflicting defeats on Charette's forces, but died on the battlefield.

Hébert (Jq-René), 1757–guill 24 March 1794. The son of a goldsmith from Alençon, H. had passed a rather obscure and disreputable existence in Paris prior to the Rev, but soon made his niche after 1789 in publishing the famous radical journal, the *Père Duchesne*. A Cordelier and a member of the Commune insur-rectionnelle in Aug 1792, Hébert was substitute to the Commune's *procureur* from Dec 1792. Arrested by the Commission des Douze on 24 May 1793, his release won popular acclaim and served as prelude to the *journée* of 31 May. He and his clique helped coordinate the *journée* of 5 Sept 1793; attacked the Dantonists; and became involved in the dechristianisation movement in the capital. Attacked by Robespierre and Saint-Just as an extremist, however, he was arrested and tried on trumped-up charges.

Hédouville (Gabriel-Marie-Théodore-Jos, comte de), 1755–1825. From an ancient noble family from the region of Laon, H. was a low-ranking officer in 1789. The Rev opened up a brilliant career for him: he campaigned with Hoche on the Rhine in 1793; in the W against the Chouans in 1796–7; in W France again in 1799–1800; and continued his career under Napoleon.

Henriot, see HANRIOT

Henry-Larivière, see LA RIVIÈRE

Hérault de Séchelles (Marie-J), 1760–guill 5 Apr 1794. An aristocrat who since 1785 had been a brilliant and youthful deputy prosecutor in the Paris parl, and who was connected with philosophic salons, H. de S. welcomed the Rev. Elected by Paris to the Leg Ass. he started as a Feuillant but evolved towards the left. In the Convtn, where he represented the Seine-et-Oise, he organised the new administration in the dept of Mont-Blanc; presided over the Constitution Committee which drew up the 1793 Constitution; joined the CPS; and made several journeys *en mission*. His moderation was increasingly marked, however, and following the disclosure of links with the alleged 'foreign plot', he was arrested. He was executed with the Dantonists.

Hermann (Armand-Martial-Jos), 1759–guill 6 May 1795. H. passed from a distinguished position in the judicature of Artois in the AR to high judicial office in the Pas-de-Calais. A compatriot of Robespierre, the latter brought him to Paris, where he became president of the Rev Tribunal. He presided over many of the most notorious trials, but by early 1794 was seen as too moderate and was replaced by Dumas. Violently attacked after Thermidor, he was eventually executed.

Hervilly (L-Ch, comte d'), 1755–emgtn 14 Nov 1795. A career soldier violently opposed to the Rev, d'H. was prominent in the king's defence during the *journées* of 20 June and 10 Aug 1792. He then emigrated, and commanded the *émigré* force involved in the Quiberon Bay disaster, where his lack of rapport with the Chouan leader Puisaye contributed to the defeat. Wounded in action, he returned to Britain to die.

Hoche (L-Lazare), 1768–97. This distinguished general started life as a stable-boy, joined the *Gardes-françaises* and had achieved the rank of corporal by 1789. He sprang to prominence combatting the Duke of York at Dunkirk then with the Army of the Moselle driving the Austrians out of Alsace in 1793–4. A general from Oct 1793, he was briefly imprisoned as a political threat and on release was sent to put down insurrection in W France. He was markedly successful in this, and he also defeated the Quiberon Bay expedition in July 1795, though his plans for an invasion of Ireland in 1796 came to nothing. Appointed to the Army of the Sambre-and-Meuse in Feb 1797, the threat of armed occupation of Paris which he and his army posed in the summer of 1797 helped the Fructidor coup succeed. He died at the height of his powers.

Houchard (J-Nic), 1740–guill 15 Nov 1793. Career soldier who had achieved the rank of captain in 1789, H. served on the N front when war broke out. He commanded the Army of the Moselle from Apr 1793 and the Army of the North from Aug 1793, winning a brilliant victory at Hondschoote. When subsequently his army was forced onto the defensive, however, he was arrested and brought before the Rev Tribunal.

Huguenin (Sulpice), 1750–1803. H. had had a chequered career under the AR, including a spell in legal practice. He sprang to prominence in Paris by his involvement in a number of the early *journées*. President of the Commune on 10 Aug 1792, he was also heavily involved in the Sept Massacres. The Council of Ministers sent him on a number of missions to Lyon, Chambéry and Brussels, but he behaved badly, enriching himself, and in Sept 1793 was arrested. Released after Thermidor, he spent the rest of his life in obscurity.

Hugues (Victor) or 'Victor-Hugues', 1762–1826. From a merchant family, Victor H. had gone to Saint-Domingue at an early age, and only returned to France in 1793. Radical, and well regarded in the Convtn, he was sent back to the W Indies in an official capacity, and coordinated the war against the British in the Caribbean. He withdrew in 1798, but in 1799 was appointed governor of Guiana. He subsequently retired to become a simple planter, and was eventually to die a landowner in the Gironde.

Imbert-Colomès (Jq-P), 1725–1809. From a wealthy merchant family from Lyon, I.-C. was mayor of Lyon 1788–90, and became highly unpopular for repressing a riot in the city in Feb 1790. He emigrated, and became an active agent of the Bourbons. He returned to Lyon in 1797 and was elected to the C500, where he became a prominent Clichyen. On Fructidor, he fled to Geneva, then London.

Isnard (Maximin), 1751–1825. Son of a wealthy landowner from Grasse, I. was a perfume manufacturer in Draguignan in 1789. Elected to the Leg Ass. and then the Convtn, he came to be viewed as a Girondin, though he was more radical and more rpbcn than most of his colleagues. In Mar 1793 he was elected to the CGD. As president of the Convtn from 16 May 1793, he uttered threats against the Paris Commune which made him a prime Girondin suspect after 2 June. He fled arrest and remained in hiding until Dec 1794. He re-entered the Convtn, then was elected to the C500, on which he sat until 1797, subsequently retiring from nat politics.

Javogues (Claude), 1759–exctd Oct 1796. A lawyer in Montbrison in 1789, J. made his name in local politics before being elected to the Convtn. His radical spell *en mission* in the Rhône-et-Loire, the Ain and the Haute-Loire won him the suspicion of the CPS and he was recalled in Spring 1794. He was a prominent critic of Robespierre, but was imprisoned as a terrorist after Thermidor, then amnestied in 1795. His involvement in the babouvist Grenelle Camp incident led to his execution by military commission.

Jean Bon Saint-André, see SAINT-ANDRÉ

Joséphine (Empress), see TASCHER DE LA PAGERIE

Joubert (Barthélemy-Catherine), 1769–battle 15 Aug 1799. A Burgundian law student with military ambitions, J. volunteered in 1791, served with distinction and won speedy promotion. In spite of a brief period as a prisoner, by 1796 he was a general, and he fought impressively in successive Italian campaigns. Resigning his command to come to Paris to pursue conspiratorial political contacts, he subsequently returned to Italy and was killed at the battle of Novi.

Jourdan (J-B), 1762–1833. Son of a surgeon from Limoges, J. had served in the army from 1778 until 1784 and then become a successful cloth merchant. He joined the Nat Guard, then rejoined the army, becoming general in July 1793 and leading the French forces at Wattignies and Fleurus. He fell out with the CPS and was dismissed, but returned after Thermidor to fight in the campaigns of 1795 and 1796. In Apr 1797 he was elected to the C500 where, in 1798, he was responsible for introducing the 'Jourdan Law' instituting conscription. He returned briefly to the army, only to be defeated at Stockach in Mar 1799. He tried to check Bonaparte's rise, was dismissed from the C500 after Brumaire, but resumed his military career under Napoleon.

Julien 'de Toulouse' (J), 1760–1828. A Protestant pastor in Sette, then Toulouse under the AR, J. became involved in local politics before being elected to the Convtn. A Montagnard and briefly member of the CGS, he was linked with Chabot and only avoided arrest over the Compagnie des Indes scandal by fleeing. He returned to the Convtn after Thermidor. A theophilanthropist in Paris under the Directory, he later became a lawyer in Turin.

Jullien 'de la Drôme' (Marc-Ant), 1744–1821. Originally from the Dauphiné, J. was working in Paris in 1789 as a private tutor. He was *suppléant* for the Drôme in the Leg Ass., and was elected to the Convtn by the same dept. Prominently anti-royalist during the king's trial, he lay low for most of the remainder of the Terror, and then turned to literature.

Jullien 'de Paris' (Marc-Ant), 1775–1848. Patriotic *wunderkind*, son of J. de la Drôme, J. was taken under Robespierre's wing in 1793 and sent as roving emissary for the CPS to Bordeaux and to Nantes (where he reported against Carrier). On Robespierre's fall he was imprisoned. Amnestied in 1795, he was implicated in the Babeuf plot, and fled France to embark on a career in military administration in Italy under the protection of Bonaparte.

Kellermann (Fs-Christophe), 1735–1820. Long-serving career officer, originally from Strasbourg, K. was enthusiastically patriotic in 1789 and was rewarded with command over Alsace in 1791. A general by 1792, he commanded at Valmy; drove the Piedmontese back through Savoy; took Lyon in 1793, but was then imprisoned. He re-emerged from late 1794 to help Bonaparte in Italy and to pursue his military career, albeit in a minor way, under the Empire.

Kéralio, see ROBERT (Madame Robert)

Kersaint (Armand-Guy-Simon Coetnempren, comte de), 1742–guill 4 Dec 1793. Patriotic naval officer from an ancient Breton family, K. acted as consultant to the Constit Ass. on naval matters, and was an administrator in the dept of Paris and *suppléant* to the Leg Ass., which he joined in Apr 1792 and sat with the Girondins. He proposed the establishment of the CGD in Jan 1793. Stridently critical of the king before 10 Aug, he changed his views completely, voted for imprisonment rather than death and resigned over the Convtn's decision in Jan 1793. He took to hiding after the purge of the Girondins, but was captured and sent before the Rev Tribunal.

Kilmaine (Ch-Edouard-Saul Jennings de), 1751–99. A cavalry captain, born in Ireland but brought up in France, K. served in the N from 1792 and in May

1793 was made general. His career was broken by a spell of imprisonment during the Terror. He defended the Convtn during the Prairial rising and was dispatched to Italy. In 1797 he commanded the occupation army in Italy and in Mar 1798 was appointed to the Army of England. He was terminally ill, however, and he resigned Jan 1799.

Kléber (J-B), 1753–1800. Son of a Strasbourg building worker, K. served in the Austrian army, but in 1789 was a inspector of fortifications in E France. He volunteered in 1792; fought in 1793 at first at Mainz, then in the Vendée, where he was made a general; and participated in the victory at Fleurus. Following brilliant victories in Germany in 1795–6, he retired, but he was brought back for the Egyptian campaign, during which he was assassinated.

La Bourdonnaie or **La Bourdonnaye** (Fs-Régis), 1767–1839. A career soldier originally from Angers, La B. joined the *émigré* forces at Coblenz and fought in France with Condé in 1792. He subsequently fought alongside the Chouans, but benefited from the 1795 amnesty to return to local politics in the Maine-et-Loire under the Directory, before entering nat politics after 1800.

Labrousse (Clotilde-Suzanne), 1747–1821. Mystic and prophetess, the protégée of Dom Gerle in the early 1790s, Suzanne L. was said to have predicted the Rev. She was imprisoned in Italy in 1792, but was freed by the French and came to Paris in 1798.

Laclos (P-Ambroise-Fs Choderlos de), 1741–1803. The author of *Les Liaisons dangereuses* (1782) served 11 years prior to the Rev as an officer in the engineers. In 1788 he became the secretary of Orléans and an important organiser of the patriot party. One of the first Jacobins, he had evolved towards republicanism by Varennes. He re-entered the army, only to be imprisoned in Mar 1793 as an Orleanist, but after Thermidor was freed and spent the rest of his life in the army.

Lacombe (Claire, or 'Rose'), 1765–?. An actress with rev convictions Rose L. came to Paris in 1792 and was involved in the *journée* of 10 Aug. She became prominent in the *Société des citoyennes républicaines révolutionnaires* until its closure by the government on 30 Oct 1793. Arrested as a Hébertist supporter in Mar 1794, she was subsequently released and returned to acting.

Lacoste (Elie), 1745–1803. A doctor at Montignac in the Périgueux, Elie L. was elected to the Leg Ass. and the Convtn, where he sat among the Montagnards. He was frequently *en mission* and joined the CGS in Nov 1793. He was opposed to Robespierre by Thermidor, but was imprisoned under the reaction for terrorist offences. Amnestied in 1795, he returned to his medical practice.

Lacoste (J-B), 1753–1821. A lawyer from Mauriac elected deputy for the Cantal in the Convtn, L. spent much of his time *en mission*. Arrested as a terrorist after Thermidor, he was amnestied and entered the bureaucracy, becoming a prefect under Napoleon.

Lacoste (J de). 1730–1820. A lawyer who had achieved high rank within the naval bureaucracy under the AR, L. was responsible for the installation of the rev regime in the W Indies before being appointed Navy Minister in March 1792. He was dismissed in July; was tried but acquitted by the Rev Tribunal in 1793; and re-entered the bureaucracy.

Lacretelle (J-Charles-Dominique de), 1766-1855. L. was making his way in the legal and literary worlds when the Rev broke out. He worked on the *Journal des débats*; was active as a Jacobin, then a Feuillant; and served as secretary to La Rochefoucauld-Liancourt. Forced into hiding under the Terror, he returned to Parisian journalism after Thermidor, and became a leader of the *jeunesse dorée*. Implicated in the Vendémiaire rising, he was imprisoned for two years at Fructidor, but had returned to politics by 1799. After Brumaire, he returned to private life and literary endeavour.

Lacroix or **Delacroix** (Sébaste-Marie-Bruno de), 1764–guill 20 Apr 1794. From a well-off bourgeois family, L. threw himself enthusiastically into rev journalism in 1789. Pro-Robespierre, he acted as commissary for the executive power, but his links with the Hébertists in Parisian sectional politics were his downfall. He was arrested and executed as an accomplice of Hébert.

Lacroix (J-F de), see DELACROIX

Ladmiral (Henri), *c* 1735–guill 18 June 1794. An unemployed clerk, L. seems to have become suddenly obsessed in 1794 with the plan to assassinate Robespierre. In the end, he tried Collot-d'Herbois instead, failed and was executed. He probably acted on his own initiative rather than as a royalist agent.

Lafayette (Marie-Jos-Paul-Roch-Yves-Gilbert Motier, marquis de). 1757–1834. A wealthy liberal aristocrat, L. was a hero in France on account of his part in the American War of Independence when, at the Ass. of Notables in 1787, he called for the convocation of the EG. Closely associated with the reform movement in 1787–8, he was elected by the nobility of the Auvergne to the EG in 1789, and on 15 July was appointed commander of the new Parisian Nat Guard. Hated by Marie-Antoinette for his part in the *journées* of 5 and 6 Oct 1789, he was to enjoy massive popularity at the time of the Fête de la Fédération in July 1790. He lost much popular support, however, for his support for Bouillé in the Nancy mutiny and for his role at Varennes and after, when he supported the 'Triumvirate' and was instrumental in the massacre of the Champ de Mars. He was appointed commander of the Army of the Centre in 1792, but lost all credibility when he left his army to try to rally the Leg Ass. against the Jacobins following the *journée* of 20 June 1792. The fall of the king led to his defection to the enemy, but he was imprisoned by the Allies down to Sept 1797. He returned to France under Napoleon.

Lajard (P-Auguste de), 1757–1837. From a *robin* family based in Montpellier, L. pursued a military career before the Rev, and became an aide of Lafayette in the Parisian Nat Guard from 1789 until 1792, when he rejoined the army. He was briefly War Minister in June–July 1792, proving a staunch constitutional royalist, but was subsequently denounced, whereupon he emigrated, returning to France after Brumaire.

Lakanal (Jos), 1762–1845. A Doctrinaire schoolteacher before the Rev, L. was elected by his native Ariège to the Convtn. He served frequently *en mission* but achieved most prominence by his solid work on the Education Committee, re-organising all levels of French education. In the C500, he helped install the Institut, and in 1798 was sent to organise the new depts on the right bank of the Rhine. His career in education continued under Napoleon.

Lally-Tollendal (Trophime-Gérard, marquis de), 1751–1830. A cavalry captain, L.-T.'s Neckerite sympathies got him elected by the Parisian nobility to the EG. Chairman of the Constitution Committee, he advocated, along with *Monarchiens* Mounier and Bergasse, a bicameral legislature. When these proposals were defeated in the Ass. in Sept, he emigrated to Switzerland. He returned temporarily in 1792 in an attempt to help Louis XVI escape, but then passed into Britain. He returned to France after Brumaire.

Lamarck (J-B-P-Ant de Monet, chevalier de), 1744–1829. The great evolutionary theorist, a pupil of Jussieu, had enjoyed court favour but still was appointed to the Muséum d'histoire naturelle in 1795 and the Institut in 1796.

Lamarque (Fs), 1753–1839. A lawyer from the Périgueux, L. sat in the Leg Ass. and the Convtn, and was one of the deputies who were handed over to the Austrians by Dumouriez in April 1793. He returned to France in 1796, and was a neo-Jacobin in the C500. He returned to his legal career under Napoleon.

Lamballe (Marie-Thérèse-Louise de Savoie-Carignan, princesse de), 1748–assass 3 Sept 1792. Widow of the prematurely debauched prince de Lamballe, the princesse de L. became the close confidante of Marie-Antoinette, whom she served as *surintendante* of the queen's household. She was interned with her mistress in the La Force prison in Aug 1792 where she fell victim to the Sept Massacres.

Lameth (Alexandre-Théodore-Victor, comte de), 1760–1829. Cavalry colonel in 1789, Alexandre de L. was elected by the nobility of Péronne to the EG. He was swift to join the Third Estate; was prominent on the 'Night of 4 Aug'; and became a leader of the patriot party and one of the so-called 'Triumvirate' (with Duport and Barnave). He supported the king after Varennes, but rejoined the army in 1791. In Aug 1792 he was serving with the Army of the North when he decided to join Lafayette in fleeing. He was imprisoned by the Allies however, and only released in 1795. Under Napoleon he was to be a prefect.

Lameth (Charles-Malo-Fs, comte de), 1757–1832. A career soldier like his brothers, Charles de L. was elected by the nobility of Artois to the EG where he sat on the left and was reputed a liberal. He supported Louis XVI after

Varennes; then returned to the army; but fled to Hamburg in late 1792, only definitively returning to France after Brumaire.

Lameth (Théodore, comte de), 1756–1854. The eldest though the least well known of the Lameth brothers, Théodore de L. was colonel of a cavalry regiment in 1789, and served in the dept administration of the Jura before being elected to the Leg Ass. He sat on the right, supported the king and was one of the handful of deputies to oppose war in Apr 1792. In Feb 1793, he fled arrest to Switzerland, and only returned to France after Brumaire.

Lamoignon (Chrétien-Fs II de), 1735–89. A prominent figure in the Paris parl, L. was appointed Garde des Sceaux in 1787 during the Ass. of Notables. He collaborated with Brienne in the May Edicts of 1788, but was forced into resignation and died shortly afterwards, possibly by his own hand.

Lamourette (Ant-Adrien), 1742-exctd 11 Jan 1794. This Lazarist priest advised Mirabeau on ecclesiastical matters in 1789, accepted the Civ Constn and was elected bishop of Lyon. A moderate in the Leg Ass., he stepped from obscurity in a famous session on 7 July 1792 where, with the so-called *baiser Lamourette*, he persuaded all sides openly to fraternise. Appalled by the turn of events in late 1792, he returned to Lyon and was arrested and executed following the siege of the city.

Lanjuinais (J-Denis), 1753–1823. A legal consultant to the Estates of Brittany, L. rallied to the cause of the Third Estate in late 1788, was elected to the EG and was a founder-member of the Breton Club. In the Constit Ass., he was one of the architects of the Civ Constn. He returned to municipal politics in Rennes in 1791, but was elected to the Convtn, where he was closely linked with the Girondins. Proscribed on 2 June 1793, he went into hiding, only re-emerging 18 months later to be recalled to the Convtn. Elected triumphantly by dozens of depts to serve in the C Anciens, he was viewed as a royalist. He returned to Rennes in 1797, but his political career continued under Napoleon.

Lannes (J), 1769–1809. A textile worker in 1789, L. volunteered in 1792 and was soon promoted. He served in the Pyrenees from 1793 to 1795; in Italy until 1798; and from 1798 in the Orient, where he was made general in May 1799.

Lanthénas (Fs-Xavier), 1754–99. An obscure Parisian doctor in 1789, L.'s patronage by the Rolands won him election to the Convtn for the Rhône-et-Loire. Originally on the proscription lists on 31 May 1793, he was struck off by Marat for alleged harmlessness. Elected to the C500, he retired from political life in 1797.

Laporte (Armand de), 1737-guill 23 Aug 1793. A high-ranking naval bureaucrat under the AR, L. rallied to the monarchy in 1789. From Jan 1791, he had responsibility for the king's civil list, and was reputed to be the hub of a secret network of royalist funds down to the fall of the monarchy.

La Révellière-Lépeaux (L-Marie de), 1753–1824. From solid bourgeois stock in Montaigu, La R.-L. was giving botany classes in Angers when the Rev broke out, and the city elected him to the EG, where he sat on the left. Elected to the Convtn, he was a member of the Plain, opposing both the Girondins and the Commune, but an energetic one. He went into hiding after the proscription of the Girondins, but returned to the Convtn in Mar 1795 and served on the CPS. Elected to the C Anciens, he was chosen as Director. His name is particularly associated with the cult of theophilanthropy; and with the Fructidor coup against the right. His stay in office was ended by the Prairial coup of Year VII, at which juncture he left politics.

La Rivière or **Henri-Larivière** (P-Fs-Joachim-Henri de), 1761–1838. A Norman lawyer who sat on both the Leg Ass. and the Convtn, La R. was a precocious rpbcn but gravitated towards the Girondins. He was a member of the Commission of Twelve and had to flee to escape arrest in early June 1793. His efforts to foster the Federalist revolt were unavailing, and he went into hiding, only to re-emerge and to resume his place in the Convtn in March 1795. His attacks on the CPS of Year II led to his election onto the body. He evolved rapidly to the right: he was opposed to the Prairial *journées*; was suspected of royalist plotting; and in the C500 became an energetic Clichyen. A victim of Fructidor, he escaped to Germany and then passed into the entourage of Artois in London. He returned to France to resume his political career in 1814.

La Rochefoucauld-Liancourt (Fs-Alexandre-Frédéric, duc de), 1747–1827. A philanthropist, a proponent of agricultural, educational and industrial innovation and a notorious liberal, La R.-L. was elected to the EG, and chaired the sessions of the Mendicity Committee of the Constit Ass. which urged the adoption of a kind of welfare state. In 1791 he was put in charge of the military division of Normandy, and proposed that Louis XVI escape to Britain via Rouen. He emigrated himself in Aug 1792, but refused service in the *émigré* cause, visited the USA and returned to France in 1799 to spend the rest of his life devoted to philanthropic work and liberal politics.

La Rochejaquelein (Henri du Vergier, comte de), 1772–exctd 28 Jan 1794. An officer in Louis XVI's Constitutional Guard in 1791, La R. left Paris in disgust in 1792 and rallied to the Vendéan cause from Oct 1793. CinC of the rebels from late 1793, he was hunted down and killed by the rpbcn forces.

La Rouërie (Armand-Taffin, marquis de), 1756–93. Veteran of the American War, ex-Trappist, ex-*Garde-française*, La R. supported the Rennes parl in the Pre-Rev and was imprisoned in the Bastille in 1787 for his pains. In 1789, however, he was transformed into a royalist and from late 1791 was acting for the princes, setting up secret royalist committees in towns throughout W France. In late 1792 he had to go into hiding and died seemingly of exhaustion while still on the run.

'**Lasource**' (sobriquet of Marie-David ALBA), 1763–guill 31 Oct 1793. A Protestant minister in Languedoc prior to the Rev, L. was elected to the Leg Ass. and the Convtn by the Tarn. He served *en mission* in the S, and was a member of the CGS in early 1793, but his attacks on the Paris Commune and on Marat and Robespierre brought him closer to the Girondins. He was proscribed on 2 June 1793 and executed with the Girondin leaders.

La Tour du Pin-Gouvernet (J-Frédéric de), 1727–guill 28 Apr 1794. Career soldier and in 1789 military governor of Poitou and Saintonge, La T. du P. was elected to the EG where he rallied to the Third Estate. On 4 Aug 1789 he became War Minister, but he lost much popularity in the Nancy affair and he resigned in Nov 1790. He came out of retirement to defend Marie-Antoinette in her trial, and was executed himself.

La Tour Maubourg (Marie-Ch-César-Florimond de Fay, comte de), 1756–1831. A career soldier, La T.M. was elected to the EG by the nobility of Le Puy, rallied to the Third Estate and became a noted Fayettiste. He was responsible for bringing the royal family back to Paris from Varennes (with Barnave and Pétion). He returned to the army in 1791 with Lafayette, with whom he emigrated. Both men were imprisoned by the Allies, only emerging in 1797. He returned to France after Brumaire and re-entered politics.

Laumond (J-Ch-Jos), 1753–1825. Functionary who served in the intendance of Lorraine in 1789, in the financial bureaucracy in 1791 and in the Finance Commission which replaced the Ministry of Finance in 1794, L. was sent to Italy under the Directory to serve as war commissary. He became a prefect under Napoleon.

Launey (Bernard-René Jourdan de), 1740–assass 14 July 1789. De L. succeeded his father as governor of the Bastille in 1776. He was murdered by the fortress's assailants on 14 July.

Laveaux (J-Ch-Thiébault), 1749–1827. Man of letters and journalist living in Germany in 1789, L. took over the *Courrier de Strasbourg* in the early 1790s, moved to Paris and became editor of the *Journal de la Montagne*, the official mouthpiece of the Jacobin Club. Imprisoned after Thermidor, he subsequently became a teacher and a bureaucrat.

Lavicomterie (L-Th de), 1746–1809. The Rev gave this failed literary hack a chance to make his name by publishing sensationalist accounts of the crimes of kings, queens, popes, etc. He was elected to the Convtn by Paris, and served on the CGS on and off from Sept 1792 until 13 therm II. He was arrested for involvement in the Prairial *journées*, but was amnestied in 1795 and returned to private life.

Lavoisier (Ant-Laurent), 1743–guill 8 May 1794. The great chemist, the son of a wealthy merchant, advised the rev assemblies on a number of technical and scientific subjects in the early 1790s, but was guillotined for his AR past as a *fermier général*.

Lebas or **Le Bas** (Ph-Fs-Jos), 1765–suic 28 July 1794. Son of a wealthy notary from Artois, L. trained as a lawyer in the 1780s and was elected to the Convtn by the Pas-de-Calais. A member of the CGS from Sept 1793, he served *en mission* to the armies in the N and E alongside Saint-Just in late 1793 and early 1794. He was closely associated with the Robespierre fraction, partly through having married the daughter of Robespierre's landlord, Duplay, in Aug 1793, and voluntarily associated himself with their fate on 9 Thermidor, killing himself before capture.

Lebon or **Le Bon** (Ghislain-Fs-Jos), 1765–guill 16 Oct 1795. An Oratorian schoolteacher before the Rev, Joseph L. accepted the Civ Constn and became *curé* of a village near Arras. He frequented the popular society, married and in 1792 was elected mayor of Arras. He entered the Convtn as a *suppléant* following the *journées* of 31 May and 2 June 1793. His first spell *en mission* was in the Pas-de-Calais; from Mar 1794 he developed into a violent and sanguinary rep at Arras and Cambrai. He was denounced for his misdeeds after Thermidor, tried by special tribunal and executed.

Lebrun (Ch-Fs), 1739–1824. A former disciple of Maupeou, and renowned as a savant, L. was elected to the EG where he was identified with the *monarchiens*. He retired from public life in 1792, was imprisoned during the Terror but was elected to the C Anciens in 1795. Although he was seemingly uninvolved in the Brumaire coup, Napoleon chose him his third consul.

Lebrun or **Lebrun-Tondu** (P-Henri-Hélène-Marie), 1763–guill 27 Dec 1793. Ex-cleric (known as the abbé Tondu), ex-soldier, printer and journalist, L. had spent the period from 1787 to 1791 in the Austrian Netherlands. He came to Paris with a reputation as a democrat and Brissot got him a post in the Foreign Ministry and helped make him Foreign Minister following the overthrow of the king. He was still closely associated with the Girondins, and on 2 June 1793 was arrested along with his colleague Clavière. He escaped from prison but was recaptured and executed.

Le Chapelier (Isaac-René-Gui), 1754–guill 22 Apr 1794. A Breton lawyer and *anobli*, Le C. was prominent in the Pre-Rev period in Brittany and was elected to the Third Estate of the EG and was a founder of the Breton Club. He presided in the Nat Ass. on the night of 4 Aug. He is best known as the author of the *Loi Le Chapelier* of 14 June 1791 which outlawed workers' associations. A Feuillant, he was executed during the Terror.

Leclerc (Jean-Théophile-Victor), 1771–? Son of a wealthy civil engineer from central France, L. was involved in rebellion in Martinique in the early 1790s. By 1792 he was in Paris. He served on an espionage mission in Germany and then at Lyon, where he became involved with the left-wing Chalier faction. Back in Paris for the *journées* of 31 May and 2 June 1793, he launched a radical news-paper, a new *Ami du peuple*, in July, following Marat's death. His left-wing, *enragé* criticisms of the Rev Govt saw him threatened with arrest in Sept 1793. He married the rev Pauline Léon in Nov 1794; was briefly imprisoned in 1794; and subsequently disappeared from view.

Lecointre (Laurent), 1742–1805. A cloth merchant from Versailles, L. represented the Seine-et-Oise in the Leg Ass. and Convtn. A violently anti-Girondin Montagnard, he developed into a vicious anti-Montagnard after Ther-midor. He retired to private life in 1795.

Le Couteulx-Cantelau (J-Barthélemy), 1746–1818. Son of a Norman *robin*, Le C.-C. was a financier and magistrate in Rouen in 1789. Elected to the EG, he specialised in financial and commercial questions. He lay low during the Terror in Paris, but re-emerged to be elected to the C Anciens. A moderate, he rallied to Napoleon after Brumaire.

Lefebvre (Fs-Jos), 1755–1820. A career soldier from Alsace like his father, L. was *premier sergent* in the *Gardes-françaises* in 1788. He rose into the officer corps in the Rev, and by Jan 1794 was a general. His part in the campaigns of 1794 and 1795 was outstanding. Posted to a command over internal forces in 1799, he participated at Brumaire and continued his career under Napoleon.

Legendre (L), 1752–97. A Parisian butcher, L. was prominent on the *journées* of 14 July and 5 Oct 1789; was a founder-member of the Cordeliers; and distinguished himself again in the *journées* of 20 June and 10 Aug 1792. He sat in the Convtn and voted for the king's death, and was said to have urged that the corpse be cut into 84 chunks and distributed among France's 84 depts. He participated in the *journées* of 31 May and 2 June 1793 and served briefly on the CGS, though his links with Danton held him back. He participated in the Ther-midor coup, then became a reactionary, attacking Carrier and Lebon, helping to put down the insurrections of Germinal and Prairial and getting himself elected to the C Anciens.

Léon (Pauline), 1768–? Daughter of a Parisian chocolate-maker, L. participated in the rev *journées* of 1789 and 1792, and became involved with the Cordeliers before co-founding the women's society, the *Société des citoyennes républicaines révolutionnaires* in May 1793. Linked with the *enragés* in advocating radical econ-omic reform, the club was closed down in Oct 1793. She married the *enragé* Leclerc, alongside whom she was imprisoned in 1794, before disappearing from view.

Lepeletier de Saint-Fargeau (L-Michel). 1760–assass 20 Jan 1793. Magistrate in the Paris parl, L. was elected to the EG, where he rallied to the Third Estate. Liberal and reformist in the Constit Ass., he was returned to the Convtn where he sketched out far-reaching educational reforms. He was assassinated, however, before he could present them to the Convtn.

Lepeletier (Ferdinand-L-Félix), 1767–1837. Adc to the prince de Lambesc under the AR, Félix L. became a Jacobin following the death of his brother, L. de Saint-Fargeau. He became linked with Babeuf; was a member of the Société du Manège; and opposed Brumaire.

Lequinio (Jos-Marie), 1755–1814. Son of a surgeon from Sarzeau in Brittany, L. was elected by the Morbihan to the Leg Ass. and Convtn. He spent much of his time *en mission:* notably with the Army of the North, and then in the W where his cooperation with Carrier brought suspicions of extremism. He was imprisoned as a terrorist in 1795 but went into hiding to avoid arrest, and was amnestied in the same year. Though elected to the C500 in 1798, he was not allowed to sit, and turned to a career in administration.

Lescure or **Delescure** (L-Marie, marquis de), 1766–battle 3 Nov 1793. A career soldier who from 1791 was involved in counter-rev activity in W France, de L. was briefly leader of the Vendéan rebels in 1793. He died on the battlefield.

Lessart or **Delessart** (Claude-Ant de Valdec de), 1742–assass 9 Sept 1792. A *maître des requêtes* since the 1760s, de L. served in the financial bureaucracy under Necker in 1789 before himself becoming Controller-General in 1790. In Jan 1791 he was appointed Minister of the Interior, and moved to Foreign Affairs in Nov. Arrested as a royalist in Mar 1792, he was assassinated when a convoy of prisoners of which he formed part was massacred by a mob on its way from Paris to Orléans.

Letourneur (Ch-L-Fs-Honoré), 1751–1817. Captain in the engineers in 1789, L. represented the Manche in the Leg Ass. and Convtn, where he became an active member of the Military Committee. He served on the CPS in 1795 and, then, from the C Anciens, was elected Director. Closely identified with Carnot's positions, he was replaced in May 1797. The remainder of the 1790s he spent as a diplomat and as an inspector of the artillery. In 1800 he became a prefect.

Levasseur 'de la Sarthe' (René), 1747–1834. Man-midwife and surgeon in Le Mans before the Rev, L. served as a district administrator before being elected to the Convtn, where he adopted Montagnard, anti-Girondin and later anti-Dantonist positions and was frequently *en mission*. He survived the Terror but was imprisoned for his implication in the Germinal insurrection. Amnestied in 1795, he returned to his medical practice.

Lindet (J-B-Robert), 1746–1825. Lawyer from Bernay in Normandy, Robert L. represented the Eure in the Leg Ass. and the Convtn. He evolved from moderate to Montagnard opinions: he opposed the Girondins, and was elected to the CPS. *En mission* combating Federalists in mid 1793 at Lyon and in Normandy, Lindet was preoccupied from Sept with the implementation of the General Maximum through the National Food Commission. After Thermidor, he was the butt of attacks and was imprisoned for alleged implication in the Prairial rising. Involved with the babouvists, he lived this down and was Finance Minister following the Prairial coup down to Brumaire, at which point he retired to private life.

Lindet (Robert-Thomas), 1743–1823. *Curé* in Bernay in 1789, Thomas L. was elected to the EG where he sat on the left. He accepted the Civ Constn and was elected bishop of the Eure. Elected, like his brother Robert, to the Convtn, in Nov 1792 he became the first bishop to marry, and in Nov 1793, he renounced his priesthood. He served in the C Anciens from 1795 to 1798, but then passed into obscurity.

Loménie de Brienne, see BRIENNE

Louis XVI (king of France, 1774–1792), 1754–guill 21 Jan 1793. Grandson of Louis XV, Louis XVI enjoyed nat success in the American War of Independence, but never came to terms with the regime's financial problems. Well intentioned but badly advised, notably by court factions, he vacillated in 1789 just as he had done throughout the Pre-Rev. Effectively a prisoner in Paris after the *journées* of 5–6 Oct 1789, his acceptance of the new regime was never more than half-hearted. His flight to Varennes in June 1791 cost him much popular support, and forced him to accept the 1791 Constitution which, however, whether intentionally or not, he thereafter subverted. He nearly fell victim to the Paris crowd in the *journée* of 20 June 1792, then was overthrown on 10 Aug. He defended himself with dignity in his trial before the Convtn.

Louis XVII, (at first duc de Normandie; dauphin from 6 June 1789; king of France in theory from 21 Jan 1793), 1785–8 June 1795. The sickly pretender was imprisoned at the Temple prison and died after a long illness.

Louis XVIII (down to June 1795 comte de Provence; king of France in theory from 1795, effectively from 1815 to 1824), 1755–1824. Though he had been involved in the Pre-Rev, Provence was highly critical of the new regime and emigrated in June 1791. He proclaimed himself Lieutenant-General of the Kingdom and organised an *émigré* army to fight the Rpbc. Based in N Italy, he proclaimed himself regent on the death of Louis XVI in Jan 1793 and Louis XVIII after the death of the sickly 'Louis XVII' in June 1795. In 1797 he moved to Blankenburg in the lands of the duke of Brunswick, in 1798 to Russia and in 1807 to Britain, only returning to France in 1814.

Louis 'du Bas-Rhin' (J-Ant), 1742–96. Functionary in the intendance of Alsace under the AR, L. represented the Bas-Rhin in the Convtn and served in the CGS from Oct 1793 until Thermidor. He remained a Jacobin after Thermidor and sat briefly on the C500.

Louis-Philippe, see CHARTRES

Loustalot (Elisée). 1761–90. A lawyer in the Bordeaux parl, L. came to Paris in 1789 and began to work as a journalist with Prudhomme on the popular *Révolutions de Paris*. Pro-Jacobin, pro-Cordelier, he fell ill and died prematurely.

Louvet de Couvray (J-B), 1760–97. From a printing background in Paris, L. achieved fame on the eve of the Rev through his best-selling *Les Amours du chevalier de Faublas* (1787–8). He came to support the Girondins and edited a journal, the *Sentinelle*. Roland's patronage assured him election to the Convtn by the Loiret, and he achieved note as a courageous defender of the Girondin cause. He fled arrest on 2 June 1793 and hid with Guadet, Barbaroux and Buzot in Normandy and Guyenne. He came out of hiding and was recalled to the Convtn in Mar 1795, and served on the CPS. He helped draft the Constitution of Year III and the Law of Two-Thirds. He was elected to the C500, where he maintained his rpbcn sentiments.

Luckner (Nic, baron de), 1722–guill 3 Jan 1794. A German career soldier who had fought against and (since 1763) for France, L. was in 1791 made the last marshal of the old monarchy. He commanded on the Rhine in 1792, then was switched to the Army of the North *vice* Rochambeau and invaded Belgium. In late 1792, he was recalled and allowed to retire.

Luzerne (César-Henri, comte de la), 1737–99. A career sailor and colonial administrator, L. served as Navy Minister from Dec 1787 to 12 July 1789, then again in the Necker ministry following the fall of the Bastille. He resigned in Oct 1789 and emigrated.

Macdonald (Et-Jq-Jos-Alexandre), 1765–1840. Of Scottish Jacobite descent, M. served on the staff of Beurnonville and Dumouriez and in Nov 1794 was made a general. In 1795 he achieved great fame by exploits on the N. front. In 1797 he served in the N and in 1798 in Italy. Governor of Rome in 1798, he fought in S Italy alongside Championnet, whom he succeeded as commander, and brought Naples under French control, but then lost at Trebbia to Austro-Russian forces as France was forced out of Italy. He supported Brumaire and continued his career under Napoleon.

Maignet (Et-Chrisostome), 1758–1834. An Auvergnat lawyer, M. represented the Puy-de-Dôme in the Leg Ass. and Convtn. He was responsible for a substantial number of *missions*, notably in the Midi, where he organised the Orange rev tribunal. After Thermidor he went into hiding, only emerging after the amnesty of 1795. He subsequently returned to his legal practice.

Mailhe (J-B), 1754–1839. A lawyer from Toulouse, M. had served as PGS in the Haute-Garonne before being elected to the Leg Ass., then the Convtn. He presented the case for the Convtn trying Louis XVI, but otherwise lay low during the Terror. He sat in the C500; moved towards the Clichyens; was deported after Fructidor; and then returned (1800) to his legal practice.

Maillard (Marie-Julien-Stanislas), 1763–94. Obscure functionary who became an outstanding street figure in Parisian *journées* (14 July 1789, 5 and 6 Oct 1789,

Sept Massacres, etc), M. worked for the CGS under the Terror; just escaped purge as a Hébertist; and died in his bed in Apr 1794.

Maistre (Jos de), 1753–1821. The counter-rev ideologist was a Savoyard senator when the Rev broke out, and opposed France's annexation of Savoy and its territorial involvement in N Italy. By 1799, he was in the retinue of the king of Sardinia. His *Considérations sur la France* appeared in 1796.

Malesherbes (Chrétien-Guillaume de Lamoignon de), 1721–guill 22 Apr 1794. A distinguished magistrate and minister under Louis XVI, M. was linked with the 1787 Toleration Edict and, through his kinsman Lamoignon, in the promulgation of the May Edicts in 1788. He volunteered in Dec 1792 to defend Louis XVI at his trial and ultimately shared his fate.

Mallarmé (Fs-René-Auguste), 1755–1831. A lawyer from Lorraine, M. represented the Meurthe in the Leg Ass. and Convtn. He presided over the Convtn on 31 May 1793. A radical rep *en mission* in the E from late 1793, he was recalled and plotted against Robespierre. He remained a Jacobin after Thermidor, and was arrested after the Prairial rising, though subsequently amnestied. The Directory used him as a commissary in the Belgian depts and he pursued an administrative career under Napoleon.

Mallet du Pan (Jq), 1749–1801. Son of a pastor from Geneva, M. du P. had with Voltaire's patronage carved out a literary and journalistic career for himself under the AR. From 1784 he worked on the *Mercure de France* and was to gain notoriety for his anti-rev dispatches after 1789. Louis XVI used him for a secret diplomatic mission in Germany in 1792, and he did not return to France because of the fall of the monarchy. His *Considérations sur la nature de la Révolution en France* (1793) won him international fame, and from 1794, he resided in Switzerland, and from 1798 in England, where he founded the counter-rev journal, the *Mercure britannique* (1798).

Malouet (P-Victor), 1740–1814. Diplomat and colonial administrator, M. was appointed Intendant of the port of Toulon in 1788. He was elected to the EG by his native Riom, and urged the introduction of a bicameral legislature. When his plans were thwarted in the autumn of 1789, he moved towards the right. In Sept 1792 he emigrated to England, returning to France in 1801.

Manuel (P-L), 1751–guill 14 Nov 1793. Son of an artisan from Montargis, M. was a writer who had spent a period in the Bastille. In 1789 he was a private tutor in Paris, and his speeches in the Jacobins and a sensationalist book on the Bastille soon won him fame. From Dec 1791 he was the *procureur* of the Paris Commune, and though temporarily suspended for his part in the *journée* of 20 June 1792 soon won the post back. He was elected to the Convtn by Paris, but had a striking change of heart during the king's trial: he voted for the *appel au peuple* and then resigned on this issue and returned to his home town where he was subsequently arrested, to be brought to Paris and executed.

Marat (J-Paul), 1744–assass 13 July 1793. 'L'Ami du peuple' was a physician by training, and had enjoyed a stormy literary and scientific career under the AR. The violence and the democratic sentiments expressed in his journal, *l'Ami du peuple*, from Sept 1789 soon won him notoriety, and he was forced into hiding on a number of occasions. A member of the Commune insurrectionnelle, he was alleged to have had a large part in the Sept Massacres, for which he won the undying hatred of the Girondins, who attacked him fiercely in the Convtn, to which he was elected by Paris. His referral to the Rev Tribunal in Apr 1793 was crucial in the events leading to the *journées* of 31 May and 2 June 1793. His assassination by Charlotte Corday in July 1793 led to a rev cult growing up around his name.

Marbot (J-Ant), 1750–1800. M. resigned from the army on the eve of the Rev, became prominent in the dept administration of the Corrèze and was elected to the Leg Ass. In 1792 he returned to the army and fought on the Spanish front, 1793–5. By 1795 a general, he was elected to the C Anciens, where he opposed the Clichyens and supported the Fructidor coup. He returned to the army, but died of an epidemic in Genoa.

Marceau or **Marceau-Desgraviers** (Fs-Séverin), 1769–battle 19 Sept 1796. Son of an attorney from Chartres, M. joined the local Nat Guard in 1789 and then volunteered in 1791. He served in the N and W, and by Nov 1793 was a general. Commander of the Army of the West, he was victorious at Le Mans and Savenay before being switched to the Army of the Ardennes and then the Sambre-and-Meuse. He died in battle inside Germany.

Maréchal (Pierre-Sylvain), 1750–1803. Son of a Paris wine merchant, Sylvain M. trained as a lawyer but never practised, turning instead to literature. Man of letters, freemason, avowed atheist, bookseller, he threw himself into rev journalism from 1789, contributing to the *Révolutions de Paris* and becoming linked with Chaumette, Danton, Desmoulins, etc. His atheistic views may have influenced the dechristianisation campaign in Paris from late 1793. Politically marginal, he became involved in Babeuf's conspiracy, but avoided imprisonment and died an impoverished bookseller.

Maret (Hugues-Bernard), 1763–1839. Son of a doctor from Burgundy, M.'s interest in literature and in rev politics led to him creating the *Bulletin de l'Assemblée*, a precursor of the *Moniteur*. A Jacobin turned Feuillant, he was used on diplomatic missions by Lebrun-Tondu, but was imprisoned by the Austrians while returning from Italy in 1793 and not released until 1795. From 1796 he was associated with Bonaparte; helped plot Brumaire; and became his intimate adviser under the Empire.

Marie-Antoinette (Josèphe-Jeanne, queen of France from 1774 to 1792), 1755–guill 16 Oct 1793. The youngest daughter of Maria Theresa of Austria, M.-A. was married at 14 to the future Louis XVI. She lost a great deal of popularity for her extravagance, involvement in scandals (including the 'Diamond Necklace' affair of 1785), and reactionary political views. She opposed compromise with the Third Estate in the summer of 1789 and was widely blamed for Louis's political bad faith. She narrowly avoided lynching during the *journées* of 5 and 6 Oct 1789, and was an early advocate of the royal family's flight. She was viewed as the hub of the *Comité autrichien*, and passed classified military information to the Austrians in 1792. Imprisoned with her husband after 10 Aug 1792, she was tried and executed in the autumn of 1793.

Marmontel (J-Fs), 1723–99. Poet and dramatist, disciple of Voltaire, secretary of the Académie française from 1793, M. was a Parisian elector during the crisis of summer 1789. His moderate political views caused him to lie low during the Terror. He was elected to the C Anciens, but his right-wing views led to his expulsion after Fructidor.

Masséna (André), 1758–1817. An orphan who had served as a cabin-boy, then become an army officer, M. played an important part in the occupation of Nice in 1792. He was rapidly promoted thereafter, serving in Italy from 1792 to 1798. A general from 1793, he was in 1799 appointed commander of the Army of the Danube and won the crucial battle of Zurich against Austro-Russian troops. His career continued under Napoleon.

Mathieu-Dumas, see DUMAS

Maupeou (René-Ch-Augustin de), 1714–92. The Chancellor was by tradition irremovable, so this Parisian magistrate, who had been appointed to the post in 1768 and had played a major part in the struggle against the parls in the early 1770s, was in theory head of the judiciary throughout Louis XVI's reign, even though he played no administrative role whatever and lived in retirement, with his functions performed by the Garde des Sceaux.

Maury (J-Siffrein, abbé), 1746–1817. Son of a cobbler, M.'s brilliant student career led to swift preferment. By 1789 he was vicar-general of the diocese of Lombez and a member of the Académie française. He was elected to the EG by the clergy of Péronne, and proved to be the most energetic and forceful counter-rev orator in the Constit Ass. He emigrated in 1791 and by 1794 had been made cardinal. He returned to France to serve Napoleon in 1806.

Menou (Jq-Fs, baron de), 1750–1810. Career soldier from an ancient noble family from the Touraine, M. was elected to the EG, rallied to the Third Estate in June and was an active member of the Military Committee. He emerged as a leader of the Feuillants, but on the dispersal of the Constit Ass. rejoined the army. Despite being badly beaten by La Rochejaquelein in the Vendée, he had achieved the rank of general by 1793. He helped put down the Prairial rising, but failed to cope with the Vendémiaire revolt and was replaced by Bonaparte. The latter used him in his Egyptian campaign and later as military governor in Italy.

Mercier (L-Sébastien), 1740–1814. Author renowned for his famous *Tableau de Paris* (1781–8), M. edited (with Carra) the *Annales patriotiques*, then contributed to the *Chronique du mois*, which followed a Girondin line. The Seine-et-Oise elected him to the Convtn, where he proved a moderate, voting against the king's death then protesting against the proscription of the Girondins, for which he was arrested and imprisoned. He returned to the Convtn after Thermidor, sat on the C500 until 1797, but then turned to administrative and educational office.

Mercy-Argenteau (Florimond-Claude, comte de). 1727–94. Austrian diplomat, ambassador in Paris since 1766, M. was a confidant of Marie-Antoinette and was often accused of being leader of the *Comité autrichien*. His royalist plotting continued even after 1790 when he was transferred, first to Brussels, then to London.

Merlin 'de Douai' (Ph-Ant), 1754–1838. Son of a well-off farmer from the Douai region, M. was a wealthy lawyer who numbered Orléans among his clients. In the Constit Ass., his role on the Feudal Committee was important in the abolition of feudalism. He was elected to the Convtn; was frequently *en mission* during the Terror; was elected to the CPS after Thermidor; and became a dominant political figure down to the end of the Convtn, closing the Jacobin Club, breaking up the Commune and negotiating the Basle peace treaties. Elected to the C Anciens, he was appointed Minister of Justice and served briefly as Police Minister. One of the architects of Fructidor, he then served as Director, before being forced out of office by the Prairial coup. His political career continued under Napoleon.

Merlin 'de Thionville' (Ant-Christophe), 1762–1833. Son of a lawyer from Lorraine, M. forsook an ecclesiastical career with the Lazarists in 1781 and turned to the law. He served in the dept administration of the Moselle before being elected to the Leg Ass. His radical views were often heard, notably in attacks on the *Comité autrichien*. He was instrumental in organising the war effort in the N in Aug-Sept 1792. Elected to the Convtn, he was prominent *en mission* in the defence of Mainz until its capitulation in July 1793 and then in the Vendée until Nov 1793. He did not play a prominent role for the rest of the Terror, although he was a key figure in the overthrow of Robespierre. He was appointed to the CGS in Aug 1794 and, in conjunction with the *jeunesse dorée*, harassed the Jacobins. Although he sat in the C500 until 1798 he played no further political part of note and retired to private life.

Mirabeau (Honoré-Gabriel Riquetti, comte de), 1749–2 Apr 1791. Errant son of Mirabeau the economist (the so-called *Ami des hommes*), M. had gained a reputation in the closing years of the AR as a liberal polemicist. The nobility of Aix-en-Provence refused to let him stand for the EG as a noble because he did not own a fief, so he was elected by the Third Estate of the *bailliage*. A fine orator and shrewd political operator, he was dominant throughout the Summer crisis of 1789. From 1790, he was increasingly overtaken by events, as his decision to sell himself to the court attested.

Mirabeau or 'Mirabeau-Tonneau' (André-Boniface-L Riquetti, vicomte de), 1754–92. Dissolute younger brother of the great Mirabeau, the vicomte M. was a career soldier who was elected by the nobility of the Limousin to the EG and who there manifested reactionary sentiments and scandalous behaviour heavily censured by the Ass. He emigrated and formed the so-called 'Mirabeau Legion' which fought against the French in 1792 before their leader collapsed and died of a heart attack.

Miranda (Francisco de), 1750–1816. The architect of Latin American independence in the early nineteenth century, M. had served with the Spanish and French armies prior to the Rev. Lobbying in Paris in 1792 on behalf of the Spanish-American colonies, his military skills were utilised at the front, where he served with Dumouriez and fought at Valmy. Following Neerwinden and the defection of Dumouriez, he dropped out of public life and endured several spells in prison. Deported as a royalist at Fructidor, he escaped to Britain, before returning to the New World in 1806.

Miromesnil (Armand-Thomas Hue de), 1723–96. A Norman *parlementaire* who had opposed the Maupeou reforms in the early 1770s, M. was adopted by Maurepas and served as Garde des Sceaux from 1774 until 8 Apr 1787. He presided over a number of liberal reforms (abolition of torture, etc). He played no part in the Rev.

Momoro (Ant-Fs), 1756–guill 24 Mar 1794. A printer-bookseller in Paris in 1789, M. became prominent in the Cordeliers, and was among the leaders of the *fédérés* on 10 Aug 1792. He served in the dept administration of Paris, and was sent to the Vendée as a commissioner of the PEC. Increasingly linked with the dechristianising campaign in Paris, he was arrested and executed as an Hébertist.

Monge (Gaspard), 1746–1818. A well-known scientist and engineer under the AR, M. was favourable to the Rev, and was appointed Navy Minister in the PEC following the overthrow of the king. As minister down to Apr 1793 he built up the fleet and mobilised scientists for the war effort. Under the Directory he was elected to the C500 but was rarely in Paris, preferring to serve as a scientist in the train of Bonaparte in Italy and Egypt. He subsequently returned to Paris to continue his scientific career.

Montaut (L de Maribon de), 1754–1842. A king's musketeer under the AR, M. embraced the rev cause in 1789, left the army and entered dept politics in the Gers. He was elected to the Leg Ass. and Convtn, where he became a noted Maratist. He was implicated in the Germinal rising, was arrested, but later amnestied.

Montesquiou-Fézensac (Anne-P, marquis de), 1739–98. Brought up at court, M.-F. was in 1789 both an illustrious career soldier and a literary figure, member of the Académie française. He was elected by the nobility of Meaux to the EG and was quick to rally to the Third Estate. In the Constit Ass., he was esp involved in financial questions. In 1791 he was attached to the army in the S and when war broke out invaded Savoy as a rev liberator. He was threatened by political manoeuvres in Paris, however, and fled to Switzerland, only returning to France after Thermidor.

'Montgaillard' ('comte de', sobriquet of J-Gabriel-Maurice ROQUES), 1761–1841. A career soldier under the AR, M. entered secret diplomacy in the early 1790s, and assumed his sobriquet when working for Danton in Germany in 1792. By 1795 he had links with Louis XVIII, but was seemingly working for the Rpbc as a double agent throughout the Directory and Consulate.

Montlosier (Fs-Dominique de Reynaud, comte de), 1757–1838. A scion of an Auvergnat *hobereau* family, M. was elected as *suppléant* to the EG and sat in the Ass. from Sept 1789. He was politically ineffectual, emigrated to Coblenz and fought against the Rpbc in the 1792 campaign. He moved to Hamburg, then to Britain, where he evolved in the direction of Bonapartism, and returned after Brumaire and worked in the foreign ministry.

Montmorin or **Montmorin de Saint-Herem** (Armand-Marc, comte de), 1745–assass 2 Sept 1792. A diplomat under the AR, M. sat in the Ass. of Notables in 1787 and was appointed Foreign Minister in succession to Vergennes in Feb 1787. He was temporarily dismissed in July 1789, then reinstated. He worked assiduously for the court, helping to win over Mirabeau. He was the author of the dispatch to foreign powers in Apr 1791 which stated that the king was acting as a free agent, and though he resigned after Varennes, he remained court adviser and perhaps a member of the *Comité autrichien*. Arrested following the *journée* of 10 Aug 1792, he was imprisoned in the Abbaye, where he fell victim to the Sept Massacres.

Moreau (J-Victor). 1763–1813. Leader of Rennes law students supporting the Breton parl in July 1788, then an ardent democrat, Moreau joined the Army of the North in 1791 and by Apr 1794 was a general. In 1795 he succeeded Pichegru as commander of the same army, and in 1796 commanded the Army of the Rhine-and-Moselle in which post he acquitted himself brilliantly. His ascent was checked by his friendship with the royalist Pichegru and he was recalled. But he returned to the fray in Italy in 1798 at first under Schérer then as commander. He refused the offer of involvement in the kind of military coup which Bonaparte was subsequently to organise. His military career was blighted and he was to die fighting for the Russians against Napoleon.

Moulin (J-Fs-Auguste), 1752–1810. An engineer in the Paris Intendance in 1789, M. served in the Paris Nat Guard before volunteering in 1791. He fought with distinction in the Vendée and in Nov 1793 was made a general. Imprisoned briefly by Carrier, his career recovered, and he served in a number of different postings. He commanded the occupying forces in Holland in late 1797 and in Jan 1799 was appointed commander of the Army of England. He was prevailed on to replace La Révellière-Lépeaux as Director following the Prairial coup in 1799; opposed Bonaparte; and was swiftly neutralised after Brumaire, though his military career continued.

Mounier (J-Jos), 1758–1806. A lawyer from Grenoble, son of a wealthy cloth merchant, M. was a key figure in the Pre-Rev in Dauphiné and came to Paris for the EG in 1789 with a nat reputation. A leading figure in the Summer crisis of 1789 (he proposed the Tennis Court Oath), his proposal that the new constitution should be bicameral was rejected by the Constit Ass. He resigned from the Ass. in protest at the *journées* of 5–6 Oct 1789, returned to Grenoble ostensibly to stir up opposition to the Ass., but in May 1790 he emigrated to Switzerland, only returning definitively to France in 1801, to become a prefect in 1802.

Murat (Joachim), 1767–1815. Son of an inn keeper from the Lot, M. had abandoned an ecclesiastical career for the army and in 1791 was a member of Louis XVI's Constitutional Guard. He subsequently served on the N front; seconded Bonaparte in putting down the Vendémiaire rising; then followed him to Italy for the campaigns of 1796–7. He also served in Egypt, returning to France to assist in the execution of the Brumaire coup. His brilliant military career continued under Napoleon.

Napoleon, see BONAPARTE

Narbonne or **Narbonne-Lara** (L-Marie-Jq-Amalric, comte de), 1755–1813. Brought up at court, N. was a career soldier with, apparently, a great future before him when the Rev broke out. He contrived to retain credit both at court and among the constitutional royalists and in Dec 1791 was appointed War Minister. He supported the drift towards war, but in Mar 1792 was dismissed by the king. He joined the Army of the North, but was outlawed in Aug 1792 and escaped to Switzerland, then Britain. He returned to France after Brumaire to serve as officer and diplomat.

Necker (Jq), 1732–1804. Genevan banker who had been a reformist Finance Minister from 1777 to 1781, N. had produced a theoretical state of national accounts, the *Compte-rendu au Roi* (1781) which purported to show the state's finances in rosy condition, despite France's involvement in the American War of Independence. He and his followers used this against Calonne and Brienne who maintained that the state was bankrupt, and it was not surprising that Brienne's dismissal in Sept 1788 was followed by N.'s appointment. His second spell of office was ineffective: he granted the doubling of the representation of the Third Estate in the EG, but failed to resolve the question of voting by head, which would be the cause of the political crisis of mid 1789, and his handling of the meeting of the EG was inept. Dismissed on 11 July 1789, he had already left for Switzerland when the fall of the Bastille forced Louis to recall him to popular acclaim. He was increasingly marginalised by the workings of the Constit Ass., however, and in Sept 1790 emigrated to Switzerland.

Neufchâteau, see FRANÇOIS

Ney (Michel), 1769–1815. Son of a cooper from Sarrelouis, N. worked as a clerk before joining the army in 1787. The Rev allowed his promotion: by 1794 he was captain, by 1799 full general. 'The bravest of the brave' (NAPOLEON), his most brilliant exploits were to be under Napoleon.

Noailles (L-Marie, vicomte de), 1756–1804. A career soldier who had fought in America with his brother-in-law Lafayette, N. was a member of the Ass. of Notables; was elected to the EG by the nobility of Nemours; rallied to the Third Estate; was prominent on the 'Night of 4 Aug'; and sat on the left. His contributions to the work of the Military Committee of the Constit Ass. were highly useful. He joined the Army of the North in 1791, but in mid 1792 emigrated to Britain then the USA, only returning to France in 1803.

Orléans (L-Ph-Jos, duc d'; from 15 Sept 1792 known as Philippe-Egalité), 1747–guill 6 Nov 1793. As duc de Chartres (until 1785), O. led a frivolous and debauched life. He became increasingly interested in politics and was a critic of the government at the Ass. of Notables in 1787 (which he attended as a Prince of the Blood) and in the Paris parl, for which he was temporarily exiled by *lettre de cachet*. He also criticised the government in the second Ass. of Notables in 1788, and became a leader and coordinator of the 'patriot party' and political impresario of the Palais-Royal, before being elected to the EG and later the Convtn. Perennially accused of aiming for a regency, and identified with the left, he voted for the king's death and 'revolutionised' his name. He was arrested for his links with Dumouriez, however, and executed.

Oudinot (Ch-Nic), 1767–1847. Son of a businessman from Bar-le-Duc, O. served in his local Nat Guard before volunteering. He fought courageously on the Rhine, 1792–4, and then later in the 1790s, and was made general in Apr 1799 when with the Army of Helvetia. His career prospered under Napoleon.

Ouvrard (Gabriel-Julien), 1770–1846. A financier who in 1789 was dealing in colonial goods in Nantes, O. survived the Terror and in 1797 became chief contractor for the Rpbc's armed forces. He amassed thereby a colossal fortune, to which he continued to add in subsequent regimes.

Pache (J-Nic), 1746–1823. P.'s father had been in the service of the marquis de Castries, and the young P. served as tutor to Castries's children before being procured a post in the naval bureaucracy, from which he advanced to become chief steward in the king's household in the early 1780s. Roland took on this industrious and competent functionary when he was Minister of the Interior. He also served Servan in the War Ministry before being himself appointed War Minister under Girondin pressure in Oct 1792. He became increasingly Montagnard in his sympathies, however, and it was the Girondins who caused his dismissal in Feb 1793. He had his own back, however, since he was elected mayor of Paris and played an important role in the *journées* of 31 May and 2 June. His political evolution continued and he only just avoided proscription as an Hébertist in early 1794, though he was dismissed in May as mayor. He was harassed after Thermidor, but retired from public life.

Paine (Th), 1737–1809. The English radical was well known in France for his defence of the American colonists during the 1770s and early 1780s and for his riposte to Burke, the *Rights of Man*. He was elected to the Convtn by the Pas-de-Calais. He was linked with the Girondins and although he did not speak French contributed to the king's trial, urging banishment rather than death. His popularity waned thereafter, and he was excluded from the Convtn in Jan 1794 and imprisoned. He returned briefly to the Convtn after Thermidor, but then retired to private life and eventually died in the USA.

Palm (Etta; baronne d'Aelders). A Dutch feminist living in Paris, Etta P. became notorious for supporting women's rights in the Cercle social and the *Bouche de fer*. When war broke out she organised collections for the front and founded the *Cercle patriotique des amies de la vérité*. She came under suspicion of being a Prussian secret agent in 1792, however, and emigrated.

Panis (Et-J), 1757–1833. A lawyer in the Paris parl, P. was the brother-in-law of the wealthy brewer Santerre and like him was a major figure among the Parisian *sans-culottes*. He was a key figure in the *journée* of 20 June 1792; was a member of the Commune insurrectionnelle; and was prominent on 10 Aug 1792 and in the Sept Massacres. He was elected to the Convtn where he was fiercely attacked by the Girondins. He was a member of the CGS down to Jan 1794 and contributed to the overthrow of Robespierre. He remained a Jacobin; was imprisoned for being implicated in the Prairial rising; and was amnestied in 1795. He subsequently entered Parisian hospital administration.

Paoli (Pascal), 1726–1807. The famous Corsican independence leader who had failed to prevent annexation by the French in 1768 had lived in Britain until 1789. The Nat Ass. welcomed him back to France and he became a dept administrator in Corsica. When war broke out, however, the British won him over and from Apr 1793 he fought against the Rpbc. Wishing to minimise the potential embarrassment he might cause, the British obliged him to live in exile in London.

Paré (Jules-Fs), 1755–1819. Danton had employed this carpenter's son as his clerk prior to the Rev and he used him again when he was Minister of Justice in autumn 1792. P. was promoted to Minister of the Interior in Aug 1793 but was manifestly not up to the job and, attacked from both the left and the right, resigned in Apr 1794. He subsequently served as a directorial commissary in the dept of the Seine and in military hospital administration.

Pâris (Ph-Nic-Marie de), 1763–suic 31 Jan 1793. Son of an architect, P. had served in the army under the AR. He seems to have formed the plan of assassinating one of the regicides in the Convtn and, lighting upon Lepeletier de Saint-Fargeau in an inn on 20 Jan 1793, murdered him. He committed suicide while at large.

Pastoret (Claude-Emmanuel-Jos-P), 1755–1840. A legal theorist who was a *maître des requêtes* from 1788, P. showed sufficient enthusiasm for the Rev to become the PGS of the dept of Paris. He was elected to the Leg Ass. by Paris, sat on the right and rallied to the monarchy. He was forced into hiding in the provinces but re-emerged after Thermidor to be elected to the C500 where he gained a reputation as a Clichyen. He fled deportation after Fructidor, taking refuge in Switzerland and Italy and only returning to France to pursue a political career after Brumaire.

Payan (Claude-Fs de), 1766–guill 28 July 1794. An artillery officer from the Dauphiné, P. renounced the army for politics and became a fervent Jacobin in Valence before coming to Paris in 1793 to a job in the CPS bureaucracy. He succeeded Chaumette as *procureur* of the Commune in March 1794, and worked to make the Commune a docile instrument of the committees of government. He fought for Robespierre at Thermidor and was executed the following day.

Périer (Claude), 1742–1801. A Dauphinois industrialist, P. placed his château at Vizille at the disposal of the Estates of Dauphiné during the Pre-Rev in that province. He moved to Paris at some time in the 1790s and made a fortune in financial operations under the Directory.

Périer (Jq-Constantin), 1742–1818. An engineer and industrialist best known for installing steam-driven pumps at Chaillot in Paris for water haulage, P. manufactured cannon for the war effort.

Perregaux (J-Frédéric), 1744–1808. A Swiss banker who made a fortune out of financial dealing in the early 1790s, P. was imprisoned then exiled under the Terror. In 1796 he formed with Récamier and Desprez the Caisse des comptes courants which made enormous loans to the government.

Pétiet (Claude-L), 1749–1806. Military administrator then Breton sub-delegate under the AR, P. was elected PGS of the Ille-et-Vilaine in 1790. From 1793 he contributed to administering the rpbcn war effort against the Vendéans. He was elected to the C Anciens, and became an effective War Minister in Feb 1796, losing his post for being too moderate. In 1799 he was elected to the C500, but under Napoleon pursued an administrative career.

Pétion or **Pétion de Villeneuve** (Jérôme), 1756–suic 20 June 1793. A lawyer from Chartres serving in 1789 as sub-delegate in the Orléanais, P. was elected to the EG. A supporter of negro emancipation, he was viewed as a member of the radical clique which included Buzot and Robespierre, and he was widely dubbed 'Pétion the Virtuous' to Robespierre's 'Incorruptible'. In 1791 he was entrusted with bringing the royal family back from Varennes, and was subsequently involved in the agitation which led to the Champ de Mars massacre. In Nov 1791, supported by the radicals as well as (for machiavellian reasons) the court, he was elected mayor of Paris, and as such contributed to the overthrow of the king. He was shocked by the Sept Massacres, however, and when he was elected (by the Eure-et-Loir) to the Convtn he rallied to the Girondins, and voted the *appel au peuple*. Discredited by the defection of Dumouriez as well as by his own political vanity, he fled arrest in June 1793, first to Brittany then to Guyenne and seems to have committed suicide when on the run.

Phélippeaux (Ant Le Picard de), 1768–99. Career soldier who had been Bonaparte's schoolboy rival, P. emigrated in 1791, fought with Condé's forces in 1792, then in 1796–7 and died fighting the French in the Middle East.

Philippeaux (P), 1756–guill 5 Apr 1794. A lawyer from Le Mans, P. was elected to the Convtn by the Sarthe. He voted the *appel au peuple*, but was more a Dantonist than a Girondin. Sent *en mission* to W France, his *colonnes mobiles* strategy for combatting the Vendéans, though approved by the CPS, went badly awry. At loggerheads with Rossignol and Ronsin and attacked back in Paris by the Hébertists, he was recalled and in Mar 1794 arrested as an accomplice of Danton.

Philippe-Egalité, see ORLÉANS

Pichegru (J-Ch), 1761–1804. Son of poor peasants from E France, P. had entered the army in 1783, though his background held him back from promotion. A democrat in the ranks once the Rev broke out, by Oct 1793 he was general in command of the Army of the Rhine. He worked with Hoche and the Army of the Moselle to drive the Allied forces out of Alsace, then in Feb 1794 was appointed to the Army of the North and contributed to the great successes of the summer campaign, pushing into Belgium and Holland. In 1795 he helped put down the Germinal rising. He became increasingly converted to royalism and entered into secret relations with the princes. Replaced by Moreau in his command, he retired temporarily from the army and was in 1797 elected to the C500. His political career was baulked by the Fructidor coup, which he escaped by fleeing to London. He worked with the *émigrés* thereafter and died after capture on a mission to France under Napoleon.

Pinel (Ph), 1745–1826. The famous doctor and pioneering psychiatrist had been working in Paris since 1778. As doctor attached to the Paris Hôpital Général he is usually credited with releasing the insane from their chains and instituting more humane treatment.

Pons 'de Verdun' (Ph-Laurent), 1759–1844. A lawyer and poet, P. was elected to the Convtn by the Meuse and sat with the Montagnards. He remained a staunch rpbcn after Thermidor in both the Convtn and the C500, but resumed his legal career under Napoleon.

Pons 'de l'Hérault' (André), 1772–1853. Originally from Sette in the Hérault, P. had abandoned an ecclesiastical career for the sea. He played a crucial role in the capture of Toulon in 1793, and was elected to the C500 in 1798 though his candidature was refused on grounds of age. He was to re-emerge into politics under Napoleon.

Portalis (J-Et-Marie), 1745–1807. Napoleon's minister of religion was a lawyer from a bourgeois family in Provence and spent much of the early 1790s in opposition or in hiding. He was elected to the C Anciens in 1795, but his Clichyen opinions made him flee to Switzerland to avoid arrest at Fructidor. He returned to Paris after Brumaire.

Poullain-Grandprey (Jos-Clément), 1744–1826. A magistrate at Mirecourt in 1789, P.-G. became PGS of the Vosges in 1790 before being elected to the Convtn. He reported to the Ass. on the contents of the *armoire de fer*. He was regarded as a moderate, and lay low for most of the Terror. After Thermidor, he was sent *en mission* to Lyon and the E to combat terrorists. In the C Anciens (until 1797), then the C500 (until 1799), he attacked royalists and approved the Fructidor coup, but became discontented with the evolution of the Directory and helped bring about the Prairial coup. He opposed Brumaire and returned to his legal career under Napoleon.

Précy (L-Fs Perrein, comte de), 1742–1820. A career soldier under the AR, P. was appointed one of the commanders of Louis XVI's Constitutional Guard in 1791. In 1792 he retired to his estates in Charolais, but came out of retirement to lead the Lyon rebels in 1793. He managed to take a small party of followers into Switzerland in Oct 1793 as Lyon fell to the rpbcn forces. By 1797 he was working as a royalist agent in France, but was arrested after Brumaire and imprisoned.

Priestley (Jos), 1733–1804. The famous English chemist, discoverer of oxygen, was best known in France for his vigorous defence of the Rev against Burke. On 14 July 1791 his house in Birmingham was wrecked by a 'Church and King' mob. He was accorded honorary French citizenship in Aug 1792 and two depts elected him to the Convtn, though he declined to sit. In 1794 he emigrated to the USA.

Prieur 'de la Côte-d'Or' or **Prieur-Duvernois** (Claude-Ant), 1763–1832. Son of a Burgundian tax official, P. was an officer in the engineers in 1789. The Côte-d'Or elected him to the Leg Ass. and Convtn, where he became noted for his staunch republicanism and administrative competence. He was elected to the CPS in Aug 1793, and specialised in military affairs, which necessitated frequent absences from Paris *en mission*. His part in the 'organisation of victory' meant that he, like Carnot, avoided proscription after Thermidor. He was elected to the C500, but in 1798 returned to the army and subsequently became a wallpaper manufacturer.

Prieur 'de la Marne' (P-L), 1756–1827. A lawyer from Châlons-sur-Marne, P. was elected to the EG where he sat on the left. He showed competence in calming the W depts following the flight to Varennes. After service as PGS of the Marne, he was elected to the Convtn, where he was appointed to the CGD and sent *en mission* to the armies and to Brittany. On 10 July 1793 he was elected to the CPS and spent most of the Terror *en mission*. Compromised in the *journées* of Germinal and Prairial, he went into hiding and only re-emerged at Brumaire, when he returned to his legal career.

Proli or **Proly** (P-J-Berthold), 1752–guill 24 Mar 1794. P. was often alleged to be the illegitimate son of Maria Theresa's minister, Kaunitz. He spent most of the 1780s living in Paris in extravagant fashion, but by 1791 was running a radical newspaper (*Le Cosmopolite*) and posing as a left-winger. His mission in 1793 to stop Dumouriez from defecting failed in circumstances which cast a shadow over his loyalty to the regime. He then began to set up a network of militants in the Paris sections, fell under suspicion as a foreign spy and was arrested with Hébert and executed.

Provence (comte de), see LOUIS XVIII

Prudhomme (L-Marie), 1752–1830. A journalist originally from Lyon, P. was responsible for a great deal of polemical pamphlet literature in Paris during the Pre-Rev, and in July 1789 began to publish the radical weekly, the *Révolutions de Paris*. The journal ended in early 1794, when Prudhomme was imprisoned. Under the Directory he became a printer-bookseller.

Puisaye (Jos-Geneviève, comte de), 1754–1827. A *hobereau* from Normandy, P. was a soldier under the AR and was elected by the nobility of the Perche to the EG. He rejoined the army in 1791 and rallied to the Federalist revolt in Normandy in 1793. After the 'battle' of Pacy-sur-Eure, he passed into Brittany then organised an extensive network of peasant rebels, the Chouans, and entered into contact with London and the princes. From Sept 1794 he was in London and organised the fateful Quiberon Bay expedition in 1795. Much of his credit was lost by the failure at Quiberon, but he managed to reconstitute his Chouan network. His links with the princes and with the British government were less strong, however, and he eventually retired, emigrating to Canada, then to Britain.

Puységur (L-P de Chastenet, comte de), 1726–1807. An illustrious career soldier under the AR, P. was appointed War Minister in Nov 1788. He was dismissed on 12 July 1789, but remained loyal to the king and personally defended the royal family on 10 Aug 1792. He then emigrated, only returning to France under Napoleon.

Quinette (Nic-Marie), 1762–1821. A notary from Soissons, Q. was elected to the Leg Ass. and Convtn by the Aisne. A staunch rpbcn, he was sent *en mission* to the armies before being elected to the CGD. However, he was handed over to the Austrians in Apr 1793 by Dumouriez on his defection, and only returned to France in Dec 1795. He sat in the C500 from 1795 to 1797 and was appointed Minister of the Interior in the last months of the Directory. He became a prefect under Napoleon.

Rabaut-Pommier (Jq-Ant), 1744–1820. A Protestant pastor from Montpellier, R.-P. was elected to the Convtn by the Gard and tended to be pro-Girondin. He fled arrest in June 1793, but was captured and imprisoned in Dec 1793. Released after Thermidor he sat in the Convtn before being elected to the C Anciens, on which he served down to 1798. He became a pastor again under Napoleon.

Rabaut Saint-Etienne (J-Paul), 1743–guill 5 Dec 1793. A Protestant pastor in Languedoc like his brother, R. S.-E. was elected to the EG after having played a role in negotiating the Edict of Toleration of 1787. A constitutional royalist, he remained in Paris after 1791 and wrote for the *Moniteur* and the *Feuille villageoise*. Elected to the Convtn by the Aube, he accepted the Rpbc, but voted for the *appel au peuple*. A member of the Commission of Twelve, and widely identified as a Girondin, he fled arrest on 2 June 1793, but was discovered and executed.

Ramel (J-P), 1760–guill 2 Apr 1794. Originally from Cahors, R. was a lawyer in Toulouse in the late 1780s. He sat in the prov ass. of Quercy; became PGS of the Lot; and was elected to the Leg Ass., where he proved a moderate. He joined the Army of the E Pyrenees in 1792, but despite some successes fell foul of Jean Bon Saint-André, was suspended from his functions in Dec 1793 and later executed.

Ramel or **Ramel-Nogaret** (Dominique-Vincent), 1760–1829. A lawyer from Carcassonne, R. was elected to the EG and was prominent in discussion of financial affairs in the Constit Ass. He represented the Aude in the Convtn, in which he voted the *appel au peuple* and was a key member of the Finance Committee. Elected to the C500, in Feb 1796 he was appointed Finance Minister. During his ministry down to July 1799, paper currency was withdrawn and the 'bankruptcy of the two-thirds' stabilised government finance. He returned to private life in 1799.

Raynal (Guillaume-Thomas-Fs, abbé), 1713–96. *Philosophe* best known for his radical *Histoire des Deux Indes* (1770), R. had become rather conservative by the 1790s and lay low.

Réal (P-Fs), 1757–1834. Attorney at the Châtelet in 1789, R. joined the Jacobins and became linked with Danton and Desmoulins. A moderate, he was none the less respected both in the Jacobins and the Commune. He was temporarily imprisoned after the fall of Danton, and on his release pursued a legal and administrative career. He helped plan the Brumaire coup.

Rebecque, see CONSTANT

Rebecqui (Fs-Trophime), 1760–suic 1 May 1794. Active in the Pre-Rev and then in local politics in Provence, R. represented the Bouches-du-Rhône in the Convtn. He was closely associated with Barbaroux and through him with the Girondins, and voted for the *appel au peuple*. He fled Paris in early June 1793 and tried to organise the Federalist revolt in the S, but in despair eventually threw himself into the sea and drowned.

Reinhard (Ch-Frédéric), 1761–1837. Son of a Protestant pastor from Württemburg, R. was working as a private tutor in Bordeaux in 1789 and became friendly with the future Girondins, who in 1792 secured him a diplomatic post in London. He later served in Naples (1793), Germany (1795) and Italy (1798–9), before being appointed Foreign Minister in the last months of the Directory. He returned to diplomatic service under Napoleon.

Renault (Aimée-Cécile), 1774–guill 1794. Daughter of a Parisian paper-worker, Cécile R. tried to assassinate Robespierre in May 1794.

Rétif or **Restif de la Bretonne** (Nic-Edme), 1734–1806. This prolific and colourful author, the 'Rousseau des Halles' was a shrewd observer of the Rev in Paris. The Convtn granted him a pension of 2,000 liv in 1795.

Reubell or **Rewbell** (J-Fs), 1747–1807. A diligent lawyer from Alsace, R. was elected to the EG where he gained a reputation as a radical reformer. PGS of the Haut-Rhin in 1791, he represented the same dept in the Convtn and though still radical was not associated with any party, and was usually away *en mission*, inc a spell in besieged Mainz. After Thermidor, he served on the CGS and CPS and was elected to the C500. He became a Director in 1795 and specialised in foreign affairs, in which he proved a fervent 'annexationist', esp as regards the left bank of the Rhine. He returned to the C Anciens in May 1799, but then retired to private life after Brumaire.

Réveillon. A wealthy industrialist, the owner of a wallpaper factory in the Faubourg Saint-Antoine in Paris which employed 300 workers. His intemperate talk about wage cuts in Apr 1789 triggered off the 'Réveillon riots'.

Rewbell, see REUBELL

Richelieu (Armand-Emmanuel-Sophie-Septimanie Vignerot du Plessis, duc de), 1766–1822. A court noble under the AR, R. emigrated in 1789 and fought for Russia against the Turks in 1790. In 1791–2 he acted as a royalist secret agent in central Europe, and in 1793 fought with the *émigrés* against the Rpbc.

Rivarol (Ant), 1753–1801. This well-known author became a royalist journalist in the Rev and from 1790 contributed to the *Actes des apôtres*. In June 1792 he emigrated.

Robert (P-Fs-Jos), 1762–1826. Originally a lawyer, R. became prominent in the Cordeliers Club, and played an important part in events leading to the massacre of the Champ de Mars. He was a member of the Commune insurrectionnelle and served as Danton's secretary in the Ministry of Justice in Aug 1792. Elected by Paris to the Convtn, he sat on the left, though his reputation as a hoarder led to his house being pillaged on 27 Sept 1793. He abandoned politics for trade in 1795.

Robert (Louise-Félicité Guinement Kéralio, Madame), 1758–1821. Wife of the above, Madame R. was a prolific woman of letters in her own right, and became involved in Parisian radical politics and journalism alongside her husband.

Robespierre 'le jeune' (Augustin-Bon-Jos [de]), 1764–guill 28 July 1794. Augustin R.'s career was undoubtedly furthered by his brother's reputation. He represented Paris in the Convtn where he attacked the Girondins and fulfilled an important spell *en mission* in S France and on the Italian front from July 1793 to Jan, then Feb–June 1794. He associated himself with his brother's fate on 9 Thermidor and was guillotined the following day.

Robespierre (Maximilien-Fs-Isidore [de]), 1758–guill 28 July 1794. Son of a lawyer, Maximilian R. was a scholarship boy at the Collège Louis-le-Grand in Paris (where he got to know Desmoulins) before returning to become a lawyer in his native Arras. Elected to the EG, he became notorious for his pro-Jacobin, democratic views. During the session of the Leg Ass., he built up his support in the Paris Commune and dabbled in rev journalism. A member of the Commune insurrectionnelle in Aug 1792, he was elected to the Convtn in triumph by Paris. He urged the execution of the king and soon fell out with the Girondins, with whom he was in open conflict by May–June 1793 and supported their expulsion. He was elected to the CPS in July 1793. Though his name was often linked with Saint-Just and Couthon, he played a general role in determining policy and presenting it in the Convtn. Hostile to the dechristianising movement, he spoke in favour of religious toleration late 1793–early 1794 and instituted the Cult of the Supreme Being. His fears that the Rev might be subverted by a 'foreign plot' led to him accepting the purge of the Hébertists and the Dantonists, and he was also closely linked with the hated Law of 22 Prairial which speeded up the procedure of the Rev Tribunal. It is uncertain how he saw the Rev developing by July 1794, but his apparent desire for a further purge brought his enemies together in the successful coup of 9 Thermidor.

Rochambeau (Donatien-Marie-Jos de Vimeur, vicomte de), 1750–1813. A career soldier like his father the comte, R. put down the slave revolt in Saint-Domingue in 1792–3 with great ferocity. He also fought against the British in the Caribbean in the 1790s.

Rochambeau (J-B-Donatien de Vimeur, comte de), 1725–1807. A career soldier who was one of the French heroes of the American War of Independence, R. was identified with the reform movement during the Pre-Rev, in the Orléans prov ass. and in the Ass. of Notables. He was placed in command of the Army of the North in 1791. In 1792 he quarrelled with Dumouriez and resigned. He was arrested under the Terror but subsequently released.

Roederer (P-L), 1754–1835. A *parlementaire* from Metz, R. was a *suppléant* to the EG and joined the Constit Ass. in Oct 1789. Solid and dependable, he assisted in tax reforms and also worked as a journalist. PGS of the dept of Paris in 1791, he won enemies for defending Louis XVI on the *journée* of 10 Aug 1792. He went into hiding when the Girondins were proscribed, but reappeared after Thermidor. He was elected to the Institut and also contributed to the *Journal d'économie publique, de morale et de politique*. He was to prove an ardent supporter of the Brumaire coup.

Roland de la Platière (J-Marie), 1734–suic 15 Nov 1793. A royal factory inspector in Lyon in 1789, R. was sent by Lyon manufacturers to lobby for them in Paris in 1791. He and his wife there strengthened links with the Amis des Noirs, Brissot, Pétion, Buzot, etc. In March 1792 he was made Minister of the Interior and though dismissed on 13 June he was popular enough to be reinstated following the *journée* of 10 Aug. He was shocked by the Sept Massacres, which distanced him from the Montagnards in the Convtn. His inept handling of the *armoire de fer* issue attracted much hostility, as did his pro-Girondin attitude over the king's trial. He resigned as minister on 23 Jan 1793. He escaped proscription in June 1793 by fleeing from Paris, but committed suicide when he heard of his wife's execution.

Roland (Marie-Jeanne or Manon Phlipon, Madame), 1754–guill 9 Nov 1793. Daughter of a Parisian engraver, wife of Roland de la Platière since 1780, this ambitious woman used her salon as a coordinating centre for the Girondin faction. She was arrested following the *journées* of 31 May and 2 June 1793 and guillotined while her husband was still on the run.

Romme (Ch-Gilbert), 1750–suic 17 June 1796. Tutor to Count Stroganoff in Russia in the late 1780s, Gilbert R. was elected to the Leg Ass. and Convtn by his native Puy-de-Dôme. *En mission* with Prieur de la Côte-d'Or in Normandy in Apr 1793, he was imprisoned for two months by the Federalist rebels. He returned to Paris, was a keen educational reformer, and was prominent among those supporting the introduction of the Rev Calendar. A Jacobin even after Thermidor, he was implicated in the Prairial rising, condemned to death and, committing suicide on the way to the scaffold became one of the so-called 'martyrs of Prairial'.

Ronsin (Ch-Ph), 1751–guill 24 Mar 1794. Of peasant stock, R. was a failed dramatist who made a name for himself as a speaker in the clubs. An officer in the Paris Nat Guard from 1789, and from 1793 a major figure in the 'sansculottised' Ministry of War under Bouchotte, he was sent to W France and was an acerbic critic of the generals combating the Vendéans. He was recalled to Paris in Dec 1793, however, and imprisoned. Though released in Feb 1794, he urged a popular insurrection against the committees of government, and was consequently arrested and executed with the Hébertists.

Rossignol (J-Ant), 1759–dep 1802. A jewellery-worker in Paris, R. was prominent in street action in the *journées* of 14 July 1789 and 20 June and 10 Aug 1792. Sent to W France with Ronsin, he was responsible for Westermann's dismissal. Appointed commander of the Army of the Coasts of La Rochelle, he was recalled but then reinstated after pressure from the Paris Commune. Imprisoned after Thermidor, he was amnestied in 1795; compromised in the Babeuf plot and temporarily imprisoned; and involved in the *machine infernale* attack against Napoleon in 1800 and deported.

Roucher (J-Ant), 1745–guill 27 July 1794. Poet and precursor of romanticism, R. welcomed the Rev in 1789, but soon shrank from what he saw as its excesses. He was arrested in Oct 1793 and executed two days before Thermidor.

Rouget de l'Isle (Claude-Jos), 1760–1836. This soldier-musician is best known as the composer (in ?Apr 1792) of the 'Marseillaise'. He was imprisoned as a suspect during the Terror; rejoined the army after Thermidor; and then became a member of the entourage of Tallien.

'Rousselin' (sobriquet of Alexandre-Ch-Omer Rousselin de Corbeau, comte de SAINT-ALBIN), 1773–1847. Scion of an ancient noble family from Dauphiné, R. was a student when the Rev broke out, and became an enthusiastic rev and an associate of Desmoulins. When only 20 years old, the CPS sent him as civil commissary to Troyes, but he was soon hauled before the Rev Tribunal as a Dantonist. He was saved by the Thermidor coup, and became an influential bureaucrat under the Directory.

Roux (Jq), 1752–suic 10 Feb 1794. Parish priest in the Saintonge under the AR, Jacques R. came to Paris in 1790; was elected *vicaire* in the parish of Saint-Nicolas-des-Champs; and became a militant in the Cordeliers Club and in the Gravilliers section, urging more radical economic policies on the government. He became a member of the Commune; was involved in the *journées* of 25 Feb, 31 May and 2 June 1793; on 25 June 1793 headed a delegation at the bar of the

Convtn on this question; and influenced the *journée* of 5 Sept, though in fact he was imprisoned on the same day. He gave way to despair in his cell and committed suicide.

Roux de Fazillac (P), 1746–1833. A high-ranking army officer who welcomed the Rev, R. de F. represented the Dordogne in the Leg Ass. and Convtn and became a violent critic of the Girondins. He was often *en mission* from the Convtn. Under the Directory he served as directorial commissary in the Dordogne, then retired after Brumaire.

Rovère (Jos-Stanislas-Fs-Xavier, marquis de), 1748–dep 1798. From a *hobereau* background – though he claimed under the Terror to be the son of an artisan – R. had a disreputable military career under the AR but came to the fore in the annexation to France of his native Comtat Venaissin. Elected to the Convtn by the Bouches-du-Rhône, he served *en mission* in Lyon in Feb, and in the Vaucluse from June to Nov 1793. On 9 Thermidor he led the anti-Robespierrist forces alongside Barras, and became a violent anti-Jacobin in the Thermidorian Convtn. In Oct 1795 he was arrested as a crypto-royalist, but he was released and elected to the C Anciens. He was deported at Fructidor, and died in Guiana.

Royer (J-B), 1733–1807. Son of a doctor, R. was a *curé* in 1789 and was elected to the EG as a *suppléant*, serving from March 1790. He accepted the Civ Constn and was elected bishop of the Ain, which he went on to represent in the Convtn. Proscribed for protesting against the expulsion of the Girondins, he was released after Thermidor; sat again in the Convtn and then, until 1798, in the C500; and, as newly elected bishop of the Seine, helped Grégoire regroup the constitutional clergy. He retired from his bishopric at the Concordat.

Royer-Collard (P-Paul), 1763–1845. A sectional politician in Paris in the early 1790s, the lawyer R.-C. was a notorious moderate and went into hiding after the *journée* of 31 May 1793. In 1797 he was elected by the Marne to the C500, but he was expelled at Fructidor and became an ardent counter-rev plotter. He followed a teaching career under Napoleon, re-entering politics in 1815.

Royou (Jq-Corentin), 1745–1828. A lawyer from Quimper, 'the monarchy's Marat' (DANTON) R. produced, with his brother (see below) the notoriously ultra-royalist *Ami du Roi*. His journalism continued after his brother's death, but in the late 1790s he returned to legal practice.

Royou (Th-Maurice, abbé), 1741–94. R. was an ecclesiastic in his native Brittany before, in the late 1770s, turning to journalism. A counter-rev from 1789, he founded the royalist journal, the *Ami du Roi* with his brother in June 1790. Threatened with arrest in 1794, he went into hiding, became ill and died.

Rühl (Ph-Jq), 1737–suic 30 May 1795. A Lutheran minister in Strasbourg under the AR, R. served in the administration of the Bas-Rhin before being elected to the Leg Ass. and the Convtn. An avowed Montagnard, he served *en mission* in the E as well as on the CGS. He retired from active politics after Thermidor on grounds of age, but was implicated in the Prairial rising and committed suicide in his cell on the eve of his trial, thus becoming a 'martyr of Prairial'.

Sade (Donatien-Alphonse-Fs comte de; known as marquis de), 1740–1814. The infamous S. had spent much of his adult life under the AR in prison for his scandalous life and writings. In the Bastille until just before 14 July 1789, he was freed as a *lettre de cachet* victim. He became active in sectional politics in Paris, even becoming president of the Section des Piques, but was arrested as a moderate in Dec 1793. Released after Thermidor, he began publishing again. After Brumaire, Napoleon had him confined for good.

Saint-Albin, see ROUSSELIN

Saint-André (André Jean Bon), 1749–1813. A Protestant pastor from Montauban, Jean Bon St-A. was elected to the Convtn by the Lot. A Montagnard, his forceful views were widely respected. He supported the purge of the Girondins and entered the CPS in June 1793. At first *en mission* with the armies, he came to specialise in all matters concerning the navy. He was stationed in Brest from Sept 1793 until Jan 1794, and later participated in naval skirmishes with the British in May–June 1794. He was sent *en mission* to the coastal departments of the S between July 1794 and Mar 1795, and though arrested as a terrorist shortly afterwards was soon amnestied. The Directory sent him as consul to Smyrna, but he was imprisoned when he got there and only released under the Consulate. Napoleon made him a prefect.

Saint-Cyr, see GOUVION SAINT-CYR

Saint-Huruge (Victor-Amédée de la Fage, marquis de), 1750–1810. A rather disreputable and down-at-heel nobleman who made a career in the Rev as a street figure and popular militant, St -H. was arrested in 1794 as a Dantonist, but was released after Thermidor and became a leader of the *jeunesse dorée* before passing into obscurity.

Saint-Just (L-Ant-Léon), 1767–guill 28 July 1794. Son of a cavalry officer, St-J. was too young in 1789 to have made much of a career for himself. Austere and fanatical, he became linked with Robespierre even before being elected to the Convtn by the Aisne. He made a startling political début in his speeches during the king's trial, and went on to help draft the 1793 Constitution and attack the Girondins. Elected a member of the CPS on 30 May 1793, he was closely linked with Robespierre and Couthon, but was away *en mission* for much of the Terror: from Oct 1793 until Jan 1794 in Alsace accompanied by Lebas, then with the Army of the North on several occasions in 1794. He attacked both Dantonists and Hébertists in the Spring of 1794; personally sponsored the Laws of Ventôse; and on 9 Thermidor supported Robespierre and was executed along with him.

Saint-Priest (Fs-Emmanuel Guignard, comte de), 1735–1821. A soldier and diplomat under the AR, St -P. entered the king's council in Dec 1788 as Minister without Portfolio. He was dismissed on 12 July 1789 but recalled alongside Necker after the fall of the Bastille and placed in charge of the Royal Household (from Aug 1790 the Interior). A royalist with a reputation for favouring hard-line policies, he resigned in Dec 1790 and emigrated, but remained active as an agent of the king in the courts of Europe. In 1795 he became chief minister of Louis XVIII at Verona and followed his master to Blankenburg.

Saladin (J-B-Michel), 1752–1812. A lawyer from Amiens, S. represented the Somme in the Leg Ass. and Convtn. A Jacobin and Montagnard, he was, however, a moderate and protested at the proscription of the Girondins, for which he was arrested. Freed after Thermidor, he returned to the Convtn. He thereupon became a specialist in denouncing terrorists and was sent *en mission* to E France to clear up any remnants of Jacobinism. He opposed the Law of Two-Thirds, but was elected to the C500 where he was a noted Clichyen. At Fructidor, he went into hiding, only re-emerging in 1799.

Saliceti (Ant-Christophe), 1757–1809. An Italian lawyer who was elected to the EG by Corsica, S. sat on the left. He was PGS in Corsica in 1791 before representing the island in the Convtn. He served *en mission* in Corsica and Italy in 1793–4. Arrested as a terrorist in 1795, he was amnestied and from 1796 operated as a commissary of the Directory attached to the Army of Italy, where he worked alongside his fellow Corsican, Bonaparte. In 1797 he was elected to the C500, where he supported neo-Jacobin policies. He was used by Bonaparte after Brumaire.

Salles or **Salle** (J-B), 1760–exctd 20 June 1794. A doctor in Lorraine in 1789, S. represented Nancy in the EG where he proved a moderate. Elected to the Convtn by the Meurthe, it was he who proposed the idea of the *appel au peuple* during the king's trial. Inevitably, he was proscribed after 2 June 1793. He fled arrest but was soon captured and executed.

Sanson. Dynasty of executioners since the early seventeenth century. Ch-Henri was responsible for the execution of Louis XVI and died shortly afterwards, repentant it was said. He was succeeded by his son Henri who presided over the remainder of the Terror and beyond.

Santerre (Ant-Jos), 1752–1809. A wealthy and paternalistic brewer from the Faubourg Saint-Antoine, S. was an elector in Paris in 1789, participated in the seizure of the Bastille and became a sectional commander of the Nat Guard. He helped organise the *journées* of 20 June and 10 Aug 1792. Influence through the Paris Commune won him the rank of general by July 1793 and he was sent to the Vendée to command a force of Parisian volunteers. He was not a military success, however, and was recalled by the CPS in Apr 1794 and arrested. Released after Thermidor, he returned to private life.

Scellier (Gabriel-Toussaint), 1756–guill 1795. A lawyer from Noyon, S. found promotion in the courts of Compiègne and Paris before being appointed judge, then (after the Law of 22 Prairial) vice-president of the Rev Tribunal. He was sent to the guillotine after Thermidor with Fouquier-Tinville.

Schérer (Barthélemy-L-Jos), 1747–1804. From a middle-class family in E France, S. had served in the Austrian army before being transferred to the French army in which he achieved the rank of captain in 1785. A general in 1794, he was extremely active on the N and E fronts in the same year. He was subsequently transferred to the Army of the Alps, then promoted commander of the Army of the E Pyrenees (May 1795), then of the Army of Italy (Sept 1795). Lack of political backing for his military successes in Italy led him to resign, but he was soon back in harness, with the Army of the Interior, then of the Rhine. On 23 July 1797 he was appointed War Minister, but he soon resigned and went to fight in Italy. Things went badly, however, and he resigned, retiring to private life.

Schneider (J-Georges, or 'Euloge'), 1756–guill 10 Apr 1794. Distinguished German priest, savant and freemason who in 1789 was official preacher in the court of the duke of Württemberg, S. became a fanatical rev almost overnight, the 'Marat of Strasbourg'. In Feb 1793, he was appointed public prosecutor in the criminal court of the Bas-Rhin. He undertook a far-ranging proscription of political dissidents; renounced his orders; and married. Saint-Just and Lebas, *en mission* in Alsace, brought him to heel and sent him to certain execution in the Rev Tribunal in Paris.

Ségur (L-Ph, comte de), 1753–1830. Soldier and diplomat under the AR, S. supported the Rev and in 1791 was sent to Berlin to try to wrest Prussia away from alliance with Austria. He failed and, as the Rev became more extreme, he withdrew to private life, only re-entering public life after Brumaire, and becoming Napoleon's master of ceremonies.

Ségur (Ph-Henri, marquis de), 1724–1801. After a distinguished military career, S. served as War Minister from 1780 to 1787. He was responsible for a number of reforms, the most notorious of which was the so-called Ségur Ordinance of 1781 which restricted high posts in the army to nobles of ancient lineage. He took no part in the Rev.

Sergent or **Sergent-Marceau** (Ant-Fs), 1751–1847. From a humble background, S. made his name with his popular engravings. A sectional militant and Jacobin, he played a part in organising the Sept Massacres and was elected to the Convtn by Paris. A Montagnard, he was most involved in committee work concerning works of art. He fled at Prairial; was amnestied in 1795; became military hospitals inspector; but then emigrated under Napoleon.

Sérurier (J-Mathieu-Philibert), 1742–1819. A long-serving career soldier, the Rev brought S. promotion. He served in the Army of the Var in 1792–3 and was a general by June 1795. He fought in Italy throughout the late 1790s and helped Bonaparte in the Brumaire coup. Under Napoleon he was to be governor of the Invalides.

Servan or **Servan de Gerbey** (Jos), 1741–1808. An army officer who had contributed articles on military science to the *Encyclopédie*, S. hitched his career to the Girondins, and thanks to their influence served as War Minister from Mar 1792. Dismissed in June, he was reinstated following the *journée* of 10 Aug. He resigned in Oct and was in May 1793 appointed commander of the Army of the W Pyrenees. He was dismissed and imprisoned following the fall of the Girondins but was released after Thermidor and entered the military bureaucracy.

Sèze (Raymond, comte de), 1748–1828. The scion of an ancient noble family from Guyenne, S. was a well-known lawyer in Paris in 1789. He acceded to Louis XVI's request that he serve as his defence counsel, for which he suffered imprisonment during the Terror.

Sicard (Roch-Ambroise Cucurron, abbé), 1742–1822. Founder and director of the institution for deaf mutes in Bordeaux, S. was called to Paris in 1789 to take over the similar institution founded by the abbé de l'Epée. He was imprisoned in 1792 but was later released and held a number of educational and academic posts under the Directory and Empire.

Siéyès (Emmanuel-Jos, abbé), 1748–1836. Ecclesiastic *malgré lui* under the AR, with a good position in the church bureaucracy, S. was a member of the prov ass. of the Orléanais in 1787. In 1788–9, he wrote the famous pamphlets *Essai sur les privilèges* and *Qu'est-ce que le tiers état?* and worked with the Orleanist patriot party. He represented the Third Estate of Paris in the EG, and was soon prominent: he urged the union of the orders; composed the Tennis Court Oath; and contributed to the Declaration of the Rights of Man. He was an active committeeman in the Constit Ass., notably in matters concerning administrative reorganisation. Elected to the Convtn, this 'monk of the Revolution' (ROBESPIERRE) voted for the king's death, but generally lay low. He came more out of his shell after Thermidor and served on the CPS and concerned himself with constitutional and diplomatic questions. He was elected to the C500; chosen as ambassador in Berlin in 1798; was elected Director in 1799; and plotted the Brumaire coup with Bonaparte, becoming a member of the provisional consulate down to Dec 1799.

Sijas (Prosper), 1759–guill 29 July 1794. Chief functionary in the Ministry of War under Bouchotte and a faithful supporter of Robespierre, S. was guillotined after Thermidor.

Sillery (Ch-Alexis-P Brulat, comte de Genlis, marquis de), 1737–guill 31 Oct 1793. A career soldier, he married Mlle de Saint-Aubin (who was to keep her title the comtesse de Genlis) in 1780. Elected by the nobility of Champagne to the EG, S. was quick to rally to the Third Estate and was viewed as an Orleanist.

He represented the Somme in the Convtn, where he voted the *appel au peuple*. He was arrested because of his links with Dumouriez and Orléans, but was executed alongside the Girondins with whom he had no political link whatever.

Simon or **Simond** (Philibert), 1755–guill 13 Apr 1794. A Savoyard priest who became vicar-general of the Bas-Rhin in 1790, S. made his name as a radical in Strasbourg politics before being elected to the Convtn. Linked with the Allobroges, he was sent *en mission* to organise the dept administration in the newly annexed Mont-Blanc; participated in the *journée* of 31 May 1793; and was a radical rep *en mission* in the Alps in late 1793. But he was viewed as a Dantonist, and was arrested in early 1794 and executed alongside Gobel, Chaumette and others.

Simonneau or **Simoneau**, ?–assass 3 Mar 1792. Mayor of Etampes in 1792, S. refused to respond to popular pressure by fixing bread prices and was assassinated by a rioting crowd. On the initiative of the Feuillants, the Leg Ass. held a funeral service in his honour.

Sotin de la Coindière (P-J-Marie), 1764–1810. A lawyer in Nantes, S. was sent to Paris with more than 100 of his compatriots under the Terror to be tried for rev offences by the Rev Tribunal. He was acquitted, stayed in Paris and became a commissary in the Seine dept. Merlin de Douai had him appointed Police Minister in July 1797, and he played a crucial part in the success of the Fructidor coup. In Feb 1798 he resigned and became a diplomat.

Soubrany (P-Amable de), 1750–suic 17 June 1795. A rich cavalry officer under the AR, S. served as mayor of his native Riom before being elected by the Puy-de-Dôme to the Leg Ass. and Convtn. He was often *en mission* under the Terror, esp with the armies. Involved in the Prairial rising, he committed suicide on the way to the scaffold, thus becoming one of the 'martyrs of Prairial'.

Soulavie (J-L Giraud-), 1752–1813. Priest and would-be man of letters, S. was vicar-general of Châlons in 1789. He welcomed the Civ Constn and in 1792 married. Linked with Chabot, Bazire and Collot-d'Herbois, he was sent to Geneva in May 1793 as acting consul. Imprisoned after Thermidor as a terrorist, he was amnestied whereupon he returned to literature.

Soult (Nic-Jean de Dieu), 1769–1851. Son of a Languedoc notary, S. was only a corporal in the army in 1789, but he was soon promoted once war broke out. He served with the Army of the Moselle from 1793 to 1794; with the Sambre-and-Meuse from 1794; and on the Rhine from 1797. He became a general in Mar 1799 and played a crucial part with the Army of Helvetia in the battle of Zurich.

Staël (Madame de, sobriquet of Anne-Louise-Germaine Necker, baronne de STAEL-HOLSTEIN), 1766–1817. Daughter of Jq Necker, she married Staël, the Swedish ambassador in Paris, in 1786. Originally pro-Rev, she emigrated in the Autumn of 1792, but returned after Thermidor and, along with Benjamin

Constant, began to organise the Cercle constitutionnel, which combated the Clichyens and tried to influence the Directors. Supporter of a liberal regime, she opposed Bonaparte.

Stofflet (Nic), 1752–exctd 24 Feb 1796. Son of a miller from Lunéville, S. was working as a gamekeeper in Anjou in 1789. From 1793 he was leader of the Anjou rebels and linked with the Vendéans under Cathelineau to fight the battle of Cholet. He took command of all the rebel forces on the death in Mar 1793 of La Rochejaquelein. He negotiated an armistice with the Rpbc in May 1795, but by early 1796 had resumed hostilities. Ambushed, perhaps treacherously, he was captured and shot.

Suard (J-B-Ant), 1733–1817. Friend of the *philosophes*, member since 1784 of the Académie française and tolerant theatre censor from 1774 till 1790, S. engaged in counter-rev pamphleteering at the beginning of the Rev, but was soon lying low. He returned to royalist journalism after Thermidor but was exiled to Switzerland, only returning to France in 1799.

Taillefer (J-Guillaume), 1764–1835. A doctor, T. represented the Dordogne in the Leg Ass. and the Convtn. An energetic Montagnard, he served *en mission* in the SW in the Autumn of 1793; and remained a Jacobin after Thermidor. He served as a bureaucrat in the late 1790s and returned to his medical practice after Brumaire.

Talleyrand or **Talleyrand-Périgord** (Ch-Maurice de), 1754–1838. Licentious ecclesiastic who had served as *agent général* of the clergy from 1780, T. was appointed bishop of Autun in Oct 1788. He was elected to the EG, rallied to the Third Estate and was a positive reformer in the spheres of finance, education and religion. He celebrated mass at the Fête de la Fédération in 1790, but renounced his bishopric at the promulgation of the Civ Constn. Briefly ambassador in Britain in 1792, he was forced into exile following the overthrow of the king. He returned in Sept 1795, and largely through the influence of the Cercle constitutionnel was appointed Foreign Minister in 1797. Cynical (he acquiesced in the independent policy-making of Bonaparte) and largely successful, he resigned in the last months of the Directory and rallied to Bonaparte.

Tallien (J-Lambert), 1767–1820. An ambitious clerk who won notoriety as a promoter of fraternal societies and as a radical journalist on his *Ami du citoyen*, T. was a member of the Commune insurrectionnelle and was prominent on the *journée* of 10 Aug 1792 and in the Sept Massacres. Elected to the Convtn by the Seine-et-Oise, he attacked Louis XVI and the Girondins with great ferocity. He participated in the *journée* of 31 May 1793 and in Aug was sent (with Ysabeau) *en mission* against federalism in the SW. They entered Bordeaux on 19 Oct 1793 and introduced severe repressive policies. T. also met in the gaols of Bordeaux Thérèse Cabarrus whom he married. Back in Paris in Mar 1794 he was attacked by Robespierre and helped plot the coup of 9 Thermidor. A leading Thermidorian, he was elected to the CPS; he had the Rev Tribunal suppressed; he caused the closure of the Jacobin Club; and he had Carrier and other terrorists arraigned. His political influence was bolstered by the salon presided over by his wife, but when they separated his past caught up with him. Though elected to the C500 he did not play a prominent political role and in 1798 embarked on a new career in diplomatic service.

Tallien (Madame), see CABARRUS

Talmont (Ant-Ph de la Trémoïlle, prince de), 1766–exctd Jan 1794. This Breton nobleman had served as adc to Artois in Germany before returning to France and becoming involved in the Vendéan rising. Demoralised by the rebels' defeats, he was captured and executed.

Talon (Ant-Omer), 1760–1811. Parisian magistrate from an illustrious *robin* family, T. was made Lieutenant Civil of the Châtelet in 1789. He won little but criticism for his handling of the case of the insurgents of 5–6 Oct 1789 and the Favras affair, and in June 1790 resigned so as to sit as *suppléant* in the Constit Ass. An active royalist, he helped win over Mirabeau and was heavily involved in court intrigue. Compromised by the disclosure of the contents of the *armoire de fer*, he fled to the USA, returning to France under Napoleon.

Target (Gui-J-B), 1733–1806. A distinguished lawyer linked with the *philosophes* and a member of the Académie française, T. became involved in the 'patriot party in 1788–9 and was elected to the EG by Paris. A great committeeman, he helped in framing the constitution and in administrative, legal and ecclesiastical reforms. Under Napoleon, he was to be a major contributor to the Code Civil.

Tascher de la Pagerie (Marie-Josèphe-Rose; from 1779, Joséphine de Beauharnais; from 1796, Joséphine Bonaparte; from 1804 to 1809, empress), 1764–1831. A Creole from a distinguished Martiniquais family, Joséphine was imprisoned as an aristocrat under the Terror (her husband, Alexandre de Beauharnais, was executed). On her release she became attached to Barras, and through him met Napoleon Bonaparte, whom she married in Mar 1796. The two were divorced in 1809.

Terwagne, see THÉROIGNE DE MÉRICOURT

Théot (Catherine), 1716–17 Sept 1794. Norman visionary who claimed to be the mother of God and who under the AR had been imprisoned in the Bastille, Catherine T. was holding seances in 1794 in which she was alleged to claim that Robespierre was the new Messiah. Vadier of the CGS reported on her to the Convtn on 17 June 1794 in such a way as to smear Robespierre and the Cult of the Supreme Being.

'Théroigne de Méricourt' (sobriquet of Anne-Joseph TERWAGNE), 1762–1817. Originally from Luxemburg, T. was living in Paris in 1789. She welcomed the Rev; was active in the *journées* of 14 July and 5–6 Oct 1789; was an enthusiastic speaker in the Cordeliers and Jacobins; and held a salon attended by Siéyès, Pétion, Romme, Ronsin, Desmoulins, Momoro and others. Visiting Liège in 1791 she was imprisoned by the Austrians and on her release was welcomed back triumphantly to Paris. She was involved in the *journées* of 20 June and 10 Aug 1792, but her sympathies were with the Girondins. She was attacked and publicly flogged by radical women in May 1793, never recovered and died insane.

Thibaudeau (Ant-Claire), 1765–1854. A lawyer from Poitou, T. had served as *procureur-syndic* of the Poitiers prov ass. in 1787. He was elected to the Convtn, and sat among the Montagnards but never spoke. He came out of the shadows after Thermidor: he served on the CPS and CGS; he had the proscribed Girondins reinstated in the Convtn; he attacked the Maximum and other rev legislation; he strongly opposed the Germinal and Prairial risings; and he helped draft the Constitution of Year III. Elected to the C500, he followed a moderate line and seemed to have links with the Clichyens. Under Napoleon he became a prefect.

Thibault (Anne-Alexandre-Marie), 1747–1813. A *curé* elected to the EG by the clergy of Nemours, T. welcomed the Civ Constn and was elected bishop of the Cantal. He was elected to the Convtn and though linked with the Girondins did not share their fate. He specialised in financial matters; in Nov 1793 renounced his priesthood; and in 1795 was elected to the C500. He retired to private life in 1799.

Thirion (Didier), 1763–1815. A professor of rhetoric in E France with the Oratorians in 1787, T. established himself as a lawyer in Metz before going on to represent the Moselle in the Convtn. A staunch rpbcn, he voted for the king's death, attacked the Girondins and called for the institution of the Maximum in May 1793. From Sept to Nov 1793 he served *en mission* in the Vendée but was recalled at Couthon's behest, and became increasingly jaundiced towards the committees. He supported the overthrow of Robespierre, but remained a Jacobin and was imprisoned after the Prairial rising. Amnestied in 1795, he turned to teaching, then to administration.

Thouret (Jq-Guillaume), 1746–guill 22 Apr 1794. Son of a notary, T. was a lawyer, and was appointed *procureur-syndic* of Normandy's prov ass. in 1787. He was elected to the EG; was on four occasions president of the Constit Ass.; and played an important role in securing legal, constitutional, ecclesiastical and administrative reforms. He recommenced his legal career in 1791, but fell under suspicion during the Terror and was executed as an alleged Dantonist.

Thuriot (Jq-Alexis), 1753–1829. Prominent in the storming of the Bastille, the Champenois lawyer T. represented the Marne in the Leg Ass. and Convtn, where he sat among the Montagnards. Often *en mission*, he served in the CPS from July to Sept 1793, and then again following Robespierre's overthrow (in which he, as acting president of the Convtn on 9 Thermidor, played a key role). He remained a Jacobin and though arrested on grounds of implication in the Prairial rising, was amnestied in 1795.

Toulongeon (Fs-Emmanuel, vicomte de), 1748–1812. T. had renounced an ecclesiastical career to become a cavalry officer, and played a prominent role as a liberal noble in the Pre-Rev in Franche-Comté. He was elected to the EG and was swift to rally to the Third Estate. In the Constit Ass. he was a respected influence on military, educational and economic matters. He lay low during the Terror and in 1795 was appointed to the Institut.

Tourzel (Louise - Elisabeth - Félicité - Françoise - Armande - Anne - Marie - Jeanne - Josèphe de Croy d'Havré, marquise de), 1749–1832. Appointed governess of the king's children in 1789, Madame de T. played a key role in the flight to Varennes under the alias of the baronne de Korff. She returned to Paris with the royal family, was imprisoned in late 1792 and just avoided assassination in the Sept Massacres.

Treilhard (J-B), 1742–1810. A lawyer originally from Brive, but since the 1770s attached to the Paris parl, T. was elected to the EG by Paris and specialised in legal and ecclesiastical reforms during the Constit Ass. He was elected by the Seine-et-Oise to the Convtn, in which he was a moderate. Between missions to Belgium in Jan 1793 and the SW in the Summer of 1793 he served on the CPS from Apr to June 1793. He lay low during the Terror, but was elected to the CPS again after Thermidor. He served in the C500 until 1797; acted as negotiator in the abortive peace talks with Britain in 1797; and was a Director from May 1798 to June 1799. Under Napoleon, he returned to the law, making an important contribution to the framing of the Code Civil.

Tronchet (Fs-Denis), 1723 – 1806. A Parisian lawyer, T. was elected to the EG and played a role in the Constit Ass. in the reform of the law and the abolition of feudalism. Louis XVI chose him as his defence counsel in the king's trial, and he prudently lay low thereafter. He was elected to the C Anciens, and was associated with judicial reform. He would contribute towards the making of the Code Civil under Napoleon.

Tronson du Coudray (Guillaume-Alexandre), 1750–dep 27 May 1798. A Parisian lawyer who was royalist and counter-rev from 1789, T. de C. defended Marie-Antoinette at her trial. He was a prominent Clichyen in the C Anciens until Fructidor when he was deported.

Truguet (Laurent-J-Fs), 1752–1839. Career naval officer and diplomat, T. was placed in command of Mediterranean defence in 1792. Imprisoned under the Terror, he rejoined the navy on his release, but was appointed Navy Minister in Nov 1795. An active minister, he organised the unsuccessful Irish expedition. On his resignation in July 1797, he became Spanish ambassador.

Turreau de Linières (L), *c* 1760–1796. Son of a financial bureaucrat, T. was a soldier who was elected *suppléant* for his native dept of the Somme and who then served in the Convtn. A Montagnard, his spell *en mission* in W France with Bourbotte (notably his alleged massacre of rebels on Noirmoutier in Apr 1794) was too radical for many of the deputies and he was recalled. Commissary with the Army of Italy in 1795, he entered military administration under the Directory but died soon afterwards.

Turreau (L-Marie), 1756–1816. A career soldier under the AR, T. achieved the rank of general in Sept 1793. He served on the Spanish front as well as in the W, where he became notorious for his *colonnes infernales* and for his brutal scorched earth policies towards rebel areas. He was suspended for this after Thermidor and only ended his period of disgrace in 1797. He then served in the E and in Italy.

Vadier (Marc-Guillaume-Alexis), 1736–1828. A former army officer, and in 1789 a magistrate in Pamiers, V. was elected to the EG but achieved no prominence in the Constit Ass. Elected to the Convtn by the Ariège, however, he proved a stern critic of the Girondins, and was elected to the CGS in Sept 1793. He attacked the Dantonists, then used the Catherine Théot affair to embarrass Robespierre, whose religious policies he opposed. He plotted the Thermidor coup, but found himself attacked as a terrorist thereafter. In Apr 1795, he, Billaud-Varenne, Collot-d'Herbois and Barère were sentenced to deportation. V. escaped and hid, and, though amnestied in 1795, later became implicated in the Babeuf plot, for which he was imprisoned. He was freed under caution in the late 1790s.

Valazé or **Dufriche-Valazé** (Ch-Eléonore du Friche de), 1751–suic 30 Oct 1793. A lawyer from Alençon, V. was elected to the Convtn; became associated with Vergniaud and the Girondins, who met to coordinate policy at his home; and voted the *appel au peuple*. Tried with the Girondins, he died in prison before reaching the scaffold.

Varlet (J), ?1764–?1832. An unemployed Parisian of no real profession, V. was an assiduous Cordelier and Jacobin as well as an enthusiastic participant in street action (*journées* of 10 Aug 1792, 31 May 1793, etc). His *enragé* policies had him expelled from the Jacobin Club in early 1793. Despite spells in prison, he escaped the purge of the Hébertists in 1794. He surfaced under the Directory supporting Babeuf, then in 1799 as a member of the Club du Manège.

Vauban (Jq-Anne-Jos Le Prestre, comte de), 1754–1816. This career soldier was linked with Orléans prior to the Rev, but emigrated in 1791; joined Condé's forces at Coblenz; and fought against the Rpbc in 1792 as Condé's adc. He assisted Puisaye in the Quiberon expedition, then worked in the coordination of Chouan resistance. He returned to France under the Consulate.

Vaublanc (Vincent-Marie Viénot, comte de), 1756–1845. A soldier under the AR, V. was elected to the Leg Ass. by the Seine-et-Marne and was a noted constitutional royalist. He disappeared from political life during the Terror, but was involved in sectional politics in Paris at the time of the Vendémiaire rising.

A Clichyen in the C500, he had to flee arrest at Fructidor. He returned to France after Brumaire and continued in politics under Napoleon and the Restoration.

Vaudreuil (L-Ph de Rigaud, marquis de), 1724–1802. A naval officer elected by Castelnaudary to the EG, V. sat on the right and served on the navy committee. He defended the royal family physically during the *journées* of 5–6 Oct 1789, and emigrated to Britain in 1791, returning to France only under Napoleon.

Vauquelin (L-Nic), 1763–1829. Pharmacist, close friend and ally of Fourcroy, V. became a professor at the Ecole des Mines and the Ecole polytechnique in 1795, as well as a member of the Institut.

Vergennes (Ch Gravier, comte de), 1717–1787. Career diplomat, V. was Foreign Minister from 1774 until his death in Feb 1787. His death at that time removed a source of sound political advice at a testing time for the monarch.

Vergniaud (P-Victurnien), 1753–guill 31 Oct 1793). A disciple of Turgot in his youth, V. became a lawyer in Bordeaux and after serving in local administration was elected to the Leg Ass. and the Convtn by the Gironde. In both assemblies he was seen as one of the major leaders of the Girondin group. Though stern critics of the government in the summer of 1792, he and his colleagues tried unsuccessfully to come to terms with the king on the eve of 10 Aug 1792. In the Convtn he led the attacks against the Commune and the Montagnards, and increasingly exasperated even deputies of the Plain over the king's trial. A stern critic of the Montagnards in Spring 1793, he was proscribed on 2 June 1793, and executed with the other Girondins in Oct.

Vernier (Théodore), 1731–1818. A lawyer from Lons-le-Saulnier, V. was elected to the EG, and specialised in financial matters in the Constit Ass. Elected to the Convtn by the Jura he sat with the Plain, and after protesting against the proscription of the Girondins escaped arrest by emigrating to Switzerland. He was recalled to the Convtn in Dec 1794 and subsequently served on the C Anciens. He supported Bonaparte in the Brumaire coup.

Viala (Jos-Agricol), 1780–battle July 1793. Like Bara, V. was a young man transformed into a myth as a result of dying heroically while fighting against the enemies of the Rpbc: in his case, against royalists outside Avignon.

Villaret de Joyeuse (L-Th), 1748–1812. A career naval officer, V. was given command of the French fleet in Brest in 1793. He became a hero for skirmishing with the British in May–June 1794 thereby allowing a crucial shipment of American grain to reach France. He was elected to the C500 in 1797 but, regarded as a Clichyen, was imprisoned after Fructidor. He was recalled to naval service by Bonaparte.

Villatte or **Vilatte** (Joachim), 1768–guill 7 May 1795. Son of a doctor from the Limousin, V. was working as a schoolteacher in Limoges when the Rev broke out. He came to Paris in 1792; joined the Jacobins; participated in the *journée* of 10 Aug; and became a juryman in the Rev Tribunal. He fell under suspicion, however, and was imprisoned just prior to Thermidor. He remained in gaol and was executed as a terrorist.

Vincent (Fs-Nic), 1767–guill 24 March 1794. Son of a gaoler, V. was a petty clerk who made a career for himself in popular politics in Paris. A Cordelier, deeply involved in the organisation of the *journée* of 10 Aug 1792, he secured an important post in the military bureaucracy under Bouchotte and became a forceful political influence on the conduct of the war. Denounced with Ronsin and briefly imprisoned in Dec 1793, he seemed to be preaching insurrection on his release, and was arrested and executed as an Hébertist.

Virieu (Fs-Henri, comte de), 1754–battle 15 Oct 1793. An army officer from an ancient Dauphinois family, V. was involved in the Pre-Rev in Grenoble before being elected by the nobility of the Dauphiné to the EG. He was swift to rally to the Third Estate and was prominent on the night of 4 Aug, but his liberal, bicameralist views were increasingly overtaken by events, and he evolved into a hard-line royalist. He was in Lyon when the city rebelled against the Convtn, and he became one of the rebels' military leaders. He was attacked and killed as he tried to leave the city with his followers.

Volney (sobriquet of Constantin-Fs CHASSEBOEUF), 1757–1820. Author well known for his *Voyage en Egypte et en Syrie* (1787) and for his *Les Ruines* (1791), V. represented Anjou in the EG. A moderate who came to have links with the Girondins, he was imprisoned during the Terror and visited the USA between 1795 and 1798. He supported Bonaparte in the Brumaire coup.

Voulland (J-Henri), 1751–1801. A lawyer from Nîmes and friend of Rabaut Saint-Etienne, V. served in the EG before being elected by the Gard to the Convtn. A staunch Montagnard, he served in the CGS from Sept 1793 to Sept 1794, but fell foul of the Thermidorian reaction, and was arrested and imprisoned. Amnestied in 1795, he became a bookseller and died penniless.

Westermann (Fs-Jos), 1751–guill 5 Apr 1794. Son of an Alsatian surgeon, W. had served as a soldier before settling down as a magistrate in Strasbourg. He became a municipal official in Haguenau on the outbreak of the Rev, and was to be one of the leaders of the *fédérés* involved in the *journée* of 10 Aug 1792. Friendly with Danton, he was sent as a commissary of the PEC to the Army of the North. In Apr 1793 he was almost brought down by his links with Dumouriez, but in May was sent to the Vendée. Despite some successes here, he was subject to much criticism – he was dubbed 'the butcher of the Vendée' – and he was recalled in Jan 1794. Arrested as a Dantonist, he accompanied his friend to the scaffold.

Willot (Victor-Amédée, comte de), 1755–1823. W. was captain in the grena-

diers in 1789 and from 1793 to 1795 was attached to the Army of the E
Pyrenees. He was subsequently sent to W France, but Hoche had him dismissed
as a royalist. Elected to the C500 in 1797 and a prominent Clichyen, he was
deported after Fructidor but escaped to Britain and the USA, only returning to
France in 1814.

Wimpffen or **Wimpfen** (Georges-Félix), 1744–1814. A distinguished career
soldier elected to the EG by the nobility of Caen, W. specialised in military
matters in the Constit Ass. He returned to the army in 1792; defended Thionville
in Aug 1792; and was appointed commander of the Army of the Coasts of Cherbourg. He rallied to the Federalist revolt in Normandy, however, and following
its defeat went into hiding for the remainder of the 1790s. He was rehabilitated
after Brumaire.

Ysabeau (Claude-Alexandre), 1754–1831. An Oratorian priest, Ysabeau
welcomed the Civ Constn and was elected vicar-general of the bishop of the Indre-
et-Loire. He renounced his priesthood and married, however, and was elected by
the Indre-et-Loire to the Convtn, where he sat with the Montagnards. *En mission*
(with Tallien) in Bordeaux and the SW in Autumn 1793, he was recalled in May
1794. He helped plot the Thermidor coup; served *en mission* again in the SW;
and was a member of the CGS in Aug 1795. He served in the C Anciens down
to 1798, then entered the bureaucracy.

XI. GLOSSARY OF FRENCH
REVOLUTIONARY TERMS

abbé, (1) abbot; (2) courtesy title given to all clerics.

accapareur, monopolist, hoarder (esp of grain).

affouage (droit d'), collective right (common in E France) to take firewood from communal woods. Reaffirmed in legislation in 1802.

agent national, direct representative of central government at district and municipal levels, created by the law of 14 Frimaire II/4 Dec 1793, charged with surveillance of rev legislation. Suppressed 17 Apr 1795.

agiotage, speculation.

aides (AR), indirect taxes, notably on wines and spirits. Abolished in 1790.

aînesse (droit d'), prerogatives of the eldest child (esp important in noble families). Abolished in 1790–1.

alarmiste (neol 1793–4), spreader of false news, rumour-monger.

Allobroge, member of the 'Allobrogian Society' (*Société des Allobroges*), a club formed in Paris in 1792 by Savoyard expatriates demanding the annexation of Savoy to France.

amalgame, merger into single fighting units of volunteers and troops of the line, achieved in infantry regiments in Spring 1794.

amis des noirs, 'Friends of the Blacks': political club and pressure group for negro emancipation founded by Brissot in 1788.

anarchiste (neol 1791–2), 'anarchist': used at first by the right of Jacobins and after Thermidor of all who had been prominent in politics in Year II.

Ancien, member of the 'Council of Elders' (C Anciens) established by the Constitution of Year III.

Ancien Régime (neol 1789), Ancien (in sense of former, rather than old) Régime.

anglomane (1) (AR) anglophile; (2) supporter of bicameral legislature on the British model (esp in Autumn 1789).

anobli, recently ennobled commoner.

anticipations, instalment loan made by financiers to the AR government, anticipating forthcoming tax income.

appelants, members of the Convtn who in Jan 1793 voted that the fate of Louis XVI be referred to the people at large in a referendum, the so-called *appel au peuple*.

appel au peuple, referendum e.g. regarding popular acceptance of the Constitution of Year III; but used esp as regards the plebiscite proposed by Girondin deputies during the trial of Louis XVI to determine the king's fate.

appel nominal, roll-call of all deputies to pronounce openly on an issue; used notably in the trial of Louis XVI.

aristocrate, epithet first used against the noble opponents of reform in 1787–8, but by 1793 used to refer to all alleged supporters of the AR whatever their status, and as a moral and political term rather than as a social category.

armées révolutionnaires, 'people's armies', semi-regular units composed of popular militants, formed in 1793 and disbanded in early 1794, which were esp prominent in promoting economic and religious aspects of the Terror.

armoire de fer, iron wall-safe in the Tuileries, discovered in Nov 1792 in which Louis XVI had kept correspondence which compromised Mirabeau, Lafayette, Dumouriez *et al*.

arrêt du conseil, decree of the king's council.

arrondissement, (1) one of 12 administrative subdivisions of Paris introduced in the Autumn of 1795, and replacing the 48 sections which had existed since 1790; (2) the main subdivision of departments, created by the law of 28 pluviôse VIII/17 Feb 1800, and roughly corresponding to the districts which had been abolished in 1795.

assemblées primaires, 'primary assemblies': meetings of active citizens under the two-tier electoral systems established by the Constitutions of 1791, Year III and Year VIII; their main political function was to choose electors of the deputies to the Nat Ass.

assemblées provinciales, 'prov assemblies': representative bodies of local notables, instituted by Necker in Berry in 1778 and extended elsewhere by his successors, which Brienne (in June 1787) established in all *pays d'élection*.

assermentés, priests who had sworn the oath of allegiance to the Civ Constn.

assiettes (AR), representative diocesan assemblies in Languedoc which divided up the tax burden fixed by the prov estates.

assignat, initially a government bond, but from 1790 the rev paper currency which was in principle 'assigned' (secured) on the nationalised property of the church.

ateliers de charité, public workshops, normally on the roads, utilised in the last decades of the AR and esp in the early years of the Rev as a form of relief in times of hardship.

aubaine (droit d') (AR), right of the crown to claim the estate of aliens who died on French soil. Abolished 6 Aug 1790.

autel de la patrie, civic altar, popularised by the Fête de la Fédération in Paris in July 1790.

Autrichienne (l'), 'the Austrian woman' (with pun on *chienne*, 'bitch'): insulting epithet for Marie-Antoinette.

aveu (AR), written declaration containing the act of recognition by a vassal of his seigneur, and itemising all obligations.

avocat-général (AR), deputy prosecutor in a parl.

babouviste, political supporter or proponent of the ideas of Babeuf.

bailliage, sénéchaussée (AR), royal courts (with certain exceptions the former were situated in the N, the latter in the S). The jurisdictional boundaries of the largest were used as the framework for elections to the EG in 1789.

banalités (AR), much detested seigneurial monopolies, under which peasants were obliged to use their seigneur's mill, oven, wine-press, etc, in return for (often extortionate) payment.

ban des vendanges (AR), seigneur's right to fix the date on which the wine-harvest was to begin.

banvin (AR), exclusive right of seigneurs to sell their wine for a fixed period (usually 30–40 days) after the wine-harvest.

barbets, disaffected smugglers, deserters, etc, who in the late 1790s conducted a guerrilla war against the rev authorities in the Var and the Alpes-Maritimes.

barrières, customs posts surrounding Paris erected by the *Ferme Générale* from 1784 and which were targets for crowd action in the crisis of July 1789.

basoche, bazoche, body of clerks attached to the parls of Paris and some other prov cities.

bicamériste, supporter of a British-style bicameral legislature.

bienfaisance, beneficence, philanthropy (often contrasted with supposedly undiscriminating Christian charity).

biens communaux, common lands, commons.

biens de mainmorte, see MAINMORTE.

biens dominiaux, see BIENS NATIONAUX.

biens ecclésiastiques, see BIENS NATIONAUX.

biens des émigrés, see BIENS NATIONAUX.

biens nationaux, 'national lands': nationalised property of the church (*biens ecclésiastiques*: by the decrees of 2 Nov 1789 and 13 May and 16 July 1790), of the royal domain (*biens dominiaux*: by the laws of 19 Dec 1789 and 9 Mar 1790) and of *émigrés* (*biens des émigrés*: by decrees of 9 Feb and 17 July 1792), sold off throughout the 1790s.

blancs, royalists (term used esp in the Vendée wars).

bleus, republican soldiers (because of their blue uniforms), then by extension all supporters of the Rpbc (used esp in the Vendée wars).

bocage, woodland landscape typical of W France.

bonnet phrygien, bonnet rouge, red cap used decoratively from 1789 and which from mid 1791 became the fashionable coiffure of *sans-culotte* militants and a symbol of republican spirit. From 1792 it was also an official emblem of state.

bordier, bordagier, share-cropper (*métayer*), esp in SW France.

bourgeois, originally the citizen of a town; by the late eighteenth century, used (in opposition to peasants, nobles) to denote the urban notables, and in 1789 the upper fraction of the Third Estate.

bras nus, 'the bare-armed': Michelet's way of referring to plebeian members of the Parisian popular movement.

brassier, day-labourer (esp in SW).

brissotins, supporters of Brissot in the Leg Ass. and Convtn (often used synonymously with Girondins).

Brumaire, coup of 18 Brumaire Year VII/9 Nov 1799 overthrowing the Directory and instituting the Consulate with Napoleon Bonaparte as First Consul.

bureaucrate (neol), office-worker, functionary.

bureau des finances, see TRÉSORIER DE FRANCE.

bureaux de bienfaisance, home-relief boards established in every commune by the law of 27 Nov 1796/16 frim V.

buveur de sang, 'blood-drinker': term of abuse used esp after Thermidor to denote the sectional personnel and Jacobins of Year II.

cabaret, bar, drinking establishment.

cahiers de doléances, books of grievances drawn up at every stage (parish, guild, *bailliage*, etc) of the electoral procedure for the EG in 1789.

'ça ira', rev song, first heard in 1790, and with violently anti-aristocratic verses added from 1793.

Caisse d'escompte, discount bank, created by Turgot in 1776 and modified by his successors, bedrock of government credit in the final years of the AR; abolished in 1793.

calotins (from *calotte*, skull-cap), popular and denigratory name for priests, and by extension supporters of the non-juring clergy.

canton, administrative subdivision of the department between district and commune levels; esp important during the Directorial period.

capitainerie (AR), office, or jurisdictional area, of captain of the royal hunt.

capitaliste, wealthy person (NOT capitalist) deriving income from investment in bonds, annuities, etc, and from other financial operations.

capitation, poll-tax created in 1695 and supposed to be levied on nobles, though in fact usually assessed according to the rolls of the *taille*.

capitouls (AR), municipal magistrates of Toulouse.

carmagnole, jacket, originally from Savoy, which in 1793 became a revolutionary emblem; by extension, a revolutionary dance; a song; a militant; or a soldier of the Rpbc.

cas prévôtaux (AR), offences within the jurisdiction of the *prévôts* of the *maréchaussée*, who were concerned with internal security and policing.

casuel, perquisites of any office, but esp those which parish priests derived from baptisms, marriages, funerals, etc. *Droits casuels* were seigneurial dues which fell adventitiously (e.g. *lods et ventes*).

cens (AR), quitrent that peasants were obliged to pay to their seigneurs. Rarely onerous by 1789, it was still seen as the classic symbol of feudal dependence.

cens électoral, the property qualification for the franchise introduced in the Rev.

censive (AR) (1) property on which the *cens* was payable; (2) synonym for *cens*.

centième denier (AR), 1 per cent tax on transactions involving property and venal offices.

cercles constitutionnels, clubs composed of pro-rpbcn sympathisers, created in Paris and provincial cities from mid 1797.

certificat de civisme, documentary proof of political orthodoxy and civic virtue delivered under the Terror, usually by *comités de surveillance*.

Chambre des Communes, see COMMUNES.

chambre des enquêtes, see PARLEMENTS.

chambre des requêtes, see PARLEMENTS.

champart (AR), usually onerous and highly detested seigneurial due in kind constituting a fraction (which varied from a third to a twentieth, according to region) of the peasant's grain harvest.

chasse (droit de) (AR), absolute hunting monopoly enjoyed by nobles and seigneurs.

Châtelet, the most important civil and criminal jurisdiction in AR France, situated in Paris. The Grand Châtelet was its prison.

chauffeurs (neol 1797), bandit gangs (esp in N and W France) who tortured their victims into disclosing the whereabouts of their wealth by burning their feet.

chef-lieu, administrative capital (of a department, district, etc).

chevaliers du poignard, name given the noblemen who in a public demonstration of support for Louis XVI (and possibly with the ulterior motive of abducting him) invaded the Tuileries on 28 Feb 1791.

chiffonistes, chiffonniers, name for members of counter-rev gangs in Arles and the Midi.

Chouans, royalist insurgents (mainly peasants) in W France.

ci-devant (neol 1792–3), of, or pertaining to, the AR; also used as a noun to denote the powerful and prestigious under the AR, esp aristocrats.

Cinq Grosses Fermes, 'Five Great Farms': the area within which collection of the main indirect taxes was in the hands of the *Ferme générale*.

citoyens actifs, 'active citizens': those under the 1791 Constitution who had the necessary requirements (ownership of property, etc) to enjoy both civic rights and political rights such as the right to vote.

citoyens passifs, 'passive citizens': those under the 1791 Constitution enjoying civic rights (freedom of expression, etc) but not political rights.

civisme, civic virtue. Its opposite was *incivisme*.

clichiens, clichyens, right-wing deputies under the 'First Directory', and their supporters.

closier, economically dependent peasant (esp in W France).

cocarde, cockade, used as an emblem of political opinion.

cocarde tricolore, official red-white-and-blue cockade, originating in the July crisis of 1789, derived from the combination of the colours of Paris (red, blue) with that of the king (white).

collecte (AR), responsibility, usually held on a rota basis within a parish, for the collection of royal taxes.

colombier (droit de) (AR), right to own a dovecote, a symbol of seigneurial status.

colonnes infernales, 'infernal columns': the units used during the Vendée wars deliberately to spread devastation and destruction in rebel areas.

colonnes mobiles, 'mobile columns': concentrated troop formations of approximately 200 men which from 1795 to 1796 regularly combed rebel areas in W France to root out Chouans.

Comité autrichien, the alleged 'Austrian Committee', the court faction opposed to the Rev and involving the (Austrian) Marie-Antoinette.

Comité central révolutionnaire, coordinating committee established in Paris a couple of days prior to the *journée* of 31 May 1793 and which planned the purge of the Contvn.

comités d'arrondissement, post-Thermidor name for Parisian *comités de surveillance*, or *comités révolutionnaires*.

Comité des dépêches, see CONSEIL DU ROI.

Comité de salut public, title sometimes used at local level by self-important *comités révolutionnaires*.

Comité de l'hôtel-de-ville, see COMITÉ DES ÉLECTEURS.

Comité des électeurs, *ad hoc* committee of former electors of the Paris deputies in the EG who met in the Hôtel-de-Ville during the summer crisis of 1789 and became the basis of the Paris Commune.

comités de surveillance, (1) local committees of revolutionary militants, officially created by a decree of 21 Mar 1793, which were entrusted with ensuring the execution of revolutionary legislation during the Terror; (2) committees of the Leg Ass. and Convtn, created 25 Nov 1791 to investigate possible crimes of *lèse-nation*. In Oct 1792, the Convtn's committee became the CGS (*Comité de sûreté générale*).

Comité des Trente, 'Committee of Thirty': rallying-point for *patriote* sentiment in 1788–9, and including among its members Duport, Talleyrand, Mirabeau and Siéyès.

comités révolutionnaires, generic name for local *comités de surveillance*.

commende (AR), administration of an ecclesiastical benefice by a layman, in theory only temporary, in practice often definitive.

commissaires aux accaparements, local commissioners entrusted with the execution of the law of 26 July 1793, which stipulated the death penalty for hoarders. They often dealt more generally with problems of food supply.

commissaires aux armées, political commissaries (under the Terror, normally deputies) sent to the armies to supervise the war effort in much the same way that the reps en mission were sent out into the provinces.

commissaires du pouvoir exécutif, functionaries entrusted with general surveillance of the execution of legislation; functionaries with this title in 1795 replaced the PGSs attached to the depts.

Commission des Douze, (1) shortlived committee of the Leg Ass. established on 17 June 1792 to aid ministers in the conduct of the war: a kind of embryonic CPS; (2) 12-man committee appointed by the Convtn under Girondin pressure on 18 May 1793 to investigate the threat of subversion from the Paris Commune. Abolished on the *journée* of 31 May 1793.

Commission des Onze (1) *ad hoc* committee of 11 members formed in the Jacobin Club on the *journée* of 31 May 1793 to coordinate the actions of the sections in collaboration with the Commune; (2) Constitution Committee created 18 Apr 1795 to draft a new constitution (ultimately the Constitution of Year III).

Commission des Vingt-et-Un, 21-man committee established in the Convtn on 26 Dec 1794 to review the conduct of former members of the CPS and CGS (notably Billaud-Varenne, Collot-d'Herbois, Vadier and Barère).

commissions administratives or **commissions exécutives,** administrative committees, 12 in number, which were established 1 Apr 1794/12 germ II to replace ministers, and which lasted down to the end of the Convtn.

communauté (1) all inhabitants of a parish; (2) an urban professional group (e.g. apothecaries); (3) a religious community.

Commune, municipal government of Paris, 1789–95

commune (neol 1792), the smallest administrative unit, approximately equivalent to a parish.

Commune insurrectionnelle, name adopted by the renovated municipal government of Paris from 9–10 Aug 1792 which was instrumental in the overthrow of Louis XVI and heavily involved in the Sept Massacres.

Communes, Chambre des Communes, 'House of Commons': way of referring to the Third Estate during the summer crisis of 1789.

compagnies de Jéhu (de Jésus, du Soleil), violent gangs of royalist militants who during the 'White Terror' hunted down and assassinated ex-Jacobins, esp in Lyons and in S France.

Compagnie des Indes, East Indies Company, established 14 Apr 1785 to stimulate trade with the E. Suppressed 3 Apr 1790, its winding-up in 1792–3 led to a scandal of corruption involving Fabre d'Eglantine.

compagnon (1) journeyman; (2) journeyman member of a *compagnonnage.*

compagnonnages, clandestine workers' organisations, strong in the building trades and traditional crafts.

'complot aristocratique', the 'aristocratic plot' according to which the aristocracy were conspiring to subvert the Rev. Belief in the plot was esp widespread in July 1789 and resurfaced sporadically in the early 1790s.

'complot de l'étranger', the 'foreign plot' allegedly organised by Pitt and his agents in France in 1793–4.

compoix (AR), cadastral registers which were used as the basis for tax assessment in certain *pays de taille réelle* such as Languedoc.

Conseil du roi (AR), king's council, suppressed in the 1791 Constitution. Its main subcommittees were also sometimes given this title, notably the *Comité des dépêches* which handled prov business, petitions and dispatches, and the *Comité des finances.*

conseil exécutif provisoire, council of ministers established on the *journée* of 10 Aug 1792. The epithet *provisoire* was later dropped, and the council lasted until the suppression of ministries in Apr 1794, though its powers were increasingly eroded by the CPS.

constitutionnels (1) title sometimes accorded the Fayettiste group in 1790–1; (2) the constitutional clergy (those who adhered to the Civ Constn 1790); (3) members of cercles constitutionnels under the Directory.

consul (1) (AR) name for municipal magistrates in S France; (2) (AR) judges in commercial tribunals in Paris and in Toulouse; (3) one of the heads of the executive (the most important of whom was First Consul Bonaparte) following the *coup d'état* of 18 Brumaire,

contrainte de sole (AR), customary obligation for individual farmers to observe time-honoured collective rotation systems of the land. Abolished 5 June 1791.

contribution, tax (generally preferred to AR term *impôt*).

contribution patriotique, extraordinary direct tax aimed at meeting urgent state commitments established at Necker's request by the Constit Ass. on 1 Oct 1789.

conventionnel, member of the Convtn, 1792–5.

corvée (AR), forced labour service: the *corvée seigneuriale* existed mainly where feudalism in 1789 was still rigorous; the *corvée royale*, established in 1737, which normally took the form of labour on roads, was more widepread, but had been commuted into cash payments in many areas.

Cour plénière, 'Plenary Court' created 8 May 1788: packed with high dignitaries, who were to be responsible for registering royal edicts, this court (which never met) was intended to be more docile than the parl which it was supposed to replace.

cour souveraine, the 'sovereign courts' were in theory those which judged without appeal; but the phrase was sometimes used as a synonym for the parls.

crapauds du Marais, 'toads of the marshes (or the Plain)': pejorative way of referring to centrist deputies in the Convtn.

crétois, deputies of the 'Crest' of the 'Mountain' (*Montagne*) – the last surviving Montagnards in the Thermidorian Convtn, liquidated or neutralised following the Prairial *journées*.

culottes dorées, the 'golden breeches': a sans-culotte way of referring to the better-off.

culs blancs, the 'white arses': infantrymen in the Rev armies (whose uniform included white trousers).

curé, parish priest, who held a *cure* (cure of souls).

Dantoniste, alleged supporter of Danton.

dauphin, son and presumptive heir of the king of France.

décade, the period of 10 days which replaced the week in the Rev Calendar.

décadi, the tenth day of the *décade*, instituted by the Rev Calendar, and a day of rest.

décimateur, tithe-owner, sometimes a layman, very often an ecclesiastical dignitary rather than the *curé*. In return for the tithe, the tithe-owner was supposed to contribute towards the upkeep of the parish (church buildings, stipend of the *curé*, alms to the poor, etc).

décime (AR), tax which the church levied on its members.

décrets des deux-tiers, decrees of the Convtn, 22 and 30 Aug 1795/5, 13 fruct III which stipulated that two-thirds of the new legislature under the Constitution of Year III should be drawn from the existing Convtn.

défenseurs de la patrie, soldiers (term used esp of invalids and disabled veterans).

Déficit (Madame), insulting title for Marie-Antoinette, used esp 1787–9.

défrichement, land-clearance, encouraged by the government after 1766, but in a way that tended to favour seigneurs and led to peasant hostility over attempts to infringe on common lands.

dépôts de mendicité, workhouses for beggars and vagrants established from 1767.

dérogeance, loss of privileges attaching to nobility as a result of engaging in work considered demeaning (menial trades, manual labour, etc).

dîmes inféodées (AR), impropriated tithes (tithes enjoyed by a layman).

districts (1) electoral divisions of Paris, 60 in number, created for elections to the EG in 1789 and which were replaced by 48 sections in the municipal law of 21 May 1790; (2) main administrative subdivision of departments: an important agency for rev legislation in Year II, they were abolished in 1795.

domaine congéable (bail à), kind of lease esp favourable to tenants, common in Brittany. The landlord was held to own the land and the tenant all buildings on it.

don gratuit, 'voluntary gift', the size of which was periodically agreed by the Ass. of the Clergy, and which comprised a payment to the crown in lieu of taxation. The term was also sometimes used of the financial obligations of other corporate bodies.

doublement du tiers, the 'doubling of the Third (Estate)': the right of the Third Estate (conceded by Necker on 27 Dec 1788) to elect a number of deputies to the EG equal to those of the other two orders.

Droite, 'the Right': originally the group of deputies who sat to the right of the president of the Constit Ass. from Sept 1789, and who included most rightwing members.

droits casuels, see CASUEL.

échevin (AR), municipal magistrate (esp in Paris and N France).

égaux, supporters of Babeuf's 'Conspiracy of Equals' (*conjuration des égaux*).

électeurs (1) individuals who in the multi-tiered system of election to the EG elected the deputies for Paris, and who played a major part in the political crisis of the summer of 1789; (2) individuals chosen in primary assemblies of active citizens to elect deputies to the Leg Ass. and Convtn; (3) electors, the German princes and bishops with the right to elect the Holy Roman Emperor.

élections (AR), main subdivisions of the *généralités*.

embrigadement, fusion into a single *demi-brigade* of one battalion of line soldiers and two battalions of volunteers (the main means by which the *amalgame* was achieved in 1793–4).

émigrant, émigré (both terms are found), individuals, not only nobles, who left France on political grounds during the Rev.

enfants de la patrie, often used to describe bastards, orphans and foundlings (*bâtards, orphelins, enfants trouvés* under the AR).

enragé, injurious epithet variously used and esp (1) by aristocrats to describe Jacobins in 1790–1; (2) to describe the sectional militants led by Jacques Roux, Varlet, Leclerc, etc, who demanded stringent economic legislation in the Spring and Summer of 1793, which the Rev Govt gradually adopted.

état civil, registry, and registration, of births, marriages and deaths, which became a state monopoly by the law of 20 Sept 1792.

exagéré (neol), political extremist, ultra-revolutionary.

exclusif (1) set of prescriptions, regulating trade under the AR between France and those of its colonies not controlled by chartered companies; (2) post-Thermidor term of abuse to describe Jacobins, who were alleged to have wished to exclude from the Rpbc those they adjudged lacking in civic virtue.

fabrique, (1) fabric (of church); (2) vestry; (3) small business, involving a couple of workshops.

factieux, 'seditionaries': pejorative term used esp of Jacobins.

fanatisme, 'fanaticism': under the Terror the conventional way of describing catholicism.

faubourgs, suburbs, or, as in Paris, former suburbs (e.g. Faubourg Saint-Antoine, Faubourg Saint-Marcel) by 1789 within city walls; and by extension, the labouring population of the faubourgs.

fayettiste, supporter of Lafayette.

fédéralisme, federal political system favoured by Girondin deputies (e.g. Brissot, Buzot) in the Convtn; and supposedly the main programme of the 'Federalist Revolt' consequent on the purge of Girondin deputies from the Convtn in the *journées* of 31 May and 2 June 1793.

fédéraliste, supporter of *fédéralisme* (esp used pejoratively of the Girondins).

fédération, demonstration of patriotic fervour, the first of which occurred in the provinces in late 1789 and which became highly popular throughout France following the Fête de la Fédération in Paris in July 1790.

Fédération (Fête de la), ritualistic ceremony proclaiming national unity, originating in the provinces and popularised by the decision of the Constit Ass. to mark the first anniversary of the fall of the Bastille in 1790 by an elaborate festival on the Champ de Mars in Paris.

fédérés, individuals, including many Nat Guardsmen, sent from the provinces to Paris to celebrate the Fête de la Fédération: esp in 1790 and then again in 1792, when many *fédérés* were involved in the overthrow of Louis XVI.

féodalité, literally 'feudalism': the political and social system of the AR, including feudal and seigneurial elements but also venality of office, tithes, social privilege, aristocratic hierarchy, etc.

fermage, system of tenancy, differing from *métayage* (which involved payments in kind) in being based on cash payments.

fermier, (1) tenant leasing land under the system of *fermage*; (2) contractor responsible for the collection of a tax, a tithe, a seigneurial due, etc; (3) tax-farmer (often referred to as *fermier général*).

Ferme générale, see FERMIER GÉNÉRAL.

fermier général, (AR) tax-farmer responsible for the collection of most indirect royal taxes: the much detested *Ferme générale* was abolished in 1790, and many individual *fermiers généraux* ended up on the scaffold during the Terror.

feu (AR), hearth and, by extension, the family living around it; often the basis of tax assessment.

Feuillants, constitutional monarchists, including Lafayette, Duport, Barnave, Bailly, the Lameth brothers, who split away from the Jacobin Club following the flight to Varennes and established their own organisation in a monastery of the Strict Bernardines (*feuillants*); also used from late 1791 to denote moderates and royalists.

fief. By the late eighteenth century this feudal term denoting seigneurial subjection was used more or less synonymously with seigneurie or any noble property.

Floréal (*loi du 22 [an VI]*/22 May 1798), Directorial coup aimed at eliminating the strong left-wing delegation elected in the Year VI elections.

forain, individual who possessed land within a parish but normally resided outside it (often in a town).

fournée, batch of prisoners brought before the Rev Tribunal.

franc, unit of currency, approximately equivalent to the livre: the latter term was more widely used under the AR but was increasingly displaced by the former from the late 1790s.

franc-alleu (AR) allodium, freehold land exempt from all feudal and seigneurial obligations.

franc-fief (AR) 'frank-fee': payment made to the crown by any commoner purchasing a seigneurie.

franc-salé (AR) allocation of free salt to certain privileged individuals (royal officials, etc) and institutions (monasteries, hospitals, etc).

fraternisation, ritualistic act of political union between fellow patriots, often synonymous with an act of *fédération*.

fraternité et secours (décret de), decree of 19 Nov 1792 offering 'fraternity and aid' to all subject peoples wishing to overthrow the yoke of the AR.

frontières naturelles, the doctrine of 'natural frontiers' (i.e. the Alps, the Pyrenees and the Rhine) first adumbrated under the Leg Ass, and which became an important consideration in foreign policy during the Directorial period.

Fructidor, coup d'état, of 4 Sept 1797/18 fruct V by which Directors Barras, La Révellière-Lépeaux and Reubell purged the Directory and the Councils of right-wing members.

gabelle (AR) (1) the much-hated salt-tax, suppressed in 1790, assessed according to theoretical rather than actual consumption; (2) in popular parlance, used indiscriminatingly for all taxes on consumption. See also PAYS DE GABELLE.

gabelou, official of the *Ferme générale* responsible for the collection of the salt-tax; excise officer.

Garde constitutionnelle, royal bodyguard, comprising 1,800 men, allowed Louis XVI by the decree of 30 Sept 1791. Disbanded by the Leg Ass., 29 May 1792.

Garde du corps législatif, bodyguard of 1,500 men appointed to protect the C500 and C Anciens.

Garde du Directoire, bodyguard of 360 men instituted by the Constitution of Year III to protect the Directors.

Garde nationale, 'Nat Guard': citizens' militia, originating in the rev crisis of July 1789 with the aim of maintaining internal order and national defence. Organised by a series of laws, 1789–91.

Gardes-françaises, infantry regiment of the royal household under the AR, deserters from which were instrumental in the capture of the Bastille in July 1789. Incorporated into the Paris Nat Guard in Aug 1789.

garenne (droit de), (AR) right of seigneurs to enjoy a monopoly of maintaining rabbit-warrens.

gendarmerie (1) (AR) cavalry troop attached to the household of various royal personnages; (2) name adopted by the reformed *maréchaussée*, the paramilitary police force, from Dec 1790.

générale, drum roll calling citizens to arms.

généralité, main fiscal and administrative unit of AR France.

gens sans aveu, individuals unable to have a respectable person vouch for them: tramps, vagrants.

Germinal (journées de), unsuccessful popular insurrection in Paris, 1–2 Apr 1795/12–13 germ III, in the name of radical political and economic policies.

Girondins, loosely organised political grouping in the Leg Ass and Convtn including deputies from the department of the Gironde (Vergniaud, Guadet, Gensonné) and others (Brissot, Buzot, Isnard, etc).

glanage (droit de) (AR), customary right of the poor of a parish to glean from cultivated fields following the harvest.

glandée (droit de) (AR), customary right of villagers to allow their pigs the run of communal woodland.

gouverneur, see GOUVERNEMENT.

gouvernement (AR), main military regions into which France was divided. Each was headed by a *gouverneur*, drawn usually from the very highest aristocracy.

gouvernement révolutionnaire, title most usually ascribed to the emergency government centred on the CPS which emerged from 1792 onwards and ended after Thermidor.

Grand'Chambre, most senior and most prestigious chamber of the Paris parl which dealt with all high-priority business.

Grand Châtelet, see CHÂTELET.

Grand Conseil (AR), sovereign jurisdiction charged with settling disputes between parls.

'Grande Nation' (neol 1796–7), 'the Great Nation': i.e. France, as it expanded to incorporate new territory and to organise other states.

Grande Peur, panic fear which swept through France in late July and early Aug 1789 triggering off the attack on, and the abolition of, feudalism.

Grand Livre de la Bienfaisance Nationale, 'Great Register of National Beneficence': introduced by the law of 22 flor II/11 May 1794 which established a far-ranging pensions scheme for the rural poor.

Grand Livre de la Dette Publique, unified register of the national debt, introduced by Cambon on 24 Aug 1793 and petering out from 1794.

Grands Bailliages (1) 47 royal courts established by the May Edicts 1788 (but which never met) aimed at breaking the power of the parls; (2) also sometimes used to refer to the larger *bailliages* which provided the framework for elections to the EG.

greniers à sel (AR) (1) storehouses for salt; judicial and administrative agency, or jurisdiction, relating to the *gabelle*.

greniers d'abondance, grain warehouses, established by the decree of 9 Aug 1793, for times of dearth.

guet et garde (AR), labour obligation (usually commuted into cash) whereby peasants were supposed to provide the watch for their lord's chateau.

guillotine sèche, the 'dry guillotine': deportation, usually to Guiana, which was used against political offenders notably in the Thermidorian and Directorial periods.

Hébertiste, supporter of Hébert, the editor of the *Père Duchesne*, whose power base was in the Paris sections and Commune.

hobereau, 'sparrow-hawk', 'hobby': denigratory way of referring to a member of the country gentry.

hospice de l'humanité, hospital, hôtel-dieu.

hôtel-de-ville, town hall. The Paris Hôtel-de-Ville was the seat of the Commune.

impartiaux (1) the right in the Constit Ass., 1789–90; (2) members of the Plain in the Convtn.

impôt territorial, see SUBVENTION TERRITORIALE.

incivisme (neol), lack of civic virtue, an indictable offence under the Terror.

incroyables, extravagantly dressed young royalists in the Thermidorian period (term often used synonymously with *muscadins*).

indulgents, name given to Danton, Desmoulins and their followers who from late 1793 were calling for clemency and a relaxation of the Terror.

insermentés, priests who refused the oath of allegiance to the Civ Constn.

insoumis, absentee conscripts, 'draft-dodgers'.

Intendants, or **Intendants de justice, police et finances,** the main agents of the crown in the provinces under the AR. There was one in each *généralité*.

jacquerie, violent peasant insurrection.

jeunesse dorée, 'gilded youth', the dandified gangs of youths organised after Thermidor, notably, in Paris, by Fréron, and which went around attacking former militants and Jacobins.

journalier, day-labourer.

journée (1) 'day' on which some action of great political significance occurred (e.g. 14 July 1789, 10 Aug 1792); (2) a day's labour and, by extension, wage-payment for a day's labour.

journée des tuiles, 'day of the tiles': 7 June 1788, when the people of Grenoble threw tiles, etc, from the rooftops on soldiers called in to suppress the opposition to the crown of the parl of Grenoble.

jurade (AR), the set of municipal officials (*jurats*) of Bordeaux under the AR.

jurande (AR), elected leadership of a guild.

laboureurs, upper fraction of the peasantry, who owned a plough and hired labour. In some regions, however, all peasants were referred to by this term.

lanterner (neol), to hang individuals, aristocrats, etc from a lamp-post (*lanterne*).

lèse-majesté, treason, lese-majesty (until late 1791).

lèse-nation, neologism adapted in 1789 from *lèse-majesté*: treasonous attack on the state (Cf. similar coinings: *lèse-constitution, lèse-Convtn, lèse-patrie,* even *lèse-jacobinisme,* etc.)

lettre de cachet (AR), sealed administrative missive, signed by the monarch and countersigned by a minister, containing a detention order against an individual: the order was to be executed swiftly, secretly and with no recourse to the courts.

lettres de jussion (AR), royal order requiring registration of a law, and overriding parl remonstrances.

lettres de rémission, royal pardon.

levée en masse (neol), law of 23 Aug 1793 mobilising the French nation for the war effort.

lit de justice (AR), solemn session of the parl in the presence of the king (who was positioned on a raised ceremonial 'bed' of cushions) at which the monarch forcibly registered an edict, overriding the parl's remonstrances.

livre (1) one pound weight (between 380 and 552 grammes, depending on the locality); (2) the basic monetary unit of the kingdom since the times of Saint Louis, whose exact value varied according to its place of origin.

livre tournois, 'the livre of Tours': the basic state money of account since 1667.

lods et ventes (AR), onerous seigneurial due, payable when property changed hands through sale.

loi agraire, 'agrarian law', in fact simply the idea of redistributing property by expropriating the wealthy and producing a more egalitarian system of land-holding.

loi des otages, law of 12 July 1799/24 mess VII under which the relatives of *émigrés* resident in France could be held responsible for *émigrés'* subversive actions.

Madame, title given to the wife of Monsieur, the oldest of the monarch's younger brothers.

Mademoiselle, courtesy title accorded the oldest daughter of the brothers and uncles of the king.

mainmortable, see MAINMORTE.

mainmorte (1) *gens de mainmorte* or *mainmortables*, relatively few in number in 1789, were serfs under heavy personal dependence and whose rights to transmit property were circumscribed by their seigneur; (2) *biens de mainmorte* were properties owned by monasteries, hospitals, etc, which were inalienable.

maîtres des requêtes (AR), select group of venal lawyers and bureaucrats (67 in 1789), from whose ranks major royal administrators (counsellors of state, intendants, etc) were drawn.

mandats territoriaux, paper money introduced in Mar 1796, but which followed the disastrously depreciatory crash of the assignat and were withdrawn in Feb 1797 (when they were worth 1 per cent of their face value).

Manège (Salle du), riding hall in which the Constit Ass., the Leg Ass. and the Convtn held their sessions from 9 Nov 1789 to 9 May 1793; where the C Anciens met from 1795 until 21 Jan 1799; and which was subsequently hired out to the neo-Jacobin Club du Manège.

manœuvrier, manouvrier, day-labourer, esp in heavy work.

Marais (literally 'the Marsh'), the Plain – that is, the centrist deputies in the Leg Ass. and the Convtn.

marc d'argent, silver mark worth 52 liv. Payment of taxes to this value was the proposed condition of eligibility for being a deputy in 1789, along with ownership of land. The stipulation was dropped in the Constitution of 1791.

maréchaussée (AR), paramilitary mounted police force, reorganised as the gendarmerie in 1790.

Marseillaise, written by Rouget de l'Isle, originally the 'Chant de guerre pour l'armée du Rhin' (1792). The song became the national anthem, 14 July 1795.

martyrs de Prairial, the six Montagnard deputies (Bourbotte, Duquesnoy, Duroy, Goujon, Romme, Soubrany) sentenced to death for their alleged involvement in the Prairial rising and who were executed or committed suicide on 16 June 1795.

Maximum, set of price-fixing regulations: the law of 4 May 1793 introduced regulations concerning grain; the law of 29 Sept 1793 (the so-called 'General Maximum') generalised them for all articles of prime necessity including (in theory) wages.

meneur, agitator.

menu peuple, the common people, esp of the towns.

merveilleuses, provocatively fashionable women of the Directorial period (e.g. Madame Tallien, Madame Hamelin).

'Mesdames', Louis XVI's aunts, Madame Victoire and Madame Adelaide, whose emigration to Turin in Feb–Mar 1791 caused a mild political storm.

métayage, sharecropping: form of tenancy whereby the tenant (*métayer*) shared the harvest with the landlord, usually in lieu of cash payments; the most widespread form of tenancy in AR France.

métier (1) loom; (2) (AR) corporate professional grouping, corporation.

Midi, the south of France.

milices bourgeoises, urban militias, by 1789 used mainly for ceremonial purposes, but which often became the embryo of the Nat Guard during the summer crisis of 1789.

milice, or **milice provinciale** (AR), prov militia, instituted in 1688, manned by a form of conscription and occasionally incorporated into the regular army; suppressed 6 Mar 1791.

modérantisme, political system of moderation (by 1793 synonymous with federalism, royalism, etc).

monarchiens, Anglophile deputies of the Constit Ass. who in the Summer and Autumn of 1789 advocated a British-style bicameral legislature.

Monsieur, courtesy title of the monarch's oldest younger brother: at the outbreak of the Rev, the title was borne by the comte de Provence, future Louis XVIII; in 1796 it passed to the comte d'Artois, future Charles X.

Montagne, name given left-wing deputies (Montagnards) headed by Danton and Robespierre who occupied benches at the top and on the left of the steep-banked Salle du Manège.

municipalité, administrators (mayor, etc) of each *commune*.

muscadins, 'dandies': royalist youths (term used from 1793 and applied to the *jeunesse dorée* in the post-Thermidor period).

nationaliser (neol), to make national, have adopted by the nation, popularise in a rev way.

noblesse d'épée, the old 'sword nobility', which had allegedly won its noble status through feats of arms.

noblesse de cloche, individuals who achieved noble status through municipal office (e.g. in Paris, Toulouse).

noblesse de robe, individuals whose noble status derived from office in the royal bureaucracy.

noirs (1) supporters of a return to the AR (esp in the autumn of 1789); (2) negroes.

noyades, mass drownings of refractory priests and others in the mouth of the Loire outside Nantes organised by Carrier in late 1793 and early 1794.

octrois, tolls on merchandise entering towns. Abolished on 19 Feb 1791, but gradually restored from Oct 1798.

officier, holder through purchase of an administrative post in the royal bureaucracy.

ordres, the three orders, namely the clergy, the nobility and the Third Estate, into which Ancien Régime society was conventionally divided.

ouvriers, manual, semi-skilled and skilled workers.

pacage (droit de), customary collective right to pasture livestock in woodland.

pacte colonial, see EXCLUSIF.

pacte de famille, 'family compact': the diplomatic alliance uniting, since 1761, the branches of the Bourbon family on the thrones of Spain and France.

pacte de famine, alleged conspiracy, imputed in the eighteenth century to merchants, ministers and even to members of the royal family, to starve the populace by withholding corn from the market until its price had reached very high levels.

pairs, peers: the apex of the French aristocracy, comprising in 1789 the princes of the blood, six high ecclesiastics and nearly 40 dukes.

Palais-Royal, Parisian residence of the duc d'Orléans which from 1780 became a commercial centre and in the late 1780s a base for rev activity.

panthéoniste, member of the neo-Jacobin Panthéon Club, 1795–6.

parcours (droit de), customary right of villagers to pasture their livestock on the common lands of neighbouring villages.

parlements, the major high courts of appeal under the AR, 13 in number in 1789. The most important, the Paris parl, comprised a number of courts, the most senior of which was the *Grand'Chambre*, as well as three *chambres des enquêtes*, one *chambre des requêtes*, the criminal court known as the *Tournelle*, and a number of other chambers.

pataud, pejorative term used by Vendéan rebels to denote 'patriot'.

patente, direct tax introduced in 1791, levied on all traders, craftsmen and manufacturers.

patriotes, 'patriots': a title first used in 1787–8 of opponents of Calonne and Brienne, then after 1788 of opponents of the parls, and then more generally of all supporters of the new ideas in 1789.

patriotes de 1789, three battalions of ex-Montagnards formed to defend the Convtn against the rebel royalist sections in the Vendémiaire rising.

pays conquis, see PAYS D'IMPOSITION.

pays d'élection, (AR) areas without prov estates, whose financial administration was run by *bureaux de finances* in collaboration with the local Intendant.

pays d'imposition, tax areas (esp the more recently annexed provinces, or *pays conquis*) where tax administration was directly under the Intendants, and where there were no prov estates, *bureaux des finances*, etc.

pays de gabelle, region within which the salt-tax (*gabelle*) was fixed at a uniform rate. In 1789, these were the *pays de grande gabelle* (where the price of salt was

12–13 sous per liv); *pays de petite gabelle* (6–8 sous); *pays de salines* (2–6 sous); *pays rédimés* and *pays de quart-bouillon* (less than 2 sous), and *pays exempts* (3–6 deniers).

pays de grande culture, area of open-field cultivation, esp in N and NE France, characterised by large-scale farming, esp of cereals.

pays de petite culture, area (esp in W and S France) where polycultural subsistence farming was the rule, and where the units of cultivation were small.

pays de petite gabelle, see PAYS DE GABELLE.

pays exempts, see PAYS DE GABELLE.

pays rédimés, see PAYS DE GABELLE.

pays de salines, see PAYS DE GABELLE.

pays de taille personnelle, see TAILLE.

pays de taille réelle, see TAILLE.

pays d'états, (AR) areas which had local representative assemblies of the three estates which in particular contributed towards the assessment and collection of royal taxes.

péage (AR), toll on roads, bridges, fords, etc. About 600 were alleged to exist on the eve of the Rev.

pêche (droit de) (AR), monopoly of fishing enjoyed by seigneurs. Abolished 28 Nov 1793.

pékin (neol 1797), pejorative military slang for representative of the civil authority, and by extension for civilians in general.

Petites Maisons, Parisian poor-house, notorious as a home for lunatics.

philippotins, supporters of Philippeaux (NOT Philippe, duc d'Orléans).

philosophes, 'philosophers': the writers and thinkers of the French Enlightenment.

physiocrates, followers of the set of economists associated with Quesnay which emphasised the importance of a strong agricultural interest.

piteux, feeble Jacobin pun, designating counter-rev supporters of William Pitt and individuals worthy of pity for their political stupidity.

Plaine, the 'Plain': middle-ground deputies who tended to sit in the lower middle reaches of the steeply banked sides of the Salle du Manège in which the Leg Ass. and the Convtn met.

portion congrue, stipend which parish priests received in those parishes where the tithe-owner was an outsider: in 1786 stipendiary levels were raised from 500 to 700 liv for a *curé*, and from 200 to 350 liv for a *vicaire*, though these levels were still regarded as risibly low.

Prairial (coup d'état du 30), the so-called '*journée* of the Councils' which purged Merlin de Douai and La Révellière-Lépeaux from the Directory (18 June 1799).

Prairial (journées de), unsuccessful Parisian popular rising (20–3 May 1795/1–4 prair III).

prébende, prebend, benefice of any cleric, esp the dignitary of a cathedral.

préséance, ceremonial and conventional customs of precedence and superiority, esp rife under the AR.

prévôt des marchands (AR), head of the municipal administration of Paris.

prévôté (AR), exceptional jurisdiction (the best known of which was that of the *prévôts* of the *maréchaussée*).

princes possessionnés, rulers of the small German principalities enclaved within E France and guaranteed by the Treaty of Westphalia (1648).

privilégiés, privileged groups and individuals; by 1789, becoming synonymous with the nobles and clergy.

procureur (AR), attorney, procurator. The term was replaced by *avoué* in the Rev.

procureur de la commune, elected official in each commune whose responsibility it was to defend the interests of the community; in towns with a population over 10,000, *procureurs* were permitted to appoint deputies (*substituts*).

procureur du roi (AR), royal officials (suppressed in Aug 1790) attached to the main financial and judicial bodies and responsible for protecting the crown's interests.

procureur-général-syndic, elected officials who from 1790 were attached to the administration of each department and who represented the judicial power and ensured the application of laws. They were suppressed by the Law of 14 Frimaire II/4 Dec 1793. Under the Directory, they were replaced by *commissaires du pouvoir exécutif*.

procureur-syndic, official operating at district level, 1790–5, in the same way as the *procureur-général-syndic* at dept level.

provinces de l'étranger effectif, 'effectively foreign provinces': indirect tax areas outside the jurisdiction of the *Cinq Grosses Fermes*. Normally these were provinces relatively recently incorporated into France, and they were characterised by a customs regime which in many respects was more favourable to foreign trade than trade with the rest of France.

provinces réputés étrangères, 'provinces reputed foreign': indirect tax areas outside the jurisdiction of the *Cinq Grosses Fermes*, and enjoying a customs regime different from and often less favourable than the area of the *Fermes* or the *provinces de l'étranger effectif*.

purs, hard-line royalists.

quart-bouillon, see PAYS DE GABELLE.

quartier d'hiver (1) army's winter quarters; (2) by the eighteenth century a direct tax, supplementary to the *taille*, allegedly levied to pay for the army's winter quarters.

question, torture: *la question préparatoire* was used to secure a confession; *la question préalable*, to secure names of accomplices. The former was abolished in 1780, the latter (in theory at least) in May 1788.

queue de Robespierre, 'Robespierre's tail': Thermidorian description for Montagnards after the fall of Robespierre.

rapporteur, member of a committee or council entrusted with presenting business.

redevances, generic term for dues, esp seigneurial ones.

réfractaires, individuals opposed to rev laws (used esp of refractory priests, who rejected the Civ Constn).

régale, royal prerogative of enjoying the revenues of vacant sees.

régicides, members of the Convtn who voted for the death of Louis XVI in 1793. Those still alive in 1816 were exiled by the restored Louis XVIII.

régie, collection of taxes by state functionaries (as opposed to tax farmers).

remontrances, 'remonstrances': formal objections which sovereign courts (esp the parls) could make to the king framing objections to laws which seemed to infringe the 'fundamental laws of the kingdom'.

rentes constituées, standard form of credit whereby a borrower agreed to pay the lender an annual percentage sum of the principal in perpetuity: used by state and corporate bodies as well as private individuals.

rentiers, middle- and upper-class individuals living off unearned income.

représentants aux armées, see REPRÉSENTANTS EN MISSION.

représentants du peuple, members of the Nat Ass in the 1790s.

représentants en mission, deputies sent out from the Convtn from Mar 1793 to rally the provinces and supervise the war effort. Those attached to the rev armies were also referred to as *représentants aux armées*.

république, AR sense of 'popular government' only transformed into meaning 'form of government without a monarch' in 1790–1.

républiques sœurs, name given, in the late 1790s, to the new republics established under French control (Cisalpine, Helvetian, Roman, etc).

retrait féodal, right of seigneurs to intervene in a property sale involving a vassal and make the purchase themselves at the same price.

révolte nobiliaire, resistance to royal reforms by nobles and parls in 1787 and 1788.

richérisme, doctrine, popular among lower clergy in 1789, originated by Edmond Richer (1559–1631) who advocated a stronger representation of the lower clergy in ecclesiastical governance.

robin (AR), 'wearer of the robe': magistrate, high state functionary.

rolandin, rolandiste, supporter of Roland, Girondin.

roturier, commoner.

salut et fraternité, form of greeting much used in rev correspondence 1793–4.

sans-culottes (neol 1791), small property-owners and artisans active in Parisian sectional politics; and by extension, all who supported egalitarian and radical policies, esp in 1793–4.

sans-culottides, the five last days of the year in the Rev Calendar (6 in leap years), unattached to any of the 12 months.

séance royale, ceremonial session of the parl and, after May 1789, of the EG and Nat Ass. in the presence of the monarch.

sectionnaires, politically active members of the Paris sections.

sections, the 48 units of local government, replacing the 60 districts of

1789–90, into which Paris was divided by the municipal law of 21 May 1790 and which became the framework for popular militancy from 1792.

seigneurie, seigneurie: conventionally divided into *domaine*, containing manor-house, main farm buildings, etc; and the *censives*, land owned by peasants under seigneurial obligations.

sénéchaussée, see BAILLIAGE.

septembriseurs, pejorative name for *sans-culotttes*, *fédérés* and others held responsible for the Sept Massacres 1792; and after Thermidor, used generally for all militants and Jacobins of Year II.

serment de haine à la royauté, oath of allegiance demanded of all public functionaries in Aug 1792.

serment de haine à la royauté et à l'anarchie, oath of allegiance to the Rpbc demanded of all public functionaries on 20 Mar 1797 on pain of deportation.

serment du Jeu de Paume, 'Tennis Court Oath': collective oath taken by the Third Estate (with a single exception) at their meeting on 20 June 1789 not to disperse until a constitution had been agreed.

servage, serfdom.

sociétés fraternelles, 'fraternal societies': early radical clubs formed in Paris 1790–1, often as associates and affiliates of the Cordeliers Club.

sociétés populaires, general term applied to local clubs and societies, esp from 1791 until the downfall of popular militancy in 1794–5.

subvention territoriale, unitary land-tax in kind advocated in response to the threat of state bankruptcy by Calonne and Brienne in 1787.

Suisses de Châteauvieux, the Swiss regiment whose mutiny at Nancy in Aug 1790 became a *cause célèbre* between left and right in the Ass.

suppléant (neol), substitute deputies to the EG and to successive legislatures, elected at the same time as the deputies and called to sit in case of the latter's death, ministerial appointment or expulsion.

suspect, in general terms, those whose political orthodoxy was in doubt; in particular terms, those categories of individuals (royalists, federalists, dismissed public functionaries, relatives of *émigrés*, etc) designated suspect by the law of 17 Sept 1793.

syndic (AR), representative of a parish, a corporation, etc, who defended the interests of the community in question before the law.

taille (AR), the main royal direct tax, created in 1439. Its form of assessment varied: in *pays de taille personnelle*, it was based on movable wealth; in *pays de taille réelle* (situated mainly in S France), on land.

taillon (AR), supplement to the *taille*, created in 1549.

taxation populaire, compulsory sale, at a price adjudged 'fair', of foodstuffs and other commodities, imposed by direct action.

temple, name given in 1793 to many disaffected churches: e.g. Notre-Dame in Paris was renamed 'Temple de la Raison'.

temple de l'humanité, hospital.

terrage, synonym of *champart*.

terreur blanche, 'White Terror' of 1794–6 (in distinction to the 'Red' Terror of 1793–4) during which royalist vigilantes harassed former popular militants.

terrier, register containing legal documents relating to seigneurial dues and land-ownership.

terroriste (neol 1794), a term used almost solely retrospectively about those involved in the Terror, 1793–4.

théophilanthropie, set of religious and philosophical beliefs of deist inspiration, advocated by key political figures (esp La Réveillière-Lépeaux) from 1796 until its formal abolition in 1801.

Thermidor, the *journée* of 9 Thermidor II.

tiers consolidé, 'the consolidated third': the capital of the national debt after the 'two-thirds liquidation' of 1797 had reduced its value.

Tiers Etat (or **Tiers**), the Third Estate of the Estates General of 1789, and, by extension, the French nation generally excluding the nobility and clergy.

tirage, drawing of lots within communities to designate conscripts for the *milice provinciale* under the AR.

Tournelle, the main criminal court of the parl of Paris.

traite des noirs, traite des nègres, slave-trade.

traites (AR), duty levied on the import of merchandise and on its transportation between provinces.

trésoriers de France (AR), officials grouped normally into a *bureau de finances* in each *généralité* which had jurisdiction over a wide range of financial matters.

triage, right claimed by seigneurs in certain circumstances to appropriate one-third of communal woodlands: utilised esp from the late 1760s following the enclosure of commons.

tribunes, public galleries (of Nat Ass., Jacobin Club, etc).

tricolore, see COCARDE TRICOLORE.

tricoteuses, 'the knitter women': lower-class women who attended sessions of the Nat Ass., Paris Commune, etc. A decree of the Commune on 26 Dec 1793 had allowed women to knit while attending sessions.

triumvirat (1) usual way of referring to *patriote* leaders Barnave, Alexandre de Lameth and Adrien Duport; (2) sometimes used after Thermidor to refer to Robespierre, Saint-Just and Couthon; (3) in the 1770s, the term had been used about royal ministers Maupeou, Terray and d'Aiguillon.

'Trois Comités', used under the Terror to denote the CPS, the CGS and the Committee of Legislation.

tutoiement, use of more familiar and fraternal *tu* form of address, current even in official parlance in Year II.

tyran, Louis XVI (after 1791).

ultra, ultra-révolutionnaire, revolutionary extremist (e.g. used by Robespierre of Hébert in Dec 1793).

ustencile, (AR), tax in lieu of the food, drink, heating, etc, which the population was supposed to provide *gratis* to royal troops; collected as a supplement to the *taille*.

vaine pâture, customary right of villagers to pasture their livestock on common lands.

Vainqueurs de la Bastille, title given by Constit Ass. to between 800 and 900 persons who were able to establish their claim to have participated actively in the capture of the Bastille on 14 July 1789.

vandalisme (neol 1793), despoliation of churches, destruction of works of art.

vassal, by 1789 used in non-technical feudal sense to denote any peasant.

vénalité des charges, des offices, system current throughout the royal bureaucracy under which offices were purchasable and hereditary.

Vendéen, supporter of the counter-rev insurrection in W France centred in the dept of the Vendée.

Vendémiaire, popular, right-wing revolt in Paris, 5 Oct 1795/13 vendém IV.

Ventre, 'belly': pejorative way of referring to centrist deputies, esp under the Directory.

vérification des pouvoirs, ratification of credentials – the issue which in the summer of 1789 became the cause of political crisis, as the deputies of the Third Estate refused to verify their credentials save in the presence of the other two orders.

vicaire, assistant to the *curé* in a parish.

vingtième, royal tax equivalent to one-twentieth of income levied at different occasions in the eighteenth century, and in particular from 1782 to 1786.

visites domiciliaires, domiciliary raids, house-to-house searches (esp for arms and suspects under the Terror).

XII. THE REVOLUTIONARY CALENDAR

THE REGULAR CALENDAR*

	vendémiaire	brumaire	frimaire	nivôse	pluviôse	ventôse
1	SEPT 22	Oct 22	Nov 21	Dec 21	Jan 20	Feb 19
2	23	23	22	22	21	20
3	24	24	23	23	22	21
4	25	25	24	24	23	22
5	26	26	25	25	24	23
6	27	27	26	26	25	24
7	28	28	27	27	26	25
8	29	29	28	28	27	26
9	30	30	29	29	28	27
10	OCT 1	31	30	30	29	28
11	2	NOV 1	DEC 1	31	30	MAR 1
12	3	2	2	JAN 1	31	2
13	4	3	3	2	FEB 1	3
14	5	4	4	3	2	4
15	6	5	5	4	3	5
16	7	6	6	5	4	6
17	8	7	7	6	5	7
18	9	8	8	7	6	8
19	10	9	9	8	7	9
20	11	10	10	9	8	10
21	12	11	11	10	9	11
22	13	12	12	11	10	12
23	14	13	13	12	11	13
24	15	14	14	13	12	14
25	16	15	15	14	13	15
26	17	16	16	15	14	16
27	18	17	17	16	15	17
28	19	18	18	17	16	18
29	20	19	19	18	17	19
30	21	20	20	19	18	20

germinal | *floréal* | *prairial* | *messidor* | *thermidor* | *fructidor*

Day	germinal	floréal	prairial	messidor	thermidor	fructidor
1	Mar 21	Apr 20	May 20	Jun 19	Jul 19	Aug 18
2	22	21	21	20	20	19
3	23	22	22	21	21	20
4	24	23	23	22	22	21
5	25	24	24	23	23	22
6	26	25	25	24	24	23
7	27	26	26	25	25	24
8	28	27	27	26	26	25
9	29	28	28	27	27	26
10	30	29	29	28	28	27
11	31	30	30	29	29	28
12	APR 1	MAY 1	31	30	30	29
13	2	2	JUNE 1	JULY 1	31	30
14	3	3	2	2	AUG 1	31
15	4	4	3	3	2	SEP 1
16	5	5	4	4	3	2
17	6	6	5	5	4	3
18	7	7	6	6	5	4
19	8	8	7	7	6	5
20	9	9	8	8	7	6
21	10	10	9	9	8	7
22	11	11	10	10	9	8
23	12	12	11	11	10	9
24	13	13	12	12	11	10
25	14	14	13	13	12	11
26	15	15	14	14	13	12
27	16	16	15	15	14	13
28	17	17	16	16	15	14
29	18	18	17	17	16	15
30	19	19	18	18	17	16

Jours complémentaires: 1 = 17 Sept; 2 = 18 Sept; 3 = 19 Sept; 4 = 20 Sept; 5 = 21 Sept; 6 (1795 and 1799 ONLY) = 22 Sept.

* See explanatory notes on p. 428–9.

The Convtn agreed, on 5 Oct 1793, to replace the Gregorian calendar with a rpbcn calendar commemorating the new era in human history which they alleged had begun following the overthrow of Louis XVI. It was agreed, then and in a further debate on 24 Oct, that the new era should date from 22 Sept 1792, when the newly elected Convtn had proclaimed the Rpbc. Nomenclature and final details were fixed on 24 Nov/4 frim II. Thus there was no 'Year I' except in retrospect.

The introduction of the calendar formed an important part of the 'dechristianisation' movement of 1793–4, and should also be seen as part of the move towards metrication (the 7-day week was replaced by the *décade* of 10 days) inaugurated as early as 1790. Typically, too, it was agreed to base the new calendar in 'nature' by according each day and month a name drawn from the natural world.

The calendar continued in use until 31 Dec 1806.

THE REVOLUTIONARY YEARS, 1793–1800

Year II: (22 Sept: in fact Oct 1793)–21 Sept 1794
Year III: 22 Sept 1794–22 Sept 1795
Year IV: 23 Sept 1795–21 Sept 1796
Year V: 22 Sept 1796–21 Sept 1797
Year VI: 22 Sept 1797–21 Sept 1798
Year VII: 22 Sept 1798–22 Sept 1799
Year VIII: 23 Sept 1799–22 Sept 1800

THE REVOLUTIONARY MONTHS

Each month had 30 days. At the end of the year were tacked on 5 (in leap years, 6) extra days called at first *sans-culottides* and, from 24 Aug 1795/7 fruct III, *jours complémentaires*.

vendémiaire = the month of vintage
brumaire = the month of fog
frimaire = the month of frost
nivôse = the month of snow
pluviôse = the month of rain
ventôse = the month of wind
germinal = the month of germination
floréal = the month of flowering
prairial = the month of meadows
messidor = the month of harvest
thermidor = the month of heat
fructidor = the month of fruit

428

CALENDAR CONCORDANCE FOR THE PERIODS FROM 22 SEPT 1795 TO 29 FEB 1796 AND FROM 22 SEPT 1799 TO 29 FEB 1800

To circumvent the problems caused by the leap years 1796 and 1800, an extra jc was tacked on to the end of Years III and VII (6 jc = 22 Sept 1795, 1799). Thus from the beginning of Years IV and VIII to the leap day in the following Feb, the following calendar equivalence applied (see overleaf, p. 430).

Day	*Vendémiaire*	*Brumaire*	*Frimaire*	*Nivôse*	*Pluviôse*	*Ventôse*
1	Sept 23	Oct 23	Nov 22	Dec 22	Jan 21	Feb 20
2	24	24	23	23	22	21
3	25	25	24	24	23	22
4	26	26	25	25	24	23
5	27	27	26	26	25	24
6	28	28	27	27	26	25
7	29	29	28	28	27	26
8	30	30	29	29	28	27
9	Oct 1	31	30	30	29	28
10	2	Nov 1	Dec 1	31	30	29
11	3	2	2	Jan 1	31	
12	4	3	3	2	Feb 1	
13	5	4	4	3	2	
14	6	5	5	4	3	
15	7	6	6	5	4	
16	8	7	7	6	5	
17	9	8	8	7	6	
18	10	9	9	8	7	
19	11	10	10	9	8	
20	12	11	11	10	9	
21	13	12	12	11	10	
22	14	13	13	12	11	
23	15	14	14	13	12	
24	16	15	15	14	13	
25	17	16	16	15	14	
26	18	17	17	16	15	
27	19	18	18	17	16	
28	20	19	19	18	17	
29	21	20	20	19	18	
30	22	21	21	20	19	

XIII. SELECT BIBLIOGRAPHY

The list is merely the tip of the iceberg of works consulted. For fuller bibliographical guidance, see R. J. Caldwell, *The Era of the French Revolution. A bibliography of western civilization, 1789–99*, New York & London 1985. Place of publication is London for works in English, Paris for works in French unless otherwise stated. English translations are given where possible.

BOOKS AND ARTICLES CITED

Almanach royal (1789).

Archives parlementaires.

F. A. Aulard (1889–1923), *Recueil des actes du Comité de salut public*, 27 vols.

F. A. Aulard (1889–97), *La Société des Jacobins. Recueil de documents pour l'histoire du Club des Jacobins de Paris*, 6 vols.

F. A. Aulard (1910), *The French Revolution. A political history, 1789–1804*, 4 vols.

R. Baticle (1909–10), 'Le plébiscite sur la constitution de 1793', *La Révolution française*, lvii, pp. 494–524; lviii, pp. 5–30, 117–55, 193–237, 327–41 and 385–410.

D. Bien (1974), 'La réaction aristocratique avant 1789: l'exemple de l'armée', *Annales. Economies. Sociétés. Civilisations*, xxix, pp. 23–48 and 503–34.

C. Bloch and A. Tuetey (eds) (1911), *Procès-verbaux et rapports du comité de mendicité de la Constituante (1790–1)*.

P. Bois (1960), *Paysans de l'Ouest*. Le Mans.

E. Boursin and A Challamel (1893), *Dictionnaire de la Révolution française. Institutions, hommes et faits*.

F. Braesch (1912), 'Essai de statistique de la population ouvrière de Paris vers 1791', *La Révolution française*, lxiii, pp. 289–312.

R. Brécy (1981), 'La chanson révolutionnaire de 1789 à 1799', *Annales historiques de la Révolution française*, liii, pp. 279–303.

C. Brinton (1930), *The Jacobins*. New York.

G. Cabourdin and G. Viard (1978), *Lexique historique de la France d'Ancien Régime*.

L. Cahen and R. Guyot (1913), *L'Œuvre législative de la Révolution*.

P. Caron (1947), *Manuel pratique pour l'étude de la Révolution française*.

J. A. Chaptal (1819), *De l'Industrie française*, 2 vols.

G. Chaussinand-Nogaret (1985), *The French Nobility in the Eighteenth Century: from feudalism to enlightenment*. Cambridge.

C. Clerget (1905), *Tableaux des armées françaises pendant les guerres de la Révolution*.

R. Cobb (1961, 1963), *Les Armées révolutionnaires: instrument de la Terreur dans les départements*, 2 vols.

O. Connelly *et al.* (1985), *Historical Dictionary of Napoleonic France, 1799–1815*.

F. Crouzet (1985), *De la Supériorité de l'Angleterre sur la France: l'économique et l'imaginaire, XVIIe–XXe siècles*.

R. Darnton (1979), *The Business of Enlightenment. A publishing history of the 'Encyclopédie', 1775–1800*. Cambridge, Mass.

A. Daumard and F. Furet (1961), *Structures et relations sociales à Paris au milieu du XVIIIe siècle.*

Décembre-Alonnier (1866–8), *Dictionnaire de la Révolution française*, 2 vols.

L. Duguit and H. Monnier (1898), *Les Constitutions et les principales lois politiques de la France depuis 1789.*

M. Edelstein (1982), 'La noblesse et le monopole des fonctions publiques en 1789', *Annales historiques de la Révolution française*, liv, pp. 440–43.

J. Egret (1977), *The French Pre-Revolution, 1787–8.* Chicago.

R. Estivals (1965), *La Statistique bibliographique de la France sous la monarchie au XVIIIe siècle.*

abbé Expilly (1780), *Tableau de la population de la France.*

G. Feyel (1984), 'La presse provinciale au XVIIIe siècle: géographie d'un réseau', *Revue historique*, cclxxii, pp. 353–74.

Figuères (1901), *Les noms révolutionnaires des communes de France.*

M. Fleury and P. Valmary (1957), 'Les progrès de l'instruction élémentaire de Louis XIV à Napoléon III, d'après l'enquête de Louis Maggiolo (1877–9)', *Population*, xiii, pp. 71–92.

R. Forster (1960), *The Nobility of Toulouse in the Eighteenth Century*, Baltimore.

J. Godechot (1968), *Les Institutions de la France sous la Révolution et l'Empire.*

J. L. Godfrey (1951), *Revolutionary justice: a study of the organisation, personnel and procedures of the Paris Revolutionary Tribunal.* Chapel Hill, N. Carolina.

D. Greer (1935), *The Incidence of the Terror in the French Revolution. A statistical interpretation*, Cambridge, Mass.

D. Greer (1951), *The Incidence of the Emigration during the French Revolution*, Cambridge, Mass.

F. A. Helié (1880), *Les Constitutions de la France.*

E. Herbin de Halle (1803), *Statistique générale et particulière de la France et de ses colonies*, 7 vols.

P. Higonnet (1985), 'The social and cultural antecedents of Revolutionary discontinuity: Montagnards and Girondins', *English Historical Review*, c, pp. 513–44.

P. Higonnet and J. Murphy (1973), 'Les députés de la noblesse aux Etats-Généraux de 1789', *Revue d'histoire moderne et contemporaine*, xx, pp. 230–47.

Histoire de l'édition française. ii. *Le livre triomphant, 1660–1830* (1984).

L. A. Hunt (1976), 'Committees and communes: local politics and national revolution in 1789', *Comparative Studies in Society and History* xviii, pp. 321–46.

L. A. Hunt (1984), 'The political geography of Revolutionary France', *Journal of Interdisciplinary History*, xiv, pp. 535–59.

L. A. Hunt (1984), *Politics, culture and class in the French Revolution*, Berkeley and Los Angeles, Calif.

J. Jaurès, *Histoire socialiste de la Révolution française.*

M. Kennedy (1982), *The Jacobin Clubs in the French Revolution*, Princeton, New Jersey.

A. Kuscinski (1920), *Dictionnaire des Conventionnels*.

C. E. Labrousse, R. Romano and F. G. Dreyfus (1970), *Le Prix du forment en France au temps de la monnaie stable, 1726–1913*.

A. Lajusan (1911), 'Le plébiscite de l'an III', *La Révolution française*, lx, pp. 5–37.

C. Langlois and T. Tackett (1980), 'Ecclesiastical structures and clerical geography on the eve of the French Revolution', *French Historical Studies*, xi, pp. 352–70.

A. Le Bihan (1967), *Loges et chapitres de la Grande Loge et du Grand Orient de France, deuxième moitié du XVIIIe siècle*.

F. Lebrun ed (1980), *Histoire des catholiques en France du XVe siècle à nos jours*.

F. Lebrun (1986), 'Reynald Secher et les morts de guerre de la Vendée', *Annales de Bretagne*.

G. Lefebvre (1924), *Les Paysans du Nord pendant la Révolution française*, 2 vols.

G. Lefebvre (1962, 1964), *The French Revolution*, 2 vols.

G. Lefebvre (1963), *Etudes sur la Révolution française*.

E. Lemay (1977), 'La Composition de l'Assemblée nationale constituante: les hommes de la continuité', *Revue d'histoire moderne et contemporaine*, xxix, pp. 341–63.

R. Le Mée (1971), 'Population agglomérée, population éparse au début du XIXe siècle', *Annales de démographie historique*, pp. 455–510

E. Levasseur (1903), *Histoire des classes ouvrières et de l'industrie en France de 1789 à 1870*.

M. Marion (1923), *Dictionnaire des institutions de la France aux XVIIe et XVIIIe siècles*.

M. Marion (1914–31), *Histoire financière de la France depuis 1715*, 4 vols.

A. Martin, R. Frantschi and V. G. Mylne (1977), *Bibliographie du genre romanesque française, 1751–1800*, London.

J. Massin (1963), *Almanach de la Révolution française*.

J. Massin (1965), *Almanach du Premier Empire, du 9 thermidor à Waterloo*.

A. Mathiez (1919), *Le Club des Cordeliers pendant la crise de Varennes et le massacre du Champ de Mars*.

A. Mathiez (1927), *La Vie chère et le mouvement social sous la Terreur*, 2 vols.

C. J. Mitchell (1984), 'Political divisions within the Legislative Assembly of 1791', *French Historical Studies*, xiii, pp. 356–89.

M. Morineau (1977), 'France', in G. Parker and C. Wilson (eds), *An Introduction to the Sources of European Economic History, 1500–1800*. Vol. I. *Western Europe*, pp. 155–89.

M. Morineau (1980), 'Budgets de l'Etat et gestion des finances royales en France au XVIIIe siècle', *Revue historique*.

R. F. Necheles (1974), 'The Curés in the Estates General of 1789', *Journal of Modern History*, xliv, pp. 425–44.

R. R. Palmer (1941), *Twelve Who Ruled: the year of the Terror in the French Revolution*, Princeton.

A. Patrick (1972), *The Men of the First French Republic: political alignments in the National Convention of 1792*, Baltimore.

A. Poitrineau (1965), *La Vie rurale en Basse-Auvergne au XVIIIe siècle*.

"*Population*" (1975), special number, 'Démographie historique'.

M. Reinhard (1971), *Nouvelle histoire de Paris: la Révolution, 1789–99*.

A. Robert, E. Bourloton and G. Cougny (1891), *Dictionnaire des parlementaires français, 1789–1889*, 5 vols.

Robinet, A. Robert and J. Le Chaplain, (1899) *Dictionnaire de la Révolution et de l'Empire 1789–1815*, 2 vols.

D. Roche (1978), *Le Siècle des lumières en province. Académies et académiciens provinciaux, 1680–1789*, 2 vols.

G. Rudé (1959), *The Crowd in the French Revolution*, Oxford.

S. F. Scott (1973), *The Response of the Royal Army to the French Revolution: the role and development of the line army, 1787–93*, Oxford.

S. F. Scott and B. Rothaus (eds) (1985) *Historical Dictionary of the French Revolution, 1789–1799*.

A. Soboul (1958a), *Les Sans-culottes parisiens de l'an II*.

A. Soboul (1958b), *Les Campagnes montpelliéraines à la fin de l'Ancien Régime*.

J. Suratteau (1971), *Les Elections de l'an VI et le coup d'état du 22 floréal an II*.

M. Sydenham (1961), *The Girondins*.

T. Tackett (1986), *Religion, Revolution and Regional Culture in Eighteenth-century France: the ecclesiastical oath of 1791*, Princeton, New Jersey.

C. Tilly (1964), *The Vendée*, Cambridge, Mass.

J. Vidalenc (1963), *Les Émigrés français*, Caen.

M. Vovelle (1984), *The Fall of the French Monarchy, 1787–1792*, Cambridge.

G. Walter (1941, 1951), *Répertoire de l'histoire de la Révolution française*, 2 vols.

G. Walter and A. Martin (1936–43), *Catalogue de l'histoire de la Révolution française*, 5 vols.

INDEX

Readers are advised that an entry may appear more than once on a page; that page references in bold indicate main references; and that the same abbreviations as in the text have been used for forenames.